Lonely Planet Publications
Melbourne | Oakland | London | Paris

D0370345

Damien Simonis

Venice

The Top Five

1 Burano and Torcello
Enjoy a quiet retreat among pastel houses and ancient mosaics (p91)

2 Peggy Guggenheim Collection
Tour the capricious collector's gallery of modern art (p62)

3 Basilica di San Marco
Admire the treasure-filled cathedral at the heart of the city (p50)

4 Grand Canal
Glide past mansions to emerge in the Bacino di San Marco (p48)

5 Palazzo Ducale
Visit the Gothic seat of 1000 years of Venetian power (p55)

Contents

Published by Lonely Planet Publications Pty Ltd
ABN 36 005 607 983

Australia Head Office, Locked Bag 1, Footscray
Victoria 3001, ☎ 03 8379 8000, fax 03 8379 8111
talk2us@lonelyplanet.com.au

USA 150 Linden St, Oakland, CA 94607
☎ 510 893 8555, toll free 800 275 8555
fax 510 893 8572, info@lonelyplanet.com

UK 72–82 Rosebery Ave, Clerkenwell, London,
EC1R 4RW ☎ 020 7841 9000, fax 020 7841 9001
go@lonelyplanet.co.uk

France 1 rue du Dahomey, 75011 Paris
☎ 01 55 25 33 00; fax 01 55 25 33 01
bip@lonelyplanet.fr, www.lonelyplanet.fr

© Lonely Planet 2004
Photographs © Juliet Coombe and as listed (p238), 2004

All rights reserved. No part of this publication may be
copied, stored in a retrieval system, or transmitted in any
form by any means, electronic, mechanical, recording
or otherwise, except brief extracts for the purpose of
review, and no part of this publication may be sold or
hired, without the written permission of the publisher.

Printed through The Bookmaker International Ltd
Printed in China

Lonely Planet and the Lonely Planet logo are trade-
marks of Lonely Planet and are registered in the US
Patent and Trademark Office and in other countries.

Lonely Planet does not allow its name or logo to be
appropriated by commercial establishments, such as
retailers, restaurants or hotels. Please let us know of any
misuses: www.lonelyplanet.com/ip.

Although the authors and Lonely Planet have taken
all reasonable care in preparing this book, we make
no warranty about the accuracy or completeness of
its content and, to the maximum extent permitted,
disclaim all liability arising from its use.

The Author

DAMIEN SIMONIS

As a young backpacker with not a word of Italian and barely two brass lire to rub together, Damien first landed in Venice way back in his Dark Age. Enchanted like most by his first encounter with the countless little bridges, blind alleys and winding canals, Damien was left with a lasting, but for many years dormant, impression. Indeed, he finally returned only many years later while on assignment for Lonely Planet. Like an old flame never quite forgotten, the charming old queen of the sea once again worked her magic. Things had changed in the meantime. Italian had become Damien's second language and so he began to see and hear the city in a clearer and closer fashion. Having lived in Milan and distant Palermo, and crisscrossed the bootlike peninsula on assignment and off, he could put the unique one-time merchant empire into clearer context. Sure, cracks began to appear beneath the make-up, but that only endeared him more to the place, which he now gets back to just as often as he possibly can. As he learns to tread an ever finer path through the labyrinth of lanes (it's always fun to discover another short cut) and potter about in boats on the lagoon that surrounds the city, our man in Venice can only confess that he has become more hooked than ever before. Even when at home in faraway Stoke Newington, London, he can taste that slightly bitter afternoon *spritz* as the sun goes down.

PHOTOGRAPHER
JULIET COOMBE

As a full-time freelance travel photojournalist, Juliet has taken pictures which have appeared in more than 200 Lonely Planet guidebooks. She has won the prestigious British Guild of Travel Writers award for Travel Photographer of the Year. When she is not circumnavigating the world writing and taking pictures, you will find her plotting her next assignment in her 1840s London warehouse by Spitalfields market. Of the 120 cities Juliet has been to, Venice is still her true love, because of its ethereal charm and theatrical setting. It may be one of the world's most photographed, filmed and written about places, but however many times she goes there, whether it be for the Carnevale in February or the Venice International Film Festival in August, she always finds something new and inspiring to rekindle her passion for La Serenissima.

Lonely Planet books provide independent advice. Lonely Planet does not accept advertising in guidebooks, nor do we accept payment in exchange for listing or endorsing any place or business. Lonely Planet writers do not accept discounts or payments in exchange for positive coverage of any sort.

Introducing Venice

The clap, clap of water thudding against the sides of the airport waterbus quickens as you head south from the mainland across the shimmering lagoon. In the distance rise the slender bell towers of Murano and, just beyond, Venice. Woven together like a fine piece of Burano lace from a myriad of islets, Venice still has the self-assured, almost quietly arrogant feel of the 1000-year merchant empire that was known as the Most Serene Republic and long dominated the eastern Mediterranean.

While you approach this impossible city, built upon islets and platforms of countless pylons slammed over the centuries into the mud of the lagoon, its people go about their business, traipsing about the lanes and along canals, up and down the countless bridges. They have no cars to race around in! And so the air hums to the sound of padding feet, chatter resonating off the walls along narrow lanes and busy squares.

The roads of Venice are made of water. Fire engines, police, ambulances and taxis tootle about as wheeled vehicles would in other cities. Only here they are all boats and the speed limit is 5km/h. Not that anyone seems to enforce the limit. Suntanned taxi drivers pound about in their expensive, oak-panelled vessels, dodging gondoliers with their boatloads of enthralled visitors.

Venetians are unperturbed. Used to the incredible, indigestible accumulation of natural and constructed beauty that surrounds them, and seemingly indifferent to the slow rotting decay of that same beauty, they sometimes give the impression of being unaware that Venice has long ceased to be one of the centres of the European universe. Venice was and remains a sore point with the rest of Italy, a source of envy and irritation. Throughout its history, rivals as varied as the popes, Milan, Genoa, Padua, Imperial Spain and the Turks sought to break the haughty masters of the Adriatic. Often they came close. Nowadays, other Italians consider the city to be as stuck-up as ever.

Venice is unique, and not only for its watery home. The city's builders seem to have delighted in variety: from the great mosaics of Basilica di San Marco and Torcello to the sober Gothic majesty of the Frari, from the simplicity of Romanesque to the discipline of Palladio, from the sensuality of Veneto-Byzantine to the extremes of baroque, the concentration of architectural gems is astonishing. The same is true of its art – the march past of greats from the Venetian school seems infinite. Some of their works are scattered in galleries far from home,

Lowdown

Population 63,000 (275,000 for whole municipality, including islands and mainland)
Time zone (GMT/UTC + 1 hour)
3-star double room Around €200
Coffee at the bar Less than €0.90
Coffee on Piazza San Marco Up to €9!
Takeaway pizza slice €1.50 to €3
Gelato €1.50 to €2.50 (one or two flavours)
Vaporetto ticket €3.50 (single ride)
Consideration Walk single file along narrow streets to let people past
Vaporetto etiquette If you're near the exit, get off at intermediate stops to let other passengers on and off

but the number of masterpieces by Tiepolo, Tintoretto, Veronese, Titian and others still to be seen in the city is the equivalent of death by chocolate for art-lovers.

There is more to Venice than history, art and architecture. Exploring the lagoon's islands is essential to a broader understanding of the whole. Contemplate Venice from the long Adriatic barrier that is the Lido, and you can't help thinking that the place must be a figment of your imagination. Over on Murano, glassmakers continue to create crystal dream shapes at their blast furnaces, while on Burano a handful of dames still patiently sew together extraordinarily intricate lace. Back in town, people also take their leisure seriously, whether getting down to a succulent seafood meal by a canal or sidling up to a *bacaro* (old-style bar) for *cicheti* (snacks) and a glass of *prosecco* (sparkling white wine). Early evening tipplers favour a *spritz*, a refreshing, fiery red shot of *prosecco* mixed with soda and bitters.

But the proud city is slowly expiring. International organisations fight to preserve its monuments and engineers debate how to stem Adriatic floods. Press coverage of the battle to clean the lagoon of toxic waste alternates with alarmed reports on building subsidence. Everyone, from the mayor of Venice to ministers in Rome, from art historians in Britain to architecture buffs in the USA, expounds unendingly about the need to do *something*.

Perhaps they have missed the point. The lifeblood of a city is its people, and the people of Venice are voting with their feet. Since the 1950s, the population has more than halved. Housing is too expensive, transport too complicated, jobs too scarce. Talk to Venetians and you get the uncanny feeling you are on a sinking ship. One day it may truly be just a theme park open daily from eight till late.

For the moment you can still feel the pulse, and Venice has returned from the brink of extinction before. This city defies its admirers and detractors alike. Above all, it is elusive. The tides rise and fall every six hours, pushing the water first this way then that along the canals. More than a 'sight', Venice seems to be time and motion itself.

DAMIEN'S TOP VENICE DAY

After a long stretch and a little lazy staring out of my boutique hotel room window, it's time to get up for a cappuccino, pastry and paper on the nearest square – Campo Santa Maria Formosa perhaps. Suitably confused by the day's Italian political news, I wander the *calli* (streets) down to Riva degli Schiavoni to contemplate the busy lagoon spectacle before heading west to the Palazzo Ducale – a giddy trip down the Republic's glorious memory lane. Not wanting to overdo the sightseeing, I take the slow No 1 vaporetto up to Rialto and then disappear down the narrow lanes around the markets for some lunchtime *cicheti* and wine. I then catch a couple of vaporetti to reach Burano and Torcello for a peaceful wander, coming back in time for an early evening *spritz* before proceeding to a seafood splurge at, say, Al Covo in Castello. To finish up, I can't help wandering back into Piazza San Marco late at night as the cafés close and silence sets in. Wow.

My Essential Venice

- Admiring the grandeur of **Basilica di San Marco** (p50), the city's awe-inspiring cathedral
- Cruising past the mansions that line the **Grand Canal** (p48)
- Taking a break on peaceful **Burano** (p91)
- Sipping a **spritz** (p138) on Campo Santa Margherita on a sunny afternoon
- Mucking about in a **gondola** (p13), a unique vessel designed for the lagoon city and a great way to be taken for a romantic ride

City Life

City Life

According to Tiziano Scarpa, at the forefront of young Venetian contemporary writers, Venice is a fish. Look at a map and you can see what he means. To thrive, a fish needs nice clean water to flit about in. Has this one been left high and dry? Venice, with its crumbling walls, sometimes stinky canals and ever-present crowds of tourists, continues to fascinate and enchant outsiders and its own residents alike. The city that grew out of the lagoon is uniquely captivating. But it has serious problems that mostly go unobserved by the casual visitor. Various physicians have been called to the patient's bedside over the years. Many therapies have been applied, from cultural infusions to restoration campaigns. The patient is alive but certainly not out of danger. Some observers insist that one day the city will truly become an open-air museum, the lifeblood of its people drained away elsewhere and a day charge applied at points of entry.

VENICE TODAY

What makes a city is not so much its monuments, art and glorious history. What makes a city is its inhabitants. Venice has no shortage of the aforementioned attributes, but its people are ebbing away like an outbound lagoon tide. International organisations and generations of politicians have kept applying Band-Aids to major sores, ranging from worsening tidal flooding to the need to restore the grand buildings and works of art that constitute Venice's fabulous legacy to the world. But no-one has thought of a way to stop ordinary Venetians leaving. As the local resident population drops, the social infrastructure of the city comes under greater pressure. Shops close, services disappear, it becomes harder to get things done and…more people leave. Since 1990 several big companies, banks and other financial institutions have abandoned Venice for the mainland – one of the latest was the insurance giant Le Assicurazioni Generali, which abandoned its San Marco location for a soulless spot on the mainland.

Many would love to stay, and many more non-Venetians would like to move in. With world-class architecture, arts and Oriental studies faculties, among others, Venice has a vibrant university and intellectual life, if on a modest scale. In what other city are people obliged by the lack of cars to get about mostly on foot? Apart from the benefits in terms of noise and air pollution, the absence of cars has helped preserve a social cohesion long lost in other centres. People greet each other in the streets and squares, and stop for a chat or a drink before continuing on their way. There is a spontaneity about the place and its people that's missing in bigger, busier, more terrestrial urban centres.

But all is not well. Since the 1950s the population has dropped by two-thirds. Why? The city can be frustrating. You can't park your car outside the front gate (you can't park one anywhere!), and everything costs more because transport and distribution by

Canalside dining near the Gallerie dell'Accademia, Dorsoduro

boat is more costly and complex than on land. Jobs in anything but the public service and tourism-related services are hard to come by. Indeed, most of the jobs outside tourism left for the mainland long ago. Venice survives largely because of tourism, but the flip side is a constant run on local housing for use as hotel space and second homes for nonresidents. Buying is thus prohibitive and rents continue to soar. When locals are evicted to make way for such development, they frequently throw in the towel and move to the mainland – less aesthetically pleasing but eminently more practical. Nothing (or little) is done to alleviate the distorting effects of these phenomena or to help Venetians stay – the middle classes are particularly squeezed, as there is at least some social housing set aside for poorer residents. As customers disappear, shops close. In southern Dorsoduro, for instance, one local resident laments that where once there were half a dozen bakeries to choose from there is now one. Finding a shop that sells widgets is increasingly becoming a trial.

Hot Conversation Topics

- Will those lagoon barriers really keep the floods out? And will they ever be completed?
- Who was behind the mysterious Mulino Stucky fire?
- Those speeding motorboats and their *moto ondoso* (wakes) are bad for buildings, the lagoon and more peaceful vessels – something needs to be done.
- Can you eat well anywhere in Venice?
- Is it fair to evict Venetians so that buildings can be converted into hotels?
- It's wonderful to live in a city without car noise, but what a pain not to be able to park outside your front door!
- There's water, water everywhere, including sometimes the ground floor hall.
- All these tourists!
- Clubs, what clubs?

But the city is not only under demographic assault. The very lagoon in which it stands and which protected the city for centuries is eating away at it. Floods, pollution and overfishing are all helping destroy the lagoon and its city. If nothing serious is done, we are told, the city may well be uninhabitable before the century is out.

In the meantime, locals go about their business like phantoms in among the tourists. Although at times (especially on hot summer days) it seems impossible to even move for all the crowds, in general Venetians (and non-Venetians resident here) seem to have developed coping mechanisms. It is almost as though they don't see all the day-trippers. Outsiders who stay longer, however, often find the city and its tiny mixed populace surprisingly welcoming.

Seemingly unable to think of ways to attract more stable business and draw people back to live in Venice, the town authorities try to make up for it with a rich palette of cultural offerings. The six-month-long Biennale Internazionale d'Arte (Biennial International Art Exhibition) and its architecture equivalent in alternate years, coupled with other major and frequent one-off exhibitions, are a treat for locals. But even there it is hard to escape the conclusion that all is done to attract more tourism, a short-term boon to the coffers but a fickle beast.

CITY CALENDAR

Venice is renowned for its contemporary art and cinema get-togethers. If you can manage it, timing your visit to coincide with one of the city's big shindigs will add an extra festive dimension to your discovery of Venice. Otherwise, as a general rule, the best time of year to visit is spring, from about April to June (although Easter is busy with school groups). July and August can be unpleasantly hot and muggy, and late autumn to December wet. If you don't mind the cold, you can get lucky in winter (around January–February) with crisp blue skies and a relative scarcity of tourists. See also Holidays, p220.

JANUARY
REGATA DELLA BEFANA
The first of more than 100 regattas on the lagoon throughout the year is held on the day of the Epiphany (6 January).

FEBRUARY
CARNEVALE
This is the major event of the year, when Venetians don spectacular masks and costumes for a week-long party in the run-up to Ash Wednesday. The starting dates for Carnevale in the next few years are 17 February 2004, 1 February 2005 and 21 February 2006. See the boxed text on p10.

Rites of Spring

Venetians have been celebrating the approach of spring with their Carnevale (Carnival) since at least the 15th century. In those days private clubs organised masked balls, and popular entertainments included such fun as bull-baiting and firing live dogs from cannons! By the 18th century Venice was home to hedonism and the licentious goings-on of Carnevale lasted two months.

Things quietened down after the city's fall to Napoleon in 1797 and Carnevale died when Mussolini banned the wearing of masks. Revived in 1979, it has become the world's best-known baroque fancy-dress party, as extravagant as Rio's Carnaval is riotous.

The festivities begin on a Friday afternoon with La Festa delle Marie, a procession through the city. This is a precursor to the official opening on Saturday, when a masked procession leaves Piazza San Marco around 4pm and circulates through the *calli* (streets). The next day there are jousts and other mock military tournaments.

The following Friday afternoon's highlight is the Gran Ballo delle Maschere (Grand Masked Ball) in Piazza San Marco. Anyone with proper costume and mask who is able to dance the quadrilles and other steps of a few centuries ago may join in. Tickets can cost in excess of €200, plus the outlay for costume hire.

Saturday and Sunday are given over to musical and theatrical performances in Piazza San Marco. Also on the Sunday, a beautiful procession of decorated boats and gondolas bearing masked passengers wends its way serenely down the Grand Canal.

During the course of the festivities plenty goes on outside the main events – street performers fill the main thoroughfares and squares. Campo San Polo is often given over to children's theatre, jugglers and the like.

APRIL
FESTA DI SAN MARCO
The feast day of St Mark, the city's patron saint, when men give their beloved a bunch of roses, is on 25 April.

MAY
VOGALONGA
The 'long row' is a good-natured long-distance rowing regatta, held in the first half of the month. This event began in November 1974, when a group of Venetians held their first race off the Isola di Burano in protest against pollution and *moto ondoso* (motorboat wakes) in the lagoon caused by the growing use of motorboats for business and pleasure. Since then it has developed into a friendly free-for-all, with 3000 to 5000 or more participants and around 1000 boats of all descriptions (powered by human muscle) participating in the 32km jaunt from the Bacino di San Marco up to Burano via Sant'Erasmo and back down to the Grand Canal via Murano and Cannaregio.

FESTA DELLA SENSA
This feast day falls on the second Sunday of May and marks the Feast of the Ascension (*Sensa* in Venetian). Already an important day in the Catholic calendar, it takes on a special significance in Venice. Every year since Ascension Day 998, when Venetian forces left to regain control of Dalmatia, the city has celebrated the Sposalizio del Mar (Wedding with the Sea) – see the boxed text on p39. These days the mayor takes on the ducal role. The fun culminates in regattas off the Lido.

LATE MAY–EARLY JUNE
PALIO DELLE QUATTRO ANTICHE REPUBBLICHE MARINARE
The former maritime republics of Amalfi, Genoa, Pisa and Venice take turns to host the colourful historic Regatta of the Four Ancient Maritime Republics, in which four galleons, crewed by eight oarsmen and one at the tiller, compete for line honours. The challenge will be held in Venice again in 2007. In 2003 the Venetians were beaten into second place by Amalfi (celebrating their fourth victory in a row) on their home turf.

JUNE
VENEZIA SUONA
The streets and squares of Venice burst into musical life during Venice Plays, an annual music fest. Bands of all descriptions fill the evening air with good musical cheer on the third or final Sunday of the month. Performances run from 4pm to 10pm.

JUNE–OCTOBER/NOVEMBER
BIENNALE INTERNAZIONALE D'ARTE
This major international exhibition of visual arts started in 1895 and was held every even-

numbered year from the early 20th century. The 1992 festival was postponed until 1993 so that there would be a festival on the Biennale's 100th anniversary in 1995. It is held in permanent pavilions in the Giardini Pubblici, and at other locations in Venice, including parts of the Arsenale, Palazzo Grassi and Palazzo Correr. In alternate years the less well-known Biennale Internazionale d'Architettura (Biennial International Architecture Exhibition), the architecture version, is staged. In 2003 a new element was added with the first month-long Festival Internazionale di Danza Contemporanea (International Festival of Contemporary Dance) from mid-June.

JULY
FESTA DEL REDENTORE
The Feast of the Redeemer is marked by yet another regatta on the Grand Canal. The main celebrations, however, take place at the Chiesa del Redentore on Giudecca on the third weekend of the month. The Senato (Senate) ordered the construction of this church in 1577 in thanksgiving for the end of a bout of the plague. Every year thereafter, the doge (leader, duke), members of the Senato, other VIPs and sundry citizens celebrated by crossing the canal over a provisional pontoon bridge to give thanks. The doge is no more but the tradition has continued. All sorts of boats fill the Canale della Giudecca to join in the festivities, as the cityfolk wander to and fro across the pontoon. The night before, people eat a traditional meal of roast duck and sit back to enjoy fireworks.

AUGUST/SEPTEMBER
MOSTRA DEL CINEMA DI VENEZIA
The Venice International Film Festival, Italy's version of Cannes, is organised by the Biennale committee and held annually at the Palazzo della Mostra del Cinema on the Lido.

SEPTEMBER
REGATA STORICA
This historic gondola race along the Grand Canal is preceded by a multifarious parade of boats, many decorated in 15th-century style and powered by crews in period costume. Venetians first organised a rowing race in 1274, and have been doing it ever since. This regatta, one of the most important, is held on the first Sunday of the month. The mansions along the canal are draped in silks, flags and

other festive decorations for the big day. The parade is followed by a series of four races in different categories. The races start at Castello and proceed west up the canal to the former convent of Santa Chiara, where the boats turn around a *bricola* (pylon) to pound back down to the finishing line at Ca' Foscari, cheered on by the locals. The main event is the men's *caorline* (broad, snub-nosed lagoon vessels) race – the men need all their muscle power to make these seaborne beasts surge ahead…

NOVEMBER
FESTA DELLA MADONNA DELLA SALUTE
This procession over a pontoon bridge across the Grand Canal to the Chiesa di Santa Maria della Salute on 21 November is to give thanks for the city's deliverance from plague in 1630.

Top Five Quirky Events
- **Regata delle Cento Vele (Hundred Sails Regatta)** A splendid race held in summer (mid-June in 2003) and involving the traditional lagoon sailing vessels with triangular sails (this kind of sailing is known as *vela al terzo*). The prize is the Coppa del Presidente della Repubblica (President's Cup). The boats also parade in the Bacino di San Marco and along the Grand Canal.
- **Sagra di San Pietro di Castello (Festival of St Peter of Castello)** A busy local festival on the last weekend of June with music, drinking and eating at the steps of the church that was once the city's cathedral. It is one of the city's longest-standing and most traditional festivals.
- **San Pellegrino Cooking Cup** A rather bizarre and light-hearted series of races around the lagoon held over the first weekend of July, in which participants combine sailing with onboard cooking.
- **Sagra del Pesce (Fish Festival)** The island of Burano comes truly alive for a weekend in September (dates vary) for this annual fish festival. Stands sell fish and polenta, washed down with white wine and accompanied by traditional music. In the afternoon, the city's only mixed men's and women's rowing regatta takes place off the island.
- **Festa del Mosto (Grape Juice Festival)** On the island of Sant'Erasmo, where wine grapes are still grown – although the final product is hardly world-class – the grape harvest is celebrated in October (dates vary) with this festival dedicated to the fruit of the vine. Food, music and wine (fermented grape juice after all!) are part of the day's fun on Venice's 'garden island'.

CULTURE

IDENTITY

Just what is a Venetian? Some would say an inward-looking and dying species. The lagoon city that spread its rule across all of northeastern Italy, as well as territories up and down and beyond the Adriatic, for two and a half centuries, was once a proud and independent-minded place. With around 63,000 permanent residents (275,000 in the whole municipality, which encompasses the other lagoon islands, Chioggia, Mestre, Marghera and other bits of the mainland), Venice is not what it was. Back in the 1950s some 170,000 people were resident in the city. And the downward demographic trend is continuing – some say the point of no return has already been passed.

Of the permanent residents today, many in fact come from other parts of Venice's former territories or even further. Although many purebred Venetians might not like to admit it, the Republic frequently received transfusions of new blood and happily granted citizenship to newcomers (particular in trying times, such as when the plague wiped out more than half the city in 1348).

The people of the Veneto region (population 4.54 million) in general have a reputation akin to that of the Scots – canny with money. They are said to be hard-working and thrifty but not necessarily the life of the party. The Venetians are a bit of a case unto themselves. The city long considered itself apart from the rest of Italy and even today you get the feeling that the sentiment has changed little since Italian unification. There is a reserved air about the place, not unfriendly by any means, but slightly impenetrable. The impression is no doubt reinforced by the fact that, long ago stripped of much of its economic importance and overrun by *foresti* (non-Venetians), locals find themselves living in closed and ever diminishing circles.

Demographically, the place seems condemned. Talk to the average Venetian about his or her city and it is hard not to detect a note of despair. Said one: 'Venetians have the feeling that nothing is done for them. Those who have made lots of money just buy up houses and keep them empty or rent them out to tourists. And the little people find they have to go.' A common complaint from those who have moved to the mainland is that the middle class gets it in the neck. As one put it: 'Not rich enough to buy a house here and not poor enough to be eligible for subsidised housing.' And so the slow exodus continues, and the lifeblood of Venice seeps away.

LIFESTYLE

Living in Venice presents its challenges. To get anywhere you either walk or catch a ferry. The latter is frequently as time-consuming as the former, and so the city hums to the sound of padding feet. There are certain unwritten rules. Walking in single file in narrower streets allows more purposeful individuals to move ahead – a little like a human bus and taxi lane.

Commuting this way means you will sooner or later run into people you know. This can slow the day down, especially if you decide on a quick afternoon *spritz*.

Even the simplest daily matters are approached differently. How much shopping you can do is limited by what you can carry – no weekend shopping excursions in the car. Locals still use the fruit and fish markets, abhorring the deep-frozen stuff. Rubbish collection is simple – leave plastic bags of refuse outside the front door on the *calle* (street) and the rubbish boat will pass along the nearest canal to collect it. Moving house involves hiring a removals boat. If you have a large enough window overlooking a canal, so much the better – it's easier to hoist up from the boat than to drag furniture around to a street entrance. Living on the ground floor is not a great idea. Humidity and damp are predictable problems on the lagoon, and when tidal floods hit you can find the entrance hall filling up with water.

The pace of life is refreshingly human, slowed down by the absence of cars (boats are not supposed to travel at more than 5km/h inside Venice proper). On summer weekends many locals chug out to the Lido for a day at the beach. Others, as befitting the former glory of the maritime republic, prefer a good row (see Sport, p16).

Gondolas & Co

There was a time when the only way to get about effectively in Venice was by boat. But things have gradually changed over the past few centuries as more and more canals and other waterways have been filled in and bridges have been added. Today Venice is really a pedestrian city and not, as it's often romantically imagined, a boat town. Of course, the canals are the only way to move goods around, but your average Venetian will walk to get from A to B. Only when they have to get from one end of town to the other will they bother with vaporetti, while the *traghetti* (commuter gondolas) come in handy for crossing the Grand Canal at strategic points and cutting down walking detours to bridges.

All this means that mucking about in a gondola is nowadays a tourist activity. Back in the 16th century, someone calculated the number of gondolas in use in Venice and came up with the figure of 10,000. It would be interesting to know how they worked it out. At any rate, considerably fewer ply the canals today (there are about 400 licensed gondoliers). In those distant times, gondola owners painted them every colour of the rainbow, and those with money to spare went to enormous lengths to bedeck them with every imaginable form of decoration. Finally, the Senato decided in 1630 that this was getting out of hand and decreed that gondoliers could paint their vessels any colour they wanted as long as it was black. Nothing has changed since.

No-one knows for sure the origin of the term 'gondola', but it seems probable that it came from the Near East. These people-movers don't just come in the standard size you see every day on the canals: special ones come out to play for regattas. They include the *dodesona* (with 12 oarsmen), the *quatordesona* (14 oarsmen) and the *disdotona* (18 oarsmen). The *gondolino da regata*, or racing gondola, is longer and flatter than the standard model.

More observant visitors will soon start to make out other types of vessel, used for work and pleasure. Perhaps the most common is the *sandolo* and its little brother, the *sandoletto*, with squared-off prow and stern. Two standing oarsmen power them along, although a skilled oarsman can row either one alone. The *vipera* is similar to the *sandolo* but pointed at each end – having no stern, it can be rowed in either direction. It was introduced by Austrian customs officials; if they suddenly found bandits scooting away behind them, it wasn't necessary to turn around to chase them! More common is the *mascareta*, used for pleasure rowing about the lagoon.

Plying the canals is a series of heavy, sluggish-looking transport vessels powered with outboard motors. Known as *peate*, they are the city's workhorses and are used for everything from vegetable deliveries to house removals. The *bragozzo* is similar, but sometimes has sails on two masts. Typical of light lagoon-going transport vessels is the *caorlina*. It usually sports a single big sail on a long, slanted yardarm, although at regattas you will also see them being rowed – hard work!

In times past, the construction and maintenance of all these vessels required the expertise of the *squerarioli*, master carpenters and shipbuilders, who often came from the mainland (as that is where the timber came from). *Squeri*, the small-scale shipyards where they carried out their trade, once dotted the city. By 1612 the *squero* near the Chiesa di San Trovaso (Map pp256-8) employed 60 masters and scores of apprentices, who built not only gondolas but also trading vessels. It still operates today. Another *squero* (Map pp256-8), further west on Rio dell'Avogaria, is now run by an enterprising American who came to Venice to learn about the trade and liked it so much he stayed.

Making a good gondola is no easy task – seven different types of wood are employed to make 280 pieces for the hull alone. Also, it has to be asymmetrical. The left side has a greater curve to make up for the lateral action of the oar, and the cross section is skewed to the right to counterbalance the weight of the gondolier.

Nowadays, a master craftsman can build a gondola in about a month. Your standard model costs from €20,000. If you want more fancy ornament, the price starts to rise. A really 'pretty' gondola can cost more than €50,000. Only senior and experienced gondoliers tend to go for such luxury. They do so in part as a sign of their standing within the profession, and also in the hope of attracting more or better-off customers. A newly arrived gondolier, however, will satisfy himself with a simple, second-hand vessel to get started in the business. A well-made gondola will last at least 30 years and often longer.

FOOD
Venetian Cuisine

Some commentators, such as Venice's own historian Alvise Zorzi, claim that true Venetian cuisine has all but disappeared. Whether or not this is true is open to debate, and one hopes that Zorzi's faith in the rebirth of interest in good cooking (and eating!) will save any traditions that might have been on the verge of extinction.

It is true that eating in Venice is more costly than elsewhere in Italy. This is partly due to the greater expense of waterborne transport. In some restaurants there is undoubtedly an element of cheek involved too, despite all protests to the contrary. Venetians are a little like farmers – always crying poor and claiming imminent financial disaster.

Traditional Venetian food revolves around products fished in the lagoon and out to sea. Increasingly, the fish and other products you see in the markets are shipped in from other parts of the country, the inevitable result of increased demand and overfishing. Much seafood is seasonal. Anything that's on menus year round is imported at least part of the time. That in itself is no problem, but often products are deep-frozen *(congelati)* and largely tasteless. Better Venetian restaurants pride themselves on their use of fresh fish and seafood bought that morning at the markets, and vary their menus according to what they find.

STAPLES

The basic staple in northeast Italian cuisine is humble indeed – polenta. This maize-based stodge is to Venetians what couscous is to North Africans. It comes in different forms, although generally it arrives at the table in yellow slabs, lightly grilled. A less common version is made of a fine maize and has the colour and consistency of porridge. By itself, it really is a little sad, but used to soak up sauces and the like during a meal, it can be quite tasty.

No-one could be expected to live on polenta alone. Two dishes form the next basic rung up. *Risi e bisi* is a kind of risotto broth with peas. Despite the often lurid green appearance, it is really very tasty when properly prepared. Sometimes it's served with ham and parmesan cheese. In the Veneto, people take their peas seriously – some towns even stage Pea Parties (Sagra dei Bisi). It takes all sorts.

Perhaps even more common is *pasta e fagioli* (in Venetian, *pasta e fasioi*). This is a peasant dish *par excellence* that people unable to afford much meat have been munching for centuries. To the basic mix of short pasta, dried *fava* beans, onion, olive oil, salt and pepper, you can add pretty much anything you want to make it more interesting.

SNACKS & STARTERS

Cicheti and *antipasti*, or snacks and starters, are Venetian specialities. A classic snack or starter is *sarde in saor*, sardines fried up in an onion marinade, a favourite since the 13th century. Anything fishy fried up in *saor* tastes pretty good. The secret is in the *saor* marinade, which comes out extra tasty with a few pine nuts thrown in. Onions played a big part in traditional Venetian cuisine, especially for those at sea, as a preventative measure against scurvy.

A feast of cicheti *(snacks) at the Osteria alla Patatina (p128)*

Variations on the *baccalà* (dried cod) theme are legion. It is good served up with polenta, which absorbs some of the fish's natural saltiness. A classic is *baccalà mantecato*, mashed cod prepared in garlic and parsley.

Another delicacy is *granseole* (large spider crabs that live at the bottom of the Adriatic), at their best from October to December. *Cape sante*, or coquilles St Jacques, often feature with pasta, but as a snack are fried in olive oil and garlic, with parsley, lemon and a little white wine added at the last minute. *Moeche* (small shore crabs fished when shedding their shells, in March–April and November–December) are also good but tend to be expensive. *Peoci* (Venetian for mussels, known as *cozze* in Italian), *schie* (microscopic prawns) and other shellfish all feature prominently, and the list of bite-sized seafood items served up for *cicheti* is as long as the sea is deep. The Venetians also tend to have their own names for everything – the best advice is to get in there and pick and choose. Among the meat starters is *cotechino*, a type of pork sausage served up with mustard.

Verdure fritte (vegetables fried in breadcrumbs) are also good. A particular Venetian obsession is artichokes (*carciofi* in Italian, *castraure* or *articiochi* in Venetian dialect). If you hang around produce markets you may well see buckets of carefully cut-out *fondi di articiochi* (artichoke hearts) in water. Locals swear that, fried up with parsley and garlic and accompanied by a slab of steak, *articiochi* will send your taste buds to heaven.

PRIMI PIATTI (FIRST COURSES)
Risotto, which is basically a rice-based stew (think of the Spanish paella and you'll begin to get the idea), comes in many varieties. Among the possible ingredients are mushrooms, courgettes (zucchini), sausage, quail, trout and other seafood, chicken and spring vegetables. Not to be missed is *risotto nero*, coloured and flavoured with the ink of cuttlefish *(seppia)*.

Only a few types of pasta, such as *bigoli* (a kind of thick, rough spaghetti), really have a long standing in the Venetian tradition. *Bigoli* is ideal for seafood sauces, which stick to it better than to other pastas. A classic is *bigoli alla busara*, with scampi and a very mild red sauce. If you talk to the Milanese about *bigoli* they will giggle like school kids – for them, a *bigolo* is slang for a boy's naughty bit. Gnocchi, made of potato, is strictly speaking a Veronese speciality, but has been absorbed into the Venetian tradition.

Among the soups, the best known is *sopa de pesse* (which in Italian is *zuppa di pesce*, fish soup).

SECONDI PIATTI (SECOND COURSES)
Seafood is popular but often expensive. The prices you see for some fish are per *etto* (100g). Look at the fine print – otherwise you might get an unpleasant surprise. The cost of fresh fish is high, so cheap meals generally mean frozen fish is used. Common fish types include *branzino* (sea bass; good when boiled), *orata* (bream) and *sogliola* (sole).

Those not keen on seafood will on occasion be frustrated in Venice, as many *osterie* (traditional restaurant/bars) and restaurants specialise in watery delights and offer few, and in some cases no, meat alternatives.

This is not to say meat dishes do not exist. Of land-going critters, pork and its derivatives figure high in the more traditional foods, along with items such as liver *(fegato)* and even spleen (*milza*; an acquired taste) or cow udder *(mammella di vacca)*. Don't worry – all the more standard cuts of beef *(manzo)*, lamb *(agnello)*, veal *(vitello)* and so on are available. Try boiled meats with *radicchio trevisano* (bitter red chicory), eaten baked, in risotto or with pasta.

If you were to try only one meat dish in Venice that you had never had before (or even if you had), it would have to be *carpaccio*. We all know that the Bellini was invented in the Cipriani family's Harry's Bar (see the boxed text on p139), but less well known is that the idea to serve up plates of finely sliced raw beef in a simple sauce was also 'cooked up' there. The sauce is a mix of mayonnaise, crushed tomato, cream, mustard and a dash of Worcestershire sauce. The Ciprianis named it after Vittore Carpaccio, because at the time the artist was the subject of a big exhibition in Venice. A common variation on the theme sees the beef slices bathed in lemon, *rucola* (rocket lettuce) and shavings of *grana* cheese. Nowadays you can find *carpaccio* of other items too, such as tuna.

SPORT

Venetians like their *calcio* (football) as much as any Italians, but fans have precious little to crow about at the moment. With their team, Venezia, at the bottom of the second division and risking further relegation, the island stadium at Sant'Elena has become a sad sort of place.

Rowing is a more local passion, although clubs complain of declining interest. Nine rowing associations dot Venice, Mestre and the lagoon and locals compete in frequent regattas all year round. Some of the most important are gala events (see the City Calendar section, pp9–11) and attract passionate local support. *Voga alla veneta* (Venetian-style rowing, ie standing up) is the local style, but Venice has produced world champions of *voga all'inglese* (the English seated version). *Voga alla vallesana* is a rowing style where one person uses two oars.

Venetians like sailing too. Old-style sailing, or *vela al terzo,* involves traditional, shallow-hulled lagoon vessels rigged up with vaguely triangular main sails. Yachting is virtually impossible in the treacherous lagoon.

See the Sport, Health & Fitness section of the Entertainment chapter (p148) for tips on getting involved in rowing, as well as other sporting activities.

LANGUAGE

Italian in Venice comes with its own unique flavour. Since the unification of Italy into one kingdom in the latter half of the 19th century, the issue of language has been vexed up and down the country. Venice is no exception.

Standard Italian, with its roots in the Tuscan dialect of Dante, is spoken by pretty much everyone, but often with a strong local lilt. Influenced by Venessian (one of several dialects making up what linguists refer to as Venet, the language of the Veneto region), Venetians to one extent or another clip and chop consonants. *Ciao bello!* (hi handsome!) becomes *ciao beo!* in the local tongue. Many locals stick grimly to their dialect, although others tend to mix Venessian with Italian – giving Italian speakers from other parts of the country the impression at times that they understand everything, only to be confounded halfway through a sentence.

Documents from the time of the Republic show a disconcerting mix of Italian and Venetian (Venessian). Only with modern standardisation and universal schooling in the course of the 20th century have dialects, or dialect-Italian mixes, been relegated to a clearly second place in Venice and elsewhere in Italy.

ECONOMY & COSTS

The ignominious fall of the Venetian Republic in 1797 had its economic fallout. The Austrians favoured their own Adriatic port, Trieste, over Venice, although they did establish the railway line that links the city with the mainland and Milan to this day.

Inevitably, the city stagnated. While Italy's northwest embarked on a programme of industrialisation in the 1880s, the northeast remained stubbornly rural and poor. Well after the end of WWI, more than 60% of the region's workforce was involved in agriculture.

Industrialisation came mainly with the creation and expansion of Porto Marghera in the 1920s. In the following decades, the port and the metallurgy, chemical and petrol industries became major employers. But it was only well after WWII that small-scale industry began to take off around the

How Much?

Pizza – €6 to €10

Good mid-range meal – €40 to €60

Return trip along the Grand Canal – €5

An afternoon *spritz* – €2

Admission to the Palazzo Ducale – €11

One litre of mineral water in a bar – €2 to €3

Big beer – €4

Big *panino* (sandwich roll) – €3 to €5

Public toilet – €0.50

One day's bicycle hire on the Lido – €9

Veneto. By the late 1980s, only 7% of the population worked in agriculture, while 40% worked in manufacturing and 53% in services. At 4.54 million, the whole Veneto region contains around 7.5% of the country's population, but contributes 12% of exports. Since the early 1980s, the Veneto region has experienced steady growth, outstripping much of the rest of the country.

Tourism plays a pivotal role in the life of the Veneto, and above all in Venice. The Veneto as a whole contributes 13% of all Italy's tourist revenue. Although Venice has not remained untouched by the worldwide dip in tourism since the terrorist attacks in New York on 11 September 2001, tourism remains strong. In 2002 more than 3.5 million people stayed at least one night in Venice. Estimates on day-trippers range from 15 million to 20 million a year! Italians make up the biggest proportion of the city's customers, followed by Germans and Americans.

Venice is the third most expensive city in Italy after Rome and Milan. Property prices are artificially inflated by the hordes of holiday flat-owners from all over the world and limited space. Rents too are high. Indeed, everything costs a lot in Venice, in large part due to the complicated infrastructure and huge maintenance costs.

GOVERNMENT & POLITICS

Venice is the capital of the Veneto region (one of 20 regions in Italy), which extends west to Verona and the Lago di Garda and north into the Alps. The region is subdivided into seven provinces, of which the area around Venice – Venezia – is one (provinces are named after the main town in each). The other provinces are Belluno, Padua (Padova), Rovigo, Treviso, Verona and Vicenza.

Since 1927, the *comune*, or municipality, of Venice has comprised the islands of the lagoon (including Murano, Burano, Torcello, the Lido and Pellestrina), as well as Mestre, Porto Marghera and Chioggia on the mainland. Locals often divide the lot into three general areas: *terraferma* (mainland), *centro storico* (Venice proper, including Giudecca) and the *estuario* (all the remaining islands).

Traditionally, Venice is divided into six *sestieri* or municipal divisions: San Marco, Castello, Cannaregio, Dorsoduro, Santa Croce (Santa Crose) and San Polo. Nowadays, the territory of the *comune* is divided into 13 *quartieri*. The *sestieri* and the island of Giudecca (which is part of the Sestiere di Dorsoduro for administrative purposes) are grouped into the first two of these 'quarters'. The remaining 11 *quartieri* cover the lagoon islands and the mainland.

The present *sindaco* (mayor), Paolo Costa, has been in power at the head of a centre-left coalition since his predecessor, the charismatic left-winger Massimo Cacciari, vacated the position in May 2000.

Mistrust of government in Venice is as strong as anywhere in Italy. There is a feeling that little is done to address the city's acute long-term problems: rapidly diminishing population, flooding, pollution, and the extra high cost of housing, exacerbated by a recent hotel-building frenzy. Rather than actively encouraging new businesses to set up in Venice and aiding people to get access to housing, Venice's town fathers, for all the noise they make, seem content to allow the city to slip further down the slope into an open-air museum.

Costa's biggest challenge could come from the push by certain Venetian organisations for separation from the mainland parts of the Venice municipality, principally Mestre. Since 1979 there have been three referendums on the subject, and although the 'no' vote has always won in both Venice and Mestre, the gap has narrowed over the years. Many Venetians claim their city would be better served by a town hall that concentrates its energy and resources on solely Venetian issues. At the time of writing the date for a fourth referendum had yet to be set.

Strangely, at the same time, Costa is trying to *increase* Venetian influence on the mainland by promoting the setting up of a loose 'greater Venice' body that would take in several mainland local councils (including a hypothetical future Mestre council) and coordinate policy across the region. Could this be a timid imperialist reawakening?

ENVIRONMENT

Venice is under siege. For the most part, public attention on the city's ailments has focused on flooding and the chilling cry of *'Venezia sprofonda!'* ('Venice is sinking!')

THE LAGOON

For hundreds of years the city's greatest defence was its unique lagoon position. Now the one-time guarantor of Venice's survival seems bent on the inexorable eradication of the city.

The territory of the Comune di Venezia extends over 457.5 sq km, of which 267.6 sq km are lagoon waters, canals and so on. On the mainland, the city's boundaries take in 132.4 sq km. The *centro storico* is just 7.6 sq km of land, while the remaining islands together total 49.9 sq km.

It is tempting when gazing across the lagoon to think of it as a simple extension of the sea. No impression could be more mistaken. The Adriatic forces its way into the lagoon through three port entrances *(bocche di porto)* that interrupt the bulwark of narrow sandbanks strung north to south in a 50km arc between the mainland points of Jesolo and Chioggia.

The lagoon was formed by the meeting of the sea with freshwater streams running off from several Alpine rivers. It is like a great shallow dish, crisscrossed by a series of navigable channels. These were either the extension of river flows or ditches created by the inflow of seawater. One of the deepest is the Grand Canal (Canal Grande), which runs through the heart of the city. It is thought to have been an extension of the Brenta (which has since been diverted south).

No-one knew the lagoon better than the Venetians – whenever invaders threatened (such as in 1379–80, during the Battle of Chioggia), the Venetians would pull up buoys marking the course of navigable channels and so pretty much close access to the city. The channels are marked today by lines of wooden pylons *(bricole)*.

More than 40 islands and islets dot the lagoon. The better-known ones include the Lido, Pellestrina, Murano, Burano and Torcello. The tinier ones have served as convents, quarantine stations, hospitals and cemeteries. Today some belong to the city of Venice, while others are privately owned. A couple have been converted into luxury hotels. Some, such as San Michele, are easily accessible, while others have been abandoned to decay.

The busy Canale di Cannaregio seen from the Ponte delle Guglie (p113)

City Life – Environment

A Sinking City

Venice can be flooded by high tides. Known as *acque alte*, these mainly occur between November and April, flooding low-lying areas of the city like Piazza San Marco. Serious floods are announced several hours before they reach their high point by the sounding of 16 sirens throughout the city and islands. Although there is nothing new about the phenomenon (disastrous floods have been recorded since at least the 13th century), the wailing of the sirens is becoming an increasingly common part of the Venetian winter.

When floods hit, buy a pair of Wellington boots (gumboots; *stivali di gomma*) and continue sightseeing. Raised walkways *(passerelle)* are set up in Piazza San Marco and other major tourist areas of the city (you can pick up a map of them at the tourist office) and the floods usually last only a few hours. If the flood level exceeds 1.2m you can be in trouble, as even the walkways are no use at that level.

Since 1900, Venice has sunk by 23cm (some claim the real figure is much higher), partly due to rising sea levels and partly due to subsidence. Climate change could cause a general global rise in sea levels of 40cm to 60cm by 2100, which would make the city uninhabitable if no preventative measures are taken. Floods have become increasingly common and even occur out of the usual wet season. The city was inundated in June 2002, an unprecedented and unseasonal event that bodes ill.

Another major concern is that the waters of the canals are incredibly polluted. Until the years after WWII, the Adriatic Sea's natural tidal currents flushed the lagoons and kept the canals relatively clean. But the dredging of a 14m-deep canal in the 1960s, to allow tankers access to the giant refinery at Porto Marghera, changed the currents. Work is now underway to clean the sludge from the city canals. In the wake of the *Prestige* oil tanker disaster off Spain in 2002, the Veneto regional government called on Rome to ban oil tankers from the lagoon – a tough demand as that would do nothing for Porto Marghera's refineries. Fears of an oil spill in the lagoon remain ever present but at least single-hull tankers of the *Prestige* type have been banned.

As though all this were not enough, the saltwater – even when unpolluted – is corroding the city's foundations. Alarm bells are ringing and the city fathers have warned that if efforts are not made to counteract the corrosion, canalside buildings could start to collapse.

The good news, perhaps, is that a plan to install mobile flood barriers (known as the Mose project) at the main entrances to the lagoon, after decades of political stalling over their pros and cons, finally seems to be going ahead. In 2002 the central government in Rome approved the first phase around the Malamocco lagoon entrance (the main shipping lane into the lagoon), which will include a semicircular breakwater to reduce the effect of high seas pushed up the Adriatic by southerly winds, and a lock for waiting ships while the barriers are up. In all, 79 mobile barrier gates will be installed. They will be activated when floods of one metre or more above mean sea level threaten the lagoon.

Although Rome has given the green light, it has done so without having finalised the finances. Moreover, many remain sceptical about whether the system will even work. Theories on what should be done and alternative projects abound. A recent one is a German plan to build a series of road bridges from Punta Sabbioni to Chioggia. The cunning part is that when serious flood tides hit, part of the bridge would tip over into the water to form a flood barrier. Others say floodgate systems used in other cities, such as Rotterdam, are a more effective option. If the Mose system really does go ahead, both its supporters and detractors will be praying it works. If it fails, it will not only be an extraordinarily costly white elephant, but Venice's long-term fate could be sealed.

The 7.6 sq km of Venice today weren't always there. The islands that together formed Rivoalto were a fraction of the area now covered. The very shallowness of the lagoon allowed the next step. Along the edge of the deeper channels, the inhabitants began to expand their tiny islands. They did this by creating platforms on which to build new structures. Pine pylons were rammed into the muddy lagoon floor, then topped by layers of Istrian stone. The action of the seawater on the wood caused a process of mineralisation that hardened the structure, while the upper stone layers were impervious to the tides. It was an ingenious solution and the method has remained pretty much the same to the present day.

The lagoon is under threat. Petrochemical waste is dumped into it from the Porto Marghera plants. The digging of a major transit channel for tankers in the 1960s and other interventions have radically altered the natural flushing mechanisms. This and overfishing put pressure on the fragile marine life. The blatant disrespect of motorboat drivers for lagoon speed limits causes *moto ondoso*, the damaging waves that eat away at Venice's buildings but also destroy the mud banks *(barene)* that help keep the lagoon alive. Huge sums are spent on preserving the *barene* – but nothing is done to bring the boat drivers to heel.

If the lagoon and the many related environmental issues interest you, pop into **Punto Laguna** (Map pp256-8; ☎ 041 529 35 12; Campo Santo Stefano, San Marco 2949; ☯ 2.30-5.30pm Mon-Fri). It has a range of brochures, some in English, as well as videos and computers on which to search out specific information.

GREEN VENICE

Surprisingly for a city built out of the water, an extraordinary amount of greenery decorates Venice's private gardens. Public parks, however, are in short supply. The only ones of note are the Giardini Pubblici, created at the Castello end of town under Napoleon at the expense of a great deal of fine buildings, the rather small Giardini Papadopoli, near the bus station, and Parco Savorgnan, in Cannaregio.

Although there is frequent debate on recycling, refuse collection remains a basic affair. People leave plastic bags out on the street on collection days and the lot is tossed into rubbish barges. On those occasions when recycling has been attempted, recyclable and nonrecyclable rubbish has always ended up being tossed together into the same barges plying the city's main canals.

Arts & Architecture

Arts & Architecture

Venice was by tradition a city of practical people – merchants interested above all in the business of trade. This is not to say that the city and its people were aesthetically indifferent – quite the opposite is evident in its periods of artistic greatness. In architecture in particular, the city is adorned with an array of jewels that span the early medieval Byzantine to the neoclassical Renaissance splendour of Palladio.

In the visual arts, the lagoon city was a little slower off the mark. The most glorious period in Venetian painting came with the late Renaissance, taking in the 15th and 16th centuries and sputtering to a close in the early decades of the 17th century. Some masterly flashes followed in the form of the Tiepolos and Canaletto, but like the Republic itself, the power and the glory belonged to the past. Venice attracted as well as bred artists – many big names came from surrounding mainland territories of the Veneto.

Other arts, such as music and literature, seem to have excited Venetians considerably less. A handful of exceptions tend to prove that rule.

The contemporary scene in a sense continues the historical trend. Reduced to a backwater when the Republic fell in 1797, Venice never completely recovered culturally. Sure, artists were at work through the 19th century and into the 20th century (as best seen in the Galleria d'Arte Moderna, p63) but true greatness rarely sparkled. The high notes of the art scene today come from the outside, particularly in the form of the temporary shows of the Biennale Internazionale d'Arte (p10).

ARCHITECTURE

Of the early centuries in the life of Venice, no visible sign remains. The bulk of the city's surviving architectural testimony dates from the 11th century.

VENETO-BYZANTINE

East was West. That Venice stood apart from the rest of Italy is never clearer than in the city's monuments, whose inspiration is a mixture of Western and Byzantine influences. The obvious starting point is not in Venice at all, but on the island of Torcello.

Top 10 Notable Buildings
▪ Basilica di San Marco (p50)
▪ Palazzo Ducale (p55)
▪ Chiesa di Santa Maria della Salute (p60)
▪ Chiesa di Santa Maria dei Miracoli (p78)
▪ Chiesa di San Giorgio Maggiore (p90)
▪ Libreria Nazionale Marciana (p54)
▪ Arsenale (p81)
▪ Ponte di Rialto (p75)
▪ Ca' Rezzonico (p59)
▪ Mulino Stucky (p89)

While Venice proper was still a motley collection of muddy refugee settlements, Torcello was a booming focal point. Its people raised the **Cattedrale di Santa Maria Assunta** (p92), a singular lesson in cross-cultural experimentation. Essentially following the Byzantine style that can be seen in the basilicas of Ravenna, its builders were also influenced by the Romanesque developments to the west. The iconostasis separating the central nave from the presbytery, in this case made up of six thin columns, was a prime feature of Eastern Orthodox churches. The apses (dating to the 7th and 9th centuries) are the single clearest echo of the Romanesque style born in the Lombard plains to the west.

The real treasures are inside. Craftsmen from Ravenna created extraordinary mosaics, including the 12th- to 13th-century *Madonna col Bambino* (Madonna and Child) in the semidome of the central apse. Some art historians rate this work more highly than anything done in Constantinople itself.

Use of mosaics dates from Roman times and continued under the Byzantine Empire. In Venice, the use of a gold background became the norm. Nowhere is that clearer than in the dazzling décor of the city's star attraction, **Basilica di San Marco** (p50). This also started off as a three-nave basilica when founded in the 9th century to house the remains of St Mark. Later, two wings were added to create a Greek-cross form, again a Byzantine idea (and based on the Church of the Holy Apostles in Constantinople). To the casual observer, the clearest signs of its Eastern form are the five domes – add a couple of minarets and you could almost think yourself in Istanbul (ie Muslim Constantinople). Less visible from the outside, but still another characteristic that separates the basilica from Western churches, is the narthex (or atrium) wrapped around the front and side of the church up to the arms of the cross.

The basilica, with bits and pieces added on and redone over the centuries, is a bit of a hodgepodge. Romanesque elements are clear in the main entrances, and Gothic and even Renaissance contributions demonstrate the difficulty of easily categorising some monuments, built and altered over centuries.

The Romanesque Chiesa di San Giacomo dell'Orio in Santa Croce (p64)

ROMANESQUE

The architectural expression of Europe's reawakening, this style that swept across Western Europe made less of an impact on Venice. In some cases it was mingled with Byzantine building styles. Much of what was built in more purely Romanesque style was later demolished and replaced.

One reasonable surviving example is the **Chiesa di San Giacomo dell'Orio** (p64) in Santa Croce. Here you can see all the classic elements of the style. The Romanesque church tended to be squat and simple, with up to three apses. Decoration was minimal and the semicircle dominant. Doorways and windows, in the church as well as in the square-based and equally squat bell towers, were capped by semicircular arches. Architectural or sculptural ornament was otherwise virtually absent from most Romanesque buildings, at least in the earlier days. The pretty cloisters at the **Museo Diocesano d'Arte Sacra** (p85), just east of the Palazzo Ducale, are a perfect specimen of Romanesque simplicity.

As the grander Gothic fad caught on, church authorities had few qualms about rebuilding churches from scratch, seeing little value in the Romanesque versions, judged too simple and modest for the Lord's houses. Oddly enough, the bell towers that stood beside them were frequently left intact.

GOTHIC

In the 13th century, Gothic winds began to prevail in Venice, although the more sensual Byzantine aesthetic continued to inform artistic and architectural thinking. One way of identifying Venetian Gothic is by looking at the windows. Where you see them in clusters, with their tops tapering to a point, you can be reasonably sure the building you are looking at is Gothic (or perhaps a remake!). It is, however, a very Venetian twist on the theme – the shape of the windows is a hallmark of Byzantine and Eastern influences.

Of the city's great Gothic monuments, the **Palazzo Ducale** (p55) stands out. It is a remarkable creation and representative of the unique turn the style took in Venice. What you see is a mixed result: building started in the early 15th century, with several extensions and then reconstruction after fires in the late 16th century. The graceful porticoed facades facing the Bacino di San Marco and the square are given a translucent quality by the use of white Istrian stone and pink Verona marble. Elsewhere the decoration is restrained. This is less the case on the side nearest Basilica di San Marco: the carving on the Porta della Carta and Arco Foscari are fine examples of the intricacy reached in Gothic sculpture.

The two greatest Gothic churches in Venice were built earlier, at the height of the style's sway. The **Chiesa di Santa Maria Gloriosa dei Frari** (p66) was completed in 1443 (after a century's work), while the **Chiesa dei SS Giovanni e Paolo** (aka San Zanipolo; p82) was completed in 1368. Both are magnificent edifices on a Latin-cross plan. Decoration of both lasted long after construction was completed and reflects changing tastes. The Frari, a tower of elegance in brick, eschews almost completely the twisting lacelike external decoration typical of French and German Gothic. SS Giovanni e Paolo is partly decorated in marble and shows signs of the transition to the Renaissance. The churches are interesting for several reasons. Their relative sobriety of style underlines the fact that, throughout Europe, the Gothic style took many shapes and forms. These massive churches also symbolised the rivalry of two of Christendom's most important orders, the Franciscans (who built the Frari) and the Dominicans (SS Giovanni e Paolo).

Many architects at work in Venice were Lombards. Mauro Codussi (aka Coducci; c. 1440–1504), from Bergamo, was responsible for the imposing facade of the **Chiesa di San Zaccaria** (1483; p84), although much of the florid Gothic flavour (see the apse, for example) is the work of another architect, Antonio Gambello.

RENAISSANCE

The Renaissance cracked over Italian and then European society like a burst dam. Revelling in the rediscovery of the greats of classical literature, philosophy, science and art, writers, thinkers and artists embarked on a frenzied study of the ancient and an impatient search for the new. This was most publicly reflected in construction. Rejecting the clerical haughtiness of the Gothic and the Eastern rigidity of the Byzantine, architects of this new age put classical models to their service in a quest for harmony and rationality.

If Gothic churches soared high into the heavens, reminding people of their smallness compared with the Almighty, Renaissance grandeur spread laterally, luxuriating in the power of the human mind and the pleasure of the human eye. While tall Gothic spires might be topped by the cross, a building such as the Libreria Nazionale Marciana is low, flat-roofed and topped by statues. It is a house of learning.

Doorway of the Gothic Chiesa dei SS Giovanni e Paolo in Castello (p82)

Of course, it is not as simple as that. Among the identifying signs in Venetian Renaissance building is a proclivity for spacious rounded arches on all levels (usually two but sometimes three storeys). Fluted half-columns often feature on the upper storey, but otherwise ornamentation is generally restrained. The classical triangular pediment borne by columns is another common touch, seen clearly at the front of Andrea Palladio's Chiesa di San Giorgio Maggiore.

During this period, three of the city's master architects were from out of town. Jacopo Sansovino (1486–1570), whose real name was Tatti, was born in Florence and lived and worked there and in Rome. Michele Sanmicheli (1484–1559) came from Verona, but he, too, was drawn to Rome. The sack

The Power of Palladio

Although Palladio (1508–80) was active in Venice, the greater concentration of his work is in and around Vicenza. Palladio's name has a far greater resonance for a wide audience than any of his contemporaries, largely because his classicism was later taken as a model by British and American neoclassicists. The White House in Washington DC owes much to Palladio.

Palladio is best known for his **villas** (p196) in the Venetian hinterland. Of them, La Villa Rotonda (just outside Vicenza) is among the most famous. The villas were built for local nobility or those well-to-do Venetians who had turned their backs on the sea. They were conceived with a double role in mind – pleasure dome and control centre over agricultural estates.

Steeped in the classicism of Rome that had inspired much Renaissance architecture, Palladio produced buildings rich with columns and triangular pediments and occasionally with a central dome (as in La Villa Rotonda). Palladio's version of Renaissance architecture is often described as 'archaeological' due to his unswerving recourse to antiquity.

Palladio was made Venice's official architect on the death of Sansovino in 1570. His single greatest mark on the city was the **Chiesa di San Giorgio Maggiore** (p90) on Isola di San Giorgio Maggiore. Even in the distance, seen from Piazza San Marco, its majesty cannot fail to impress. He also built the Chiesa del Redentore on the same island.

It is probably no accident that Palladio received commissions to work his particular magic in such relatively isolated corners of the city. Bereft of significant surroundings, these grand churches, with their weighty columns, high domes and strong classical facades, command respect – and are best contemplated at a distance.

Palladio died before finishing many of his projects, including San Giorgio Maggiore. For their completion, we are largely indebted to Vincenzo Scamozzi (1552–1616), who faithfully carried out their designer's plans. Scamozzi did his own thing, too, designing the Procuratie Nuove in Piazza San Marco (completed by Baldassare Longhena).

of that city in 1527 spurred them both to pack their bags. Sansovino moved to Venice and Sanmicheli back home. Both remained from then on in the service of the Republic. Palladio (1508–80) was from Padua – read more about him in the boxed text above.

Sansovino dominated the Venetian scene. He had a hand in 15 buildings, among them **La Zecca** (the Mint; p54), the **Palazzo Dolfin-Manin** (p103) on the Grand Canal, **Ca' Grande** (p100) and the **Chiesa di San Francesco della Vigna** (p83). Perhaps the most prominent testimony to Sansovino's work in Venice is his **Libreria Nazionale Marciana** (aka Biblioteca di San Marco, or Libreria Sansoviniana in memory of its creator; p54).

Sanmicheli's most important contribution to La Serenissima was **Palazzo Grimani** (built 1557–59; p103). The Republic's leaders kept him busy engineering defence works for the city and Venice's scattered possessions.

Quite a deal older than the others, Pietro Lombardo (1435–1515) was another out-of-towner. While he was chiefly a sculptor, his latter years were occupied principally with building. One pleasing result was the **Chiesa di Santa Maria dei Miracoli** (1489; p78).

BAROQUE & NEOCLASSICISM

The 17th century in the Venetian building industry was dominated by Baldassare Longhena (1598–1682). A master of baroque, which took to florid ornament in seeming reaction to what some plainly considered the austerity of the Renaissance, Longhena cannot be said to have fallen for the most extreme of its decorative excesses.

His masterpiece is the **Chiesa di Santa Maria della Salute** (p60), the great dome of which dominates the southeastern end of the Grand Canal and not a few Venetian postcards. An octagonal church, its classical lines are a reminder of Palladio, but the sumptuous external decoration, with phalanxes of statues and rich sculpture over the main entrance, shows where Longhena was headed. To see where he ended up, you only need to look at the opulent facade of giant sculptures of the **Ospedaletto** (p86), northeast of Piazza San Marco.

In Venice's last century of independence, neoclassicism came into vogue. One of the senior names of the period was Giorgio Massari (1686–1766). Inspired by Palladio, his more lasting works include the **Chiesa dei Gesuati** (p59), **Palazzo Grassi** (p101) and the completion of **Ca' Rezzonico** (p59) on the Grand Canal.

THE PRESENT DAY

Palladio frequently found himself up against the conservative habits of the town fathers. His plans for the Palazzo Ducale and for a new Rialto bridge were overruled. The attitude persists to this day, but not necessarily with the same happy results. A design for a magnificent building on the Grand Canal by Frank Lloyd Wright, and Le Corbusier's plans for a hospital in the area of the former Macello Comunale in Cannaregio, are among many to have received the thumbs down.

This is not to say that nothing has been done. Probably the best known of Venice's modern architects was Carlo Scarpa (1906–78). He designed the entrance to the Istituto Universitario di Architettura di Venezia in Santa Croce (p110) and redesigned the inside of several museums, most notably the Palazzo Querini-Stampalia (p86). He also worked on pavilions for the Biennale in Castello from 1948 to 1978.

Venice, a labyrinth of canals, tight streets and urban planning restrictions, leaves little room for innovative building. However, the Venice city council has commissioned the Spanish architect Santiago Calatrava to design a fourth bridge across the Grand Canal between Piazzale Roma and Ferrovia. Just why this all-steel bridge is needed is not entirely clear to Venetians – a less strategic crossing point is barely imaginable given the presence of the perfectly handy Ponte dei Scalzi nearby. The new bridge is due to open in August 2004. Outside the city, Frank Gehry has presented his exciting Venice Gateway project as part of the revamped Marco Polo airport. A series of buildings seemingly half-covered in flowing drapes (or spinnakers according to the official interpretation) will symbolise the air, the sea and the dynamism of the Veneto region. Approval seems a long way off.

VISUAL ARTS

Venice's artistic golden era coincided with its expansion across northeastern Italy. It was a happy combination, for as Venice became the capital of a considerable land empire, it attracted artists from its newly acquired territories. All of this happened as the winds of the Renaissance finally began to wash over the region in the first half of the 15th century. Many of the greatest names in Venetian art did not come from Venice, and many moved around in search

> **Top Five Museums**
> - Palazzo Ducale (p55)
> - Museo Correr (p54)
> - Ca' Rezzonico (p59)
> - Museo della Fondazione Querini-Stampalia (p87)
> - Palazzo Mocenigo (p66)

of patrons, so that much of their work was either produced in other cities or has found its way to distant collectors' homes and galleries.

The Venetian Renaissance peaked with the greats in the 16th century. A handful of geniuses studded the following centuries, which were otherwise increasingly lacklustre.

The arrival of Napoleon in 1797 was a disaster. In the years of his Kingdom of Italy (1806–14) he and his forces systematically plundered Venice and the region of their artistic treasures. Many were whisked away to Paris, while countless others were sold off at hasty auctions.

Venice, no longer an independent capital, sank into provincial obscurity and its art went with it. The 19th century was a mostly stuffy and academic time, and more adventurous outbursts through the 20th century, while interesting, rarely resulted in greatness. Today Venice largely wallows in its glorious past. A plethora of galleries flog a variety of lazy lounge-room art and unconvincing commercial contemporary stuff. Only a handful make a serious attempt to be at the cutting edge of present-day trends. The major exception is the Biennale (p10), an international contemporary art fest staged every two years at venues across the city.

PRELUDE

Before the Renaissance made itself felt, Venice followed a largely pedestrian trail. The glory of its mosaic tradition dominated the Middle Ages, and the likes of Paolo Veneziano (c. 1300–62), perhaps Venice's most notable Gothic-era artist, could not break free from the Byzantine mould. His *Madonna col Bambino* (Madonna and Child; in the Gallerie dell'Accademia, p60) is a perfect example. The almost expressionless face of the Virgin Mary and the Christ child inside the almond with a gold background are typically Eastern iconic touches.

Some of Venice's best Gothic sculpture is represented in the tombs of the dogi (leaders, dukes) Michele Morosini and Marco Corner in the Chiesa dei SS Giovanni e Paolo. The latter was done by a Pisan, Nino Pisano (c. 1300–68). Sculptors never achieved the renown of some of their counterparts elsewhere in Italy, notably Florence and Rome. Renaissance tombs of several dogi in the same church are among the city's most important Renaissance sculpture.

The real innovative impetus in painting came from the mainland. Tuscans like Donatello and Filippo Lippi worked in Padua and influenced the work of Padua's Andrea Mantegna (1431–1506). Although Mantegna never worked in Venice, he became the conduit between that city and the fresh new Florentine artistic vision. He embraced the new idea of depicting perspective and injected a lifelike warmth and movement into his paintings.

The Renaissance was, in essence, a joyous rediscovery of classical Greek and Roman art, which served as a launch pad to shoot away from the didactic, motionless world of Gothic art, itself a more lively outgrowth of the still more instructive and largely religious Romanesque era.

This new wave brought another big change. Although some Gothic-era artists had begun to sign their work, it was only with the Renaissance that painters and sculptors truly began to emerge from centuries of artisan anonymity. That said, artists continued to operate as small businesses, running workshops and often having only a supervisory role in the execution of many orders. For this reason paintings are often attributed to an artist's workshop rather than the fellow himself. In some cases doubt remains over whose brushes were used. Although no longer anonymous, most artists are known to us by sobriquets – Il Veronese was from Verona, Tintoretto was the 'Little Dyer' because his father was a *tintore* (dyer).

Various Venetian painters, among them Jacopo Bellini (c. 1396–c. 1470) and Murano-born Antonio Vivarini (c. 1415–c. 1480) came into contact with Mantegna but it was Antonio's brother Bartolomeo (c. 1432–99) who picked up the baton. Altarpieces by him can be seen in the Frari (p66), San Giovanni in Bragora (p84) and SS Giovanni e Paolo (p82) churches, as well as in the Gallerie dell'Accademia. He filled his best and most lively paintings with a vivacious colour and crystal luminosity that were altogether new in Venice.

THE BELLINI BOYS & CO

Jacopo Bellini's sons Giovanni (1432–1516) and Gentile (1429–1507) proved less reticent about plunging into the new artistic wave than their father, who no doubt kept a keen eye on the order book and preferred to deliver what his clients wanted. Gentile had a crystal-clear eye for detail, evident in works such as *Processione a Piazza San Marco* (Procession to St Mark's Square; Gallerie dell'Accademia). A specialist portraitist in his early career, he was sent to Constantinople in 1479 to do Sultan Mehmet II's profile (now in London's National Gallery).

Giovanni shone out still more. The clarity of his characters, dominating their landscape backdrops, betrays Mantegna's influence, but Bellini extracts greater variety in tone and colour, creating a new softness and meditative quality. He also experimented with oil, which would replace tempera (powdered pigments mixed with egg yolk and water). His works are scattered across the globe but some can be admired in the Gallerie dell'Accademia, Museo Correr (p54) and elsewhere.

The younger Bellinis had set the ball rolling and the following generation bubbled with enthusiastic artists. Among them were Vittore Carpaccio (1460–1526), Lorenzo Lotto (c. 1480–1556), Cima da Conegliano (c. 1459–c. 1517) and Giorgione (1477–1510), the last two from the provinces. Carpaccio has left us some wonderful scenes that give us clues as to what the Venice of his day might have looked like, but the most extraordinary works come from Giorgione. He eschewed the usual route of the workshops, wrote poetry and music, and danced to his own tune. Credited with inventing the easel and teaching Titian, Giorgione was a man out of time. He painted *La Tempesta* (The Storm), now in the Gallerie dell'Accademia, without having first drawn his subject – a striking step into new territory. The subject itself was way ahead of its time.

THE GLORY

Venice might have been slow to catch on to the Renaissance, but with the dawning of the 16th century came the immortals.

Titian (Tiziano Vecellio; c. 1490–1576) was a 'sun amidst the stars', as one admirer put it. Born at Pieve di Cadore, Titian brought an unprecedented poetic approach to painting, full of verve and high drama. Confirmation of his status as leading artist of his day came in 1518 with the unveiling of his monumental *Assunta* (Assumption) in the Chiesa di Santa Maria Gloriosa dei Frari. His fame spread across Europe and he executed portraits of the greatest leaders of his day, from Habsburg emperor Charles V to Francis I of France. Relatively little of his work remains in Venice. A few pieces adorn the churches of Santa Maria della Salute (p60), the Gesuiti (p80) and San Salvador (p53). His most poignant work is in the Gallerie dell' Accademia. The *Pietà* (the dead Christ supported by the Virgin Mary), intended for his burial chapel, was finished by Palma il Giovane. Titian was carried off by the plague before he could finish it.

Titian was a hard act to follow, but he had fierce competition from Venice's Jacopo Robusti, better known as Tintoretto (1518–94), and Paolo Caliari, or Il Veronese (1528–88).

Tintoretto is regarded as the greatest of all Mannerists in Italy, going beyond Michelangelo's lead away from the more classical Renaissance, and right up with the singular El Greco in Spain. Indeed the latter, who studied in Venice in 1560, may have encountered Tintoretto. Some of their works show surprising similarities.

Mannerism is one of those twilight phases in the history of art, falling between the splendours of the late Renaissance and the excesses that would come with baroque in the 17th century. It is characterised in painting by a yearning to break with convention and a certain wilful capriciousness in the use of light and colour. In his earlier stages, Tintoretto's paintings are dominated by muted blues and crimsons and spectral figures. He also relished three-dimensional panoramas (see his *Crocifissione*, or Crucifixion, in the Scuola Grande di San Rocco, p76) and a swift, airy brushstroke. Much of his work is dominated by the dramatic use of shafts of light penetrating the dark. The Scuola Grande di San Rocco is a Tintoretto treasure chest, but also look for his masterpieces in the Palazzo Ducale (p55), Gallerie dell'Accademia and elsewhere in the city.

Il Veronese, too, was busy in the Palazzo Ducale. His grand canvases are mostly resplendent with lively colour and signal a penchant for architectural harmony. He liked to have all sorts of characters in his paintings, something that brought him uncomfortably close to the Holy Inquisition. His *Ultima Cena* (Last Supper), done for the Chiesa dei SS Giovanni e Paolo, included figures the Inquisitors found impious, including a dog and a jester. It is unlikely Veronese's defence of freedom of artistic expression won the day. The Inquisition was viewed unkindly by La Serenissima and so it decided on the face-saving solution of proposing another title for the painting, *Convito in Casa di Levi* (Feast in the House of Levi, Gallerie dell'Accademia).

Other artists of this epoch worth bearing in mind include Palma il Vecchio (1480–1528), originally from Cremona, and his grandson Palma il Giovane (1544–1628). Various works have been attributed to the former, but the younger Palma was more prolific. He finished Titian's final work, the *Pietà*. The Oratorio dei Crociferi (p80) is jammed with his work.

Another busy family were the Da Pontes, aka the Bassano because they were from Bassano del Grappa (see p204). Francesco Bassano il Vecchio worked in the first half of the 16th century. Four of his descendants stayed in the family trade: Jacopo (1517–92), Francesco Bassano il Giovane (c. 1549–92), Leandro (1557–1622) and Gerolamo (1566–1621). Of the lot, Jacopo stands out. His works can be seen in his hometown and the Gallerie dell'Accademia.

ROCOCO & CITY VIEWS

The 18th century was marked by the steady decline of the Venetian Republic. In the arts, a handful of greats kept the flag flying before the end finally came.

Venice's greatest artist of the century and one of the uncontested kings of the voluptuous rococo style was Giambattista Tiepolo (1696–1770). Tiepolo lived most of his life in the lagoon city but spent his last years working for royalty in Madrid. You can see some examples of his work in the Chiesa dei Scalzi (p77), the Gesuati (p59) and Ca' Rezzonico (p59). The Gallerie dell'Accademia has a fair smattering of paintings too. His son Giandomenico Tiepolo (1727–1804) worked with him to the end, returning to Venice after his father's death. Some caricatures of his, now housed in Ca' Rezzonico, presage the Spaniard Goya and the Frenchman Daumier.

On a completely different note, Antonio Canal, aka Canaletto (1697–1768), became the leading figure of the *vedutisti* (landscape artists). His almost painfully detailed *vedute* (views) of Venice, filled with light, were a kind of rich-man's postcards. Many of the well-to-do visitors to 18th-century Venice took home with them such a souvenir. Canaletto was backed by the English collector John Smith, who lived most of his life in Venice, bringing Canaletto a steady English clientele. This led to a 10-year painting stint in London. His success with foreigners was such that few of his paintings can be seen in Venice today. There are a couple in the Gallerie dell'Accademia.

Francesco Guardi (1712–93) became the Republic's chosen artist to paint official records of important events, such as the visit of Pope Pius VI. Guardi opted for a more interpretative approach than Canaletto. His buildings almost shimmer in the reflected light of the lagoon. One of the few of his major works in Venice is the *Incendio di San Marcuola* (Fire at San Marcuola) in the Gallerie dell'Accademia.

Born in Possagno, Antonio Canova (1757–1822) was the most prominent sculptor to emerge in late-18th-century Italy. He debuted in Venice, but by 1780 he had shifted to Rome, where he ended up doing most of his work. A few of his early forays, such as *Dedalo e Icaro* (Daedalus and Icarus), remain in Venice, in the Museo Correr. You could also head for Possagno (see p205).

TO THE PRESENT

Few Venetian names stood out after the Republic's fall in 1797. Francesco Hayez (1791–1882) started in Venice but spent most of his life in Milan, where his work ranged from a strict neoclassicism to the more sentimental Romanticism.

Gino Rossi (1884–1947), whose career took him from Symbolism to a growing interest in Cubism, was one of Venice's biggest names in the first half of the 20th century. He frequently exhibited at the city's pre-WWI art expos in Ca' Pesaro.

One of the few noteworthy names to emerge since WWII is Emilio Vedova (born 1919). Setting out as an Expressionist, he joined the Corrente movement of artists, who opposed the trends in square-jawed Fascist art. Their magazine was shut down in 1940. In postwar years, Vedova veered more towards the abstract. Some of his works can be seen in the Peggy Guggenheim Collection (p62) and there are a couple in the Galleria d'Arte Moderna (p63).

Fabrizio Plessi (born 1940), although born in Bologna, is seen by many Venetians as one of their own. He has long lived, studied and worked here and become known for his video art. Water is, appropriately, a central theme in his installations and sculptures, for which he combines all sorts of materials (anything from iron to straw) with videos. In 2001 Plessi transformed the facade of Museo Correr in Piazza San Marco into a sheet of streaming colour and light that made it seem like an otherworldly waterfall.

LITERATURE

Venice does not enjoy a senior place in the history of Italian letters and, perhaps surprisingly, has only occasionally taken centre stage in the minds of great writers from abroad. In modern times the lagoon city's mysterious location has, however, generated several strands of entertaining detective stories.

IN THE LIFE OF THE REPUBLIC

Not a great deal of literary consequence went on in medieval Venice. Francesco Petrarca (Petrarch; 1304–74), one of the 'big three' behind the birth of literary Italian in Florence, came to live in Venice for some years in the latter part of his life, although he preferred Padua. He had already gained considerable fame for his sonnets in Italian, although he continued to write much in Latin as well.

One of the earliest Venetian writers of any importance was Leonardo Giustinian (1388–1446). A member of the Consiglio dei Dieci (Council of Ten) and author of various tracts in Latin, he is remembered for his *Canzonette* (Songs) and *Strambotti* (Ditties). They are a mix of popular verses wrought in an elegant Venetian-influenced Italian.

The shining literary light of early Renaissance Venice was Pietro Bembo (1470–1547), who in his *Rime* (Rhymes) and other works defined the concept of platonic love and, above all, gave lasting form to Italian grammar.

Bembo worked with Aldo Manuzio on a project that would help revolutionise the spread of learning – the **Aldine Press** (p111). From 1490 on, Manuzio and his family became the most important publishing dynasty in Europe. He produced the first printed editions of many Latin and Greek classics, along with a series of relatively cheap volumes of literature, including Bembo's *Cose Volgari* (Ordinary Things).

Playwright Carlo Goldoni (see Theatre & Dance, p33) by far overshadowed the competition in the 18th century. Giorgio Baffo (1694–1768) is known above all for his risqué dialect verse (he was a pal of Casanova and particularly enamoured of the female behind), while Francesco Gritti (1740–1811) satirised the decadent Venetian aristocracy. The bulk of the latter's work is collected in *Poesie in Dialetto Veneziano* (Poetry in the Venetian Dialect).

MODERN TIMES

EM Forster, better known for his Florentine introduction to *A Room With a View*, gave Venice a run in his first novel, *Where Angels Fear to Tread*. A young English widow flits off on the Grand Tour, marries an Italian (tut tut), dies tragically and leaves behind a young child being raised, much to the family's horror, as an Italian!

Henry James set his *Aspern Papers*, a brief tale of a literary researcher determined to get his hands on an American poet's love letters from his aged and reclusive one-time lover, in the lagoon city in the 1880s. Weightier is *The Wings of the Dove*, in which the penniless Merton Densher foists himself on the ailing heiress Milly Theale in the romantic setting of Venice. The hopes of Densher and his secret lover, Kate Croy, go rather awry.

If you were to pick up just one piece of fiction concerning Venice, Thomas Mann's absorbing *Der Tod in Venedig* (Death in Venice; 1912) should be it. The city itself seems to be the main protagonist, reducing Gustav von Aschenbach, its feeble human 'hero', to a mere tragic shadow. In all its mysterious beauty, the cholera-struck city seems at the same time cloyingly infectious and coldly indifferent.

Thudding heavily back to earth, Ernest Hemingway was in maudlin form when he penned *Across the River and into the Trees* in post-WWII Venice. It is hard not to imagine Hemingway seeing himself in his Colonel character, as he mooches about between lagoon hunts and monosyllabic trysts – middle-aged and cantankerous.

A backpacker takes time out to read in Campo Bandiera e Moro

Top Five Books

- *Death in Venice*, Thomas Mann
- *Night Letters*, Robert Dessaix
- *The Comfort of Strangers*, Ian McEwan
- *The Wings of the Dove*, Henry James
- *Across the River and into the Trees*, Ernest Hemingway

In 1963 a Venetian business association inaugurated the Campiello prize (won that year by Turin's Primo Levi for his *La Tregua*), which has become one of the country's most prestigious literary awards.

Among several scribblers at work today, Paolo Barbaro (Venetian by adoption) is one of the few Italian writers active in the city today. He has taken the Campiello prize three times, the last in 1995 for *La Casa con le Luci* (House of Lights). His novels are generally set in Venice or his hometown of Padua, and in recent years he has written several personal musings on the lagoon city. In the latest, *Venezia – La Città Ritrovata* (Venice Revealed), he struggles to come to terms with the wintry lagoon city again after several years' absence.

In the latest wave of modern Italian literature is Tiziano Scarpa, whose first novel, *Occhi sulla Graticola* (1996), set in the student ambience of the lagoon city, revolves around several love stories which have at their epicentre a porno cartoonist.

A modern hit was Ian McEwan's *The Comfort of Strangers*, an early novel (1981) in which an outsider rocks a marital boat. It was made into a forgettable film in 1990.

Erica Jong, the doyenne of erotic fem lit, took a leap of the imagination in *Serenissima* (1987) by placing a Hollywood actress in autumnal Venice, where she finds herself transported back to the 16th century and living out a torrid affair with Bill Shakespeare!

Every night for 20 nights, a man just diagnosed with an incurable disease writes a letter in Robert Dessaix's *Night Letters* (1997). In the letters the reader is swept around in a whirlwind of past and present, tale and musing.

Numerous crime writers have found rich inspiration in Venice. Donna Leon's inspector Guido Brunetti resolves case after case in Leon's burgeoning series of detective stories, all set in the city. Try *A Venetian Reckoning*, *The Anonymous Venetian*, *Acqua Alta* and *A Sea of Troubles*. Michael Dibdin created another Venetian detective, Aurelio Zen, who tends to roam all over Italy. One set in the detective's hometown is *Dead Lagoon*.

MUSIC

Venice was the first European city to throw opera open to a wide public by establishing public opera houses in the first half of the 17th century. Some important names were busy before this too.

THE CLASSICS

Just because the first great names of Venetian music start from the 17th century does not mean there was no music in Venice before. Church, court and popular music abounded, and some of it has been rediscovered. Massimo Lonardi, who plays the lute, has resurrected sounds of the past.

The greatest musical name to come out of Venice was Antonio Vivaldi (1678–1741), born in Castello. A gifted violinist from an early age, he completed his first important compositions in 1711. By the time he died, he had left a vast repertory behind him: some 500 concertos have come down to us today. He was not simply prolific, but innovative, perfecting the three-movement concerto form and introducing other novelties that allowed greater room for virtuoso displays. Surely his best-known concerto is *Le Quattro Stagioni* (The Four Seasons).

Overshadowed by the genius of Vivaldi was Tomaso Albinoni (1671–1750), something of a dilettante who nevertheless produced a small body of exquisite music. Notable are the *Sinfonie e Concerti a 5*. His single best known piece today is the airy *Adagio in G Minor*.

Bruno Maderna (1920–73), composer and conductor, was at the forefront of the avant-garde in 20th-century European classical music.

OPERA

Claudio Monteverdi (1567–1643), born in Cremona, is considered the father of modern opera. He cut his teeth as a composer at the court of the Gonzaga family in Mantua (Mantova) and his *Orfeo* (Orpheus; 1607) has been acclaimed as the first great opera. Monteverdi's relationship with the Gonzagas was unhappy and he snapped up Venice's offer to make him music director at Basilica di San Marco in 1613.

Until 1637, opera and most chamber music was the preserve of the noble classes, performed in private sessions. This changed in Venice, which threw open the doors of the first public opera houses. As the only composer with any experience in the genre, the elderly Monteverdi wrote his two greatest surviving works: *Il Ritorno di Ulisse al suo Paese* (The Return of Ulysses) and *L'Incoronazione di Poppea* (The Coronation of Poppea). In each, Monteverdi created an astonishing range of plot and subplot, with strong characterisation and powerful music. Although he was not Venetian, the city liked to consider him one of its own – he was buried with honours in the Frari.

MUSIC IN VENICE TODAY

The modern music scene in Venice is dominated by opera and classical concerts by top Italian and foreign companies, who maintain a full programme at the PalaFenice and Malibran theatres (p147) and from 2004, it is hoped, the rebuilt La Fenice.

On a cheesier note, baroque music groups regularly stage works by Vivaldi and company at various venues, mostly churches and other little-used religious locations, for tourists. One that has gone beyond that and produces its own compositions is Rondò Veneziano.

Top Five CDs

- *Le Quattro Stagioni* (The Four Seasons), Antonio Vivaldi
- *Adagio in G Minor*, Tomaso Albinoni
- *Orfeo*, Claudio Monteverdi
- *Il Liuto a Venezia*, Massimo Lonardi (16th-century Venetian music for lute)
- *Piatti Roventi*, Pitura Freska

Young folk left utterly indifferent by these offerings seek solace in a small local music scene. Jazz, blues and rock can all be seen in Venice and, more importantly, Mestre. Until 2002 Pitura Freska led the Venetian reggae wave. In their wake other reggae bands have been left to keep the scene alive, among them Ciuke e I Aquarasa, which does a mix of reggae, ragamuffin and rock.

Venice and the surrounding area have also produced notable jazz musicians, such as Pietro Tonolo and Massimo Donà.

CINEMA

Back in the 1980s, a film archive in Venice found that the city had appeared, in one form or another, in 380,000 films (feature films, shorts, documentaries and so on). However, the city has starred in its own right in surprisingly few great flicks, tending rather to take bit parts.

From the early 1920s, Venetians Othello and Casanova got their fair share of runs on the silver screen. A good one was the 1927 *Casanova* by Alexandre Volkoff, with scenes shot in the city.

As the German film industry collapsed in the wake of Hitler's rise to power, mostly shifting to Hollywood, Venice began to get a bit of a run there too. Ernst Lubitsch's *Trouble in Paradise* (1932) probably has a lot more to answer for than the director could have imagined. In his studio re-creation of the lagoon city, he has a gondolier (dubbed with the voice of Enrico Caruso) singing that great Neapolitan song *O Sole Mio*. So that's where that modern tourist request came from!

Another Hollywood Venice was constructed for *Top Hat* (1935), one of the all-time great musicals starring Fred Astaire and Ginger Rogers.

Orson Welles had a go at *Othello* in 1952, a film he shot partly in Venice but mostly in Morocco. The antithesis of this was standard Hollywood schmaltz, of which *Three Coins in the Fountain* (1954), directed by Jean Negulesco, is a fairly telling example. A year later, Katherine Hepburn fronted a more substantial production, David Lean's *Summertime*.

Steve McQueen and a band of US sailors plan to rob the casino in 1961's *The Honeymoon Machine*. It's a fairly silly film but some of the shots of Venice are good.

Morte a Venezia (Death in Venice), Luchino Visconti's 1971 rendition of the

Top Five Films

- *The Wings of the Dove*, Iain Softley
- *Morte a Venezia* (Death in Venice), Luchino Visconti
- *Pane e Tulipani* (Bread and Tulips), Silvio Soldini
- *The Venice Project*, Robert Dornhelm et al
- *Othello*, Orson Welles

Thomas Mann novel, has a suitably ashen-looking Dirk Bogarde in the main role of Aschenbach. Perhaps less well known, but a better film, was Federico Fellini's *Casanova* (1977), starring Donald Sutherland. In this version of the life of the self-confessed lover and adventurer, we are given a more subtle look at the unhappy soul of a man who seems almost condemned to his role. Donald Sutherland was no stranger to Venice when he played Casanova. In 1973 he starred with Julie Christie in Nicolas Roeg's *Don't Look Now*. Based on a Daphne du Maurier novel, it shows Venice at its crumbling, melancholy best (or worst, depending on your point of view).

More recently, Venice has made appearances in *Indiana Jones and the Last Crusade* (1989) and Woody Allen's *Everyone Says I Love You* (1996), while films set in the city include the screen version of Ian McEwan's novel *The Comfort of Strangers* (1990), Oliver Parker's *Othello* (1995) and Henry James' story of love and betrayal, *The Wings of the Dove* (1997), starring Helena Bonham-Carter. *Dangerous Beauty* (1998), directed by Marshall Herskovitz, is a raunchy and somewhat silly romp through 16th-century Venice seen through the eyes of a courtesan. In *The Venice Project* (1999), starring Lauren Bacall and Dennis Hopper, Roland the artist in Venice, California, and his sister the countess in the family Venetian estate are not amused to find out their father had bequeathed his art collection to the Italian state. Venice also has a bit part in the 2003 version of *The Italian Job*, a fairly silly heist story set mainly in Los Angeles that was funnier in its original 1969 Roman guise with Michael Caine.

A charming Italian film, Silvio Soldini's *Pane e Tulipani* (Bread and Tulips; 1999) charts a housewife's unlikely escape from urban drudgery to the canals of Venice, where she embroils herself in all manner of odd occurrences.

Venice stars in several flicks by the city's controversial film-maker and erotophile, Tinto Brass. Born in 1933 and trained as a lawyer, Brass has directed a mountain of films, some of them teetering on a razor's edge between serious cinema and porn. Whatever you make of his films, many agree that his vision of his home town is among the most acute (if you can see past the sex, that is). His latest effort, *Senso '45* (2002), is set in the lagoon city in the closing stages of WWII, with the protagonists the wife of an Italian minister and her dashing SS lover.

THEATRE & DANCE

Oh God, Venetians groan as they peruse the programme at the city's main theatre, the Teatro Goldoni (p147). More bloody Goldoni! The 18th-century playwright Carlo Goldoni (1707–93) bestrides the Venetian stage much as Shakespeare dominates the English world's theatrical memory. Goldoni's stormy life saw him moving from one city to another, at times practising law but dedicating most of his energies to the theatre. From 1748 in particular, the prolific playwright produced dramas and comedies at an extraordinary rate.

Goldoni single-handedly changed the face of Italian theatre, abandoning the age-old commedia dell'arte, with its use of masks, a certain rigidity in storytelling and concentration on standard characters. This form of theatre had dominated the stages and public squares of Italy, and to a large extent France, for the previous couple of centuries, but Goldoni would have none of it. Instead, he advocated more realistic characters and more complex plots. *Pamela* (1750) was the first play to dispense with masks altogether.

Some of his most enduring works came during the 1750s and '60s. Among the best known are *La Locandiera* (The Housekeeper), *I Rusteghi* (The Tyrants; written in Venetian dialect) and *I Malcontenti* (The Malcontents). His decision to move to Paris was not an entirely happy one. With the exception of *Il Ventaglio* (The Fan), he produced little of note in the French capital, where, overtaken by the French Revolution, he lost his pension and died in penury.

While talking of theatre classics, William Shakespeare's *The Merchant of Venice*, starring Shylock and a host of colourful characters, is mandatory reading for a distant Elizabethan view of what in those days must have seemed an extraordinarily exotic and bizarre city.

The modern theatre scene is not all Goldoni and Shakespeare reruns. Local theatre groups and a few small companies stage modern plays, both Italian and foreign, mostly in Mestre. Tiny avant-garde and experimental theatrical hideaways lend a smidgen of local creativity, sometimes in dialect, to the Venice scene. For more information see Theatre, Opera & Dance in the Entertainment chapter (p146).

Since 2003 contemporary dance has received a thorough workout during the Biennale arts extravaganza, with the month-long Festival Internazionale di Danza Contemporanea (International Festival of Contemporary Dance) from mid-June.

History

History

To transport yourself back to the origins of La Serenissima Repubblica (the Most Serene Republic) – damp early days of refugees who chose the dubious swampy safety of the Venetian lagoon over the hazards of the lawless Italian mainland – get out of Venice. The grand *palazzi* (palaces), busy canals and splendid squares – none of these existed in the beginning. Strike out for the distant scrub-covered flats of Torcello, in the north of the lagoon, where the first mainlanders sought haven as the edifice of empire and the rule of law on the mainland crumbled before the barbarian invasions at the beginning of the Dark Ages. That's how it began. And now let's wind forward a little.

THE RECENT PAST

On 14 May 2003 the Italian Prime Minister, Silvio Berlusconi, paid a quick visit to the lagoon city to mark what might be the end of the beginning. After 30 years of debate, bickering, slander and foot-dragging, the Italian government had finally decided to set in motion work designed to protect Venice from the increasingly damaging tidal floods. Politicians on the left and environmentalists continue to maintain that the expensive plan (see the boxed text on p19) will prove an incredible white elephant. And at the time of inaugurating the project no long-term financial plan for its completion had been approved.

Water has dominated the history of the city from the beginning, and this particular phase of Venice's history started with record inundations on 4 November 1966. Never in living memory had such disastrous flooding been seen – the city looked set to be submerged. Ever since, debate has raged on how to protect the city, from the Mose (Modulo Sperimentale Elettromeccanico, or Experimental Electromechanical Module) system of flood barriers now finally decided on, to lesser measures such as raising pavement levels. The present mayor, Paolo Costa, has long supported the Mose project in tandem with other measures. His predecessor, the charismatic left-wing philosopher Massimo Cacciari, tended to side with environmentalists, who regularly brandish impact studies showing the system cannot work. Venetians are more than sceptical about the whole thing. Enormous sums of money have already been spent on studies and many feel that not a few politicians and lobbyists have benefited along the way.

Costa had replaced Cacciari when the latter stepped down in the hope of becoming president of the regional Veneto assembly in 2001. He failed in that attempt as Berlusconi's right-wing Forza Italia party swept to power across the country and the president's position was taken by Giancarlo Galan. Cacciari has returned to lecturing but remains waiting in the political wings.

Berlusconi's presence in Venice was, as usual, a source of controversy. Since becoming prime minister in 2001, the media magnate turned self-appointed political white knight has made a lot of promises but seemed mostly intent on passing laws to serve his own complicated purposes. The social and political climate has heated up, with massive demonstrations, bomb attacks and even the assassination of a senior government advisor. Venice got to feel some of the heat in August 2001, when a bomb ripped through the court buildings in Rialto just hours before Berlusconi was due to arrive for a lightning visit.

On, in retrospect, a lighter note of terror, seven young Venetian 'nationalists' invaded Piazza San Marco in May 1997 with a truck dressed up as an armoured vehicle and scaled the

TIMELINE	c. 1500 BC	218–203 BC	15 March 49 BC
	Veneti tribes arrive in northeastern Italy	Veneti ally with Rome in struggle against Hannibal during the Second Punic War	Roman citizenship conferred on people of the province of Venetia

Campanile to place a home-made Venetian flag high up for all to see. The police were lying in wait and quickly hauled them off. The aim of this rather quixotic operation? A reminder to Venetians of their glorious past, exactly 200 hundred years after the last doge (leader, duke) capitulated to Bonaparte and ended Venetian independence.

Largely untouched during WWII, Venice nevertheless suffered with the rest of Italy in the postwar years. The industrial zone of Marghera (which had been created under Mussolini in the 1920s) had been heavily bombed but, worst of all, people suffered shortages of just about everything. By the mid-1950s things were beginning to look up, but new challenges lay ahead. The population of 170,000 started to move, slowly at first and then with increasing rapidity. Venice is pretty but also pretty inconvenient. People left in search of work on the mainland. As tourism began to take off and outsiders began to buy up property in Venice for conversion into hotels and holiday residences, Venetians began to find the high cost of living increasingly untenable.

Relics from the 7th to 13th centuries in the Museo di Torcello (p92)

The process has continued to this day. One can only ask if the city, once the heart of a great trading empire, is destined, one way or another, to sink back into the lagoon from which it emerged in the dark years following the eclipse of the Roman Empire.

FROM THE BEGINNING

Legends suggest refugees from ancient Troy founded colonies in northeast Italy, just as the mythical Trojan Aneas landed in what would one day become Rome. A more sober reading of events sees Celtic tribes, the Veneti, moving in from the east around 1500 BC. Founders of the city of Patavium and staunch allies of Rome, the Veneti would eventually be absorbed into the expanding empire and granted full Roman citizenship in 49 BC. For centuries thereafter they shared the empire's fate and lived mostly in peace, far from the frontier-expanding wars of the legions.

All good things come to an end, and by the opening of the 5th century AD, Italy was under threat as the empire slowly crumbled. In 402 Alaric led a Visigothic invasion through the province of Venetia. His hordes sacked the port and bishopric of Aquileia and pillaged cheerfully all the way to Rome. Many Veneti fled to the islands in the lagoon that stretches along part of the province's Adriatic coast, returning when the invaders were expelled. More barbarian invasions followed, the most terrible by Attila the Hun in 452, and refugees increasingly opted to stay on the islands. The nascent island communities elected tribunes and in 466 met in Grado, south of Aquileia. There they formed a loose federation and established a degree of self-rule. Little evidence supports Venice's traditional 'foundation' date of 25 March 421.

In the meantime, the Western Roman Empire collapsed. Britain, Spain, Gaul and North Africa had all fallen, or were about to fall, into barbarian hands by 476, when the last,

AD 402	25 March 421	540	726
Alaric leads Visigothic invasion of Italy, forcing many to flee northeastern towns for Venetian lagoon islands	Traditional foundation date for Venice	Byzantine occupation of Italy	Orso Ipato elected doge of the Venetian lagoon communities

ineffectual emperor, Romulus, capitulated to the German Odoacer. Odoacer in turn was replaced by the Ostrogoth Theodoric, who proclaimed himself king in 493 and installed himself in Ravenna.

A DOGE IS BORN

In 535, the ambitious leader of the Eastern Roman Empire, Justinian, decided to turn the tide and recover Italy. Venetia (roughly equivalent to the modern Veneto region), the islands and Ravenna were quickly bound into the Eastern, or Byzantine, Empire, whose capital was Constantinople (modern Istanbul). The retaking of Italy and other former imperial territory proved costly and the successes short-lived, truncated by the Lombard invasion from France in 568. As the Lombards swept across the Po plains, refugees made for the islands in unprecedented numbers.

The new migrants settled primarily on Torcello, which would for some time remain the commercial centre of the islands, Malamocco (the southern end of what today is known as the Lido), Chioggia and Rivoalto. Rivoalto, subsequently known as Rialto ('high bank'), was no more than the highest of a small huddle of islets in the middle of the Venetian lagoon.

Anti-Byzantine uprisings had in part paved the way for the Lombards, and the Venetian lagoon communities were not immune to the spirit of rebellion. They named a certain Orso Ipato as their *dux* (leader, duke) in 726. *Dux* in Venetian dialect comes out as doge – and in this figure (another 117 doges followed) would reside the office of head of the Venetian state for the ensuing millennium. Orso and some of his successors found it hard to resist turning their appointment into an hereditary monarchy. Such temptation had its price: Orso was assassinated; two of his immediate successors were deposed, one of them blinded and sent into exile. Blinding became the common fate of later leaders who fell into disgrace. What slowly emerged was an electoral office, kept in check by two councillors and the Arengo (a popular assembly).

The Lombards were replaced by the Franks, who tried to invade the islands. They foundered in the lagoon, whose treacherously shallow waters only locals could navigate. In the end, Charlemagne, crowned Holy Roman Emperor in a muddy political deal with the Pope in Rome in 800, agreed to leave the so-called Duchy of Venetia to its own devices. It thus became the only part of northern Italy to remain anchored in the Byzantine sphere of influence.

THE REPUBLIC & ITS BODY SNATCHERS

The hero of the battle against the Franks was Agnello Partecipazio, from Rivoalto. He was elected doge in 809 and the cluster of islets around Rivoalto became the focus of community development. They were virtually impregnable to all who did not know how to navigate the deep-water channels that crisscross the lagoon. The duchy now began to come into its own. Its commercial and naval fleets were already the most powerful in the Adriatic, and Venetian ships were trading as far away as Egypt.

At home, Partecipazio had a fortress built on what would later be the site of the Palazzo Ducale. To the east, a church to St Zachariah (San Zaccaria) was going up at Byzantine expense. As the islands of Rivoalto were too small, too few and often too waterlogged for sustained settlement, land was drained and canals cleared. Most impressive of all, the land mass was extended by driving great clusters of wooden pylons into the muddy depths as foundations.

As Byzantine power waned, the duchy, which would become known as La Serenissima Repubblica, assumed greater autonomy. What it needed was a symbol to distinguish it from its official patrons in Constantinople. Legend had it (or was now cooked up) that the

810	828	992	1094
Peace treaty between Charlemagne and Byzantium leaves Venice in Constantinople's sphere of influence	Corpse of St Mark the Evangelist smuggled from Alexandria (Egypt) to Venice	Byzantium and the Holy Roman Empire grant trading privileges to Venetian merchants	Basilica di San Marco in its present form consecrated

With This Ring I Thee Wet

Pietro Orseolo's successful campaigns to subdue the Dalmatian coast and hamstring piracy earned him the title of Dux Dalmatiae. So chuffed were he and the nobles of Venice that in 998 they ordained that the events should be celebrated every year on Ascension Day (*Festa della Sensa* in Venetian).

The doge (duke), accompanied by bishops, nobles and other important citizens, would sail out to the Lido on the ducal galley, the *bucintoro*, and carry out a brief ceremony: 'Oh Lord, keep safe your faithful mariners from storms, sudden shipwreck and the perfidious machinations of wily enemies.'

The ceremony developed in pomp and circumstance over the years and came to be known as the *Sposalizio del Mar*, the Wedding with the Sea. It became customary for the doge to cast a ring into the waves just in front of the Chiesa di San Nicolò (at the northern end of the Lido) as part of this ritual. The ceremony is still carried out by the mayor today.

evangelist St Mark (San Marco) had once visited the lagoon islands and been told by an angel that his body would rest there. A band of Venetian merchants decided to make true the prophecy and in 828 spirited the saint's corpse out of Alexandria, Egypt. To house the holy relics, the doge ordered the construction of a new basilica, which would rise next to the Palazzo Ducale. Thus was the Byzantine-imposed patron saint, St Theodore (San Teodoro or Todaro), up-staged. In Christian iconography St Mark is symbolised by a winged lion, an image soon appropriated by the city.

By the end of the century, local administration had been centred on Rivoalto (at the core of what, by the 12th century, would be known instead as Venezia, or Venice). A new series of bishoprics, independent but loyal to the Republic, was established to counteract leverage from Rome (ie the papacy) through the see of Aquileia. A board of *giudici* (judges) was created to curb abuses of power by the doge. None of this stopped Doge Pietro Candiano IV from trying to grab full power for himself. So incensed were the people that they burned down half of Venice before cornering the hapless would-be monarch in the flaming wreckage of the Palazzo Ducale and, with a stroke of the sword, sending him to his maker in 972.

Pietro Orseolo was elected doge in 991 and proved one of the Republic's most gifted leaders. By careful diplomacy, he won the medieval equivalent of most-favoured nation status in Constantinople *and* in much of the Holy Roman Empire. Constantinople went further before the century was out, virtually opening all of the Orient (the lands east of the Mediterranean) exclusively to Venetian merchants. Placing trade before all other considerations, Orseolo also courted Muslim capitals from Damascus to Cordova (Córdoba).

Venice's growing prestige and prosperity could not have been better expressed than by the oriental opulence of Basilica di San Marco, consecrated in 1094.

BYZANTIUM, BARBAROSSA & THE VENETIAN BLIND

In the wake of the First Crusade in 1095, Venice increasingly took part in naval operations in the Holy Land, almost always in return for trade concessions. But rivals Genoa and Pisa were also making their presence felt, and so Venice established the Arsenale, shipyards in the Castello end of Venice that would become the greatest industrial site in medieval Europe. Here commercial and fighting ships could be constructed more efficiently than hitherto imaginable. Venice was going to need every last one of them.

Venetian participation in the First Crusade, although limited, spoiled relations with Constantinople. In 1171 the Byzantine emperor Manuele Comnenus staged an assault on the newly formed Genoese colony in Constantinople, blaming it on the Venetians, who were promptly clapped into irons. A fleet sent to rectify this situation ended up sloping home ravaged by plague without having fired a shot. At about the same time, Venice found itself

1104	1171	1203–04	1261
Venetian victories at Jaffa and Sidon in the Holy Land; foundation of the Arsenale	After staged attack on Genoese in Constantinople, Byzantium orders arrest of all Venetians present in empire	Doge Enrico Dandolo leads Fourth Crusade and conquers Constantinople	Latin emperor of Byzantium overthrown

joining the Lombard League of Italian city states and the papacy to oppose the designs of the Holy Roman Emperor, Frederick Barbarossa, on northern Italy. Venice was more or less at war on two fronts.

A series of reverses and excommunication convinced Barbarossa to back down. Venice was quick to seize the opportunity and staged an international public relations coup by inviting Pope Alexander III and the repentant emperor to Venice in 1177. The spot where Barbarossa supposedly knelt before the Pope and was thus received back into the Christian communion is marked in Basilica di San Marco to this day.

Again at peace with the Holy Roman Empire, Venice could turn its attention back to the East, where the events of 1171 had not been forgotten. When Doge Enrico Dandolo agreed to head up the greatest armada yet put to sea in the service of God, few of the participants in this, the Fourth Crusade, could have known what he had in mind. When the Crusaders gathered in Venice it turned out they could not pay for the fleet provided. No problem, said the wily, blind, 80-year-old Dandolo, who suggested the troopers could make up for the financial shortfall by helping Venice out with a few of its own tasks before reaching the Holy Land. And so the war fleet pulled into the Golden Horn at the gates of Constantinople in 1203. In repeated assaults that lasted into the following year, Dandolo sacked and looted the city, put a western (Latin) puppet emperor on the throne and had the figure of the doge declared 'Lord of a Quarter and a Half-Quarter of the Roman [ie Byzantine] Empire' – Venice's three-eighths of the spoils. To what extent Dandolo was directly responsible for these events is unclear. Some historians suggest he did little more than play a skilful game as events unfolded, rather than plan the conquest of Constantinople.

The Eastern Empire later recovered its independence, but remained a cripple among the world's powers. It is hardly surprising that it would later cave in to the green banner of Islam under the Ottoman Turks.

Venice was now at the head of a thriving commercial empire. The city's direct control of the Adriatic was undisputed. With subject cities and bases up and down the Adriatic, dotted about the Greek mainland and on Crete, Rhodes and Cyprus, as well as in Constantinople and along the Black Sea coast, the banner of St Mark flew all over the eastern Mediterranean. The marketplaces around the Rialto teemed with produce from as far away as China – spices, silk, cotton and grain were all unloaded there for transport further into Italy and Europe.

WAR, PEACE & THE BLACK DEATH

In the course of the 13th century, Genoa's growing presence in the Black Sea and eastern Mediterranean began to upset Venice's applecart. The first scuffle came in the wake of riots between the Genoese and Venetian quarters in the Christian enclave of Acre in Palestine. This ended in an ignominious defeat for Genoa off the coast of Acre in 1258.

Three years later, Venice's luck began to look distinctly pear-shaped. In Constantinople, the Byzantines, with Genoese connivance, overthrew the Latin emperor, threatening Venice's possessions and trade routes. Venice later suffered a heavy reverse at the battle of Curzola (Korc) on the Dalmatian coast, where the Republic lost 65 out of 95 vessels and the Genoese took 5000 prisoners (among them Marco Polo).

Their conflict would simmer along throughout the 14th century, also marked by a protracted conflict with the Papal States over control of Ferrara and a rebellion at home in 1310. This was ruthlessly crushed and in its aftermath the Consiglio dei Dieci (Council of Ten) was set up to monitor security. It ultimately became a kind of CIA-cum-cabinet. From then on the Consiglio, whose members were elected in rotation from the Maggior Consiglio, wove an intelligence network in the city and throughout Europe unequalled by

1295	1380	1453	1479
Marco Polo returns home from China	Genoese defeated at Chioggia	Constantinople falls to the Turks	Peace treaty with Turkey after fall of several of Venice's Greek possessions

A Complex 'Democracy'

In early days the doge's (duke's) power was circumscribed by two councillors and ultimately the will of the people, expressed by the **Arengo**, a popular assembly. This system proved too simple and the Arengo gradually fell into disuse.

Instead, there emerged a parliamentary body known as the **Maggior Consiglio** (Grand Council), made up of members of Venice's powerful and moneyed families. Technically at least, the approval of its 480 elected members was needed for any decision of moment. By 1340 it would have more than 1200 members. The Maggior Consiglio elected the doge by an incredibly complex balloting system described below. In 1298, franchise laws known as the Serrata del Maggior Consiglio (Closing of the Great Council) effectively restricted access to the Maggior Consiglio or higher office to a caste of established noble families (although it allowed more numerous representation among these). Money alone did not constitute nobility (although this would change in the latter years of the Republic). By 1323 membership of the Maggior Consiglio had become permanent and hereditary.

The **Quarantia** (Council of Forty) was responsible for economic policy, while the 60-member **Senato** (Senate) dealt with lesser affairs. The decisions of either (which on occasion worked jointly) were ultimately supposed to be ratified by the Maggior Consiglio. With time, the Quarantia would evolve into the supreme judicial organ of the state.

The Quarantia elected three *capi* (heads) who were equivalent in status to the *consiglieri ducali*, the doge's counsellors. Six of the latter were elected, one for each of central Venice's six *sestieri* (municipal divisions created in 1171). Terms lasted for a maximum of one year and *consiglieri* could not stand again for a minimum of two years.

The *consiglieri* and the three *capi della Quarantia* convened under the auspices of the doge to elaborate the bulk of policy, distributing tasks to the Quarantia and Senato. These 10 men together were known as the **Signoria** (Signory). With the passing of time, subcommittees evolved to deal with particular issues, often made up of *savii*, or sages.

All positions were held by members of the ruling patrician class. From the 14th century some crumbs were also left to the rising middle class of *cittadini* (citizens). The biggest of them was the office of **Gran Cancelliere**, or Lord High Chancellor, effectively the head of the civil service and superior in rank to the Senators. The Gran Cancelliere could be appointed only from among the ranks of *cittadini*.

Election of the Doge

The doge was elected by the Maggior Consiglio. His was theoretically a lifelong post but his power was heavily restricted. In an attempt to blunt family rivalries and corruption, the Venetians came up with an extraordinary system of indirect voting.

The people did not vote, although technically the Assamblea General, or Arengo, had to approve the Maggior Consiglio's choice. This body elected a commission that would then elect a candidate for doge. The members of the commission were in part elected by lottery. It worked a little like shuffling a deck of cards, picking some, and then repeating the process several times before arriving at the final choice of electoral commission. Records of the 1268 election (when the rules were tightened further) show that the vote went like this:

The Maggior Consiglio chose 30 members by lot, who in turn were reduced to nine by lot. These nine elected 40 members, who in turn were reduced to 12 by lots. The 12 elected 25, who were reduced to nine. These nine elected 45, in turn reduced to 11. These 11 voted for 41 members who then voted for a candidate for doge.

The 41 were locked away and proceeded with the complex electoral business. They each scribbled down the name of a candidate, and the names of all the proposed candidates were put in an urn. As each was pulled out, the candidate's suitability was discussed (if he or anyone from his family were among the 41, they had to leave the room while the deliberations continued). Then the candidate would be interviewed and voted on — if he got 25 votes, he became doge. If not, the electors went on to the next candidate. Lorenzo Tiepolo emerged as doge from the 1268 ballot; the process took 16 days from the death of his predecessor. In earlier times, the choice of the Maggior Consiglio then went before the Arengo, the people assembled in Piazza San Marco. This was rarely more than a rubber-stamp exercise.

Once elected, the doge had to sign a *promissione*, a contract defining the limits of his power. Initially a formality, the document had become a serious check on the doge's freedom of action by the mid-13th century.

1508	1570–01	1670	1684–87
League of Cambrai formed against Venice	Turks invade Venetian-controlled Cyprus; Turkish fleet routed by Venetian- and Spanish-led fleet at Lepanto, but Cyprus falls	Crete, the last Venetian stronghold outside the Adriatic, falls to Turks after a 25-year struggle	Venice joins European alliance against Turks; Francesco Morosini embarks on series of short-lived reconquests in Turkish-held Greece

Polos Apart

For Venice, 1261 was a disastrous year. It had lost control of a trade nerve centre in Constantinople and Venetian merchants were debarred from Black Sea trading bases. The new regime in Constantinople declared open season on Venetian traders, labelling them pirates. When captured, they routinely had their eyes put out and noses lopped off.

The change in circumstances caught up with the Polo brothers, Nicolò and Matteo, trading with the Mongol Khan's representatives in the Crimea. They decided the best option was to head east and so went deeper into the unknown, ending up at the court of Kublai Khan. According to some accounts, they were in Beijing (the winter residence); others talk of the Khan's summer residence, Shang-tu (aka Xanadu).

The brothers returned to Venice in 1269 but two years later set off again, this time with Nicolò's 20-year-old son, Marco.

For the next few years, the Polos trundled around the Orient making a stash in the jewellery business. It took several years of overland travel from the Gulf of Iskenderun (Turkey) to China, but eventually they made it to Shang-tu. There Marco entered the Khan's service and travelled extensively in China for the following 17 years.

The Polos' return was somewhat disastrous, for they were robbed of much of their fortune in Trebizond (Trabzon in modern Turkey). No-one even recognised them when they finally made it home.

Marco's tales of adventure were the talk of the town, but sceptics began to consider them rather tall and they came to be known as *il milione* (the million) because there were so many. Three years after coming home, Marco was captured by the Genoese in the naval battle of Curzola and hauled off to a Genoese prison. There he dictated his Eastern adventures to a scribbler called Rustichello. Marco called his memoirs *Il Milione*. Freed in 1300, Marco returned to Venice and settled down to a quiet life. His book, known as *The Travels of Marco Polo* in English, has been the subject of constant speculation ever since his death in 1324.

any of the Republic's rivals. In this period Venice also acquired its first mainland possessions in Italy, Treviso and the surrounding territory.

Before Venice and Genoa could begin to grapple properly with one another, their merchant vessels had brought back from the Black Sea one of the most miserable imports imaginable. The nasty little rats on board the vessels of 1348 were carrying the Black Death. The effect on Venice was as horrific as anywhere, with as many as 600 people dying every day. Up and down the canals, barges plied their sorry trade: *'Corpi morti! Corpi morti!'* ('Bring out your dead!') the steersmen cried.

The two powers barely paused to absorb this blow. The climax came in 1379, when a Genoese invasion fleet appeared off the Lido and took Chioggia. On Genoa's side were ranged Padua and Hungary, busy devastating the Venetian mainland territories. Still Venice managed a minor miracle, actually besieging the Genoese in Chioggia and seeing them off in 1380.

TURKEY ON THE MARCH

By the time the Turks marched into Constantinople on 29 May 1453 and snuffed out Byzantium, Venice had in most respects reached the apogee of its power.

Since the Battle of Chioggia, the Republic had largely kept out of naval conflicts. In a series of rapid conquests early in the 15th century, it acquired a land empire stretching from Gorizia in the east to Bergamo in the west. Venice allowed the conquered cities to retain their own statutes and long had popular support from its new subjects, who found Venetian rule less capricious than that of the average Italian despot (to which they had earlier been accustomed). The local noble families, shunted aside, were clearly less enthusiastic. For the next two and a half centuries they would mostly live in peace under the standard of the winged lion, sporadic wars with Milan and other disgruntled neighbours notwithstanding.

Greek refugees poured into Venice after the fall of Constantinople and confirmed the Republic's reputation not only as the most Eastern of Western cities, but also as one of

1699	1718	1797	1814
Treaty of Karlowitz between Allies and Turks	Treaty of Passarowitz leaves Venice with its Italian mainland possessions, parts of Dalmatia and Istria, Corfu and a few Greek bases	The 1000-year La Serenissima Repubblica comes to an end as Napoleon arrives in Venice	Austria retakes possession of Venice

the most tolerant (the Orthodox population was given its own church). La Serenissima's ambassadors hammered out commercial treaties with the victorious Sultan Mehmet II but were soon confronted with a harsh new reality. By 1500 the Turks had taken most of Venice's Greek possessions.

Venice's blackening mood was not helped by news of the discovery of the New World by Columbus in 1492 and Vasco de Gama's sailing around the Cape of Good Hope from India to Portugal in 1498. The Atlantic would in time overshadow the Mediterranean, with predictable consequences for Venetian trade.

Of more immediate concern was the formation of the League of Cambrai against Venice. Pope Julius II had decided that Venice was too powerful and drummed up support from France, the Holy Roman Empire (in the person of the Habsburg ruler of Austria, Maximilian), Spain and several Italian city-states. In return for cutting Venice to pieces, all were promised rich territorial rewards. In April 1509 French forces marched on Venetian territory, and within a year Venice had lost virtually all its land empire. The coalition, however, fell apart and by 1516 Venice had fully recovered its territories.

But La Serenissima, like the rest of Italy, was being increasingly overshadowed by Europe's great nation-states: France, Henry VIII's England and the Habsburg Empire stretching from Austria to Spain and taking in the new American colonies. More than ever, Venice had to tread a subtle line to ensure survival against the unquestionably greater powers around it. And so it adopted a policy of armed neutrality, attempting to stay out of bloody European squabbles.

For some years the Republic was able to avoid trouble from Turkey too, which was otherwise engaged in Eastern Europe (Vienna came within an ace of falling to Suleiman the Magnificent in 1529). But it was only a matter of time. In 1537 Suleiman tried and failed to take Corfu. Frustrated, he quickly swallowed up a series of small Venetian-run Greek islands and two remaining bases in the Peloponnese. He then took Cyprus, an act that finally spurred united action by Christian powers. Venice, Spain and the Papal States vowed to assemble a fleet every year and return to the fight until 'the Turk' was destroyed. In 1571 a huge allied fleet led by Don John of Austria (much of it provided by Venice) routed the Turks off Lepanto in Greece. Venice urged its allies to press the victory home but in vain. Seeing allied resolve so brittle, Venice had little choice but to sue for a separate peace.

The watchword in the remaining years of the century was caution. Venice had by now embarked on the most illustrious period of its diplomatic career. In other words, from here on its single greatest weapon would be lots of fast talking.

DECLINE & FALL

As the 17th century dawned, Venice was launched into a slow decline. Although eastern Mediterranean commerce had not been eliminated by the new Atlantic trade routes, Venice was suffering, also due in part to the loss of territory to the Turks and the revocation of its trade privileges. The city's well-heeled nobs wallowed in luxury, but in the face of the great nations and empires around it, Venice had neither the will nor the manpower to equip great fleets, let alone armies.

Venice did what it could to avoid costly conflict, but in 1645 the Turks landed on Crete and launched a 25-year campaign to conquer the island. Venice then joined a coalition of Christian countries in a series of campaigns against the Turks in the late 17th century, but the gains were short-lived.

Venice managed to tootle along unmolested until French revolutionary troops under Napoleon appeared. On 12 May 1797, with Napoleon's guns ranged along the lagoon, the panicking Maggior Consiglio voted the Republic out of existence. Napoleon was charmed

1846	1861	1866	1895
First train crosses new rail bridge connecting Venice with the mainland	United, independent Kingdom of Italy declared	Venice and Veneto join Kingdom of Italy	First Biennale d'Arte Contemporanea held

by his new acquisition, describing Piazza San Marco as the 'finest drawing room in Europe'.

For around six months the Republic lived as a puppet 'democracy' under the French. In January 1798 Venice and most of the Veneto, along with Istria and Dalmatia, passed to Austria. Venice became just another playing piece to be shunted around among the great powers. For an eight-year interlude it was tied into Napoleon's Kingdom of Italy before reverting to Austria. What did the Austrians ever do for Venice? They built the rail connection with the mainland, dredged and deepened entrances to the lagoon to ease shipping access, implemented a street numbering system and invented the *spritz*. The Venetians were not impressed and joined the newly independent and united Kingdom of Italy in 1866.

During the last decades of the 19th century the city was a hive of activity. Increased port traffic was coupled with growing industry. Canals were widened and deepened and pedestrian zones laid out. Tourism took off around the turn of the century, as the fine hotels along the Grand Canal came into their own. And by 1922, La Biennale, or the Esposizione Internazionale d'Arte (International Art Expo), was firmly in place as an added attraction.

Under Mussolini, a road bridge was built parallel to the railway bridge, and this event in essence marked the shift of business and industry to what is now 'greater' Venice: Mestre and Porto Marghera. Years later these areas would bear the brunt of Allied bombing campaigns during WWII, although Venice itself came out of it unscathed.

Top Five History Books

- *A History of Venice*, John Julius Norwich
- *La Repubblica del Leone*, Alvise Zorzi
- *Venice – A Maritime Republic*, Frederic C Lane
- *Venice – The Biography of a City*, Christopher Hibbert
- *The Venetian Empire – A Sea Voyage*, Jan Morris

27 February 1918	April 1933	4 November 1966	May 2003
Austro-Hungarian planes drop almost 300 bombs on Venice	Road bridge between Venice and the mainland opened	Record floods inundate the city	After decades of debate, work starts on lagoon barriers to prevent disastrous floods

Sestieri

Sestieri

The grandest surprise for the casual stroller in Venice is that the city is not completely teeming with outsiders in the manner of a wheat field swarming with locusts. Certainly, the main trails linking the train station to Piazza San Marco and the vaporetti (ferries) of the Grand Canal are a year-round stage for the incessant, awkward pageant of international tourism. But most of Venice's visitors get little further – many are in town too briefly to venture into the unknown; others are simply too bemused by the tangle of lanes and canals that twist and bend around the cityscape like an Escher drawing. It is an uncommon pleasure to lose yourself in the backstreets and marvel in comparative calm at the many faces of this unique creation.

Of course, you will want to poke around the great monuments and art centres as well, and these are explored in this chapter. Make time to visit the outlying islands too – each is possessed of its own peculiar charm.

This chapter is divided into sections covering Venice's six *sestieri*, or old municipal divisions, plus sections on the surrounding islands and the Grand Canal.

Top Five for Children

- Grand Canal (p48)
- Campanile of Basilica di San Marco (p53)
- Bell tower of Chiesa di San Giorgio Maggiore (p90)
- Museo Storico Navale (p85)
- Giardini Pubblici (p84)

ITINERARIES

You could cobble together an endless variety of itineraries through the city.

One Day

If you're only in town for a day and it's your first ever visit, you will find it hard to resist the more obvious sights. Instead of the classic stroll from the train station to Piazza San Marco, you could catch the vaporetto down the Grand Canal to Accademia and visit the Gallerie dell'Accademia, followed by the Peggy Guggenheim collection. Proceed to the grand Chiesa di Santa Maria della Salute. After visiting this church, catch a vaporetto across the mouth of the canal to San Marco, where you can finally see what you have been waiting for: the famous square and its extraordinary basilica. If you have time and energy you could explore the innards of the Palazzo Ducale and head up to the top of the Campanile for views over the city.

If you have been to Venice before and seen the big sights, you could devote a day to something different – pick one of the *sestieri* for some exploration or 'do' the island trio of Murano, Burano and Torcello.

Three Days

In three days you can get a more solid idea of the city. You could start with the one-day itinerary outlined above. The second day could be devoted to the islands of Murano, Burano and Torcello, while the final day could be dedicated to any of a number of projects. Take a vaporetto to Rialto, for

It's Free

For one week of the year (usually in spring), entry to state museums *(musei statali)* throughout Italy is free. Since dates change, it is impossible to plan a trip around this, but keep your eyes open. Admission to all state museums is free for EU citizens under 18 and over 65. In Venice only a few museums are concerned: the Gallerie dell'Accademia, the Ca' d'Oro and the Museo d'Arte Orientale. Admission is also free for non-EU citizens aged 12 and under.

It costs nothing to wander into Basilica di San Marco (although various attractions inside entail a charge) and the same goes for many of the lesser churches.

'The finest street in the world, with the finest houses' – the Grand Canal (p48)

instance, and explore the produce markets and shops in this area before settling in to an early lunch. Proceed through the busy lanes towards the magnificent Chiesa di Santa Maria Gloriosa dei Frari and the nearby Scuola Grande di San Rocco. After such a culture hit you might wander into Campo Santa Margherita for a drink, followed by a lazy stroll through the Dorsoduro area.

One Week

Take the above three-day programme and add in a day to explore the Cannaregio area, including its Ghetto. Another day could be dedicated to the Lido, especially in summer when you might want some beach time. The following day could easily be spent exploring some of the Castello area, from the grand Chiesa di SS Giovanni e Paolo to the curious Museo dell Icone or Museo Storico Navale. A final day (not necessarily the last) should be kept aside for a mainland excursion, say to Padua or Verona.

ORGANISED TOURS

You can join free tours for a biblical explanation of the mosaics in the Basilica di San Marco. They are arranged by the Patriarcato (the church body in Venice) and take place in Italian at 11am on Monday, Tuesday, Thursday, Friday and Saturday, and at 3pm on Wednesday. Tours in English are at 11am on Monday, Thursday and Friday, and in French at the same time on Thursday. This timetable is subject to change. For more information, call ☎ 041 270 24 21.

Consult *Un Ospite di Venezia*, available from tourist offices, for details of other tours of Venetian churches and sights. The Azienda di Promozione Turistica (APT) has an updated list of authorised guides, who will take you on a walking tour of the city. Many museums can organise guided tours at a price, for example, the Palazzo Ducale. A couple of museums, such as the Museo Archeologico and the Libreria Nazionale Marciana, offer free tours.

Travel agencies all over central Venice can put you on to a range of city tours, from two-hour guided walks for €27 to gondola rides with serenade for €31 per person. An afternoon tour partly by gondola and partly on foot involves a ride through various canals, a visit to the Frari church and return to the Rialto by gondola (€32). These tours leave at 3pm

Special Tickets

A Museum Pass covers admission to the Palazzo Ducale, Museo Correr, Museo Archeologico, Libreria Nazionale Marciana, La Torre dell'Orologio, Ca' Rezzonico, Museo Vetrario on Murano, Museo del Merletto on Burano, Palazzo Mocenigo, the Casa di Goldoni and Ca' Pesaro. The ticket costs €15.50 (students aged 15 to 29 pay €10) and can be purchased from any of these museums. It is valid for three months. You can also buy a Museum Card for €11 (students €5.50) that covers the Palazzo Ducale, Museo Correr, Museo Archeologico and Libreria Nazionale Marciana only.

Further options include an €8 (students €4.50) ticket for Ca' Rezzonico, Palazzo Mocenigo and the Casa di Goldoni, and a €6 (students €4) ticket for the Murano and Burano museums. When Palazzo Fortuny finally opens it will be grouped with Ca' Pesaro at €6 (students €4). Another cumulative ticket groups the Gallerie dell'Accademia, the Ca' d'Oro and the Museo d'Arte Orientale (adult/child €11/5.50).

An organisation called **Chorus**, which is involved in the upkeep of Venice's most artistically significant churches, offers visitors a special ticket (adult/child/student €8/5/5) providing admission to 15 outstanding churches. The ticket is valid for a year. Admission to individual churches costs €2. The churches from which you can choose are, in no particular order, Santa Maria Gloriosa dei Frari, Santa Maria del Giglio, Santo Stefano, Santa Maria Formosa, Santa Maria dei Miracoli, San Polo, San Giacomo dell'Orio, San Stae, Sant'Alvise, La Madonna dell'Orto, San Giovanni Elemosinario, I Gesuati, San Pietro di Castello, Redentore and San Sebastian. The ticket, available from any of the churches, also includes the option of visiting the Tesoro (Treasury) of Basilica di San Marco. Among the more worthwhile churches to visit, if you don't want to see them all, are Basilica di San Marco (Tesoro), Santa Maria Gloriosa dei Frari, San Giacomo dell'Orio, Santo Stefano, San Polo and San Sebastian.

A handful of museums and galleries offer reductions for students and seniors regardless of where they are from. It never hurts to ask.

daily from March to October and various languages are catered for. Some start from the American Express office just west of Piazza San Marco (Map pp254-5). One travel agency to try is **Agenzia Kele & Teo** (Map pp254-5; ☎ 041 520 87 22; fax 041 520 89 13; San Marco 4930). Tourist offices also have information.

Want to be guided but remain alone? One option is the My Venice handheld audio sets. You rent these things (which look like long mobile phones) for anything from an hour (€3) to two days (€15). With the accompanying map, you can follow commentated itineraries to key parts of the city. If you want a break, just switch it off – you can't do that with human guides! You can hire the audio sets at the Venice Pavilion Infopoint (Map pp254-5). Languages catered for are Italian, English, French and German. You need to leave your passport as a guarantee that you'll return the item when you've finished.

RiViviNatura (Map pp256-8; ☎ 041 277 41 89; www.forumlagunavenezia.org; Calle dei Vitturi, San Marco 2923) organises offbeat day tours around the lagoon. There are various options and, depending on the kind of boats used (from large traditional *bragozze* under sail to a vaporetto), these trips can cost anything from €17 to €45 per person (more if you want lunch thrown in). Trips can be organised year round but you need to get in touch to see what can be tailor-made to your needs. Call ahead – there's no point popping into the tiny office unannounced. It might not always be easy to get English-speaking guides.

Manuel Vecchina (☎ 348 341 83 92) runs a rather different tour. He leads a 1½-hour evening walk based on tales and legends of ghosts and other shiver-inducing types (€20 per person). Tours take place several evenings a week in summer, starting at 8.30pm at the Rialto and winding up at the Pietà church in Castello around 10pm. Tours are conducted in English. To find out more about the myths and legends of Venice, track down Alberto Toso Fei's entertaining book, *Venetian Legends and Ghost Stories*, or check out his website (www.venetianlegends.it). Vecchina's tour was inspired by this unusual read.

GRAND CANAL (CANAL GRANDE)

Described by French writer Philippe de Commines in the 15th century as 'the finest street in the world, with the finest houses', the Grand Canal is a little dilapidated these days but still rivals the world's great boulevards. It weaves for 3.5km through the city like a huge, back-to-front 'S', with a depth of about 6m and a width ranging from 40m to 100m. Taking a vaporetto is the only way to see the incredible parade of mansions, which date from the 12th to the 18th centuries. Board vaporetto No 1 at Piazzale Roma and try to grab a seat on the deck at the back.

Not far past the train station and Canale di Cannaregio (the city's second-largest canal), and about 150m after the Riva de Biasio stop (to the right), is the **Fondaco dei Turchi** (p66). Once a Turkish warehouse and now the Museo Civico di Storia Naturale (Natural History Museum), it is recognisable by the three-storey towers on either side of its colonnade.

The canal continues past Rio di San Marcuola to **Palazzo Vendramin-Calergi** (p80), now the city casino, on the left. Further on and to the right, just after the San Stae stop, is **Ca' Pesaro** (p63), Baldassare Longhena's baroque masterpiece (built between 1679 and 1710) and home to the Galleria d'Arte Moderna and Museo d'Arte Orientale.

Shortly after, to the left, is **Ca' d'Oro** (p77), acclaimed as the most beautiful Gothic building in Venice. To the right, before the boat turns for the Ponte di Rialto (Rialto bridge), is the **Pescaria** (fish market; p75) on Campo della Pescaria, built in 1907.

The stone **Ponte di Rialto** (p75) was built in the late 16th century by Antonio da Ponte, who won the commission over architects including Palladio. The Renaissance **Palazzo Grimani**, on the left after the bridge and just before the Rio di San Luca, was designed by Sanmicheli. On the right, as the canal swings sharply to the left, is the late-Gothic **Ca' Foscari**, commissioned by Doge Francesco Foscari and now seat of the university. It is followed on the left by the 18th-century **Palazzo Grassi**, used for art exhibitions. Opposite, Longhena's massive **Ca' Rezzonico** (p59) houses a collection of 18th-century paintings and *objets d'art*.

You are now approaching the last of the canal's three bridges, the wooden **Ponte dell'Accademia** (p58). Past it and on the right is the Palazzo Venier dai Leoni, which contains the **Peggy Guggenheim Collection** (p62) of modern art. Two buildings along is the delightfully crooked Gothic **Palazzo Dario**.

On the left bank, at the Santa Maria del Giglio stop, is **Palazzo Corner**, an imposing, ivy-covered residence also known as the Ca' Grande and designed in the mid-16th century by Jacopo Sansovino. On the right, before the canal broadens into the expanse facing San Marco, is Longhena's magnificent **Chiesa di Santa Maria della Salute** (p60), which takes central place in many a postcard of the city and its canal.

SESTIERE DI SAN MARCO

Eating p124; Entertainment p139; Shopping p152; Sleeping p164

Orientation

Largely cobbled together over the centuries by reclaiming (or simply creating) land from the salty lagoon waters, the district is named after the grand basilica at its southeastern end. The area is separated from Castello, the district that occupies the tail of this fish-shaped city, by the waterways of Rio di Palazzo della Paglia, which runs just behind the Palazzo Ducale and Basilica di San Marco, and its continuation in the Rio di San Zulian, Rio della Fava and finally Rio del Fontego dei Tedeschi, which empties into the Grand Canal just north of the Ponte di Rialto. San Marco's other boundary is the serpentine swing of the Grand Canal between the Rialto and the open expanse of the Bacino di San Marco.

The glory of the Republic is long past, but Piazza San Marco remains the symbolic heart of the city, a grand ceremonial space or, as Napoleon put it, 'the finest drawing room in Europe'. To its north a web of narrow *calli* (streets) winds north towards the Ponte di Rialto. The heart of this labyrinth is known as Le Mercerie and has long been home to stores of all sorts. Most now cater more or less to tourists and many sell the kind of gewgaws you are going to wish you hadn't bought. But there are also fashion stores, delicatessens, and a sprinkling of hotels and eateries.

West of Piazza San Marco, on and around Frezzeria and Salizzada San Moisè is the city's chichi shopping scene. Just about every name in Italian fashion has set up at least one small branch around here.

BASILICA DI SAN MARCO (ST MARK'S BASILICA) Map pp254-5

☎ 041 522 52 05; Piazza San Marco; admission free; 🕙 9.45am-5pm Mon-Sat, 2-5pm Sun & holidays Apr-Oct; 9.30am-4pm daily Nov-Mar; vaporetto Vallaresso/San Marco

Basilica di San Marco is at once a remarkable place of worship and a singular declaration of commercial-imperial might. The basilica embodies a magnificent blend of architectural and decorative styles, dominated by Byzantine and ranging through Romanesque and Gothic to Renaissance. Building work on the first chapel to honour the freshly arrived corpse of St Mark (see the boxed text opposite) began in 828, but the result disappeared in a fire in 932. The next version didn't have a much happier run, for in 1063 Doge Domenico Contarini decided it was poor in comparison to the grander Romanesque churches being raised in mainland cities and had it demolished.

The new basilica, built on the plan of a Greek cross with five bulbous domes, was modelled on Constantinople's Church of the Twelve Apostles (later destroyed) and consecrated in 1094. It was built as the private ducal chapel and remained so until it became Venice's cathedral in 1807. But no-one was in any doubt that this was the city's principal church. Thus symbolically tied to the power of the doge (leader, duke), this state of affairs was an eloquent expression of the uncomfortable position of the Church in Venice, which had no intention of allowing its state interests to be subordinated to the Church (and hence Rome).

Transport

Vaporetti No 1 and N stop at various points in the *sestiere* along the Grand Canal on their run between the train station and Piazza San Marco. Stops include Rialto, Sant'Angelo, San Samuele, Santa Maria del Giglio and Vallaresso. No 82 stops at Rialto, San Samuele and San Marco.

BASILICA DI SAN MARCO

Agony in the Garden Mosaic.......1 B2	Christ Between the Virgin and
Altar Maggiore (High Altar)........2 C2	St Mark Mosaic...................6 A2
Apse...3 C2	Christ's Passion Mosaic............7 B2
Battistero (Baptistry)...............4 B2	Cripta (Crypt)...........................8 B2
Central Dome.........................5 B2	Crucifixion Mosaic...............(see 7)

East Dome.................................9 C2	
Iconostasis..............................10 B2	
Kiss of Judas Mosaic.............(see 7)	
Main Entrance into Church from	
Narthex.............................11 A2	
North Dome............................12 B1	
Oldest Mosaic on Facade........13 A1	
Pala d'Oro.............................14 C2	
Pillars from Acre....................15 A3	
Romanesque Arches over Main	
Entrance............................16 A2	
Sagrestia (Sacristy)................17 C2	
South Dome...........................18 B2	
Southern Entrance.................19 A3	
Tesoro (Treasury)...................20 B3	
Tetrarchi..............................21 A3	
Ticket Office for Tesoro.........22 B3	
West Dome.............................23 B2	

Making His Mark

The story goes that an angel appeared to the Evangelist Mark when, while on his way to Rome from Aquileia, his boat put in at the islands that would, centuries later, constitute Rialto. The winged fellow informed the future saint that his body would rest in Venice (which didn't exist at this point!). When he did die some years later, it was in Alexandria, Egypt. In 828, two Venetian merchants persuaded the guardians of his Alexandrian tomb to let them have the corpse, which they then smuggled down to their ship in port, covered in pork to dissuade customs inspections (Egypt was then a largely Muslim country).

Why would anyone bother with such strange cargo? In those days, relics (bits and pieces of saints, real or purported) had enormous value in Christian countries, so the robbers probably saw a fast buck in the operation. Secondly, any city worthy of the name had a patron saint of stature. Venice had St Theodore (San Teodoro or Todaro) but poor old Theodore didn't really cut the mustard. An Evangelist, though, would be something altogether different. Did Doge Giustinian Partecipazio order this little body-snatching mission? We will never know. Whatever the truth, it seems that *someone's* putrid corpse was transported to Venice and that everyone rather liked to think St Mark was now in their midst. St Theodore was unceremoniously demoted and the doge ordered the construction of a church to house the newcomer. That church would later become the magnificent Basilica di San Marco. St Mark was symbolised in the Book of Revelation (the Apocalypse) as a winged lion and this image came to be synonymous with La Serenissima Repubblica (the Most Serene Republic).

Legend also has it that, during the rebuilding of the basilica in 1063, the body of St Mark was hidden and then 'lost' when its hiding place was forgotten. In 1094, when the church was consecrated, the corpse (which must have been a picture of frailty by this time) broke through the column in which it had been enclosed. 'It's a miracle!' the Venetians cried. Or just dodgy plasterwork? St Mark had been lost and now was found. A grateful populace buried the remains in the crypt, where they now lie beneath the basilica's high altar.

For more than 500 years, the dogi enlarged and embellished the church, adorning it with an incredible array of treasures plundered from the East, in particular Constantinople, during the Crusades.

The arches above the doorways in the **facade** boast fine mosaics. The one at the left end, depicting the arrival of St Mark's body in Venice, was completed in 1270. Above the doorway next to it is an 18th-century mosaic depicting the doge venerating St Mark's body. The mosaics on the other side of the main doorway date from the 17th century. The one at the right depicts the stealing of St Mark's corpse, while next to it the Venetians receive the body. The three arches of the main doorway are decorated with Romanesque carvings from around 1240.

The only original entrance to the church is the one on the south side that leads to the **battistero** (baptistry). It is fronted by two pillars brought to Venice from Acre in the Holy Land in the 13th century. The Syriac sculpture *Tetrarchi* (Tetrarchs), next to the Porta della Carta of the Palazzo Ducale, dates from the 4th century and is believed to represent Diocletian and his three co-emperors, who ruled the Roman Empire in the 3rd century AD.

On the Loggia dei Cavalli above the main entrance are copies of four gilded bronze horses: the originals, on display inside, were stolen when Constantinople was sacked in 1204, during the Fourth Crusade. Napoleon removed them to Paris in 1797, but they were returned after the fall of the French Empire. It didn't occur to anyone to send them on to the original owner, the by now Muslim Istanbul.

Through the doors is the **narthex**, or vestibule (a typical Byzantine element), its domes and arches decorated with mosaics, dating mainly from the 13th century. The oldest mosaics in the basilica, dating from around 1063, are in the niches of the bay in front of the main door from the narthex into the church proper. They feature the *Madonna with the Apostles*. Look for the red marble spot in the floor. This marks where Pope Alexander III and Barbarossa kissed and made up in 1177.

The **interior** of the basilica is dazzling: if you can take your eyes off the glitter of the mosaics, take time to admire the 12th-century marble **pavement**, an infinite variety of geometrical whimsy interspersed with floral motifs and depictions of animals, made wavy by subsidence in parts. The lower level of the walls is lined with precious Eastern marbles, above which the extraordinary feast of gilded **mosaics** begins. Work started on the mosaics in the 11th century. Those in the baptistry and side chapels date from the 14th and 15th centuries, and mosaics were still being added or restored as late as the 18th century.

Notable mosaics include the 12th-century *Ascension* in the central dome; those on the

The sun sets behind one of the city's bell towers

arch between the central and west domes, dating from the same period and including *Christ's Passion*, the *Kiss of Judas* and the *Crucifixion*; the early-12th-century mosaics of the *Pentecost* in the west dome; the 13th-century lunette over the west door depicting *Christ Between the Virgin and St Mark*; the 13th-century *Agony in the Garden* on the wall of the right aisle; the early-12th-century mosaics in the left-transept (north) dome portraying the life of St John the Evangelist; those in the east dome depicting the *Religion of Christ as Foretold by the Prophets* (12th century); 12th-century mosaics in the right-transept (south) dome depicting a series of saints; and those between the windows of the apse depicting St Mark and three other patron saints of Venice, which are among the earliest mosaics in the basilica.

Separating the main body of the church from the area before the high altar is a magnificent, multicoloured marble **iconostasis** (another Byzantine element not present in Western churches). Dividing the iconostasis in two is a huge cross of bronze and silver. To each side, the Virgin Mary and the Apostles line up. In a crypt beneath the majestic marble **altar maggiore** (high altar) lie the remains of St Mark.

Behind the altar is one of the basilica's treasures, the exquisite **Pala d'Oro** (admission adult/child €1.50/1), a gold, enamel and jewel-encrusted altarpiece made in Constan-

tinople for Doge Pietro Orseolo I in 976. It was enriched and reworked in Constantinople in 1105, enlarged by Venetian goldsmiths in 1209 and reset in the 14th century. Among the almost 2000 precious stones that adorn it are emeralds, rubies, amethysts, sapphires and pearls.

The **Tesoro** (Treasury; admission adult/child €2/1), accessible from the right transept, contains most of the booty from the 1204 raid on Constantinople, including a thorn said to be from the crown worn by Christ.

Through a door at the far right end of the narthex, stairs lead to the **Galleria** (aka Museo di San Marco; ☎ 041 522 52 05; admission adult/child €1.50/1; ☷ 9.45am-5pm), which contains the original gilded bronze horses and provides access to the **Loggia dei Cavalli** (Horses Loggia). The Galleria affords wonderful views of the church's interior, while the loggia offers equally splendid vistas of the piazza. Access to the crypt and baptistry is possible only if you have specific permission from the church administrators.

The basilica's mosaics are best seen when illuminated: on weekdays from 11.30am to 12.30pm and during some of the weekend Masses.

To avoid the disappointment of being turned away at the door, dress appropriately for a religious building – no-one with bare shoulders or knees will be admitted.

CAMPANILE Map pp254-5

Admission adult/child €6/3; ⏰ 9am-9pm late Jun-Aug, 9am-7pm Apr-Jun & Sep-Oct, 9am-4pm Nov-Mar; vaporetto Vallaresso/San Marco

The 99m-tall bell tower (Campanile) of Basilica di San Marco stands apart from the church. It was raised in the 10th century and gave faithful service to the faithful for a good nine centuries. Then suddenly, on 14 July 1902, it just fell in a heap. The town fathers vowed to rebuild it brick by brick *dov'era, com'era* ('where it was and as it was'), which they did over the following 10 years. Alterations had already been made in the 12th and 16th centuries. On the second occasion, a statuette of the Archangel Gabriel was positioned at the tip of the tower to serve as an elaborate weather vane. Oddly, the tower contains just one bell, the Marangona, the only one to survive the collapse.

In more grisly times past, particularly unfortunate criminals might be condemned to be strung up in a gibbet suspended high up on the south face of the bell tower. There they would stay day and night, exposed to the elements until their sentence was done or they expired.

Take the lift to the top, from where there are views across the entire city.

CHIESA DI SAN SALVADOR Map pp254-5

Campo San Salvador; admission free; ⏰ 9am-noon & 3-6pm Mon-Fri; vaporetto Rialto

Built on a plan of three Greek crosses laid end to end, San Salvador is among the city's oldest churches, possibly dating from the 7th century (although the bulk of what you see dates from later periods). The present facade was erected in 1663. Among the noteworthy works inside is Titian's *Annunciazione* (Annunciation), at the third altar on the right as you approach the main altar. Behind the main altar is another of his contributions, the *Trasfigurazione* (Transfiguration).

To the right of the church is the former monastery of the same name, now owned by Telecom. You can get just a glimpse of one of the cloisters by peering through the window nearest the church.

CHIESA DI SANTA MARIA DEL GIGLIO

Map pp256-8

Campo di Santa Maria del Giglio; admission €2 or Chorus ticket; ⏰ 10am-5pm Mon-Sat, 1-5pm Sun; vaporetto Santa Maria del Giglio

Also known as Santa Maria Zobenigo, this church's baroque facade is a fanciful centuries-old atlas, featuring maps of European cities as they were in 1678. The facade also hides the

fact that a church has stood here since the 10th century.

The church is a rather small affair, but jammed with an assortment of paintings. Of particular interest is Peter Paul Rubens' *Madonna col Bambino e San Giovanni* (Madonna and Child with St John), the only work of his in Venice. Behind the altar lurk Tintoretto's typically moody depictions of the four Evangelists, and the church is stuffed with other works by lower-ranking Venetian painters.

Outside, the oddly out-of-place square brick building in the middle of the *campo* was the base of the church's bell tower, knocked down in 1775 because it was in danger of falling over of its own accord.

CHIESA DI SANTO STEFANO Map pp256-8

Campo Santo Stefano; admission to church free, admission to museum €2 or Chorus ticket; ⏰ 10am-5pm Mon-Sat, 1-5pm Sun; vaporetto Accademia

When you walk in here, look up at possibly the finest timber ceiling (*a carena di nave* – 'like an upturned ship's hull') of any church in Venice. Then head for the small museum to the right of the altar, where a collection of Tintoretto's paintings has been crammed. Among the most notable are the *Ultima Cena* (Last Supper), *Lavanda dei Piedi* (Washing of the Feet) and *Orazione nell'Orto* (Agony in the Garden).

Unfortunately visitors cannot get into the cloisters of the one-time adjoining monastery, as they are no longer church property. Outside, the bell tower has a fairly serious lean that is best appreciated from a distance (such as from Campo Sant'Angelo).

FONDACO DEI TEDESCHI Map pp254-5

Salizzada del Fontego dei Tedeschi 5346; admission free; ⏰ post office hours; vaporetto Rialto

From the 13th century onwards, the German trading community occupied a *fondaco* (or *fontego*, an accommodation and storage facility for foreign merchants) on this privileged site. After a fire in 1505, the present building was erected in a little under three years (1508), not bad going for the time.

It may look a little sombre now, but try to imagine the exterior adorned with frescoes by Giorgione and Titian. To help in this task, you can see some fragments in the Ca' d'Oro (p77). When they turned up at the Palazzo Ducale to pick up their payment of 150 ducats, the two artists were told their work was worth only 130 ducats. Incensed, they insisted on an independent appraisal, which confirmed the figure of 150 ducats. The artists were then told that more than 130 ducats couldn't be arranged, so they could take it or leave it. Perhaps such penny-pinching lay partly behind Titian's increasing tendency to accept commissions from abroad!

Inside, the building is simple but dignified. The Germans used the porticoed floors above the courtyard as lodging and offices, storing their merchandise below. They even had their own well, which remains. The courtyard was covered over in 1937 and the building now serves as the central post office.

LIBRERIA NAZIONALE MARCIANA

Map pp254-5
See Museo Correr

Across Piazzetta San Marco from the Palazzo Ducale lies the gracious form of what Palladio once described as the most sumptuous palace ever built. Jacopo Sansovino designed it in the 16th century. The building occupies the entire west side of the *piazzetta* and houses the Libreria Nazionale Marciana, or National Library of St Mark (aka Biblioteca di San Marco, or Libreria Sansoviniana, after its architect), and the Museo Archeologico. The library extends around the corner on the waterfront into what was once **La Zecca**, the Republic's mint. For more on the Libreria Nazionale Marciana and the Museo Archeologico, see Museo Correr below. Admission to both is through that museum.

MUSEO CORRER Map pp254-5

☎ 041 240 52 11; Piazza San Marco; admission see Special Tickets; ☼ 9am-7pm Apr-Oct, 9am-5pm Nov-Mar; vaporetto Vallaresso/San Marco

The **Ala Napoleonica**, built by the Corsican general and his lackeys as his Venetian ballroom, is now home to the Museo Correr, dedicated to the art and history of Venice. Once inside, you turn right into a hall lined with statuary and bas-reliefs by Canova. More of his creations adorn the following couple of rooms, collectively known as the Sale Neoclassiche (Neoclassical Rooms). Keeping the statues company is an assortment of 19th-century paintings (including some by Hayez), books, documents, medallions, musical instruments and other bits and bobs.

From here you slide on into the rooms dedicated to Civiltà Veneziana (Venetian Civilisation), where you can inspect coins and standards of the Republic, model galleys, maps, navigational instruments and a display of weaponry from bygone days.

Stop the Pigeons!

If you get the impression there are more pigeons in Piazza San Marco than inhabitants in the whole of Venice, you're right. Officials estimate the pesky pigeon population at around 100,000 (but how do you count them?). Tests have shown that around 15% of the flock have salmonella and can pass it on to their hapless human victims.

Attempts to deal with these flying rats have all ended in abject failure. An effort to sterilise them with chemically treated birdseed failed because they didn't swallow it. Equally unsuccessful has been the supposed ban on feeding the little beggars. There is purportedly a hefty fine for this activity, but to judge by the birdseed vendors and the throngs of delighted tourists allowing birdies to poop on their shoulders for that memorable Piazza San Marco photo, that rule died at birth.

Worse than the poop on the people is that on the monuments – the acid in bird droppings eats away at the stone. People involved in restoration pull their hair out at the thought of the vast sums spent to restore monuments, only to see the work imperilled by the toilet habits of these gormless creatures. Please don't feed them!

You are then encouraged to continue straight on to the **Museo Archeologico**, crammed mostly with Greek and Roman statues, along with a vast collection of ancient coins and ceramics. Some, but by no means all, of the material was collected in the Veneto. A couple of rooms are devoted to ancient Egyptian and Assyro-Babylonian objects. Free guided tours are available in English at 3pm on weekdays, and at noon, 3pm and 5pm on weekends (tours are also offered in Italian and French). You will be asked to show your ticket here, as you will again in the adjoining **Libreria Nazionale Marciana**.

You enter the library, in a sense, through the back door. The Sala della Libreria (Library Room) is the main reading hall, built in the 16th century to house the collection of some 1000 codices left to the Republic by Cardinal Bessarione in 1468. The ceiling was decorated by a battalion of artists chosen by Titian and Sansovino, the architect. Veronese was considered the best; his three contributions form the second line of medallions after you enter.

The Vestibolo (Vestibule) follows. The centrepiece of its ceiling ornamentation is *Sapienza* (Wisdom) by Titian. The ancient statues cluttering the floor were part of a wider collection placed here late in the 16th century. Most were later shunted over to what would eventually become the Museo Archeologico. Finally you arrive at the top end of the fine entrance stairway – a twin to the Scala d'Oro in the Palazzo Ducale across the square.

Free guided tours of the Library are available in Italian and English at 10am, noon, 2pm and 4pm on weekends.

You now have to backtrack all the way to the armoury in the Museo Correr. The western corridor of the Ala Napoleonica contains further baubles relating to the Civiltà Veneziana collection. About halfway along, a stairway leads up to two other collections. The modest **Museo del Risorgimento**, on the 2nd floor, traced the fall of the Venetian Republic and Italian unification. It has been closed for some years and is opened only occasionally to house temporary exhibitions. The **Arte Antica** collection is a kind of Noah's Ark of largely second-rate art, starting with 14th-century Byzantine painters and proceeding to Gothic art, with a series of rooms given over to Flemish and German paintings, and a room with eight works that came out of the Bellini workshop. A few items of interest by Carpaccio and Lorenzo Lotto dot the remaining rooms.

After going back downstairs, you turn left to walk through the remainder of the Civiltà Veneziana collection and so return to the ticket counter. In this section you can view paintings of Venetian scenes, society games and a large collection of miniature bronzes

The external spiral staircase of the Palazzo Contarini del Bovolo (above)

(*bronzetti*) produced mostly in Padua and depicting everything from frogs to gods.

PALAZZO CONTARINI DEL BOVOLO

Map pp254–5

☎ 041 270 24 64; Corte del Bovolo 4299; admission adult/child €2.50/2; 🕙 10am-6pm; vaporetto Rialto

This intriguing Renaissance mansion, hidden down narrow lanes off Campo Manin, takes its name from the dizzying external spiral (*bovolo* in Venetian) staircase. Built in the late 15th century, the palace maintains a hint of the Gothic in its arches and capitals. You can enter the grounds and climb the staircase, but it is perfectly visible from outside.

PALAZZO DUCALE (DOGE'S PALACE)

Map pp254–5

☎ 041 271 59 11; Piazzetta San Marco; admission see Special Tickets; 🕙 9am-7pm Apr-Oct, 9am-5pm Nov-Mar; vaporetto Vallaresso/San Marco

The Palazzo Ducale, a unique example of Venetian Gothic fantasy, was, along with its simpler predecessors, the political heart of La Serenissima for most of the Republic's existence. As the palace's name suggests, the doge called it home, but in its halls and dependencies were also housed all the arms of government, not to mention prisons. Infrared radio receivers, which pick up an audio-loop commentary, can be hired near the ticket desk for €5.50.

Established in the 9th century, the building began to assume its present form 500 years later, with the decision to build the massive Sala del Maggior Consiglio to house the members of the Grand Council, who ranged in number from 1200 to 1700. The hall was inaugurated in 1419. The whole thing rests on what amounts to a giant raft of pylons and stone blocks rammed into the muddy depths of the lagoon.

The palace's two magnificent Gothic facades in white Istrian stone and pink Veronese marble face the water and Piazzetta San Marco, respectively. Much of the building was damaged by fire in 1577, but it was successfully restored by Antonio da Ponte (who also designed the Ponte di Rialto). Thankfully, Palladio's pleas to have the burned-out hulk demolished and replaced by another of his creations fell on deaf ears. The bulk of the columns that surround the palace appear to have no bases, for the simple reason that the pavement of the *piazzetta* has since been raised almost half a metre in response to flooding!

Secret Itineraries

Lesser-known areas of the Palazzo Ducale, including the original **Prigioni Vecchie** (Old Prisons), can be visited on the **Itinerari Segreti** (Secret Itineraries) tour (☎ 041 271 59 11; adult/child €12.50/7; English-language tour 10am & 11.30am Apr-Oct, Italian 9.30am & 11am Apr-Oct, French 10.30am & noon Apr-Oct, tours in some or all of the above languages at 10am, 10.30am, 11.30am and noon Nov-Mar).

The 1½-hour tour is an intriguing look at the underside of the palace and the workings of government in the days of La Serenissima. You are taken first through some administrative offices, small rooms in which the Republic's civil servants beavered away. You then get to pass through a torture chamber, the **Sala dei Tre Capi del Consiglio dei Dieci** (Room of the Three Heads of the Council of Ten) and the Inquisitors' office.

After all this, the route winds upstairs to the **Piombi** (Leads), prison cells beneath the roof of the building. Here prisoners froze in winter and sweltered in summer. Giacomo Casanova got five years here for his apparently wayward and reckless lifestyle. The guide will show you how he made his escape. You also get an explanation of the engineering behind the ceiling of the immense Sala del Maggior Consiglio below.

The toughest prisoners ended up in the **Pozzi** (Wells), two bottom storeys of dank cells at (but contrary to popular belief not below) water level. They are closed to the public, but from all accounts, by the rather dismal standards of the Middle Ages, they could have been worse.

The ticket for this tour is separate from the normal €11 ticket. Both admit you to the Palazzo Ducale, but if you want to visit the Museo Correr and other museums on the standard ticket *and* do the Itinerari Segreti, you'll have to pay for both. You must book your place on the tour in advance.

From the loggia looking onto the *piazzetta* death sentences would be solemnly read out between the ninth and 10th columns from the left, both of them darker than the remaining columns. The sentences were usually carried out between the columns on the *piazzetta*. On occasion, the condemned person might be offered one last chance to avoid the chop. They would be directed to the third column on the seaward side of the Palazzo Ducale from the corner of the *piazzetta*. Arms tied behind their back and facing the column, they had to try to turn around the column without falling off the low marble step at its base (no longer visible). They say that no one ever managed it and that out of this rather macabre bit of Venetian humour was born a popular kids' challenge.

You enter the palace through the waterfront entrance. Beyond the ticket office and to the left is the **Museo dell'Opera**. It contains 42 capitals that once adorned the porticoes of the palace and have slowly been replaced by copies to protect the originals from further deterioration. Careful observation reveals a wealth of sculptural whimsy. On one are depicted eight emperors and kings, from Priam of Troy to Julius Caesar. The message appears to be that, compared with the illustrious lagoon Republic, they were rather small fry.

When you leave the museum you emerge into the main courtyard. The two 16th-century wells in the middle are the most exquisite in the city. Access to Antonio Rizzi's magnificent marble **Scala dei Giganti** (Giants' Staircase), at the northeastern end, is closed but you can view it

easily enough. It is topped by Sansovino's statues of Mars and Neptune, behind which the swearing-in ceremony of the doge traditionally took place. Here he would be presented with his ducal cap and swear fidelity to the laws of the Republic.

To continue, climb the **Scala dei Censori** (Censors' Staircase) up to the **Piano delle Logge**. The floor of the loggia is a classic *terrazzo alla Veneziana* (see the boxed text on p86), of which you will see more inside the building. Wander along this gallery to the loggia that looks out over Piazzetta San Marco. When you have finished here, head back to the Scala dei Censori and beyond to Sansovino's grand **Scala d'Oro** (Golden Staircase). Just before you climb these stairs up to the next floor, you pass a *bocca della verità* (mouth of truth), into which people placed denunciations against wayward citizens.

Halfway up the first flight of the Scala d'Oro, turn right and then up more stairs to reach the series of rooms comprising the **Appartamento del Doge** (Doge's Apartments). Among these, the grand **Sala delle Mappe** (Map Room) contains maps dating from 1762 depicting the Republic's territories and the voyages of Marco Polo. Also here is the standard of the last doge, Manin. You pass through several smaller rooms on the left wing before reaching the long hall known as the **Sala dei Filosofi** (Philosophy Room), so called because portraits of great philosophers once hung here. Of particular interest is Titian's *San Cristoforo* (St Christopher), a fresco above a side stairwell (signposted) and one of the few works to survive the 1577 fire. They say he finished this fresco in just three days. More rooms follow on the right wing. Continue through these, cross the Sala delle Mappe again and turn upstairs to the next floor.

The highest echelons of the government met in these rooms of the palace. You enter the **Sala delle Quattro Porte** (The Four Doors Room, named for obvious reasons), where ambassadors would be requested to await their audience with the doge. Palladio designed the ceiling and Tintoretto added the frescoes. Titian's memorable *Il Doge Antonio Grimaldi in Ginocchio Davanti alla Fede, Presente San Marco* (Doge Antonio Grimaldi Kneels Before the Faith in the Presence of St Mark) dominates the wall by the entrance.

Off this room is the **Anticollegio** (College Antechamber), which features four Tintorettos and Veronese's *Ratto d'Europa* (Rape of Europa). Through here is the splendid **Sala del Collegio** (College Room), the ceiling of which features a series of works by Veronese and a few by Tintoretto. Next is the **Sala del Senato** (Senate Room), graced by yet more Tintorettos. Senators met here in the presence of the doge and the Signoria (Signory; a council that advised the doge on policy), who sat on the high tribune.

Veronese was again at work in the **Sala del Consiglio dei Dieci** (Council of Ten Room). This council came to wield considerable power, acting as the Republic's main intelligence-gathering agency. The next room is known as the **Sala della Bussola** (Collection-box Room). Note the small box in the wall. Members of the Consiglio dei Dieci picked up denunciations left here – they were poked though a hole on the other side of the wall, rather like the way you would post a letter.

From here you follow a set of stairs to the right to the **Armeria** (Armoury), what is left of the palace's once considerable collection of arms. After this, you turn left down one flight of the Scala dei Censori and turn right into the **Andito del Maggior Consiglio** (Corridor of the Grand Council), a narrow L-shaped corridor (also known as the Liagò) off which is the **Sala della Quarantia Vecchia** (Old Council of Forty Room). This body oversaw administrative matters regarding the city. In the small **Sala dell'Armamento** (Armaments Room) next door you can see the remains of Guariento's 14th-century fresco *Paradiso* (Heaven), damaged in the 1577 fire.

On the other side of the corridor is the immense **Sala del Maggior Consiglio** (Great Council Room). This is dominated at one end by Tintoretto's replacement *Paradiso*, one of the world's largest oil paintings, measuring 22m by 7m. Among the many other paintings in the hall is a masterpiece, the *Apoteosi di Venezia* (Apotheosis of Venice) by Veronese, in one of the central ceiling panels. Note the black space in the frieze on the wall depicting the first 76 dogi of Venice. Doge Marin Falier would have appeared had he not been beheaded for treason in 1355.

The room off the northwestern corner of the Sala del Maggior Consiglio was home to the **Quarantia Civil Nuova** (New Civil Council of Forty), a kind of appeal court, while beyond lies the **Sala dello Scrutinio** (Ballot Room), where elections to the Maggior Consiglio were held. It is lined with stirring and bloody battle scenes.

From the northeastern end, a trail of corridors leads to the small, enclosed **Ponte dei Sospiri** (Bridge of Sighs). Before you reach the bridge, you pass through three small rooms,

Two 16th-century wells in the main courtyard of Palazzo Ducale (opposite)

57

the last of which contains a small collection of paintings by Hieronymus Bosch (c. 1450–1516). He must have been doing drugs!

The bridge is split into two levels, for traffic heading into and out of the **Prigioni Nuove** (New Prisons), built on the eastern side of Rio di Palazzo della Paglia in the 16th century to cater for the overflow from the Prigioni Vecchie (Old Prisons) within the Palazzo Ducale. The bridge is presumably named after the sighs that prisoners heaved as they crossed it on their way into the dungeons.

You wind your way through the cells of the Prigioni Nuove: they are small and dank, but not too bad by the standards of the times. Of course they are cleaned up and airy now, but wouldn't have been much fun when overcrowded with sick and unhappy prisoners on a bread-and-water diet.

Re-emerging from the prison, you re-cross the Bridge of Sighs to end up in the offices of the **Avogaria Comun** (Venetian magistracy) and the **Sala dello Scrigno** (Room of the Coffer). Here the *Libro d'Oro* (Golden Book) was kept. The Libro identified those noble families of impeccable Venetian descent who had the right to join the Maggior Consiglio. Interclass weddings were forbidden and a vigilant watch was maintained for fraudulent attempts to pass off unsuitable persons as nobles.

The last office you pass through before arriving back in the courtyard is the **Milizia da Mar** (Marine Militia). An office of 20 senators was set up in 1545 to organise the rapid equipping and manning of emergency war fleets whenever the need arose. The organisation began here. You then pass through a shop and downstairs to a café that leads onto the courtyard.

Exit the courtyard by what was traditionally the main entrance, Giovanni and Bartolomeo Bon's 15th-century **Porta della Carta** (Paper Door), to which government decrees were fixed (hence the name).

PALAZZO FORTUNY Map pp256-8
☎ 041 520 09 95; Campo San Beneto 3780; admission free; ⏲ depends on exhibitions; vaporetto Sant'Angelo

You'll recognise this building instantly by its two rows of *hectafores*, each a series of eight connected Venetian-style windows. Mariano Fortuny y Madrazo, an eccentric Spanish painter and collector, bought the building at the beginning of the 20th century. He left his works here and, together with another 80 by the Roman artist Virgilio Guidi, they make up the bulk of the Museo Fortuny. After years firmly shut, some rooms of the *palazzo* now open for temporary exhibitions; the whole building and its permanent collection are due to reopen in 2004.

PONTE DELL'ACCADEMIA Map pp256-8
Campo San Vidal & Campo della Carità; vaporetto Accademia

Built in 1930 to replace a 19th-century metal structure, the third and last of the Grand Canal bridges was supposed to be a temporary arrangement until a satisfactory design for a more permanent structure was produced. All that seems to have been forgotten. From the middle, the views in both directions along the Grand Canal are spellbinding. The bridge links the *sestiere* of San Marco with Dorsoduro. In front of you when you cross the bridge are the Gallerie dell'Accademia (p60).

SESTIERE DI DORSODURO
Eating p125; Entertainment pp140 & 143; Shopping p154; Sleeping p166

Orientation
Let's assume you are on the Ponte dell'Accademia, having come through Campo Santo Stefano. Once you step down off the other side of the bridge, you are in Campo della Carità. Now it's time for some serious art appreciation, with the Gallerie dell'Accademia and the Peggy Guggenheim Collection the main attractions. Between them cluster a hive of small private galleries for the aficionado.

The *sestiere* occupies the entire southern flank of Venice, looking onto the broad Canale della Giudecca and receiving the full force of the sun (blistering in summer and blissful in winter) throughout the day. The district is mostly quiet and residential, with the one major exception of Campo Santa Margherita, the nightlife hub of the city.

Transport

All Grand Canal vaporetti stop at Accademia, while the No 1 also calls at the Ca' Rezzonico and Salute stops. Along the south flank of the *sestiere*, a branch line of the No 82 and the N night vaporetti call at Zattere and San Basilio. Nos 61 and 62 also call at Zattere and San Basilio.

CA' REZZONICO (MUSEO DEL SETTECENTO VENEZIANO) Map pp256-8

☎ 041 241 01 00; Fondamenta Rezzonico 3136; admission adult/student/child €6.50/4.50/2.50, see also Special Tickets; ☉ 10am-6pm Wed-Mon Apr-Oct, 10am-5pm Wed-Mon Nov-Mar; vaporetto Ca' Rezzonico
This superb 17th- to 18th-century mansion, facing the Grand Canal, houses the **Museum of the 18th Century**. Designed by Longhena and completed in the 1750s by Massari, it was home to several notables over the years, including the poet Robert Browning, who died here. The museum includes a collection of 18th-century art and furniture and is worth visiting just for the views over the Grand Canal.

A broad staircase by Massari ascends from the ground floor to the *piano nobile* ('noble' or 1st floor). This leads to the Salone da Ballo (Ballroom), a splendid hall dripping with frescoes and richly furnished with 18th-century couches, tables and ebony statues. There follows a series of rooms jammed with period furniture, *objets d'art* and plenty of paintings. Particularly noteworthy is Tiepolo's ceiling fresco in the Sala del Trono (Throne Room), the *Allegoria del Merito tra Nobiltà e Virtù* (Allegory of Merit Between Nobility and Virtue). Tiepolo contributed several other frescoes and paintings, as did his son Giandomenico (look out for his fresco cycle taken from the Tiepolo house at Zianigo, near Mira on the mainland). Other represented artists include Pietro Longhi, Francesco Guardi, Rosalba Carriera and Canaletto.

CHIESA DEI CARMINI Map pp256-8

Campo dei Carmini 2614; admission free; ☉ 2.30-5.30pm Mon-Sat; vaporetto Ca' Rezzonico
What remains of the original 14th-century Byzantine and then Gothic church sits a little uneasily beside the richer, and perhaps less digestible, ornament of the 16th and 17th centuries. Among the paintings on view are several works by Cima da Conegliano.

CHIESA DEI GESUATI Map pp256-8

Fondamenta Zattere 909; admission €2 or Chorus ticket; ☉ 10am-5pm Mon-Sat, 1-5pm Sun; vaporetto Zattere
Built for the Dominicans (who had replaced the suppressed order of the Jesuits, or Gesuati, on this spot in 1668) by a team of architects under Giorgio Massari from 1726 to 1735, this imposing church is more properly known as the Chiesa di Santa Maria del Rosario. It contains three ceiling frescoes by Tiepolo telling the story of St Dominic – the appearance to the saint of the Virgin Mary, the institution of the rosary (hence the church's official name) and St Dominic in glory. Tiepolo also had a hand in the frescoes in the dome, while Tintoretto left behind a *Crocifissione* (Crucifixion) in his typically flowing crimsons and blues on the left side of the church nearest the altar. The statues and sculpture lining much of the interior are by Gian Maria Morlaiter (1699–1781).

Virtually next door is the little-visited **Chiesa di Santa Maria della Visitazione**, which has a curious 15th-century chessboard timber ceiling with numerous scenes depicting the Visitation and a series of portraits of saints and prophets.

CHIESA DI SAN PANTALON Map pp256-8

Campo San Pantalon 3700; admission free; ☉ 4-6pm Mon-Sat; vaporetto San Tomà
The stark, unfinished and seriously cracked brick facade dates from the 17th century, although a church was here as early as the 11th century. Inside, the greatest impact comes from the 40 canvases representing the *Martirio e Gloria di San Pantaleone* (Martyrdom and Glory of St Pantaleone), painted for the ceiling by Giovanni Antonio Fumiani. The artist died in a fall from scaffolding while at work and is buried in the church. Veronese, Vivarini and Palma il Giovane have works here too. Head for the **Cappella del Sacro Chiodo** (Chapel of the Holy Nail) to see the greatest concentration of works. To better observe the ceiling and Veronese's *San Pantaleone Risana un Fanciullo* (St Pantaleone Heals a Boy), stick coins into the slot machine to turn on the lights.

CHIESA DI SAN SEBASTIAN Map pp256-8

Campo San Sebastian 1687; admission €2 or Chorus ticket; ☉ 10am-5pm Mon-Sat, 1-5pm Sun; vaporetto San Basilio
Veronese's final resting place, this Renaissance remake of an earlier church is often attributed to Antonio Scarpagnino (c. 1505–49). Inside, Veronese went to town, decorating the

interior with frescoes and canvases that cover a good deal of space on the ceiling and walls. The organ is his work too, with scenes from Christ's life on its shutters. The ceiling paintings together seem to exude a pallid, yellowish light. Titian left a notable item here too – his *San Nicolò* (St Nicholas), first up on the right as you enter the church.

CHIESA DI SANTA MARIA DELLA SALUTE Map pp254-5
Campo della Salute; sacristy admission €1.50; ☺ 9am-noon & 3-5.30pm; vaporetto Salute

Possibly the city's most familiar silhouette (viewed from Piazzetta San Marco or the Ponte dell'Accademia), this bulging baroque beast is one of Longhena's masterpieces. Seen from close up, it's difficult to take it all in, but Longhena knew what he was doing and deliberately designed a monument to be admired from afar.

Longhena was commissioned to build the church in honour of the Virgin Mary, to whose intervention was attributed the end of an outbreak of plague in 1630. The ranks of statues that festoon the exterior culminate in one of the Virgin Mary on top of the dome. As is often the case in Venice, the church is built not on solid land but on what amounts to a huge raft of, it is said, a million tightly knit pylons hammered into the lagoon floor.

The octagonal form of the church is unusual. Longhena's idea was to design it in the form of a crown for the Mother of God. The interior is flooded with light pouring through windows in the walls and dome. Dominating the main body of the church is the extraordinary baroque *altar maggiore*, into which is embedded a Cretan icon of Mary.

Of the paintings in the church proper, only Titian's *Pentecoste* is of particular note, but admission to the sacristy is worth shelling out for: the ceiling is bedecked with three remarkable Titians. The figures depicted are so full of curvaceous movement they seem to be caught in a washing machine! The three scenes are replete with high emotion, depicting the struggles between *Caino e Abele* (Cain and Abel), *David e Golia* (David and Goliath) and finally Abraham and his conscience in *Il Sacrificio di Isaaco* (The Sacrifice of Isaac). The eight medallions by Titian, depicting saints, are small but intriguing. St Mark seems to be winking in amusement to himself, while you could swear that, under his swirling beard, San Girolamo (St Jerome) is having a quiet chuckle.

The other star of the sacristy is Tintoretto's *Le Nozze di Cana* (The Wedding Feast of Cana), filled with an unusual amount of bright and cheerful light by Tintoretto's rather morose standards.

Every year, on 21 November, a procession takes place from Piazza San Marco to the church to give thanks for the city's good health. The last part of the march takes place on a pontoon bridge thrown out between the Santa Maria del Giglio *traghetto* stop and the church.

GALLERIA DI PALAZZO CINI Map pp256-8
☎ 041 78 13 80; Piscina Forner 864; closed for restoration; vaporetto Accademia

After the overwhelming parade of Venetian masters in the nearby Gallerie dell'Accademia (see below) comes this small but curious collection of Tuscan intruders. Oddly, the main facade of this 16th-century building looks over the Rio di San Vio rather than the Grand Canal. Spread out over two floors are around 30 works, mostly from the 14th and 15th centuries. You will see a handful of works by Lippi, Piero della Francesca (*Madonna col Bambino*; Madonna and Child), Botticelli (*Il Giudizio di Paride*; The Judgment of Paris) and Beato Angelico. Mixed in are some fine pieces of 15th-century Venetian furniture, porcelain and other odds and ends.

GALLERIE DELL'ACCADEMIA Map pp256-8
☎ 041 522 22 47; Campo della Carità; admission adult/EU citizen 18-25/child under 12/EU citizen under 18 or over 65 €6.50/3.25/free/free, see also Special Tickets, audio guide €4; ☺ 8.15am-2pm Mon, 8.15am-7.15pm Tue-Sun, subject to frequent change; vaporetto Accademia

The single greatest repository of the finest in Venetian art lies here. The former church and convent of Santa Maria della Carità, with additions by Palladio, houses a swath of works that follows the progression of Venetian art from the 14th to the 18th centuries.

In 1750 the rococo painter Gian Battista Piazzetta founded the art school that later became the Accademia, Venice's official arbiter of artistic taste. The collection of paintings was assembled in 1807 and opened to the public 10 years later. The first works came from churches and other religious institutions suppressed during the brief but violent years of Napoleonic rule. Later additions came from private collections. In 1878 the galleries were hived off from the art school and passed into state control. Acquisitions have continued ever since.

From the ticket office, you pass upstairs to Room (Sala) 1, where the galleries' more or less chronological display begins. You are in what was the main meeting hall of the Scuola Grande di Santa Maria della Carità, the oldest of the Scuole Grandi (see the boxed text on p76). The magnificent timber ceiling is divided into squares; at the centre of each is a sculpted face – every one different – of an angel. The room is given over to religious art of the 14th century, including Paolo Veneziano's *Madonna col Bambino i Due Commitanti* (Madonna and Child with Two Donors).

Room 2, designed by Carlo Scarpa and with an unusual black *terrazzo alla Veneziana* floor, includes a couple of works each by Giovanni Bellini, Vittore Carpaccio and Cima da Conegliano. Note the commonality in themes adopted by all three in their depictions of the Madonna and child (for instance, the musicians at the Madonna's feet).

The most enthralling of the works is, however, Carpaccio's altarpiece *Crocifissione e Apoteosi dei 10,000 Martiri del Monte Ararat* (Crucifixion and Apotheosis of the 10,000 Martyrs of Mt Ararat). The story goes that some 10,000 Roman soldiers sent to quell rebellion in Armenia instead converted to Christianity. The Emperor was unimpressed and sent more troops. They were ordered to subject the 10,000 to the same trials that Christ had suffered if they didn't change their minds. The result was a massacre. The painting, representing a kind of collective sainthood, was a departure from the standard depiction of one or two saints in religious painting. The soldiers all have the appearance of Christ, while their executioners appear in the garb of nasty Turks – no doubt reflecting Venetian and European feelings towards the infidels of their own time.

More works by Giovanni Bellini and Cima da Conegliano adorn Room 3.

In Rooms 4 and 5 you can enjoy a mixed bag, including the work of some non-Venetians. These include Andrea Mantegna's *San Giorgio* (St George) and works by Cosmè Tura, Piero della Francesca and Jacopo Bellini. In Bellini's pieces, note the comparative stiffness of his characters, a faithful reflection of a painting style still crossing over from earlier Gothic tenets. Bellini's son Giovanni has 11 paintings here and the greater suppleness and reality of expression is clear – take, for instance, the remarkable *Madonna col Bambino tra le Sante Caterina e Maddalena* (Madonna and Child Between Saints Catherine and Mary Magdalene).

The most striking paintings in these rooms are the two rare contributions by Giorgione, *La Tempesta* (The Storm) and *La Vecchia* (The Old Woman). Both are way ahead of their time. Look at the latter closely. The lines and brush strokes, the look in the eyes, indeed the very subject matter, would be more at home in a collection of 19th-century portraiture.

In Room 6 are works by Tintoretto and Veronese, and one by Titian. In Tintoretto's *La Creazione degli Animali* (The Creation of the Animals), you can see the thick, splashy paint strokes that characterised much of this Mannerist painter's work. His use of muted crimsons and blues in *Assunzione della Vergine* (Assumption of the Virgin) reminds one of El Greco. Or rather, in Tintoretto's work you can see support for the claim that El Greco took with him to Spain a good deal of what he had learned in Venice.

The main interest in Rooms 7 and 8 is Lorenzo Lotto's *Ritratto del Giovane Gentiluomo nel Suo Studio* (Portrait of a Young Gentleman in His Studio). What's the lizard doing on his desk? Others represented here are Titian, Palma il Vecchio and even Tuscan Giorgio Vasari, better known for his history of great Italian artists.

In Room 10 you are confronted by some major works, one of the highlights of which is Veronese's *Convito in Casa di Levi* (Feast in the House of Levi). Originally called *Ultima Cena* (Last Supper), the painting's name was changed

Chiesa di Santa Maria della Salute (opposite)

at the behest of the Inquisition. The room also contains one of Titian's last works, *Pietà*. The almost nightmarish quality of the faces has a Goya-esque touch and reflects, perhaps, the fact that Titian was working on it during an epidemic of the plague. Indeed he died before finishing the work. Finally, there are some remarkable Tintorettos dedicated to the theme of St Mark. The *Trafugamento del Corpo di San Marco* (Stealing of St Mark's Body) is a mighty example of this artist's daring with a brush.

Another fine Tintoretto is his *Crocifissione* (Crucifixion) in Room 11, where you can also admire decoration by Giambattista Tiepolo salvaged from the Chiesa dei Scalzi after an Austrian bomb missed its target (the nearby train station) in 1915 and hit the church. His long frieze *Castigo dei Serpenti* (Punishment of the Snakes) was for many years rolled up and stashed away, which explains the damage evident today.

Room 12 contains minor 18th-century landscape paintings, while Room 13 has works by Jacopo Bassano, Palma il Giovane, Tintoretto and Titian. Rooms 14, 15, 16 and 16a are of less interest, although a few minor Tiepolos appear. Room 17 is crammed with small works, including a rare (in Venice) couple by Canaletto. Francesco Guardi, Pietro Longhi, Marco Ricco and Rosalba Carriera also figure here, as do some studies by Tiepolo.

Minor Veneto landscape artists *(vedutisti)* line the walls of Room 18, while Room 19 is given over to 15th- and 16th-century artists – thus breaking the chronological order established so far.

Just as you might have thought the exhibition was losing steam, you enter Room 20. The crowd scenes, splashes of red and activity pouring from the canvases in this cycle dedicated to the *Miracoli della Vera Croce* (Miracles of the True Cross) come as quite a shock. They were carried out by Vittore Carpaccio, Gentile Bellini and others for the Scuola di San Giovanni Evangelista, which is home to a relic of the True Cross. Today, much of their fascination lies in the depiction of a Venice of centuries ago, with gondolas tootling about, classic Venetian chimneys in evidence everywhere and a faithful depiction of the timber Rialto bridge that preceded the present one.

Carpaccio's extraordinary series of nine paintings recounting the life of Santa Orseola (St Ursula) follows in Room 21.

Room 22 hosts a few neoclassical sculptures, while Room 23 is actually the former Chiesa di Santa Maria della Carità. Several works from the Bellini workshops are on display. The last room (Room 24) was the Sala dell'Albergo of the Scuola Grande di Santa Maria della Carità, and is dominated by an exquisite timber ceiling and Titian's *Presentazione di Maria al Tempio* (Presentation of Mary at the Temple).

In each of the rooms there are detailed description sheets in English and Italian – remember to put them back before proceeding to the next room! When the galleries are crowded, the queues outside can be a pain – a ceiling of 300 visitors at any one time is imposed.

PALAZZO ZENOBIO Map pp256-8
☎ 041 522 87 70; Fondamenta del Soccorso 2597; vaporetto San Basilio

This grand baroque structure has housed the Collegio Armeno dei Padri Mechitaristi (Armenian College of Mechitarist Fathers) since the mid-19th century. The structure is the handiwork of Antonio Gaspari, but apart from the grand curved tympanum, the exterior of the building tells you little. Ad hoc tourist visits are not welcome, but if you could sneak in and see the Sala della Musica (Music Room), you would witness Gaspari's voluptuous décor at its baroque baubly extreme. Guided visits are sometimes organised, usually from June to September. Call ahead to find out.

PEGGY GUGGENHEIM COLLECTION
Map pp256-8
☎ 041 240 54 11; www.guggenheim-venice.it; Palazzo Venier dai Leoni 701; admission adult/student/child €8/5/5; 🕙 10am-6pm Wed-Mon & 10am-10pm Sat Apr-Oct; vaporetto Accademia

Peggy Guggenheim called the unfinished, truncated Palazzo Venier dai Leoni home for 30 years, until she died in 1979. She left behind a collection of works by her favourite modern artists, representing most of the major movements of the 20th century.

Miss Guggenheim came into her fortune in 1921 and set off for Europe from North America with no particular aim. During the 1930s she developed a voracious appetite for contemporary art (and some of the artists!). She opened an art gallery in London in 1938, the Guggenheim Jeune, and embarked on a programme of collection that continued well into 1940. Seemingly oblivious to the conflagration raging around her, she decided to return to New York from Paris only when the Nazis were at the city gates. In New York she opened the Art of this Century gallery in 1942, but five years later decided to return to Europe. By 1949 her home and museum in Venice was open to the public. The Palazzo Venier dai Leoni was so called because, it is said, the Venier family kept lions here! Peggy herself preferred the company of dogs – many of them are buried alongside her own grave in the sculpture garden.

The bulk of the collection is housed in the east wing. It is the pleasing result of an eclectic collector's whim, and the list of greats of 20th-century art is long. Early Cubist paintings include Picasso's *The Poet* (1911) and *Pipe, Glass, Bottle of Vieux Marc* (1914), and Georges Braque's *The Clarinet* (1912). There are a couple of Kandinskys, including his *Upward* (1929). Interesting works from Spain include Dalí's *Birth of Liquid Desires* (1932) – a classic example of his psycho-sick 'eroticism' – and Miró's *Seated Woman II* (1939).

It wouldn't be right if Max Ernst, Guggenheim's husband and doyen of Surrealism, was not represented. Among his many paintings on show is the disturbing *Antipope* (1942). Other names to look for include Jackson Pollock, Mark Rothko, Willem de Kooning, Paul Delvaux, Alexander Calder, Juan Gris, Kurt Schwitters, Paul Klee, Francis Bacon, Giorgio de Chirico, Piet Mondrian and Marc Chagall. The sculpture garden is sprinkled with sculptures by, among others, Henry Moore and Jean Arp.

The rear of the mansion hosts a separate collection of Italian Futurists and other modern artists from the peninsula, collected by Gianni Mattioli and now incorporated into the Guggenheim collection. Artists include Giorgio Morandi and Giacomo Balla, and there is one early work by Amedeo Modigliani.

Temporary exhibitions are held in the new wing on the west side of the garden. A highly agreeable café overlooks the garden.

SCUOLA GRANDE DEI CARMINI
Map pp256-8

☎ 041 528 94 20; Campo Santa Margherita 2617; admission €5; ☽ 9am-6pm Mon-Sat, 9am-4pm Sun; vaporetto Ca' Rezzonico

Just before you bump into the church of the same name at the southwestern end of Campo Santa Margherita, you pass on the right this *scuola*, with numerous paintings by Tiepolo and others. Tiepolo's nine ceiling paintings in the Salone Superiore (upstairs) depict the virtues surrounding the Virgin in Glory. The building facades have been attributed to Longhena. In its heyday, this was probably the most powerful of Venice's *scuole*, with a membership of 75,000 in 1675 – not bad in a city where the entire population was not much more than twice that! For more on *scuole*, see the boxed text on p76.

SESTIERI DI SAN POLO & SANTA CROCE (SANTA CROSE)

Eating p126; Entertainment p142; Shopping p155; Sleeping p167

Orientation

These two *sestieri* have been lumped together because they form a neat whole, sandwiched in between the ugly bus station of Piazzale Roma and the Ponte di Rialto. Its character changes enormously from the quiet back lanes of Santa Croce to the busier area around the Istituto Universitario di Architettura di Venezia (architecture school). Around the Ponte di Rialto a web of lanes converging on the produce markets of Rialto is peppered with shops of all sorts and some wonderful old-time eateries. The bulk of sights is made up of churches, religious confraternities and 18th-century mansions. Most notable are Ca' Pesaro, the Frari church and Scuola Grande di San Rocco, a Tintoretto feast.

CA' PESARO Map pp250-2

☎ 041 524 06 95; Santa Croce 2076; admission adult/child €5.50/3, see also Special Tickets; ☽ 10am-6pm Tue-Sun Apr-Oct, 10am-5pm Tue-Sun Nov-Mar; vaporetto San Stae

The main facade of this restored mansion fronts the Grand Canal. It has housed the

Galleria d'Arte Moderna (Modern Art Gallery) since 1902. Ca' Pesaro was designed for one of Venice's senior families by Longhena, in a muted baroque style much influenced by the harmonious Renaissance ideas of Sansovino, and finished in 1710 by Antonio Gaspari, after

Transport

A plethora of vaporetti call at Piazzale Roma and across the Ponte dei Scalzi at Ferrovia, putting you in (or very close to) the northwestern corner of Santa Croce. Otherwise, the No 1 calls at Riva de Biasio, San Stae (the N stops here too), San Silvestro and San Tomà (No 82 and N call here as well). The Rialto stop, although on the other side of the canal, is also handy (Nos 1, 4, 82 and N).

Longhena's death. He died worrying about the mounting bills! The Pesaro clan was succeeded by the Gradenigo family, the Armenian Mechitarist Fathers (who turned it into a college before moving to Palazzo Zenobio in Dorsoduro) and finally the Bevilacqua family, who turned it over to the Venice town hall for use as an art gallery.

The collection includes works purchased from the Biennale art festival, and an eclectic array of Italian and international modern art. The *androne* (main ground floor hall) is typical of the great patricians' mansions in Venice. You can look out over the Grand Canal from one side, while the inland end fronts onto a sunny courtyard dominated by a monumental fountain. A handful of statues and sculptures by 20th-century Italian artists are littered about, and temporary exhibitions are held in a side hall. As you head up the grand stairway to the first floor you will pass Auguste Rodin's *Il Pensatore* (The Thinker; 1880).

The bulk of the works are on the 1st floor. The central grand hall, or *portego*, is typical of Venetian mansions. Facing the Grand Canal and the rear courtyard, it is the main artery off which branch other rooms. While wandering around and looking at the art on the walls, don't neglect the fine frescoes from the original building on the ceilings of many rooms and the admirable *terrazzo alla Veneziana* floors. The building has been lovingly restored and faithfully reflects the grandeur to which the Republic's senior families were accustomed.

The art starts with late 19th-century Venetian works (such as Giacomo Favretto's scenes from Venice) and broadens into a series of works from the same period by other Italians. After that it gets more interesting, with works from the early Biennale years and the 1930s, such as Klimt's *Judith II (Salomé)*, and artists including Kandinsky, Chagall, Matisse, Paul Klee and Spain's Joaquim Sorolla. Next come

striking sculptures by the Milanese Adolfo Widt, and then the eclectic De Lisi collection, with works by De Chirico, Miró, Kandinsky and Yves Tanguy, among others. The following two rooms are again dedicated to Italian works from the interwar years. Max Ernst, Henry Moore and others follow in a room dedicated to the 1940s and 1950s. The final two rooms again return to Italian, and more specifically Venetian, art of the 1950s.

Proceed upstairs to the **Museo d'Arte Orientale**, one of the most important collections in Europe of Edo-period art and objects from Japan. During a two-year world tour in the 1820s, Count Enrico di Borbone amassed a store of Japanese arms and light armour (the samurai preferred ease of movement over heavy protection, judging their best defence to be their fencing skills) dating from the 17th to 19th centuries. The display is also replete with porcelain, art and all sorts of elegant household objects, from snuff boxes to ladies' toiletries cabinets. There is also some fine Chinese porcelain and a shadow puppet collection, mostly from Indonesia. The whole scene is fascinating, as the collection has been left much as it was organised in 1928, giving it a delightfully musty feel.

CASA DI GOLDONI Map pp256-8

☎ 041 523 63 53; Calle Nomboli 2794; admission adult/child €2.50/1.50, see also Special Tickets; ☉ 10am-5pm Mon-Sat Apr-Oct, 10am-4pm Mon-Sat Nov-Mar; vaporetto San Tomà

This is where Venice's greatest playwright, Carlo Goldoni, was born in 1707. The house is worth a quick visit and Goldoni fans will find a host of material on the playwright's life and works displayed in its otherwise fairly bare rooms.

CHIESA DI SAN GIACOMO DELL'ORIO
Map pp250-2

Campo San Giacomo dell'Orio 1457; admission €2 or Chorus ticket; ☉ 10am-5pm Mon-Sat, 1-5pm Sun; vaporetto Riva de Biasio

The charming, leafy *campo* is graced by the modest outline of one of Venice's few good examples of Romanesque architecture, the Chiesa di San Giacomo dell'Orio. The initial 9th-century church was replaced in 1225. The main Gothic addition (14th century) is the remarkable wooden ceiling *a carena di nave* (in the style of an upturned ship's hull). It is one of several examples in Venice and, for anyone who has tramped around the great churches of Spain, starkly reminiscent of the Muslim-influenced *artesonado* ceilings. Among the intriguing jumble of works of art are a Byzantine column in green marble, a 13th-century baptismal font and a Lombard pulpit perched on a 6th-century column from Ravenna. In front of the main altar is a wooden crucifix by Veronese, and on the wall at the rear of the central apse, a rare work by Lorenzo Lotto, *Madonna col Bambino e Santi* (Madonna and Child with Saints).

CHIESA DI SAN GIOVANNI ELEMOSINARIO Map p253

Ruga Vecchia San Giovanni 477; admission €2 or Chorus ticket; 🕙 **10am-5pm Mon-Sat, 1-5pm Sun; vaporetto Rialto**

Recently restored, this is a beautiful little Renaissance church built by Antonio Abbondi after a disastrous fire in 1514 destroyed much of the Rialto area. The church and its separate bell tower are camouflaged by the surrounding houses, so their presence comes as a bit of surprise. The frescoes inside the dome are by Pordenone, as is one of two altarpieces. Another fresco is by Titian.

CHIESA DI SAN POLO Map pp256-8

Campo San Polo 2115; admission €2 or Chorus ticket; 🕙 **10am-5pm Mon-Sat, 1-5pm Sun; vaporetto San Tomà**

Although of Byzantine origin, this church has lost much of its attraction through repeated interference and renovation. Worst of all, the pile-up of houses between it and the Rio di San Polo has completely obscured its facade. It is, however, worth your time to wander inside if you enjoy the art of Tiepolo. A whole cycle of his, the *Via Crucis* (Stations of the Cross), hangs in the sacristy. With them are other paintings and some wonderful ceiling frescoes. In the main body of the church are some works by Tintoretto and Palma Il Giovane.

CHIESA DI SAN ROCCO Map pp256-8

Campo San Rocco 3053; admission free; 🕙 **7.30am-12.30pm & 2-6pm; vaporetto San Tomà**

You are likely to wander out of the Scuola Grande di San Rocco (p76) wondering what hit you. Maybe that's why there's no charge to enter this church across the way. Although built at about the same time as the *scuola*, the church was completely overhauled in the 18th century – hence the baroque facade (easily identified by all the statues in niches and wall sculpture). It has a somewhat neglected feel

inside, but contains several paintings of interest to those who have not overdosed, including some by Tintoretto on the main-entrance wall and around the altar.

CHIESA DI SAN STAE Map pp250-2

Campo San Stae; admission €2 or Chorus ticket; 🕙 **10am-5pm Mon-Sat, 1-5pm Sun; vaporetto San Stae**

This is a fairly simple house of worship, although the facade (finished in 1709) might lead you to think otherwise. Among its art treasures are Tiepolo's *Il Martirio di San Bartolomeo* (The Martyrdom of St Bartholomew).

The facade of Chiesa di San Stae (above)

CHIESA DI SANTA MARIA GLORIOSA DEI FRARI Map pp256-8

Campo dei Frari; admission €2 or Chorus ticket; ☯ 9am-6pm Mon-Sat, 1-6pm Sun; vaporetto San Tomà

If you have seen Notre Dame in Paris or Cologne's Dom, you might be asking yourself what is so Gothic about the Frari. Built for the Franciscans in the 14th and 15th centuries of brick rather than stone, and bereft of flying buttresses, pinnacles, gargoyles and virtually any other sign of decoration inside or out, it is indeed a singular interpretation of the style. Nevertheless, some features give it away, among them the Latin-cross plan (with three naves and a transept), the high vaulted ceiling and its sheer size. A look inside is a must on any art-lover's tour of the city.

A curious element is the presence in the middle of the central nave of the *coro* (choir stalls). This is a common feature in Spain, but the stalls in most churches beyond the Iberian Peninsula tend to be kept out of the way (behind the altar, off to the side or high up at the bottom end of the cross floor plan). Was the idea an import or is it coincidence?

The simplicity of the interior (red-and-white marble floor, with the same colours dominating the walls and ceiling) is more than offset by the extravagance of decoration in the form of paintings and funereal monuments. Titian is the main attraction. His dramatic *Assunta* (Assumption; 1518) over the high altar, praised unreservedly by all and sundry as a work of inspired genius, represents a key moment in his rise as one of the city's greatest artists.

Another of his masterpieces, the *Madonna di Ca'Pesaro* (Madonna of Ca' Pesaro), hangs above the Pesaro altar (in the left-hand aisle, near the choir stalls). Also of note are Giovanni Bellini's triptych in the apse of the sacristy, Donatello's statue of *Giovanni Battista* (John the Baptist) in the first chapel to the right of the high altar, and Vivarini's *Sant'Ambrogio in Trono e Santi* (St Ambrose Enthroned and Saints) in the second-last chapel to the left of the high altar.

FONDACO DEI TURCHI Map pp250-2

☎ 041 524 08 85; Salizzada del Fontego dei Turchi 1730; due to reopen 2004; vaporetto San Stae

This 12th-century mansion belonged to the dukes of Ferrara until handed over in 1621 for use as a warehouse and way station for Turkish merchants (who operated here in spite of the centuries of at times vicious antagonism). The building now houses the **Museo Civico di Storia Naturale** (Natural History Museum).

In Venice and across the Middle East and beyond, these warehouses were set up both to house foreign merchants and to store their goods. The word *fondaco* (*fontego* in Venetian) spread, and places where Western merchants stayed and worked came to be known in Arabic as a *funduq*, from Aleppo in Syria to Alexandria in Egypt. In Arab countries, *funduq* has come to mean hotel.

The Fondaco dei Turchi was rented out to the Turks until 1858, long after the demise of La Serenissima. Although it dates to the 12th and 13th centuries, the place was restored in appalling taste in the mid-19th century. It was a little like plastic surgery gone wrong. Original features in the facade were sacrificed to the architectural fancies of the time – the odd crenellations are, for example, an unhappy addition. If the museum finally reopens, take the kids there to see the impressive 12m-long crocodile.

PALAZZO MOCENIGO Map pp250-2

☎ 041 72 17 98; Salizzada di San Stae 1992; admission adult/child €4/2.50, see also Special Tickets; ☯ 10am-5pm Tue-Sun Apr-Oct, 10am-4pm Tue-Sun Nov-Mar; vaporetto San Stae

This mansion belonged to one of the most important families of the Republic. Originally a Gothic pile, it was overhauled in the 17th century and is typical of Venetian patricians' lodgings. The 16th-century philosopher Giordano Bruno was hosted here for a time by the Mocenigo family, who then betrayed him and handed him over to the Inquisition. (He was subsequently tortured and burned at the stake in Rome for heresy.) The mansion now houses a modest museum, with clothes, period furnishings and accessories from the 17th century. It is interesting for the hints it gives you of how the other half lived in the twilight years of La Serenissima.

Sweeping stairs take you up to the *piano nobile*, divided in typical Venetian fashion. A central hall, or *portego*, divides the floor in two and is graced with period furnishings and portraits of various Mocenigo greats (the family provided seven dogi). The five big portraits are of rank outsiders, such as Charles Stuart II. A series of rooms then follows off both sides of the *portego*. The ones presumably used for public receptions have higher and mostly frescoed ceilings. Not all of the furnishings belonged to the Mocenigo family, who stopped living here in 1945.

(Continued on p75)

1

3

1 Revellers in costume during
Carnevale (p9) *2* A traveller waits
for the vaporetto outside Santa
Lucia train station (p216)
3 A gondolier plies his trade along
one of the city's many canals
(p214)

2

1 Decoration on the prow of a gondola (p13) **2** Ponte dell'Accademia, which spans the Grand Canal near the Gallerie dell'Accademia (p58) **3** A boat passes along the Grand Canal under Ponte di Rialto (p75) **4** Reflection of the Campanile of Basilica di San Marco (p53)

1 Bathing boxes on the Lido di
Venezia (p92) *2* Windsurfing on
the lagoon *3* An instructor from
Reale Società Canottieri Bucintoro
gives a rowing lesson (p148)

1 The magnificent facade of Basilica di San Marco (p50) *2* The interior of Chiesa di Santa Maria della Visitazione (p84) *3* Detail of a mosaic above the entrance to Basilica di San Marco (p50)

1 Detail of one of the many mosaics within Basilica di San Marco (p50) 2 The ornate baroque facade of Chiesa di Santa Maria del Giglio (p53) 3 Basilica del Santo (Basilica di Sant'Antonio) in Padua (p192)

1 Pedestrians stroll along the waterfront Piazzetta San Marco at dawn (p98) 2 Church domes and gondolas silhouetted against a sunset 3 Pigeons in Piazza San Marco (p54) 4 Outdoor tables at one of the cafés on Piazza San Marco (p99)

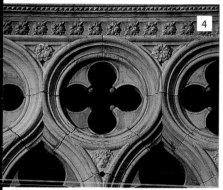

1 *La Residenza in Castello, which offers accommodation in a 15th-century mansion (p179)* 2 *The spiral staircase of Palazzo Contarini del Bovolo (p55)* 3 *One of the many palazzi that line the Grand Canal (p48)* 4 *Detail of the Gothic Palazzo Ducale (p55)*

1 A mobile fruit stall on the beach at mainland Sottomarina (p96) 2 Museo del Merletto on Burano (p91) 3 Detail of a mosaic at the Cimitero (cemetery) on Isola di San Michele (p90) 4 Locals stop for a chat on the Burano waterfront (p91)

(Continued from p66)

PONTE DI RIALTO Map pp254-5
Vaporetto Rialto

Given Rialto's importance from the earliest days of the Republic, it is hardly surprising that the city's first bridge over the Grand Canal was built here. The crossing had quite a chequered history before Antonio da Ponte (Anthony of the Bridge) built this robust marble version. Commissioned in 1588, it cost 250,000 ducats, an enormous sum in those days. When it was finally completed in 1592, all concerned must have been happy with the result – which has lasted nicely in the four centuries since.

The first bridge was little more than a dodgy pontoon arrangement thrown across the canal around 1180. A more permanent wooden structure was built in 1265, but it was cut in two in 1310 as Baiamonte Tiepolo and his fellow rebels beat a hasty retreat on horseback (see the boxed text on p104). It was repaired, but collapsed in a heap in 1444 under the weight of a crowd straining to watch the wedding procession of the Marquis of Ferrara. It was again rebuilt, as a timber drawbridge, before finally being dismantled and replaced by da Ponte's version.

RIALTO Map p253
Vaporetto Rialto

Rivoalto (later contracted to Rialto), the highest spot in the collection of islets that formed the initial nucleus of the lagoon city, was one of the areas of first settlement – although the more active part was initially on the San Marco side of the bridge. The San Polo side slowly gained the ascendance and became the main centre of trade and banking for the Republic. This is where dosh traded hands, voyages were bankrolled and news (sometimes hard to disentangle from gossip) was exchanged.

Today, the area continues to buzz with the activity of the daily produce and fish **markets** – why break the habit of 700 years? The **Fabbriche Vecchie** (Old Buildings), along the Ruga degli Orefici, were created by Scarpagnino in 1522. They were designed to accommodate markets at ground level and house offices in the upper levels. Next door is the **Palazzo dei Dieci Savi** (Palace of the Ten Wise Men). The Dieci Savi administered taxes (the building now houses the Magistrato alle Acque, or water administration). The **Fabbriche Nuove** (New Buildings), running along the Grand Canal, went up in 1555 to designs by Sansovino and became home to magistrates' courts. Other magistrates, the 'chamberlains', were housed in a separate Renaissance edifice, the **Palazzo dei Camerlenghi**, designed by Guglielmo dei Grigi. At ground level were prisons for common offenders.

The **Pescaria** (fish market), which extends into Campo delle Beccarie, was rebuilt in neo-Gothic style in 1907. They have been selling fresh fish here since 1300. While in Campo delle Beccarie, spare a thought for the Querini family. One wing of their house still looks onto the square, but the rest was demolished in 1310 in reprisal for having backed the revolt against Doge Pietro Gradenigo.

Sestieri – Sestieri di San Polo & Santa Croce (Santa Crose)

Fruit and vegetable stall at the Rialto produce markets (p158)

When School Was Cool

The name *scuola* (school) as applied to the great confraternities in Venice is perhaps misleading to a modern reader. In an era when the welfare state had not even been dreamed of, the *scuola* served as a community and religious association. Its lay members formed a brotherhood *(confraternita)* under a patron saint and, apart from acting as a religion-based club, they dealt with such matters as financial assistance to the families of members fallen on hard times. The *scuola*, along with the parish church, formed the backbone of local social life.

The division between the big six (the Scuole Grandi, dedicated to San Marco, San Rocco, San Teodoro, San Giovanni Evangelista, Santa Maria della Misericordia and Santa Maria della Carità – the latter swallowed up into the Accademia in the 18th century) and the rest (the Scuole Minori) was decreed in the 15th century. The smaller *scuole* totalled about 400, many without a church or even a fixed headquarters. Pretty much all the city's workers' and artisans' guilds had their own *scuola* and patron saint, with whom they identified strongly. As club, welfare centre and rallying point for the big parades and religious events in the city, the role of the *scuola* in Venetian society cannot be underestimated.

Early in the 19th century, most of the *scuole*, as religious institutions, were suppressed by Napoleon's administrators. Some of the richer ones (and they were well endowed) lost a good number of their works of art and precious artefacts in the course of what can only be described as heavy-handed plundering by the French. Only a few of the *scuole* were later resurrected. Some are now used, among other things, to host exhibitions and concerts.

From the docks all around Rialto, crusader fleets set sail. While men and provisions were gathered, various knights and other notables stayed in hostels just behind the Fabbriche Nuove. Many others camped out on Giudecca or around the Chiesa di San Nicolò on the Lido. Before heading off, they heard their last Mass on land for some time in the **Chiesa di San Giacomo di Rialto**. Virtually in the middle of the market, off the Ruga degli Orefici, it was supposedly founded on 25 March 421, the same day as the city.

SCUOLA GRANDE DI SAN GIOVANNI EVANGELISTA Map pp250-2

☎ 041 71 82 34, Campiello della Scuola 2454; admission free but donations appreciated; ⏰ 9am-12.30pm Tue-Thu; vaporetto Ferrovia

Codussi designed the interior of this, one of the six major Venetian *scuole*. Like San Rocco (see below), the plan is typical of the big schools, with an assembly hall (here divided in two by a line of columns) and a grand staircase up to the 1st-floor hall, which contains an altar used for religious services. Massari restyled this hall in sumptuous fashion in 1727. Many of the major works of art once housed here have been moved to the Gallerie dell'Accademia.

SCUOLA GRANDE DI SAN ROCCO

Map pp256-8

☎ 041 523 48 64; Campo San Rocco, San Polo 3052; admission adult/youth aged 18-26/child under 18 €5.50/4/1.50; ⏰ 9am-5.30pm Easter-Oct, 10am-4pm Nov-Easter; vaporetto San Tomà

Scarpagnino's Renaissance facade (exhibiting a hint of the baroque to come), with its white marble columns and overbearing magnificence, seems uncomfortably squeezed into the tight space of the narrow square below it. Whatever you make of the exterior of this *scuola* dedicated to St Roch, nothing can prepare you for what lies inside.

St Roch was born in 1295 in Montpellier, France, and at the age of 20 began wandering through southern France and Italy helping plague victims. He died in 1327 and a cult soon grew around him. His body was transferred to Venice as a kind of plague-prevention measure in 1485.

After winning a competition (Veronese was among his rivals), Tintoretto went on to devote 23 years of his life to decorating the school. The overwhelming concentration of more than 50 paintings by the master is altogether too much for the average human to digest. Chronologically speaking, you should start upstairs (Scarpagnino designed the staircase) in the Sala Grande Superiore (Upper Great Hall). Here you can pick up mirrors to carry around to avoid getting a sore neck while inspecting the ceiling paintings, which depict Old Testament episodes. Around the walls are scenes from the New Testament. A handful of works by other artists (such as Titian, Giorgione and Tiepolo) can also be seen. To give your eyes a rest from the paintings, inspect the woodwork below them – it is studded with curious designs, including a false book collection.

Downstairs, the walls of the confraternity's assembly hall feature a series on the life of the Virgin Mary, starting on the left wall with the *Annunciazione* (Annunciation) and ending with the *Assunzione* (Assumption) opposite.

SESTIERE DI CANNAREGIO

Eating p129; Entertainment pp142 & 144; Shopping p158; Sleeping p168

Orientation

Long the swampiest part of Venice and unpleasantly malarial to boot, the area owes its name to the reeds *(canne)* that grew in abundance here. For most people, this *sestiere* represents their first contact with Venice. Trains pull into Santa Lucia station and disgorge their passengers into this corner of town. Covering the whole northwestern sector of Venice above the Grand Canal, and bordering the *sestieri* of Castello to the east and San Marco to the south (at the Ponte di Rialto), it is a curious mix. The main drag leading to San Marco has a tacky, cheap souvenir feel to it, lined with shops and restaurants that in most cases have an eye on the quick euro and hope to attract new arrivals who haven't yet had a chance to learn better. The area near the train station is also laden with quick-fix hotels, some good, but many a dreary choice whose sole advantage is convenience for the train station.

And yet hidden away in the streets and along canals away from the Grand Canal side of the *sestiere* are a mix of off-the-beaten-track churches and a local hive of nocturnal activity around Fondamenta della Misericordia. This is also where you'll find the city's one-time Jewish Ghetto.

CA' D'ORO Map p253

☎ 041 523 87 90; Calle di Ca' d'Oro 3931; admission adult/student €3/1.50, see also Special Tickets; 8.15am-2pm Mon, 8.15am-7.15pm Tue-Sun; vaporetto Ca' d'Oro

This magnificent Gothic structure, built in the 15th century, got its name (Golden House) from the gilding that originally decorated the sculptural details of the facade. The facade, visible from the Grand Canal, stands out from the remainder of the edifice, which is rather drab by comparison.

Ca' d'Oro houses the **Galleria Franchetti**, an impressive collection of bronzes, tapestries and paintings. The 1st floor is devoted mainly to religious painting, sculpture and bronzes from the 15th and early 16th centuries. One of the first items you see is *San Bartolomeo*, a polyptych recounting the martyrdom of St Bartholomew. Take a closer look at the detail: the violence is remarkable, as is the saintly indifference with which Bartholomew seems to accept his torment! Much of what you see on this floor is Venetian, but one room has been set aside principally for Tuscan art.

On the 2nd floor you can see a series of fragments of frescoes saved from the outside of the Fondaco dei Tedeschi (p53). All but one are by Titian. The other, a nude by Giorgione, is the most striking, however. Also on this floor is a mixed collection, including works by Tintoretto, Titian, Carpaccio, Mantegna, Vivarini, Signorelli and van Eyck.

A big incentive for visiting is the chance to lean out from the balconies over the Grand Canal on the 1st and 2nd floors.

CHIESA DEI SCALZI Map pp250-2

Fondamenta dei Scalzi 55; admission free; 7-11.45am & 4-6.45pm Mon-Sat, 7.45am-12.30pm & 4-7pm Sun & holidays; vaporetto Ferrovia

Virtually next to the train station, this is a rare baroque extravagance. Longhena designed the church but the baroque facade was done by Giuseppe Sardi. The abundance of columns and statues in niches is a deliberate echo of the particularly extravagant baroque style often employed in Rome. The Carmelites, who had moved here from Rome several years before, specifically requested that it be so. The voluptuous decorative

Transport

Vaporetti allow you several approaches to the area. Apart from the Ferrovia stop, where an abundance of lines call, there are only two Grand Canal stops – San Marcuola (Nos 1, 82 and N) and Ca' d'Oro (No 1 and N). Lines 41, 42, 51 and 52 wing around from Ferrovia into the Canale di Cannaregio and then on around the *sestiere*'s northern lagoon shore to Fondamente Nuove, where you can also pick up vaporetti for Murano and other islands in the northern half of the lagoon.

spin continues within – the altar is a good example of baroque clearly heading for the extremes of rococo. Damaged frescoes by Tiepolo appear in the vaults of two of the side chapels.

CHIESA DELLA MADONNA DELL'ORTO Map pp250-2

Campo della Madonna dell'Orto 3520; admission €2 or Chorus ticket; 🕑 10am-5pm Mon-Sat, 1-5pm Sun; vaporetto Madonna dell'Orto

Architecture fans should find the exterior of this church intriguing. Elements of Romanesque remain (the inner arch over the main entrance, for instance) in what is largely a 14th-century Gothic structure in brick. That changes were made a century later is clear from the series of statues in niches above the two lower wings of the facade and from the triangular finish at the top. The five statues crowning the facade were added in the 18th century.

Tintoretto was a local parishioner and, although he used a good deal of his creative genius filling the Scuola Grande di San Rocco with his paintings, he found time to execute works for this church too. Among them are the *Giudizio Finale* (Last Judgment), the *Adorazione del Vitello d'Oro* (Adoration of the Golden Calf) and the *Apparizione della Croce a San Pietro* (Vision of the Cross to St Peter). On the wall at the end of the right aisle is the *Presentazione di Maria al Tempio* (Presentation of Mary at the Temple). Tintoretto is buried with other family members in the church.

In the Cappella di San Mauro is the white stone statue of the *Madonna col Bambino* (Madonna and Child) after which the church is named. The statue was supposedly found in a nearby garden in 1377 and brought here amid considerable excitement.

CHIESA DI SAN GEREMIA Map pp250-2

Campo San Geremia 274; admission free; vaporetto Ferrovia

This otherwise uninspiring 18th-century church contains the body of St Lucy (Santa Lucia), who was martyred in Syracuse in AD 304. Her body was stolen by Venetian merchants from Constantinople in 1204 and moved to San Geremia after the Palladian church of Santa Lucia was demolished in the 19th century to make way for the train station. The bell tower is a Romanesque leftover from an earlier church that stood on the same spot.

CHIESA DI SAN GIOVANNI GRISOSTOMO Map p253

Salizzada San Giovanni Grisostomo; admission free; 🕑 8.15am-12.15pm & 3-7pm Mon-Sat, 10.15am-12.15pm & 3-7pm Sun & holidays; vaporetto Rialto

This church was remodelled on a Greek-cross plan by Codussi in 1504. Since 1977 it has housed an icon of the Virgin Mary that attracts a lot of the local faithful. With all the burning incense and candles, to wander in here is to feel yourself transported to a mysterious church of the Orthodox East. Notable is Giovanni Bellini's *San Gerolamo e Due Santi* (St Jerome and Two Saints).

CHIESA DI SAN MARCUOLA Map pp250-2

Campo San Marcuola 1758; admission free; 🕑 3-6pm Mon-Sat; vaporetto San Marcuola

Although a church has been here since the 9th century, what you see was cobbled together (and not quite completed) in the 18th century by Giorgio Massari and Antonio Gaspari. Inside is an *Ultima Cena* (Last Supper) by Tintoretto. His Christ and apostles are spotlighted against a black background, giving the meal an extraordinary air. You may only be able to get in during Mass.

CHIESA DI SANT'ALVISE Map pp250-2

Campo Sant'Alvise 3025; admission €2 or Chorus ticket; 🕑 10am-5pm Mon-Sat, 1-5pm Sun; vaporetto Sant'Alvise

Built in 1388, this church plays host to a noteworthy Tiepolo, the *Salita al Calvario* (Climb to Calvary), a distressingly human depiction of one of Christ's falls under the weight of the cross. The ceiling frescoes are a riot of colour.

CHIESA DI SANTA MARIA DEI MIRACOLI Map p253

Campo dei Miracoli 6074; admission €2 or Chorus ticket; 🕑 10am-5pm Mon-Sat, 1-5pm Sun; vaporetto Fondamente Nuove

It looks like an elaborate box containing the most refined of chocolates. Pietro Lombardo was responsible for this Renaissance jewel, which is fully covered inside and out in marble, bas-reliefs and statues. They say the marble came from leftovers originally destined for use in Basilica di San Marco, but regardless of where it came from or was meant to go, the result is richly intense but without the flowery motifs that would come later with baroque. The timber ceiling is also eye-catching. Pietro and Tullio Lombardo did the carvings on the choir stalls.

The Jews of Venice

The first records of Jews in Venice go back to the 10th century. The early Jews were Ashkenazi of German and Eastern European origins. Even at this early point, acquiring Venetian citizenship was all but impossible, and so outsiders had to content themselves with regularly renewing their residence permits. In 1382, the Maggior Consiglio decreed that Jews could operate as moneylenders; in fact, it encouraged them.

As refugees of various nationalities crowded into Venice during the dark days of the League of Cambrai (see p43), the Republic decided on 29 March 1516 that all Jews residing in Venice should be moved to one area. The Getto Novo (New Foundry) was considered ideal, being far from the city's power centres and surrounded by water – a natural prison. The Ashkenazis' harsh Germanic pronunciation gave us the word *ghetto*. It should be emphasised that, although Venice gave us the word, the concept was an old one, as Jews living in Spain in earlier centuries well knew.

Jews could move freely through the city only if they wore a yellow cap or badge. At midnight a curfew was imposed. Gates around the Ghetto Nuovo were shut by Christian guards (paid for by the Jewish community) and reopened at dawn.

Deliberately excluded from most professions, Jews had few career options. Most tried to get along as moneylenders or in the rag trade. Two of the 'banks' from which moneylenders used to operate remain in evidence on Campo di Ghetto Nuovo, the **Banco Rosso** and **Banco Verde** (Map pp250-2). A third option was medicine. Jews who had lived in Muslim Spain or in the Middle East had benefited from the advances in the Arab world on this front and were considered better doctors than their Christian counterparts. Jewish doctors were allowed, in emergencies, to leave the Ghetto during curfew. It sounds bad, but everything is relative. Jews who made it to Venice were not persecuted and were free to practise their religion. Compared with their brethren in much of the rest of Europe, Venice's Jews were doing OK.

A quick look around will show you how small the Ghetto was. And the population, already in its thousands, was growing. In 1541, waves of Levantine Jews from Spain and Portugal finally made their way into Venice. Here there was a difference – they came with money, as many were wealthy and successful merchants with contacts in the Near East.

Extreme overcrowding combined with building-height restrictions had already created 'skyscrapers' around the Campo di Ghetto Nuovo – some apartment blocks have as many as seven storeys, but with very low ceilings. On top of three of them were built three modest *schole*. The **Schola Tedesca** (German Synagogue) is above the building that now houses the Museo Ebraico. Virtually next door is the **Schola Canton** (Corner Synagogue) and further around is the **Schola Italiana** (Italian Synagogue; all Map pp250-2). The last is the simplest; the largely destitute Italian Jews concerned had come from Spanish-controlled southern Italy. From the outside, the synagogues can be distinguished from the residential housing by the small domes that indicate the position of the pulpit. In the case of the German and Italian ones, the rows of five larger windows are another giveaway.

When the Levantine Jews began to arrive, even the town authorities had to admit there was no more space and ceded another small area to the Jews – the Getto Vecio (Old Foundry). So of course it came to be known as the Old Ghetto, although the converse was true (the foundry was old but the Jewish community was new). Here the Spanish and Portuguese built their two synagogues (Schola Levantina and Schola Spagnola; see p113), considered the most beautiful synagogues in northern Italy.

A final small territorial concession was wrung from the town authorities when a street east of the Ghetto Nuovo, subsequently known as the Calle del Ghetto Nuovissimo (Very New Ghetto Street), was granted to the Jews.

From 1541 until 1553, the Jewish community thrived. Their money and trade were welcome in Venice, and they also built a reputation for book printing. Then Pope Julian banned such activities. From then on, things started to go downhill. To top it off, the plague of 1630 left fewer than 3000 Jews alive.

In 1797 Napoleon abolished all restrictions on Jews. Later, under the Austrians, they enjoyed considerable liberty, if not complete freedom from prejudice. After Venice was annexed to the Kingdom of Italy in 1866, all minorities were guaranteed full equality before the law and freedom of religious expression.

Mussolini's rise to power spelled trying times for Jews in Italy. The 1938 race laws imposed restrictions, but the real torment came in November 1943, when the puppet Fascist government of Salò declared Jews enemies of the state. Of Venice's 1670 remaining Jews, quite a few were rounded up and sent to the Italian concentration camp of Fossoli (outside Modena). They were even marched out of the **Casa Israelitica di Riposo** (rest home; Map pp250-2) on Campo di Ghetto Nuovo; the home's wall bears a memorial to the victims. The next stop for about 200 of them was a death camp in Poland. Altogether, about 8000 Italian Jews were killed in the Holocaust.

Of the 500 or so Jews still living in Venice, only about 30 remain in the Ghetto. You can contact the local Jewish community on ☎ 041 71 50 12. For more on the Ghetto, you can also look online at www.ghetto.it.

I GESUITI Map p253
Salizzada dei Specchieri 4880; admission free; 10am-noon & 4-6pm; vaporetto Fondamente Nuove

The Jesuits took over this church, more properly known as the Chiesa di Santa Maria Assunta, in 1657 and ordered its reconstruction in the Roman baroque style. The conversion was completed by 1730. The facade is impressive enough – in fact, as is often the case with such sights in Venice, it seems out of place, as though it's bursting for more space to allow a greater appreciation of its splendour.

No-one could accuse the Jesuits of sober tastes. Inside, the church is lavishly decorated with white and gold stucco, white and green marble floors, and marble flourishes filling in any empty slots. Tintoretto's *Assunzione della Vergine* (Assumption of the Virgin), in the north transept, is a remarkable exception to his usual style – think of the darkness of his images in the Scuola Grande di San Rocco and you wonder where all the lightness and joy came from in this painting. Maybe there was some role-swapping going on, as Titian's *Martirio di San Lorenzo* (Martyrdom of St Lawrence) is an uncharacteristically stormy and gloomy piece (it's the first painting on the left as you enter the church). Of course, the subjects of each painting make the respective results quite logical.

Virtually across the road is the tiny **Oratorio dei Crociferi** (Map p253; Campo dei Gesuiti 4094; admission €2; 10am-12.30pm Fri, 3.30-6.30pm Sat Apr-Oct), a 12th-century oratory that was once part of a medieval hospice, renovated in the 16th century and plastered with paintings and frescoes by Palma il Giovane.

MUSEO EBRAICO Map pp250-2
☎ 041 71 53 59; Campo di Ghetto Nuovo, Cannaregio 2902/b; admission adult/student €3/2; 10am-7pm Sun-Fri except Jewish holidays Jun-Sep; 10am-5.30pm Sun-Thu, 10am-sunset Fri Oct-May; guided tours of Ghetto & synagogues adult/student €8/6.50 including museum admission, half-hourly to hourly 10.30am-5.30pm Sun-Fri except Jewish holidays; vaporetto Guglie

A modest collection of Jewish religious silverware can be found at the Jewish Museum. The guided tours (in Italian or English; other languages if booked in advance) of the Ghetto and three of its synagogues (Schola Canton, Schola Italiana and Schola Levantina) that leave from the museum are highly recommended. You can also enquire at the museum about guided tours to the **Antico Cimitero Israelitico** (Old Jewish Cemetery; Map pp262-3) on the Lido.

PALAZZO LABIA Map pp250-2
☎ 041 78 12 68; Campo San Geremia, Cannaregio 275; admission free; 3-4pm Wed-Fri; vaporetto Guglie

Now the Venice office of the RAI, Italy's national radio and TV organisation, this was once a grand 17th-century family residence. It boasts several Tiepolo frescoes inside but you need to phone ahead to arrange an afternoon visit.

PALAZZO VENDRAMIN-CALERGI
Map pp250-2
Campiello Vendramin 2040; admission free; guided tours 10.30am Sat; vaporetto San Marcuola

The canalside facade of this one-time patrician mansion is a masterpiece of restrained Renaissance elegance, behind which lurk the gambling rooms of the city's casino. The composer Richard Wagner expired here in 1883. You can wander into the ground-floor area during casino hours but you'll have to fork out to see the gaming rooms, where formal dress is obligatory. To tour the rooms Wagner took while in Venice, you must book a place on Friday between 10am and noon for the tour that takes place at 10.30am on Saturday.

SESTIERE DI CASTELLO

Eating p132; Entertainment p143; Shopping p159; Sleeping p170

Orientation

The fish's tale stretches east from San Marco, and contains a mix of the major monuments (such as the grand Chiesa di SS Giovanni e Paolo) and posh waterfront hotels facing the Bacino di San Marco. The defensive walls of the city's once mighty shipyards, the Arsenale, dominate the centre of Castello; east of here the district trails out into a mix of intensely Venetian, lively 'suburbs' and quiet extremities, such as the leafy Sant'Elena and sleepy San Pietro.

Transport

Vaporetti Nos 41 and 42 run clockwise and anticlockwise around the Castello district on their circular routes around Venice. Nos 51 and 52 do the same thing but include the Lido in their routes. They call at San Zaccaria, the main Castello stop near Piazza San Marco and calling point for various lines, including Nos 1, 5, 20 and 82, N and a branch of the LN. Giardini is the main stop for the Biennale.

ARSENALE Map pp259 & 260

Campo Arsenale 2407; admission depends on exhibitions; 🕭 depends on exhibitions; vaporetto Arsenale
For centuries the crenellated walls of the Arsenale hid from view the feverish, infernal activity of the city's shipwrights, busy churning out galleys, merchant ships and other vessels at a pace unmatched anywhere in Europe. Thousands of *arsenaloti* (Arsenale workers), each specialising in certain trades, beavered away in assembly-line fashion hundreds of years before the industrial era.

The dockyards are said to have been founded in 1104, although some historians think it may have happened a century later. What became known as the **Arsenale Vecchio** (Old Arsenal) is the core of the complex. Within it was a special storage area for the *bucintoro*, the doge's ceremonial galley (used on important occasions, such as the Sposalizio del Mar – see p39).

As the Republic's maritime needs grew and shipbuilding requirements changed, so the Arsenale was enlarged. In 1303–04 came the first expansion, known as La Tana. It occupies almost the whole length of the southern side of the Arsenale, and was refashioned in 1579 by Antonio da Ponte. The **Arsenale Nuovo** (New Arsenal) was added in 1325, followed in 1473 by the **Arsenale Nuovissimo** (Very New Arsenal). When, in the 16th century, production of much larger war vessels with a deeper draught *(galeazze)* got under way, further workshops and construction sheds were added, along with the Canale delle Galeazze. The whole was unsurprisingly walled in and top secret. The *arsenaloti* were relatively well paid and tended to be faithful to the doge and the State throughout the history of the Republic. This was proven on several occasions when they were called to arms in times of unrest or rebellion.

The Arsenale was as close as Venice (or anyone for that matter, until the 18th century) came to industrial production. And to late-medieval eyes, it must have made an enormous

impression, with all its boiling black pitch, metalworking and timber cutting. Dante was so awestruck he used it as a model scene for Hell in his *Divina Commedia* (Canto XXI, lines 7–21).

As well as shipyards, the Arsenale served as a naval base. An emergency reserve fleet of at least 25 vessels was always kept ready to set sail from inside the Arsenale, either as a war fleet or as merchant ships. As the centuries progressed, although the shortage of raw materials (especially timber) became a problem, more often than not the Republic's difficulty was finding crews. Eventually, it was obliged to employ slaves, prisoners and press gangs to fill the personnel gaps.

At its peak, the Arsenale covered 46 hectares, was home to 300 shipping companies and employed up to 16,000 people. In 1570, when requested to produce as many ships as possible for an emergency fleet, the Arsenale put out an astounding 100 galleys in just two months. The following year at the Battle of Lepanto, the last great sea struggle fought mainly with oar power and a stunning defeat of the Turks, more than half the allied Christian fleet (which included Imperial Spain) was provided by Venice.

For most of its history, Venice relied on one form or other of rowing vessel, often combined with sail. In battle, such galleys were often more manoeuvrable. By the 17th century, however, the nimble, all-sail vessels being produced in England and Holland began to show their superiority. The Arsenale never fully made the switch and, when it tried, its products often proved inferior. By this time, Venetians were increasingly turning away from the sea anyway, and the practice of buying or renting foreign vessels (and sometimes their crews) grew more common. Venice was growing soft and its people were becoming landlubbers. By the time La Serenissima fell in 1797, naval production had all but ceased. Various minor modifications were made to the Arsenale in the course of the 19th century and the area remains in the Navy's hands, although much of it is now used as exhibition space.

The land gateway, surmounted by the lion of St Mark, is considered by many to be the earliest example of Renaissance architecture in Venice; it was probably executed in 1460. Later, a plaque was installed commemorating the victory at Lepanto in 1571. The fenced-in terrace was added in 1692. At the foot of the statues (each with allegorical meaning) is a row of carved lions of varying size and type. The biggest of them, in regally seated pose, was taken as booty by Francesco Morosini

CATTEDRALE DI SAN PIETRO DI CASTELLO Map p260

Campo San Pietro; admission €2 or Chorus ticket; 🕙 10am-5pm Mon-Sat, 1-5pm Sun; vaporetto San Pietro

Although overshadowed by Basilica di San Marco in the heart of town, this church, sitting in easy somnolence on the far-removed island of San Pietro, was in fact Venice's cathedral from 1451 to 1807. Indeed the island, originally known as Olivolo, was among the first areas to be inhabited.

In 775 the original church here was the seat of a bishopric. Between then and the 16th century, it underwent several transformations. Its present appearance is basically a post-Palladian job, taking its cue in part from Giudecca's Chiesa del Redentore. Inside, various hands were at work at one point or another, including Longhena, who was responsible for, among other things, the baroque main altar. Legend says that the strange *Trono di San Pietro* (St Peter's throne) was used by the apostle Peter in Antioch and that later the Holy Grail was hidden in it. This is all rather unlikely, as the seatback of the throne is made up of a Muslim tombstone, postdating the apostle's death. The throne is located between the second and third altars on the right side of the church as you enter.

Although this was officially Venice's cathedral for so long, Basilica di San Marco was to all intents and purposes the senior church. The dogi no doubt planned it that way, having effectively excluded the clergy from any share in the running of the State. The splendour of the ducal chapel thus outshone even ecclesiastical power. The Church never really did get its own way in the Republic.

Today San Pietro rests in easy retirement, with its blinding white **campanile** of Istrian stone by Codussi leaning at an odd angle, and the **former patriarchate** dozily crumbling away next door. The latter was used as a barracks for a while and is now partly occupied by, strictly speaking, illegal apartments.

CHIESA DEI SS GIOVANNI E PAOLO
Map p253

Campo SS Giovanni e Paolo; admission free; 🕙 7.30am-12.30pm & 3.30-7.30pm; vaporetto Ospedale

This huge Gothic church (aka San Zanipolo in Venetian), founded by the Dominicans, rivals the Franciscans' Frari (p66) in size and grandeur. Work started on it in 1333, but it was not consecrated until 1430. The similarities between the two are all too evident. The use of brick and modest white stone refinements

Equestrian statue of Bartolomeo Colleoni (p117) in front of Chiesa dei SS Giovanni e Paolo (below)

from the Greek port of Piraeus. This must have required quite an effort. On its right flank is a series of Viking runes. Attempts to decipher them have brought mixed results, although by one account they are an 11th-century 'Harold was here'-style piece of graffiti left behind by Norwegian mercenaries who apparently took control of Piraeus at the time.

Over the past few years, large (and for a long time largely neglected) parts of the Arsenale have been taken over and partly restored by the city's Biennale organisation for conversion into gallery and exhibition space. These areas include the former Corderia (where ships' cables were made), the Artiglierie (guns) and various wharfs. Exhibitions thus provide ample opportunity to get inside the Arsenale, although parts remain naval property and thus out of bounds. It is possible to enter via the main entrance, although more often than not entry to exhibitions is from Campo della Tana. You pass through the lofty shipyard buildings, now empty but for the massive pillars that hold up the roof. Following these you can then head outside to view the Darsena Grande (aka Darsena Nuova), still home to coastguard and *carabinieri* (military police) vessels. You then make your away around to the main eastern sea entrance, which looks across to the Lido. Try to picture the scene of a noisy, clanking medieval shipyard as you float around admiring, say, the zany contemporary art of the Biennale.

The Infamy of Famagusta

Keep an eye out for the monument to Marcantonio Bragadin in the Chiesa dei SS Giovanni e Paolo. It is on the wall of the south aisle, virtually opposite the westernmost pillar. The monument is singular for its content, rather than for any artistic merit.

Bragadin was the commander of the Famagusta garrison in Cyprus, the last to fall to the Turks in 1570. Promised honourable terms of surrender after having endured a long siege, Bragadin decided to call on the Turkish commander Mustafa and present him with the keys of the city. Mustafa lost his head, as it were, and lopped off Bragadin's ears and nose. Several hundred Christians in the vicinity also lost their heads, rather more literally. The postbattle massacre that until now had been avoided suddenly swept like a storm across the city.

While the population of Famagusta was decimated, Bragadin rotted for a couple of weeks in prison. He was then hauled about the town under the crushing weight of sacks of stone and earth. After various other humiliations, he was tied to a stake in the execution square and skinned alive. According to one account, he passed out only when they reached his waist. The corpse was then beheaded and quartered, and the skin stuffed with straw and paraded about town. Mustafa then took it home as a trophy to present to the sultan. Some years later, a Venetian trader with considerable courage managed to steal it from the arsenal of Constantinople and return it to the Bragadin family in Venice. The remains have been in the Chiesa dei SS Giovanni e Paolo since 1596.

around windows and doorways is a clear point they have in common. A particular departure here, however, is the way in which three chapels, each of different dimensions, have been tacked – it seems almost willy-nilly – onto the church's southern flank.

The vast interior, like that of the Frari, is divided simply into an enormous central nave and two aisles, separated by graceful, soaring arches. The red-and-white chessboard floor is a further demonstration of the contemporaneity of the two buildings.

A beautiful stained-glass window made in Murano in the 15th century fills the southern arm of the transept with light. A host of artists contributed to its design, including Bartolomeo Vivarini, Cima da Conegliano and Girolamo Mocetto. It owes some of its brilliance to restoration carried out in the 1980s. Below the window and just to the right is a fine *pala* (altarpiece) by Lorenzo Lotto. On the opposite aisle wall, below the organ, is a triptych by Bartolomeo Vivarini. Noteworthy, too, are the five late-Gothic apses, graced by long and slender windows. Look out for Giovanni Bellini's polyptych of *San Vincenzo Ferreri* (St Vincent Ferrer) over the second altar of the right aisle.

In the Cappella del Rosario, off the northern arm of the transept, is a series of paintings by Veronese, including ceiling panels and an *Adorazione dei Pastori* (Adoration of the Shepherds) on the west wall.

The church is a veritable ducal pantheon. Around the walls, many of the 25 tombs of dogi were sculpted by prominent Gothic and Renaissance artists, in particular Pietro and Tullio Lombardo.

At the back of the church runs the narrow Calle Torelli, also known as Calle Cavallerizza,

after stables that once stood here. It may seem incredible now, but there was a time when nobles got around town on horseback, and these stables could house about 70 of the beasties. In 1755 Casanova was arrested in a house along this street and led off to the Piombi, the rooftop prisons of the Palazzo Ducale.

CHIESA DI SAN FRANCESCO DELLA VIGNA Map p259

Campo San Francesco della Vigna; admission free; 8am-12.30pm & 3-7pm; vaporetto Celestia

Palladio was responsible for the high and mighty facade of this Franciscan church, which takes its name from the vineyard that once thrived on the site. The remainder was designed by Sansovino. The bell tower at the back seems to all intents and purposes the twin of the Campanile in Piazza San Marco. Inside, just to the left of the main door, is a triptych of saints by Antonio Vivarini. The Cappella dei Giustiniani, to the left of the main altar, is decorated with splendid reliefs by Pietro Lombardo and his school. Off the left (northern) arm of the transept, you can enter the Cappella Santa, which houses a *Madonna col Bambino e Santi* (Madonna and Child with Saints) by Giovanni Bellini. From here you can admire the leafy cloisters too.

CHIESA DI SAN GIORGIO DEI GRECI
Map p259

Campiello dei Greci; admission free; 9am-1pm & 3-4.30pm Wed-Sat & Mon, 9am-1pm Sun; vaporetto San Zaccaria

Greek Orthodox refugees who fled to Venice from the Ottoman Turks were allowed to raise a church, 'St George of the Greeks', here in 1526.

It is intriguing above all for the richness of its Byzantine icons, iconostasis and other artworks.

CHIESA DI SAN GIOVANNI IN BRAGORA Map p259
Campo Bandiera e Moro; admission free; ☉ 9am-1pm & 3.30-7pm Mon-Fri, 3.30-5.30pm Sat; vaporetto Arsenale

Antonio Vivaldi was baptised in this church. Among the works of art inside is a restored triptych by Bartolomeo Vivarini, the *Madonna in Trono tra I Santi Andrea e Giovanni Battista* (Enthroned Madonna with St Andrew and John the Baptist). In the peaceful square just south of the church, Campiello del Piovan, the architect **Giorgio Massari** was born at No 3752.

CHIESA DI SANTA MARIA DELLA VISITAZIONE Map p259
Riva degli Schiavoni 4149; admission free; vaporetto San Zaccaria

More simply dubbed **La Pietà**, this church is best known for its association with the composer Vivaldi, who was concertmaster here in the early 18th century. Look for the ceiling fresco by Tiepolo. If you attend one of the regular concerts here you will be able to view a collection of original instruments used by Vivaldi's orchestra.

CHIESA DI SANTA MARIA FORMOSA
Map pp254-5
Campo Santa Maria Formosa; admission €2 or Chorus ticket; ☉ 10am-5pm Mon-Sat, 1-5pm Sun; vaporetto San Zaccaria

Rebuilt in 1492 by Mauro Codussi on the site of a 7th-century church, this house of worship bears a curious name stemming from the legend behind its initial foundation. San Magno, bishop of Oderzo, is said to have had a vision of the Virgin Mary on this spot. Not just any old vision, however: in this instance she was *formosa* (beautiful, curvy), which hardly seems in keeping with standard views of Our Lady. The inside of the church was damaged when an Austrian bomb went off in 1916. Among the works of art to survive is an altarpiece by Palma il Vecchio depicting St Barbara, among other saints, and the body of Christ in his mother's arms. Just to the right of the main door (as you face it from the inside) is a 16th-century Byzantine icon, *Santa Maria di Lepanto* (St Mary of Lepanto). By the first chapel on the same side of the church is displayed an 8th-century Egyptian Coptic garment, claimed to be the veil of Santa Marina (St Marina).

CHIESA DI SAN ZACCARIA Map p259
Campo San Zaccaria; admission to Cappella di Sant'Anastasia €1; ☉ 10am-noon & 4-6pm Mon-Sat, 4-6pm Sun; vaporetto San Zaccaria

If the Basilica di San Marco was the private chapel of the doge, this was his parish church (eight dogi are buried here). The Renaissance facade is the handiwork of Antonio Gambello and Codussi. Gambello started off in a Gothic vein but was already influenced by Renaissance thinking. The lower part of the facade in marble is his work. When Codussi took over he favoured white Istrian stone, and the clean curves at the top mark his take on the Renaissance.

Inside, the mix of styles could not be clearer. Against a backdrop of classic Gothic apses, the high cross vaulting of the main body of the church is a leap of faith into the Renaissance. The church has an even longer history and its earliest version dates to the 9th century.

On the second altar to the left after you enter the church is Giovanni Bellini's *La Vergine in Trono col Bambino, un Angelo Suonatore e Santi* (The Virgin Enthroned with Jesus, an Angel Musician and Saints). You cannot miss it. It exudes a light and freshness that the surrounding paintings seem deliberately to lack.

The **Cappella di Sant'Anastasia** (admission €1) is off to the right. It holds works by Tintoretto and Tiepolo, as well as magnificently crafted choir stalls. After walking through it, you then pass through another chapel to reach the **Cappella di San Tarasion** (also called Cappella d'Oro) in the apse. Its vaults are covered in frescoes and the walls are decorated with Gothic polyptychs. Twelfth-century mosaics also survive and you can wander downstairs to the 10th-century Romanesque **crypt**, left over from an earlier church on the site.

GIARDINI PUBBLICI & BIENNALE
Map p260
Vaporetto Giardini

Creation of these, the most extensive (if slightly tatty) public gardens in the city, was ordered by Napoleon in 1807. They were officially opened in 1811, just three years before his demise. In the gardens you'll find shaded benches, a few *giostre* (swings and other kids' rides) and a snack bar/restaurant. You may have noticed during your Venetian strolls that there is a surprising amount of greenery, mostly in the form of private gardens (so much so that there is a coffee-table book entitled *Secret Gardens in Venice*, by Cristiana

Moldi-Ravenna, Gianni Berengo Gardin and Tudy Sammartini).

Also here are the national pavilions of the **Biennale Internazionale d'Arte**, Venice's contemporary arts fest held from June to November every two years (p10). Together the pavilions form a kind of mini-compendium of 20th-century architectural thinking. Standing well away from the historic centre and thus uninhibited by concerns about clashing with it, the site's pavilions are the work of a legion of architects. Carlo Scarpa contributed in one way or another from 1948 to 1972, continually updating the labyrinthine Italian Pavilion and building the Venezuelan one (1954). He also did the Biglietteria (ticket office) and entrance courtyard. Other interesting contributions are James Stirling's 1991 Padiglione del Libro (Book Pavilion), Gerrit Rietveld's Dutch Pavilion (1954), Josef Hoffman's Austrian Pavilion (1934) and Peter Cox's Australian Pavilion (1988), which backs onto a canal.

MUSEO DELLE ICONE Map p259
☎ 041 522 65 81; Ponte dei Greci 3412; admission adult/student €4/2; ☺ 9am-5pm; vaporetto San Zaccaria

Also known as the Museo dei Dipinti Sacri Bizantini (Museum of Holy Byzantine Paintings) and attached to the Chiesa di San Giorgio dei Greci (p83), this museum is housed in the Istituto Ellenico (Hellenic Institute). Here you can explore the curiosities of Orthodox religious art. On display are some 80 works of art and a series of other items, including the letter from Doge Leonardo Loredan granting the Greeks permission to build their church. Foremost among the artworks are two 14th-century Byzantine icons, one representing Christ in Glory and the other the Virgin Mary with Child and Apostles. Many of the remaining works were produced by or for the Greeks in Venice and elsewhere in northern Italy.

MUSEO DIOCESANO D'ARTE SACRA
Map pp254-5
☎ 041 522 91 66; Fondamenta di Sant'Apollonia 4312; admission free, but donations welcome; ☺ 10.30am-12.30pm Mon-Sat; vaporetto San Zaccaria

Housed in a former Benedictine monastery dedicated to Sant'Apollonia, this museum has a fairly predictable collection of religious art. More interesting is the exquisite Romanesque cloister you cross in order to get to the museum. It is a rare example of the genre in Venice. The cloister is often open much longer hours than the museum. The building next door was a church until 1906, and now houses exhibition spaces.

MUSEO STORICO NAVALE Map p259
☎ 041 520 02 76; Riva San Biagio 2148; admission €1.55; ☺ 8.45am-1.30pm Mon-Fri, 8.45am-1pm Sat; vaporetto Arsenale

Lovers of model boats, from ancient war vessels to modern battleships, will want to call in here. There's plenty of stuff related to Venetian

The Renaissance facade of Chiesa di San Zaccaria (opposite)

history on the high seas in this former grain silo. Spread over four floors, the museum traces the maritime history of the city and of Italy. There are some wonderfully complex models of all sorts of Venetian vessels, but also ancient triremes, Asian men o' war, WWII warships and ocean liners. The ground floor is devoted mainly to weaponry (the usual stuff – cannons, blunderbusses, swords and sabres). Most curious are the 17th-century diorama maps of Venetian ports and forts across the city's one-time Adriatic and Mediterranean possessions.

On the 1st floor is a model of the sumptuous *bucintoro*, the doge's ceremonial barge, in among the many large-scale model sailing vessels. Napoleon's French troops destroyed the real thing in 1798. The 2nd floor is mostly given over to Italian naval history and memorabilia, from unification to the present day. Up on the 3rd floor is a room containing a few gondolas, including Peggy Guggenheim's. A small room set above the 3rd floor is dedicated to – wait for it – Swedish naval history. Curious.

The ticket also gets you entrance to the **Padiglione delle Navi** (Ships Pavilion; Map p259), on Fondamenta della Madonna near the entrance to the Arsenale. Of the various boats on display, the most eye-catching is the *Scalé Reale*, an early 19th-century ceremonial vessel last used in 1959 to bring the body of the Venetian Pope Pius X to rest at Basilica di San Marco. It was also used to ferry King Vittorio Emanuele to Piazza San Marco in 1866 when Venice joined the nascent Kingdom of Italy.

OSPEDALETTO Map p259

☎ 041 270 24 64; Barbaria delle Tole 6691; admission Sala da Musica €1.55; ⏰ 3.30-6.30pm Thu-Sat; vaporetto Ospedale

Longhena's baroque Chiesa di Santa Maria dei Derelitti (also known as the Ospedaletto, or Little Hospital) is the focal point of a hospital for elderly and poor patients that was built in the 17th century. It also served for a time as an orphanage. In an annexe is the elegantly frescoed **Sala da Musica** (Music Room), where patients and orphans performed concerts.

PALAZZO QUERINI-STAMPALIA

Map pp254-5

☎ 041 271 14 11; Castello 5252; admission adult/student/senior €6/4/4; ⏰ 10am-1pm & 3-6pm Tue-Sun Oct-Apr; 10am-1pm & 3-6pm Tue-Thu & Sun, 10am-1pm & 3-10pm Fri & Sat May-Sep; vaporetto San Zaccaria

The last of this branch of the Querini family ordained that their mansion should become home to a foundation of the same name, which it has been since the 1860s.

Never judge a book by its cover. The outer shell of this building dates from the first half of the 16th century, but the inside could not be more surprising. In the 1940s Carlo Scarpa redesigned the entrance and garden; he then did the 1st floor (which houses the foundation's library) in 1959. Scarpa decided to have some disciplined fun with shape, and, in the garden in particular, took inspiration from the Arab emphasis on geometric patterns. It may or may not appeal, but it does make a refreshing change – there is little that is 'modern' in Venice.

Of Floors & Walls

As you wander about the Palazzo Querini-Stampalia, observe the floor. The smooth speckled surface, a classic *terrazzo alla Veneziana*, could almost be a mottled carpet if it weren't a little more solid than pile. In fact it's the result of combining finely fragmented marble chips with plaster and then laying this mixture down.

Why not straight marble floors? Virtually the entire city is built on foundations of timber pylons and has all the resulting problems of subsidence that you would expect. Movement is often greater than in more stable mainland environments. Great slabs of marble have no give – they would just crack open. This mixture, when hardened, has all the feel and solidity of marble, but greater elasticity. And when cracks do appear, all you need to do is mix up a batch of the marble-plaster goo, smooth it over and allow it to dry. You don't want it to dry out completely, though. Treatment with linseed oil at least once a year is needed to keep it in good shape and to allow it to be polished.

You will no doubt have noticed this type of floor in the Palazzo Ducale, Museo Correr and some other sites – you may well have it in your hotel room! It is not so apparent in the Palazzo Querini-Stampalia, but if you get to see inside other houses or manage to stay in a hotel or mansion of sufficient history, you will often see how much these floors undulate with time – a lot better than breaking up altogether.

While on the subject of home-maintenance issues, you may also have noticed that the classic Venetian colour is a burned reddish-orange. Innumerable houses are 'painted' this way. Except it isn't really paint. A straight coat of red paint quickly fades and streaks with all the rain and humidity inevitable in the lagoon. Traditionally, the outside walls of houses were coated in a mixture of paint and crushed red bricks. Once applied and dry, it lasts much longer than standard wall paint.

On the 2nd floor is the **Museo della Fondazione Querini-Stampalia**. The core of the collection is made up of period furniture that mostly belonged to the Querinis, portraits of more illustrious family members and various papers. Among the paintings, mostly minor works, is an interesting *Presentazione di Gesù al Tempio* (Presentation of Jesus at the Temple) by Giovanni Bellini. The poor child looks like a long-suffering mummy, standing up improbably in his tightly wrapped swaddling clothes. And what's the guy on the right looking at? Well you, actually.

Just before you get to the Bellini is a small annexe off a large hall. It contains a long series by Gabriele Bella (1730–99) depicting *Scene di Vita Veneziana* (Scenes of Venetian Life). The style of painting is rather naive, if not downright childlike, but the series provides an intriguing set of snapshots of life in Venice's last century under the dogi.

Another room towards the end of the permanent exhibition is devoted to works of Pietro Longhi. It also contains some good examples of traditional Venetian furniture, characterised by its engraved and lacquered wood with painted floral motifs. Quite a few hotels have adopted a watered-down version of the style.

RIVA DEGLI SCHIAVONI Map pp254-5 & 259
Vaporetto San Zaccaria

The waterside walkway west from Rio Ca' di Dio and on to the Palazzo Ducale in San Marco is known as the Riva degli Schiavoni. *Schiavoni*, meaning Slavs, referred to Dalmatian fishermen who, from medieval times, used to cast their nets off this waterfront. For centuries, vessels would dock here amid all the chaos you might expect from a busy harbour. Boat crews, waterfront merchants, nobles, gendarmes and crooks, dressed in all manner of garb reflecting the passing parade of Greeks, Turks, Slavs, Arabs, Africans and Europeans, all jostled about these docks. It is perhaps hard to imagine the seemingly chaotic rows of galleys, galleons and, later on, sailing vessels competing for dock space or moored farther out in the Canale di San Marco. Or the confusion of rigging and containers of all sorts, the babble of languages, and the clang and clatter of arms and cooking pots as locals or seafarers prepared impromptu meals for those just arrived. The assault on the senses must have been something.

Today it remains busy, but the actors have changed. The galleons of yore have been replaced by ferries, the exotic crews and merchants by gondoliers and not-so-exotic tourists. Instead of impromptu food stalls and the smell of cooking meat, there are ice-cream stands and tourist tat. The linguistic babble remains as confusing as ever. Some of the grand old mansions now function as pricey hotels for the well-heeled out-of-towner. One of Italy's greatest writers and friend of Venice, Francesco Petrarca (Petrarch), for a time found lodgings at No 4175, east of Rio della Pietà.

SCUOLA DI SAN GIORGIO DEGLI SCHIAVONI Map p259
☎ 041 522 88 28; Calle dei Furlani 3259/a; admission €3; ☒ 10am-12.30pm & 3-6pm Tue-Sat, 10am-12.30pm Sun; vaporetto San Zaccaria

Venice's Dalmatian community established this religious school in the 15th century and the building was erected in the 16th century. The main attraction is on the ground floor, where the walls are graced by a series of superb paintings by Vittore Carpaccio depicting events in the lives of the three patron saints of Dalmatia: George, Tryphone and Jerome. The image of St George dispatching the dragon to the next life is a particularly graphic scene. Scattered about before the dragon are remnants of its victims – various limbs, the half-eaten corpse of a young woman and an assortment of bones.

Members of the *scuola* gathered upstairs for meetings and religious services. Delicate timber décor and the heavy exposed beams of the ceilings complete the scene.

SCUOLA GRANDE DI SAN MARCO
Map p253
Campo SS Giovanni e Paolo; admission free; ☒ hospital hours; vaporetto Ospedale

Standing at right angles to the main facade of the Chiesa dei SS Giovanni e Paolo is the eye-catching (well, not while the scaffolding stays up!) marble frontage of this *scuola*. Pietro Lombardo and his sons all worked on what was once one of the most important of Venice's religious confraternities. Codussi put the finishing touches on this Renaissance gem. Have a closer look and, apart from the predictably magnificent lions, you will notice the sculpted trompe l'oeil perspectives covering much of the lower half of the facade. Inside, the timber beams of the ceiling are held up by two ranks of five columns. The staircase to the upper storey is closed.

Nowadays the *scuola* is the entrance to the Ospedale Civile. Beyond, in what were the Convento dei Domenicani and the Chiesa di San Lazzaro dei Mendicanti, is the hospital proper. You are free to enter the *scuola* itself.

AROUND THE LAGOON

Eating p134; Entertainment p144; Shopping p159; Sleeping p180

Venice goes beyond the six *sestieri*. Indeed, it did not even begin on the islands that constitute them. Although the bulk of the city's visitors don't bother, it is a more than worthwhile exercise to get out to at least some of the islands.

Orientation

The island of Giudecca is virtually a part of Venice, forming a vaguely banana-shaped basin to the south of the city. A few kilometres to the east starts the long protective strip of the Lido, Venetians' local beach and sea wall. Below it stretches the razor-thin and equally long sea barrier of Pellestrina island. The most visited islands lie to the north. Murano, of glass-making fame, is first up, while further off lie the pastel-coloured Burano, known for its fishing and lace-making, and the now nearly abandoned Torcello, important for its impressive cathedral and mosaics. Several other islands are dotted about to the north and south of Venice and merit a visit.

GIUDECCA

Originally known as *spina longa* (long fishbone) because of its shape, Giudecca's name probably derives from the word Zudega (from *giudicato* – the judged), applied to rebellious nobles banished from Venice proper. There are variations on this story – the most likely seems to be that as early as the 9th century, families who had been exiled earlier (and one assumes unjustly) were given land on Giudecca by way of compensation. Until that time, the only inhabitants had been a handful of fishermen and their families. Some historians beg to differ with this and assert that the island's name comes from a period when many of Venice's Jews lived on the island before being forced into the confines of the Ghetto.

By the 16th century, the island had been extended through land reclamation to reach something approaching its present form. Merchants set up warehouses and a flourishing local commercial life made Giudecca a prime piece of real estate. Elite families (such as the Dandolos, Mocenigos and Vendramins) bought up land to build their homes-away-from-home, facing Venice to the north and ending in luxuriant gardens looking south to the open lagoon. Several religious orders also established convents and monasteries here.

With the fall of the Republic in 1797, everything changed. The noble families slipped away as their fortunes declined.

The religious orders were suppressed and the convents closed. The face of the island gradually changed through the 19th century. Replacing the pleasure domes and religious retreats came prisons, barracks and factories, and, with the latter, working-class housing grids. Descendants of the workers who powered the factories remain in the modest low-level housing, but most of the factories have long since been closed down.

Giudecca is a strangely melancholy place. A few boatyards keep busy with repair work, while a handful of shops and eateries survive on a modest local trade and the few tourists who stop long enough to want to eat here. The women's prison (which was a convent for reformed prostitutes until 1857) is still in operation. Mild building activity suggests that more life is perhaps coming to Giudecca; slightly more affordable housing than in central Venice is an attraction. Mind you, there is something for everyone, as VIPs such as Elton John also buy up getaway properties here.

CHIESA DELLE ZITELLE Map pp262–3

Fondamenta delle Zitelle; admission free; ☺ 10am-noon Fri-Sat; vaporetto Zitelle

Designed by Palladio in the late 16th century, the Chiesa di Santa Maria della Presentazione, known as the Zitelle, was a church and hospice for poor young women (*zitelle* means 'old maids', which is presumably what many of them remained). It is now used for conferences.

Transport

While vaporetti are something of an option in Venice itself and walking is often faster and more interesting, you clearly need to use the ferries to get around the islands. Lines 41, 42, 82 and N serve Giudecca regularly, the easiest approaches being from Ferrovia, Piazzale Roma and San Zaccaria. You can reach the Lido by vaporetti Nos 1, 6, 14, 51, 52, 61, 62 and 82, N and the vehicle ferry (No 17) from Isola del Tronchetto.

The other islands require a little more effort. The DM line runs from Tronchetto via Piazzale Roma and Ferrovia to all stops in Murano. No 5 runs directly from San Zaccaria in summer. Otherwise the most regular services are the 41 and 42, most easily picked up at Fondamente Nuove. You can get to Burano with the LN lines, either from Fondamente Nuove via Murano and Mazzorbo, or the longer trip from San Zaccaria via Lido and Punta Sabbioni. From Burano the T vaporetto runs every half hour to Torcello. For San Servolo and San Lazzaro, take the No 20 from San Zaccaria. The No 13 vaporetto runs to Le Vignole and Sant'Erasmo from Fondamente Nuove via Murano (Faro stop).

You can get to Pellestrina using the No 11 Lido–Pellestrina bus-and-vaporetto line. If you've hired a bicycle, you can take it across on the vaporetto for €1 (or a combined fare of €3.62 for passenger and bike if you haven't got a day ticket).

For Chioggia, bus No 11 leaves from Gran Viale Santa Maria Elisabetta, outside the tourist office on the Lido; it boards the car ferry at Alberoni and then connects with a steamer at Pellestrina that will take you to Chioggia. Alternatively, you can catch a bus from Piazzale Roma. In summer the Linea Clodia ferry runs directly from in front of the Pietà church. Once you're in the town, city bus Nos 1, 2, 6 and 7 connect Chioggia with Sottomarina (a 15-minute walk), the town's beach.

CHIESA DEL REDENTORE Map pp262-3
Campo del Redentore; admission €2 or Chorus ticket; 10am-5pm Mon-Sat, 1-5pm Sun; vaporetto Redentore

With the passing of a bout of plague in 1577, the Senato commissioned Palladio to design a church of thanksgiving. The following year the doge, members of the Senato and a host of citizens made the first pilgrimage of thanksgiving, crossing from Zattere on a pontoon bridge of boats and rafts.

Work on this magnificent edifice was completed under Antonio da Ponte (better known for his Ponte di Rialto) in 1592. The long church was designed to accommodate the large numbers of pilgrims who, from 1578 onwards, made the annual excursion. The pilgrimage still takes place today on the third Saturday in July, and it remains one of the most important events on Venice's calendar.

Inside the church are a few works by Tintoretto, Veronese and Vivarini, but it is the powerful facade that most inspires observers. Indeed, although it is uncertain why the site was chosen, there is no doubt that its open position makes the church easy to observe and admire from just about anywhere on the Fondamenta Zattere across the Canale della Giudecca. The classical cleanness of the design reminds one, if on a considerably grander scale, of the Venetian villas on the mainland (see p196).

Chiesa delle Zitelle on Giudecca (opposite)

CHIESA DI SANT'EUFEMIA Map pp262-3
Fondamenta Sant'Eufemia; vaporetto Palanca

A simple Veneto-Byzantine structure of the 11th century, this church's main portico was actually added in the 18th and 19th centuries. Down Fondamenta Rio di Sant'Eufemia are the one-time church and convent of **SS Cosma e Damiano**. They were turned into a factory and the bell tower into a smokestack!

MULINO STUCKY Map pp262-3
Fondamenta San Biagio; vaporetto Palanca

The striking neo-Gothic hulk of the best-known factory complex on the island, the Mulino Stucky, was built in the late 19th century and employed 1500 people. The windowless brick structure looks like a cathedral to industry and is hard to miss when looking across from the western end of the Zattere. It was shut in 1954 and has long sat in dignified silence. In 2000 the buildings were saved from the wrecking ball as a plan to restore them and create 138 apartments, a hotel and a congress centre got underway. If all had gone well the project would have been completed in 2005, but part of the structure was devastated by fire in mysterious circumstances in April 2003. At the time of writing, investigators were continuing to look at whether or not the fire was started intentionally.

ISOLA DI SAN GIORGIO MAGGIORE
CHIESA DI SAN GIORGIO MAGGIORE
Map pp262-3
Admission bell-tower lift €3, church admission free; 9.30am-12.30pm & 2-6pm; vaporetto San Giorgio
Palladio's grand church occupies one of the most prominent positions in Venice and, although it inspired mixed reactions among the architect's contemporaries, it had a significant influence on Renaissance architecture. Built between 1565 and 1580, it is his most imposing structure in Venice. The facade, although not erected until the following century, is believed to conform to Palladio's wishes. The massive columns on high plinths, the crowning tympanum and the statues all contain an element of sculptural chiaroscuro, if such a term is permissible, casting strong shadows and reinforcing the impression of strength. Indeed, facing the Bacino di San Marco and the heart of Venice, its effect is deliberately theatrical. Inside, the sculptural decoration is sparse, the open space regimented by powerful clusters of columns and covered by luminous vaults.

San Giorgio Maggiore's art treasures include works by Tintoretto: an *Ultima Cena* (Last Supper) and the *Raccolta della Manna* (Shower of Manna) on the walls of the high altar, and a *Deposizione* (Deposition) in the Cappella dei Morti. Take the lift to the top of the 60m-high bell tower for an extraordinary view.

Behind the church extend the grounds of the former monastery. Established as long ago as the 10th century by the Benedictines, it was rebuilt in the 13th century and then restructured and expanded in a series of projects that spanned the 16th century, finishing with the library built by Longhena in the 1640s.

Unfortunately, little or none of this can be seen, as the Fondazione Cini bought it in 1951 (saving it from a slow death by neglect, it should be added). The foundation operates various scholarly centres here. The open-air Teatro Verde, after many years of restoration, is used for occasional shows, including dance, music and theatre.

ISOLA DI SAN MICHELE
CIMITERO (CEMETERY) Map p249
Admission free; 7.30am-4pm Oct-Mar, 7.30am-6pm Apr-Sep; vaporetto Cimitero
The city's cemetery was established on San Michele under Napoleon (even the Venetians can't complain that the diminutive Corsican did nothing for them) and is maintained by the Franciscans. The **Chiesa di San Michele in Isola**, begun by Codussi in 1469, was among the city's first Renaissance buildings, built in sober style of white Istrian stone. The quiet cloister is attractive and worth a peek. Among those pushing up daisies here are Ezra Pound, Sergei Diaghilev and Igor Stravinsky. Look for their graves in the northeast sector of the island (signposted); they are in the 'acatholic' (read Protestant and Orthodox) sections. Vaporetto lines 41 and 42 from Fondamente Nuove stop here.

MURANO
The people of Venice have been making crystal and glass since the 10th century. The bulk of the industry was moved to the island of Murano in 1291 because of the danger of fire posed by the glass-working furnaces.

Venice had a virtual monopoly on the production of what is now known as Murano glass, and the methods of the craft were such a well-guarded secret that it was considered treason for a glass-worker to leave the city. See the boxed text on p160.

The incredibly elaborate pieces produced by the artisans can range from the beautiful to the grotesque – but, as the Italians would say, *i gusti son gusti* (each to his own). Watching the glass-workers in action in shops and factories around the island is certainly interesting. You can see them in several outlets along Fondamenta dei Vetrai and a couple on Viale Garibaldi. Look for the sign 'Fornace' (furnace).

Palazzo da Mula, near the Ponte Vivarini, the only bridge to span the Canal Grande di Murano, sometimes plays host to exhibitions. More often than not the subject is...glass.

By all accounts the island was graced by many fine villas and pretty gardens – the bulk of them destroyed under Napoleonic occupation after the fall of the Republic.

CHIESA DEI SS MARIA E DONATO

Map p265

Campo San Donato; admission free; ☾ 9am-noon & 3.30-7pm Mon-Sat, 3.30-7pm Sun; vaporetto Murano (Museo)

This is a fascinating example of Veneto-Byzantine architecture. Looking at the apse, however, it is impossible not to see Romanesque influences too. Founded in the 7th century and rebuilt 500 years later, the church was originally dedicated to the Virgin Mary. It was rededicated to St Donato after his bones were brought here from the Greek island of Cephalonia, along with those of a dragon he had supposedly killed (four of the 'dragon' bones hang behind the altar). The church's magnificent mosaic pavement (a very Byzantine touch) was laid in the 12th century, and the impressive mosaic of the Virgin Mary in the apse dates from the same period.

MUSEO VETRARIO Map p265

☎ 041 73 95 86; Fondamenta Giustinian 8; admission adult/child €4/2.50, see also Special Tickets; ☾ 10am-5pm Thu-Tue Apr-Oct, 10am-4pm Thu-Tue Nov-Mar; vaporetto Murano (Museo)

This museum has some exquisite pieces. The building, set in a peaceful garden, is a grand 15th-century affair that from 1659 until the early 19th century was the seat of the Torcello bishopric (until its dissolution) and then became Murano town hall. The museum was installed here in 1861, mostly on the 1st floor. On the ground floor is a display of ancient glass artefacts, mostly unearthed in tombs in Dalmatia (in the former Yugoslavia) and dating to the 1st and 2nd centuries AD (the art of glass-blowing had taken off in Palestine in the 1st century BC). Upstairs you can turn right into a room where glass-making is explained. To the left is the grand, frescoed Salone Maggiore (Grand Salon), with a display of all sorts of exquisite pieces from the 19th and 20th centuries. The surrounding annexes are dedicated to displays from preceding centuries, starting with the 15th.

Across Canale di San Donato is one of the few private mansions of any note on the island, the 16th-century Palazzo Trevisan.

BURANO

Famous for its lace industry, Burano is a pretty fishing village, its streets and canals lined with bright, pastel-coloured houses. They say the bonbon colours have their origins in the fishermen's desire to be able to see their own houses when heading home from a day at sea. Regardless of the reasons, the bright, gay colours are engaging. Given the island's distance from Venice (around 40 minutes by vaporetto), you really do get the feeling of having arrived somewhere only fleetingly touched by La Serenissima.

Give yourself time to wander into the quietest corners and shady parks. Walk over the wooden bridge to neighbouring Mazzorbo, a larger island with little more than a few houses, a couple of trattorie and open green space. A snooze in the grass takes you light years away from the marvels of Venice and somehow puts them into a harmonious perspective.

If you plan to buy lace on the island, choose with care and discretion, as these days some of the cheaper stuff is imported from Asia. That said, you can still occasionally see women working away at lacemaking in the shade of their homes and in the parks.

MUSEO DEL MERLETTO Map p264

☎ 041 73 00 34; Piazza Galuppi 187; admission adult/child €4/2.50, see also Special Tickets; ☾ 10am-5pm Wed-Mon Apr-Oct, 10am-4pm Wed-Mon Nov-Mar; vaporetto Burano

Housed on the top floor of the island's one-time lace school (it closed in 1970), here you will see pieces of handiwork that are little short of mind-boggling in the intricacy of their design. Everything from shawls to tablecloths, from gloves to napkins, is on show. Some of the 17th-century pieces, with complex relief detail and clearly the result of long and painstaking labour, are truly remarkable. In the last room hang sundry diplomas and prizes awarded at international exhibitions from the 19th century on. Recognition for the quality of the islanders' work came from as far off as Paris and Boston. For more on old lace, see the boxed text on p153.

TORCELLO

This delightful island, with its overgrown main square and sparse, scruffy-looking buildings and monuments, was at its peak from the mid-7th century to the 13th century, when it was the seat of the bishop of mainland Altinum (modern Altino) and home to some 20,000 people. Rivalry with Venice and a succession of malaria epidemics systematically reduced the island's splendour and population. Today, fewer than 80 people call Torcello home. In its now nearly abandoned state, the island gives us some idea of how things might have looked at the outset of settlement in the lagoon.

When you get off the vaporetto, you have little choice but to follow the path along the canal that leads to the heart of the island in a leisurely 10 minutes. Around the central square is huddled all that remains of old Torcello – the lasting homes of the clergy and the island's secular rulers.

A combined ticket for the Cattedrale di Santa Maria Assunta and Musei di Torcello costs €6 and can be purchased at either place.

CATTEDRALE DI SANTA MARIA ASSUNTA Map p264

Piazza Torcello; admission €3, admission to bell tower €2, or combined ticket; ☺ 10.30am-5.30pm Mar-Oct, 10am-5pm Nov-Feb; vaporetto Torcello

The island's ancient Veneto-Byzantine cathedral, Venice's first, was founded in the 7th century. What you see today dates from the first expansion of the church in 824 and rebuilding in 1008, making it about the oldest Venetian monument to have remained relatively untampered with.

The three apses (the central one dates back to the original 7th-century structure) are Romanesque in inspiration and underline its intermarriage of building styles. A jewel of simple, early-medieval architecture, the interior is still more fascinating for its magnificent Byzantine mosaics.

On the western wall of the cathedral is a vast mosaic depicting the Last Judgment. Hell (lower right side) doesn't look any fun at all. Sceptics in the 21st century may grin knowingly, but such images inspired sheer terror in the average resident of Torcello back in the 12th and 13th centuries, when the mosaics were put together.

The greatest treasure is the mosaic of the *Madonna col Bambino* (Madonna and Child) in the half-dome of the central apse. Starkly set on a pure gold background, the figure is one of the most stunning works of Byzantine art in Italy. And if you need more confirmation of the church's Eastern influences, have a look at the iconostasis set well before the altar.

Climb the bell tower for fine lagoon views.

In front of the cathedral entrance are the excavated remains of the 7th-century circular **baptistry**. Steps lead down into a small pool, a standard early-Christian model for baptistries. It was later demolished and replaced several times until in the 19th century these remains were uncovered. Fragmentary remains of construction on the site of the baptistry go back to the 4th century, indicating that the island was already inhabited under the Roman Empire.

Adjacent to the cathedral, the **Chiesa di Santa Fosca** was founded in the 11th century to house the body of Santa Fosca.

MUSEO DI TORCELLO Map p264

Piazza Torcello; ☎ 041 73 07 61; admission €2, or combined ticket; ☺ 10.30am-5pm Tue-Sun Mar-Oct, 10am-4.30pm Tue-Sun Nov-Feb; vaporetto Torcello

Across the square from the cathedral in the 13th-century **Palazzo del Consiglio** is this museum dedicated to the island. On the ground floor are some sculptural fragments from the cathedral, a 6th-century holy-water font and a curious display of Byzantine objects from Constantinople. Upstairs, among a series of rather dark religious paintings, many from the workshops of Veronese, are all sorts of odds and ends, including a 7th-century lead seal. The museum's ancient artefacts are held in the **Palazzo dell'Archivio**, just opposite the Palazzo del Consiglio. They include Roman bronze implements and figurines, some funerary stelae and statuary and other bits and pieces. The Roman items were mostly unearthed at Altino, on the mainland, but some objects have found their way into the collection without having anything to do with Torcello or the surrounding area.

The rough-hewn stone chair outside is known as the **Sedia di Attila** (Attila's Seat). Why is anyone's guess, and even the use to which the seat was put is a mystery. It is surmised that magistrates sat here to pass judgment.

LIDO DI VENEZIA

The main draw here is the beach, but the water ain't that great and the public areas of the waterfront can be less than attractive. You pay a small fortune (from €5 to €9 for a sun-lounger and €57 for a basic changing room per day) to rent a chair, umbrella and changing cabin in the more easily accessible and cleaner areas of the beach. That said,

Catamarans prepare to set sail from Lido di Venezia (below)

it is not entirely clear what, if anything, is done if you choose to plonk your towel close to the water's edge (a town ordinance technically forbids obstruction of the open beach area between the rows of cabins and the water).

The Lido forms a land barrier between the lagoon and the Adriatic Sea. For centuries, the dogi made an annual pilgrimage here to fulfil Venice's Sposalizio del Mar (Wedding with the Sea) ceremony by dropping a ring into the shallows, celebrating the city's relationship with the tides. This was done just off the **Chiesa di San Nicolò**, at the northern end of the island. After the ceremony, everyone headed to the church to hear Mass. The church today is a relatively uninteresting 17th-century structure. Nearby was one of the city's defensive forts.

A few hundred metres to the south of the church lies the **Antico Cimitero Israelitico** (Map pp262-3; Old Jewish Cemetery; guided tours in Italian & English 2.30pm Sun; adult/student €8/6.50). You can turn up at the gates or buy tickets in advance at the Museo Ebraico in Cannaregio (see p80) to tour the burial ground, said to be the second oldest Jewish cemetery in Europe after that in Worms (Germany). The cemetery is open only on Sunday for these organised visits.

The Lido became a fashionable seaside resort at the end of the 19th century, and its more glorious days are depicted in melancholy fashion in Thomas Mann's novel *Der Tod in Venedig* (Death in Venice). A wander around the streets between the Adriatic and the vaporetto stop will turn up occasional Art Nouveau (what the Italians refer to as 'Liberty style') and even Art Deco villas. One of the most extravagant is the **Hungaria Palace Hotel** (Gran Viale Santa Maria Elisabetta 28).

Today the island is fairly laid-back for most of the year, but crowded on summer weekends with local and foreign sun-seekers. The beaches are frankly better on the northern coast of the mainland (Cavallino, Jesolo and farther along the coast as far as Bibione), but the Lido is easier to reach. The place fills up for the Mostra del Cinema di Venezia (Venice International Film Festival), which takes place every year from late August to September. The cinema-fest is hosted in the snappy **Palazzo della Mostra del Cinema**.

On the lagoon side, you can see the nearby Isola di San Lazzaro degli Armeni (see p95). Closer to the shore is the former leper colony of **Lazzaretto Vecchio**.

Bus B from Gran Viale Santa Maria Elisabetta, or your bicycle, will take you to Malamocco, in the south of the island. Arranged across a chain of squares and some canals, the old heart of this town is far more reminiscent of Venice than the late-19th-century seaside conceits at the northern end of the island. The original settlement of Malamocco, besieged by the Frankish ruler Pepin in the early years of the Republic, is believed to have been an island off the Lido and has long since disappeared.

The first thing you should do on arriving at the Lido is hire a bike at **Anna Garbin** (Map pp262-3; ☎ 041 276 00 05; Piazzale Santa Maria Elisabetta 2/a; €9 per day), just off Gran Viale Santa Maria Elisabetta, a couple of minutes from the main vaporetto stop. This will allow you to explore the island, as well as (for the energetic) Pellestrina and even Chioggia to the south.

PELLESTRINA

Separated from the southern tip of the Lido by the Porto di Malamocco, one of the three sea gates between the Adriatic and the lagoon, Pellestrina is shaped like an 11km-long razor blade. Small villages of farmers and fishing families are strung out along the island, protected on the seaward side by the Murazzi, a remarkable feat of 18th-century engineering, although they don't look much to the modern eye. These sea walls, designed to keep the power of the sea over the lagoon in check, once extended without interruption some 20km from the southern tip of Pellestrina to a point well over halfway up the coast of the Lido. The Pellestrina stretch and part of the Lido wall remain. They were heavily damaged during the 1966 floods and partially restored in the 1970s. Long stretches of sparsely populated grey-sand beaches separate the Murazzi from the sea on calm days. Venetians occasionally make the effort to come here for a meal at one of the handful of small family restaurants, known for their excellent seafood.

MINOR ISLANDS
San Francesco del Deserto

The Franciscans built themselves a **monastery** (☎ 041 528 68 63; admission free, donations appreciated; ☺ 9-11am & 3-5pm Tue-Sun) on this island about 1km south of Burano to get away from it all. The island, on which evidence of an earlier Roman presence has also been found, makes an enchanting detour while exploring the islands of the lagoon. Legend has it that Francis of

Assisi himself landed here, seeking shelter after a journey to Palestine in 1220. The Franciscans deserted the island (hence the name) in 1420, as conditions had become difficult and malaria was rampant.

Another branch of the order reoccupied the island later that century, and in the 18th century they were succeeded by yet another reforming branch of the Franciscans. These various groups were united by Pope Leo XIII in the 19th century into the order of the Frati Minori and, except for an interruption under Napoleon, they have remained ever since. The monastery complex retains some of its 13th-century elements, including the first cloister. It is advisable to call before heading out, especially if you are in a group. If you turn up within the hours outlined a tour should take place, but it depends on whether or not a brother is free.

It is possible to stay in retreat on the island if you wish to participate in monastery life (prayer, catechism and a little work in the gardens if you choose). Generally people do so for a long weekend – but this is not for tourists. The emphasis is on the religious and meditative experience.

The only way there is to hire a private boat or taxi from Burano. Ask around at the vaporetto stop. You will be looking at about €80 for up to four passengers for the return trip and a 40-minute wait time.

Le Vignole & Sant'Erasmo

Welcome to the Venetian countryside! Together these two islands almost equal Venice in size, but any comparison ends there. Sparsely inhabited, these largely rural islands are covered in fields, groves and vineyards rather than endless monuments.

The southwestern part of Le Vignole is owned by the military and contains the best-preserved of a scattering of old forts, the 16th-century **Forte Sant'Andrea**. Most people content themselves with a distant view of the fort from the lagoon but it is possible to arrange visits (☎ 368 320 68 46). The low-level cannons pointing out to sea, combined with a chain strung across to the Forte di San Nicolò on the Lido rendered entry into the heart of the lagoon by enemy warships virtually impossible. The island itself long produced the bulk of the doge's wine, and its 50 or so inhabitants still live mainly from agriculture.

Together with Le Vignole, Sant'Erasmo was long known as the *orto di Venezia* (Venice's garden). About 1000 people live on the island, many around the Chiesa ferry stop. For most of its history the island has had a predominantly agricultural vocation, although the Roman chronicler Martial records the presence of holiday villas belonging to the well-to-do of the now-disappeared mainland centre of Altinum (Altino). Until the 1800s, the island bore the direct brunt of Adriatic rollers, but subsequent construction of dikes at the Porto del Lido lagoon entrance favoured the build-up of sediment that created Punta Sabbioni and largely closed the island off from the sea.

It is about a half-hour walk from the Chiesa stop to the more southern Capannone stop, and another 15 minutes east to what remains of the round Torre Massimiliana, a 19th-century Austrian defensive fort. The small nearby beach and restaurant become a weekend summer focal point for young and restless Venetians, who parade around in speedboats with music blaring, much like their young landlubber confreres do in wide-wheeled cars.

San Clemente, San Servolo and San Lazzaro degli Armeni

The island of San Clemente was once the site of a hospice for pilgrims returning from the Middle East. Later, a convent was built and from 1522 it was a quarantine station. The plague that devastated Venice in 1630 was blamed by some on a carpenter who worked on San Clemente, became infected and brought the disease over to the city. The Austrians turned the building into a mental hospital for women (the first in Europe), and until 1992 it still operated in part as a psychiatric hospital. The entire island is now a luxury hotel (see p181).

San Servolo shared these mental hospital functions from the 18th century until 1978. From the 7th to the 17th centuries Benedictine monks had a monastery here, bits of which still remain in the former hospital. Now the island is home to various cultural institutions, including the Centro Europeo de Venezia per i Mestieri della Conservazione del Patrimonio Architettonico, a rather long-winded way of saying the Venice European Restoration Centre.

Of the islets scattered about south of Venice, the most important is San Lazzaro degli Armeni. In 1717 the Armenian order of the Mechitarist Fathers (named after the founding father, Mechitar) was granted use of the island, which centuries before had been a leper colony and earlier still the site of a Benedictine hospice for pilgrims. The Mechitarists' monastery (Map pp262-3; ☎ 041 526 01 04; adult/child €6/3; ⏰ entry by guided tour only 3.25-5pm) became an important centre of learning and repository of Armenian culture, which it remains to this day. After wandering around the peaceful cloister you are taken to the church, sparkling with mosaics and stuffed with paintings (the Armenian monastery was the only one in Venice spared from pillaging by Napoleon). From there you are led to the 18th-century refectory and then upstairs to the library. The latter is divided into several rooms. The first, by which you enter, is lined by cabinets with all sorts of odds and ends, including antiquities from Ancient Egypt, Sumeria and India. The precious collections of books are followed by a room dedicated mostly to Armenian art and artefacts. An Egyptian mummy and 15th-century Indian throne dominate a room dedicated to the memory of Lord Byron, who stayed on the island in search of a little (much-needed) inner peace. True to his eccentric nature, he could often be seen swimming from the island to the Grand Canal. Lastly, a circular room contains precious manuscripts, many of them Armenian and one dating as far back as the 6th century!

CHIOGGIA

Chioggia marks the southern mainland boundary of the Venetian municipality. Invaded and destroyed by the Republic's maritime rival, Genoa, in the late 14th century, the medieval core of modern Chioggia is a crumbly but not uninteresting counterpoint to its more illustrious patron to the north. In no way cute like Murano or Burano, Chioggia is a firmly practical town, its big sea-fishing fleet everywhere in evidence. For tourist office details see the Directory (p228).

On the assumption you arrive via the Lido and Pellestrina – by far the most enchanting way to get here – you'll find yourself at the northern end of Main St Chioggia (Corso del Popolo) as soon as you set foot on dry land. Before you do anything else, head left down Calle della Santa Croce to the **Chiesa di San Domenico**, built in 1745 on the site of an earlier Dominican church. The site is a little island unto itself and the church's main claim to fame is the painting of *San Paolo* (St Paul), said to be Vittore Carpaccio's last known work. The bell tower, raised in 1200, is all that remains of the original structure.

After visiting the church, return to Corso del Popolo. A brisk walk down this cobblestoned and largely pedestrianised thoroughfare takes you to the heart of the old town. Along the way, you reach the **cathedral**. Rebuilt in the 17th century to a design by Longhena, about all that remains of the earlier structure is the bell tower, raised in 1350.

The historic centre of Chioggia is located on an island, and was transferred here from its original position in what is today Sottomarina, on the coast, after the Genoese siege of 1379–80. The reasoning was simple enough: just as water was Venice's best defence, so it would be for Chioggia. People began to repopulate the Sottomarina area only three centuries later.

Through the middle of the island runs the utterly Venetian Canale della Vena, complete with little bridges. On either side it is protected by the Canale Lombardo and Canale di San Domenico. Beyond the latter (after crossing another narrow islet), the Ponte Translagunare bridges the lagoon to link Chioggia with Sottomarina and thus the Adriatic beaches.

More interesting than the monuments is simply pottering about, ducking down the alleys that branch off like ribs to the east and west from the spine of Corso del Popolo. The **fish market** (*mercato ittico*; open Tue-Sat mornings), alongside Canale di San Domenico where the Ponte Translagunare reaches into Chioggia, is an eye-opener if you can get there at about 6am.

If you want a swim, the **beaches** at Sottomarina are pretty clean, although the water can be murky. It's a typical seaside scene, with cheap hotels, bouncy castles for kids, snack bars, tat and even the odd tacky disco.

Walking Tours

Walking Tours

Perhaps more than any other city, Venice is best discovered on foot. Clearly you can use the vaporetti to get around some places too, but often it's just as quick to get from A to B on foot. Where the vaporetti do come into their own is after a long day's exploration, to take you back to base.

The following walks cover the *sestieri*, or districts, that make up the city (San Marco, Dorsoduro, San Polo, Santa Croce, Cannaregio and Castello). The suggested routes provide possible links from one *sestiere* to the next. If you kept to the order in this chapter (and no-one is suggesting you should!), you would, at the end of several days, find yourself meandering west along the Riva degli Schiavoni in Castello towards the starting point – Piazzetta San Marco.

The routes should be viewed as suggestions for orientation. The distances given are deceptive – this is not a race and even a few kilometres can take you a day if you stop to visit sights and take your time. Let your imagination do the work and wander off wherever your nose leads you.

SESTIERE DI SAN MARCO

Ever since the rail link with the mainland opened in the 19th century, the magical symbolism of Piazzetta San Marco, the theatrical lagoonside gateway to the Most Serene Republic, has been largely lost to the city's visitors.

Walk Facts

Start Piazzetta San Marco (vaporetto San Marco)
End Piazza San Marco
Distance 4km

Stand between the two 12th-century red and grey granite columns 1 bearing the emblems of Venice's patron saints – the winged lion of St Mark and the figure of the demoted St Theodore, whom St Mark replaced. The lion faces east, perhaps to signify Venice's domination of the sea, while St Theodore (placed here in 1329) stands calmly on top of a crocodile-like dragon. The tip of his spear is pointed skywards, so perhaps he has killed his prey (some say the statue represents St George). He also holds a shield, as if to say Venice defends itself but does not seek to attack.

Imagine yourself on a galley after months at sea, making your way to La Serenissima. To some observers, the lion's and dragon's tails face each other to form the crossbeam of a perennially open gate – as if to say that Venice is open to whomever visits. At any rate, it must have been a welcome sight to Venetians returning home.

The columns were erected in 1172. In succeeding centuries, the area around them was a hive of activity, with shops selling all manner of goods and food. On a more sinister note, public executions took place between the two columns.

One of the lowest parts of the city, the Piazzetta is always the first to be covered in water when the *acqua alta* (high tidal flooding) arrives. In fact, until the 12th century there was nothing but water here. Like so much of Venice, this area is the result of landfill. The square is flanked on one side by the Palazzo Ducale 2 (p55), long the seat of power in the lagoon city, and on the other by the sumptuous 16th-century Libreria Nazionale Marciana 3 (p54).

Linked to Piazzetta San Marco is the grand Piazza San Marco, dominated by one of the world's most opulent and beautiful churches and symbol of the city, Basilica di San Marco 4 (p50). Before it rises its proud bell tower or Campanile 5 (p53). Back in 1162 the local authorities used Piazza San Marco as the stage for the city's first *caccia al toro* (bull hunt), a mad folly that would have made Pamplona's running of the bulls look orderly! Stretching west away from the Basilica on the north and south sides of the square are the elegant arcades of, respectively, the Procuratie Vecchie 6 and Procuratie Nuove 7. The former, designed by Mauro Codussi, were once

Saving Venice

Floods, neglect, pollution and many other factors have contributed to the degeneration of Venice's monuments and artworks. Since 1969 a group of private international organisations, under the aegis of Unesco, has worked to repair the damage.

The Joint Unesco–Private Committees Programme for the Safeguarding of Venice has raised millions of dollars for restoration work in the city. Between 1969 and 2000 more than 100 monuments and 1000 works of art were restored. Major projects include the Chiesa di Madonna dell'Orto, the facade of the Chiesa di San Zulian, Chiesa di San Francesco della Vigna, Chiesa di Santa Maria Formosa, Chiesa di San Nicolò dei Mendicoli, Basilica di Santa Maria Assunta on Torcello and the Old Jewish Cemetery on the Lido. All sorts of projects continue all the time. One planned for the near future is the restoration of the bronze equestrian statute of Bartolomeo Colleoni in Castello.

Funding comes from 26 private and charitable organisations from Italy and a dozen other countries. Apart from restoration work, the programme also finances specialist courses for trainee restorers in Venice. Among the higher-profile groups involved is the UK's Venice in Peril Fund, whose honorary chairman is Lord Norwich, perhaps the greatest historian of Venice in English. For UK£50 a year you can join **Venice in Peril** (☎ 020-7957 8270; www.veniceinperil.org; 5 Stamford Bridge, Fulham Rd, London SW6 1HS). The fund is presently helping to restore the Emiliana chapel on San Michele (expected to cost UK£250,000).

Important though the work of these organisations is in keeping Venice's difficulties in the public eye, more than 90% of the finance for restoration and related projects in Venice since 1966 has come from the Italian government.

the residence and offices of the Procurators of St Mark, who were responsible for the upkeep of Basilica di San Marco and the administration of sizable properties belonging to the Basilica around the square and beyond. The Procuratie Nuove were designed by Jacopo Sansovino and completed by Vincenzo Scamozzi and Baldassare Longhena.

Finally, the square is closed off by the **Ala Napoleonica 8** (p54). When Napoleon waltzed into Venice in 1797, he was so taken with the square he dubbed it 'the finest drawing room in Europe'. Not content to admire, he proceeded to demolish the church of San Geminiano to make way for a new wing that would connect the Procuratie Nuove (which he had decided to make his Venetian residence) and Vecchie and house his ballroom. At first glance it seems to blend in perfectly, but the row of statues depicting Roman emperors was a typically Napoleonic touch.

Nowadays, the square plays host to competing flocks of pigeons and tourists. Stand and wait for the bronze Mori (Moors) to strike the bell of the 15th-century **Torre dell'Orologio 9**, which rises above the entrance to the Mercerie, the series of streets that forms the main thoroughfare from San Marco to the Rialto. Or sit and savour an expensive coffee at Florian, Quadri or Lavena, the 18th-century cafés (p140) facing each other on the piazza. On occasion, you may witness a minor military ceremony to hoist or haul in the three flags – Venice, Italy and the EU. The flagpoles have been around a lot longer than the EU, so one wonders what the third flag used to be.

WEST OF PIAZZA SAN MARCO

West of the Ala Napoleonica, you find yourself on Salizzada San Moisè. Down the first street to your left, Calle Vallaresso, is a gaggle of fashion stores and **Harry's Bar 10** (p139). At No 1332 is the closed **Teatro al Ridotto 11** (in temporary use as a swank hotel restaurant).

In the 17th century, the Ridotto gained a name as the city's premier gaming house. During the twilight years of La Serenissima, Venetian nobles were wiping out their fortunes at the gaming tables. The state took a cut but this was insufficient compensation for the ruin wrought on an already shaky local economy. In November 1774, the Ridotto was shut *per tutti i tempi ed anni avvenire* ('for all time and years to come'). 'All time' was a relative term – less than 20 years later it was back in business. It remained so until the more purposeful Austrians shut it for good in the early 19th century. It is now incorporated into the Hotel Monaco.

As you approach Campo San Moisè, you pass a busy shopping street on your right, **Frezzeria 12**. In medieval days, no-one would have dreamed of opening a fashion store here: the product on sale was *frecce* (arrows). All males above a certain age had to do regular archery practice and be ready to sail off to war when necessary. Campo San Moisè is dominated by the **church 13** of the same name. Legend has it that the first church was founded in the 8th century, but the rather unrestrained baroque facade you see today is a product of the 1660s.

From here, the street widens into Calle Larga XXII Marzo, which was opened in 1881 and commemorates the surrender of the Austrians to Venetian rebels on 22 March 1848. The victory was short-lived, however, and it would be another 18 years before the Austrians received their definitive marching orders. One Italian guide rather hopefully describes this as 'the City' of Venice (in allusion to London's business district), given the presence of the local *borsa* (stock exchange) and several banks. Down Calle del Pestrin, which runs south off Calle Larga XXII Marzo, is the landward entrance to the **Palazzo Contarini-Fasan 14**. It is nothing much to look at, but legend has it that Desdemona, the wife of Othello and victim of his jealousy in Shakespeare's play, lived here.

Calle Larga XXII Marzo then contracts into Calle delle Ostreghe (Oysters St) and brings you to Campo Santa Maria del Giglio, where the **church 15** of the same name (p53) will charm you into halting your westward march.

After crossing two bridges in quick succession, you could wander south towards the Grand Canal and sidle up next to **Palazzo Corner 16** (aka Ca' Grande, or Big House), Sansovino's 16th-century masterpiece of residential building. He built it for Jacopo Corner, a nephew of the ill-fated Caterina, the queen of Cyprus (see the boxed text on p206).

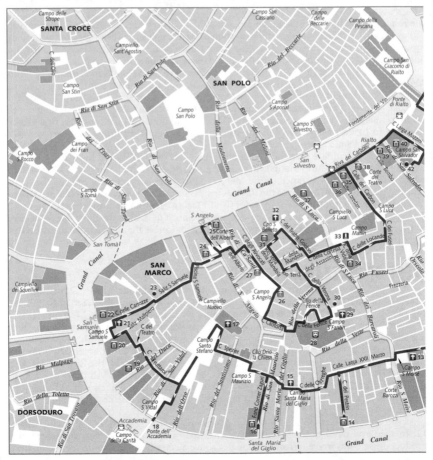

Back on the westward route, you quickly emerge in Campo San Maurizio, occasional scene of an antiques market and surrounded by elegant 14th- and 15th-century mansions, along with the church of the same name. Just off this square to the north you can sneak around to Campiello Drio la Chiesa and get a close-up look at just how much the bell tower of the **Chiesa di Santo Stefano 17** (p53) is leaning. Pause, too, when you cross the bridge leading from Campo San Maurizio to Campo Santo Stefano. Looking north, you can see how the same church is in part actually built over the Rio del Santissimo. You enter the church from Campo Santo Stefano (also known as Campo Francesco Morosini after the 17th-century doge). From the church, it is a brief stroll south across the grand expanse (a rare thing in Venice) of the *campo* to the Grand Canal and the **Ponte dell'Accademia 18** (p58) that spans it.

SANTO STEFANO TO PONTE DI RIALTO

You could cross the bridge into Dorsoduro (see p105) or instead turn back a little to the southwest end of Campo Santo Stefano, where Calle Fruttarol swings off to the northwest on a twisting and winding route towards the Ponte di Rialto.

You immediately cross a narrow canal and then another, the Rio del Duca. The building on the northwest bank, with a fine facade on the Grand Canal, is the **Ca' del Duca 19**, or Duke's House, so called because the Duke of Milan, Francesco Sforza, bought it from the

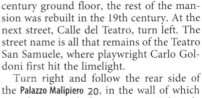

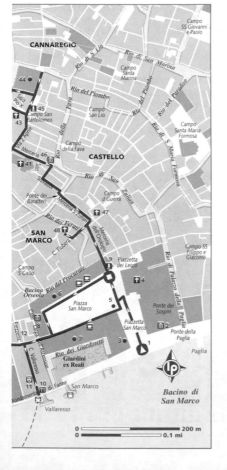

Corner family in 1461. Above the 14th-century ground floor, the rest of the mansion was rebuilt in the 19th century. At the next street, Calle del Teatro, turn left. The street name is all that remains of the Teatro San Samuele, where playwright Carlo Goldoni first hit the limelight.

Turn right and follow the rear side of the **Palazzo Malipiero 20**, in the wall of which is a plaque just before you enter Salizzada Malipiero. It reminds you that in a house along this lane, Giacomo Casanova was born in 1725.

Palazzo Malipiero forms the southern limit of the quiet Campo San Samuele on the Grand Canal. On the eastern side is the unobtrusive outline of the former **Chiesa di San Samuele 21**, and to the north the stately **Palazzo Grassi 22**, frequent host to temporary art exhibitions. Massari's 1749 design clearly shows a tendency towards neoclassicism.

Wheeling around the church, head more or less east along Calle delle Carrozze and on into Salizzada San Samuele. A number of shops, flogging everything from expensive glass to wooden sculptures of unironed shirts, line these streets. You can only wonder what Paolo Veronese, who lived at **No 3337 23**, would have thought of it all. A good lunch stop presents itself here in the form of Osteria al Bacareto (p124).

Although this itinerary barrels along towards Calle dell'Albero, unhurried strollers might like to wander down any of the several lanes around here that end at the Grand Canal. Just off Calle dell'Albero is a neat little square, the Corte dell'Albero, walled on two sides by the interesting **Casa Nardi 24** at Nos 3884–87, built in 1913 and incorporating Veneto-Byzantine architectural themes. It has a hint of the Barcelona Modernista style (and especially calls to mind the architect Lluís Domènech i Montaner) in its use of brick and the attempt to recycle a proud and distant design tradition. Facing the Grand Canal at No 3877 is Codussi's **Palazzo Corner-Spinelli 25**, later reworked by Sanmicheli.

From Calle dell'Albero you cross a tiny canal and then head south down Calle degli Avvocati, which leads directly into Campo Sant'Angelo. You may notice that a good deal of the square is raised. The two wells clue you in that directly below is a large cistern.

In 1801 the Italian musician Domenico Cimarosa died in the 15th-century **Palazzo Duodo 26** (No 3584), which in those days was the Albergo Tre Stelle. **Palazzo Gritti 27**, across the square, was built around the same period. All sorts of unpleasant things occurred in this square, according to city chronicles. In 1476 a launderer by the name of Giacomo was jailed after having taken a certain Bernardino degli Orsi under the portico of the Chiesa di Sant'Angelo Michele (now disappeared) and raped him. In 1716 the body of a violently murdered woman was discovered in one of the wells. A Florentine was accused of assaulting, robbing and killing the poor wretch. There's more where that came from, but enough. It's time to move on.

Take Calle Caotorta and cross the first bridge you see. Turn immediately left, left again and then right and you end up in Calle della Fenice, a tunnel of scaffolding along the northern wall of the star-crossed **opera house 28** (p147). With a little luck, by the time you read this the theatre will be back in business. A few steps along this street turn left again. The hotel on the tiny square (Campiello della Fenice) is covered in cannonballs used by the Austrians in their campaign to retake control of the city in 1849. Follow this little arc around and you are again in Calle della Fenice.

You now emerge into Campo San Fantin. Opposite the theatre is the **Chiesa di San Fantin 29**, whose final incarnation was wrought by either Sansovino or Pietro Lombardo.

The other main building on this square is the **Ateneo Veneto 30**, home to a learned society founded in Napoleon's time. Previously it had been the headquarters of the confraternity of San Girolamo and Santa Maria della Giustizia. The main charitable work of confraternity members was to accompany death-row criminals in their last moments before being executed. The confraternity's building was known as the Scuola di San Fantin or 'dei Picai' (the old Venetian version of 'dead men walking').

Facade of Palazzo Bembo (opposite), originally constructed in the 15th century

To proceed, take Calle della Verona north out of the square. Just before you hit the T-junction with Calle della Mandola, you cross Rio Terrà degli Assassini. In medieval times murder was a common nocturnal activity around here. Street crime got so bad that in 1128 the government banned the wearing of certain 'Greek-style' beards that, it was said, were in vogue among wrongdoers to prevent them from being identified. It was at that time too that the first all-night lamps were set burning in the dodgier parts of town – the devotional niches you still see around were created specifically for this purpose – and the Signori di Notte (Night Masters) started patrolling the lanes.

At Calle della Mandola, turn left then right into Rio Terrà della Mandola. This street bumps right into the side of the splendid **Palazzo Fortuny 31** (p58). The **Chiesa di San Beneto 32**, also in the square, was rebuilt in the early 17th century and is closed.

From Campo San Beneto, drop south along Calle del Teatro Goldoni, passing the supremely ugly Cinema Rossini, and turn left at the junction into Calle della Cortesia, which leads over a bridge and into Campo Manin. At the square's centre stands the proud **statue of Daniele Manin 33**, a lion at his feet. He led the anti-Austrian revolt of 1848–49. The square also boasts a remarkably thoughtless 20th-century contribution at its eastern end, the Cassa di Risparmio di Venezia bank. More interesting than the square itself is what lies off it, the curious **Palazzo Contarini del Bovolo 34** (p55) with its grand Renaissance open spiral staircase. Take Calle della Vida south of the square and follow the signs.

From the dead end at the Palazzo Contarini del Bovolo, the route proceeds east along Calle delle Locande to Calle dei Fuseri, which, heading north across Campo San Luca, brings you to the Grand Canal along Calle del Carbon (Coal St). Not surprisingly, Coal St leads to Coal Quay (Riva del Carbon), which until well into the 19th century was the main unloading point for the city's coal supply. Calle del Carbon, it is said, was also something of a red-light district.

To the left of Calle del Carbon are **Palazzo Loredan 35** and, one street along, **Ca' Farsetti 36**. Both started life in the 12th century as *fondachi* (or *fonteghi*). These were family houses where the ground floor, with a grand entrance on the canal, was used for the loading, unloading and storage of the merchandise upon which the wealth and standing of most of the great patrician families of Venice long depended. In some cases (as in the nearby Fondaco dei Tedeschi, a *fondaco* was more a trading house and hotel for foreign communities.

In 1826 the town hall moved its offices to Ca' Farsetti from the Palazzo Ducale. Forty-two years later, it also acquired Palazzo Loredan. You can wander into the foyer of the latter. On the corner of Calle del Carbon is a plaque announcing that Eleonora Lucrezia Corner Piscopia (of the family that once owned Palazzo Corner) was the first woman to receive a university degree – in 1678.

Just west of Ca' Farsetti, the Renaissance **Palazzo Grimani 37** was completed by Sanmicheli, although the 2nd floor was done later. It houses law courts.

Walking northeast towards the Ponte di Rialto from Calle del Carbon, you may notice the narrow, Gothic, 14th-century **Palazzo Dandolo 38**. It's just left of Bar Omnibus, a touristy restaurant that started life as a café in the 19th century. The house belonged to blind doge Enrico Dandolo, who led the Fourth Crusade to a famous victory over Constantinople in 1204. Never mind that the Crusaders were actually supposed to be toughing it out against the infidels in the sands of the Middle East rather than bludgeoning their fellow (albeit Orthodox) Christians in Byzantium (see p40)!

Wedged in between Calle Bembo and Rio di San Salvador is the magnificent red facade of **Palazzo Bembo 39**. What you see is the result of 17th-century restoration of a 15th-century late-Venetian-Gothic structure. It is almost certain that Pietro Bembo, cardinal, poet, historian and founding father of the grammar of standard Italian, was born here. On the other side of Rio di San Salvador, **Palazzo Dolfin-Manin 40**, easily identified by its portico, was designed by Sansovino and completed in 1573.

At this point, proceed inland a block along Calle Larga Mazzini. In front of you is the main entrance to the **Chiesa di San Salvador 41** (p53), among the city's oldest churches. Diagonally across from the church to the west is the **Scuola Grande di San Teodoro 42**, one of the many confraternity headquarters in Venice, now used frequently for music recitals and exhibitions.

Heading northeast, you pass the small and much interfered with **Chiesa di San Bartolomeo 43**, which at one time served as the parish church for the local German merchant community based at the **Fondaco dei Tedeschi 44** (p53). When the Republic meekly surrendered to Napoleon in 1797, an angry mob set about looting the houses of those they held responsible for such ignominy around Campo San Bartolomeo. The Venetian militia set up cannons on the Ponte di Rialto to control the unrest – the last time the guns of San Marco were fired in anger, they spilled the blood of their own people. The **statue 45** in the middle of the square is of Carlo Goldoni, Venice's greatest playwright.

BACK TO PIAZZA SAN MARCO

At this point you could head north into Cannaregio, duck across the Ponte di Rialto into San Polo or continue this itinerary back to Piazza San Marco.

Retrace your steps to the Chiesa di San Salvador and follow the narrow shopping street around its northern flank, the Merceria San Salvador. Where the street runs into a canal, you can see the late-Gothic **Palazzo Giustinian-Faccanon 46**, which for a long time housed the editorial team of the city's main newspaper, *Il Gazzettino*.

The lanes that lead from San Salvador to the Torre dell'Orologio and into Piazza San Marco are all called *merceria* (*marzaria* in Venetian dialect), referring to the merchants who traditionally lined this route. For some centuries this was one of the busiest thoroughfares in the city, directly linking Piazza San Marco with Rialto (in other words, the political with the financial lungs of La Serenissima).

The arrival of the railway in the 19th century and a new axis through Cannaregio did little to change this. The flux of *foresti* (non-Venetians) along this narrow commercial trail remains a constant. Whether you're coming from the train station or from Rialto, the

Knocking Rebellion on the Head

By 1310 Venice was in serious difficulties. Doge Pietro Gradenigo's pursuit of mainland conquest had brought upon the city a papal interdict. The pope was in no way amused by Venice's attempts to seize control of Ferrara, to which the Holy See had a long-standing claim. The Venetians had been defeated in the field, and many Venetian merchants abroad had been arrested and had their goods confiscated.

Gradenigo was not without his opponents, foremost among them the Querini family. Marco Querini, who had been in command of Venetian forces at Ferrara, claimed Venice had not given him the support he needed. Querini convinced General Baiamonte Tiepolo to lead a revolt against Gradenigo. They both lived in the San Polo area, near Rialto, and so planned to send two armed columns over the bridge. Querini's would proceed down Calle dei Fabbri to Piazza San Marco and Tiepolo's down the Mercerie. They would join in the piazza and assault the Palazzo Ducale, at which point a third force would arrive across the lagoon from the mainland.

It might have worked, but word of the plan got out. Gradenigo and his allies gathered forces in Piazza San Marco, alerted the workers of the Arsenale, who served as a kind of ducal militia in times of uncertainty, and ordered the *podestà* (mayor) of Chioggia to intercept the invasion fleet.

Things went wrong for the rebels from the start. A storm delayed the fleet, and while Querini marched on Piazza San Marco, Tiepolo's troops hung about looting in Rialto. By the time they went clattering down the Mercerie, Querini was already battling it out with ducal troopers in Piazza San Marco.

Tiepolo's boys were engaged while still in the Mercerie. The decisive moment came when a local housewife, who was leaning out of her window and bombing the rebels with anything that came to hand, pelted Tiepolo's standard-bearer on the head with a mortar (another version suggests she just leaned out the window to see what the fuss was about and accidentally bumped the mortar off her sill). The standard fell and the fight was over. Querini had already died in Piazza San Marco. The leader of the fleet was captured and summarily executed. Tiepolo beat a hasty retreat home, from where he negotiated to keep his life, but in exile.

The woman who had struck the winning blow requested the right to hang the flag of the Republic from her balcony on holidays. This she received, but she was no sentimental dummy – she also asked that the rent on her house never be raised by the Procurators of St Mark, who owned the building. In 1436, the procurators actually did raise it while a descendant of the long-deceased woman was away on military service. Thirty-two years later he demanded, and obtained, a return to the original rent.

Today a bas-relief of the woman leaning out of her window marks the spot on Merceria dell'Orologio (just above the Sotoportego e Calle del Cappello). A simple stone with the date of the incident in Roman numerals (XV.VI.MCCCX) marks the place on the ground where the standard-bearer fell.

Mercerie are to this day one of the most direct routes to Piazza San Marco. It was also thus for the conspirators in the 1310 plot to overthrow Doge Pietro Gradenigo, who came a cropper in the Merceria dell'Orologio just before the Torre dell'Orologio. See the boxed text opposite.

Where Merceria dell'Orologio begins, you can see off to the left (east) the **Chiesa di San Zulian 47** (🕙 10am-noon & 4-6pm Mon-Sat, 4-6pm Sun), founded in 829, although its present form, covered in a layer of Istrian stone, was designed by Sansovino. Inside are a few works by Palma il Giovane.

Heading right (west) from the top of Merceria dell'Orologio over the bridge, duck right into the first little lane. In the *sotoportego* (street continuing under a building, like an extended archway) just before the T-junction, you will see on your right, at No 956/b, the entrance to the **Chiesa della Santa Croce degli Armeni 48**. On Sundays only, Armenian priests from the Isola di San Lazzaro celebrate a service here. The church has been active since at least the 14th century.

Return to Merceria dell'Orologio and proceed down (south) towards the Torre dell'Orologio and pass below it. You are back in Piazza San Marco.

SESTIERE DI DORSODURO

The first buildings you bump into on crossing the Ponte dell'Accademia from the Sestiere di San Marco constitute the **Gallerie dell'Accademia 1** (p60), the city's single most important art collection. Indeed, this corner of town is a bit of an art haven. If you follow the signs for the Peggy Guggenheim Collection eastwards from the Gallerie dell'Accademia,

Walk Facts

Start Ponte dell'Accademia (vaporetto Accademia)
End Campo San Pantalon
Distance 4.8km

you soon arrive at the relatively minor collection of the **Galleria di Palazzo Cini 2** (p60).

Cross the bridge into cute Campo San Vio, one of a handful of squares that back onto the Grand Canal. Its eastern flank is occupied by **Palazzo Barbarigo 3**, whose facade is strikingly decorated with mosaics on a base of gold. They were carried out at the behest of the Compagnia Venezia e Murano, a glass and mosaics manufacturer that moved in here towards the end of the 19th century. You can't really see it from the square, but keep an eye out when you chug up or down the Grand Canal on the vaporetto. Calle della Chiesa and then Fondamenta Venier dai Leoni lead you to Venice's premier excursion into the world of international contemporary art, the **Peggy Guggenheim Collection 4** (p62). Once satiated by the art, you could do worse than have a cuppa at the gallery's coffee shop.

Back on the street, keep moving east. The next bridge brings you into a shady square. The exuberant gardens dripping over the walls, seemingly in an attempt to drop down into Rio delle Toreselle, belong to the **Palazzo Dario 5**. You can get some impression of this late-Gothic mansion from the rear, but to really appreciate it you need to see the facade – a unique Renaissance marble facing that was taken down and reattached in the 19th century – from the Grand Canal. The building looks a little unsteady and many Venetians view it with misgiving, given that most of its owners seem to have died mysterious or at least miserable deaths.

After all the bustle of the grand art galleries, it is a real pleasure to arrive in the tranquil Campo San Gregorio. The Gothic facade of the deconsecrated **church 6** of the same name boasts a graceful doorway with a Venetian pointed arch. A straggly garden on the northern flank of the square belongs to the **Palazzo Genovese 7**, built over part of what was once the abbey to which the church belonged.

As you wander under the rough-hewn portico of Calle dell'Abbazia, Longhena's dazzling white monolith, the **Chiesa di Santa Maria della Salute 8** (p60), fills your entire field of vision. Beyond, the customs offices that long occupied the low-slung **Dogana da Mar 9** are largely empty.

To stand at dawn on the **Punta della Dogana 10**, which marks the split between the Grand Canal and the Canale della Giudecca, is to feel oneself on the prow of a proud fighting vessel. Waxing lyrical? Not really. Giuseppe Benoni, who designed it in 1677, was hoping for just that effect. On top of the little tower behind you, two bronze Atlases bend beneath the weight of the world. Above them twists and turns capricious Fortune, an elaborate weather vane.

FONDAMENTA ZATTERE TO CAMPO SANTA MARGHERITA

Fondamenta Zattere runs the length of the south side of Dorsoduro along the Canale della Giudecca, from Punta della Dogana to the Stazione Marittima. It is a popular spot for a lingering *passeggiata* (the afternoon or Sunday stroll that is something of an institution in Italian life) and came to be known as the Zattere because of the giant rafts *(zattere)* that used to deliver timber from the mainland.

The first buildings of any note as you walk west are the city's **Saloni Ex-Magazzini del Sale 11** (the one-time salt warehouses). Although the facade (hard to appreciate from the street because you are standing so close) is a neoclassical job from the 1830s, the warehouses were built in the 14th century. A monopoly on the all-important salt trade was one of the foundations of medieval Venice's wealth. Why salt? In the days before fridges and electricity, the only way to preserve meat and other foodstuffs was to bury them in salt. It wasn't a perfect method but that was all people had. Salt was thus crucial to commerce. The buildings are now used in part by rowing clubs and as temporary exhibition space.

A few paces further on is the unremarkable Renaissance facade of the small **Chiesa di Santo Spirito 12**. From here boats are lined up to create a pontoon bridge across the Canale della Giudecca for the Festa del Redentore in July (see p11). About 100m separate the church from the **Ospedale degli Incurabili 13**. Put up in the 16th century to park incurable syphilis sufferers (the so-called 'French sickness' had taken particular hold across Europe at the time), who had a tendency to end up quite potty, the building was later used as an orphanage. It is now the seat of the Minors' Court. After crossing a couple of bridges, you end up in front of the imposing 18th-century **Chiesa dei Gesuati 14** (p59).

At the next bridge you hit one of the most attractive of Venice's waterways, the Rio di San Trovaso, also home to the most important of the few remaining *squeri* (gondola workshops)

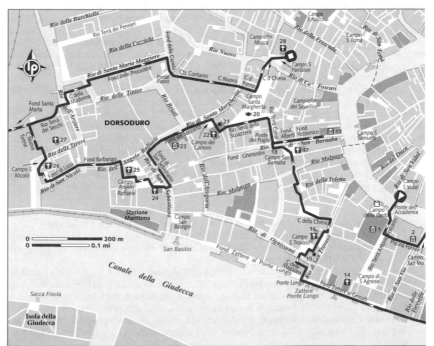

– the **Squero di San Trovaso 15**. The leafy square behind the *squero* is backed by the **Chiesa di San Tro-vaso 16** (🕑 8-11am & 3.30-6.30pm Mon-Sat, 8.30am-noon Sun), rebuilt in the 16th century on the site of its 9th-century predecessor. The associated *scuola* was home to the confraternity of *squerarioli*, or gondola-builders. Inside the church are a couple of Tintorettos.

A few hundred metres north is the fairly unprepossessing 18th-century **Chiesa di San Barnaba 17** (🕑 3-6pm Mon-Sat), which hosts a handful of paintings, including one by Veronese and a couple by Palma il Giovane. Opening times are extended during temporary exhibitions. From Campo San Barnaba wander off to the west along Fondamenta Gherardini and cross the bridge by the permanently moored greengrocer's barge. The bridge is known as **Ponte dei Pugni 18** and is one of several throughout the city where local factions, known as the Nicolotti (who wore black berets) and Castellani (who wore red berets), would regularly encounter each other for a bout of fisticuffs, sometimes good-natured, sometimes less so. The object of these *guerre dei pugni* ('fist wars') was to throw opponents into the canal, and the marks showing where to place one's feet are still in evidence. The practice was outlawed in 1705 when one such 'war' turned nasty, knives were drawn and lives lost.

Once over the bridge head east towards the Grand Canal for the magnificent 18th-century residence of **Ca' Rezzonico 19** (p59). When you're done admiring how the other half lived in Venice's glory days, turn back towards Rio Terrà Canal, which leads you north to Campo Santa Margherita. This is a real people's *platz*. Sure, any number of tourists or foreign students can be heard at the tables of the many restaurants and bars, but in the afternoon, when all the local kids come out to play, it takes on a special, living air. Henry James' words spring to mind, when he speaks of '...that queer air of sociability, of cousinship and family life, which makes up half the expression of Venice. Without streets and vehicles, the uproar of wheels, the brutality of horses, and with its little winding ways where people crowd together, where voices sound as in the corridors of a house...the place has the character of an immense collective apartment' (*The Aspern Papers*, 1888).

The square is headed at its northern end by what little is left of a former church, long ago swallowed up by residential buildings. The squat little object at its southern end was one of the city's many *scuole*, or religious confraternities, the **Scuola Varoteri 20**. The more important **Scuola Grande dei Carmini 21** (p63) caps the *campo*'s southwest corner, along with the **church 22** (p59) of the same name. Stride across Campo dei Carmini and head southwest along Fondamenta del Soccorso. The dominating mansion on your left is **Palazzo Zenobio 23** (p62), the Armenian college. Continuing along and round the corner to the left, cross the second bridge and you stand before the **Chiesa di San Sebastian 24**, Veronese's parish church (p59).

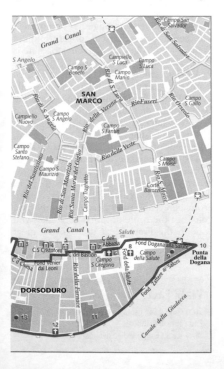

SANTA MARTA TO CAMPO SAN PANTALON

When you leave the Chiesa di San Sebastian, head into the unknown and wander around the back through the interlinked squares that take you to the Chiesa di San Basilio, better known as **Angelo Raffaele 25**. The uneven squares, with clumps of grass pressing up between the flagstones, are intriguingly quiet during the day, but take on a subdued evening buzz as locals take their places at the local trattorie.

As you cross the bridge north of Angelo Raffaele and look left (west), you'll espy the bell tower of the **Chiesa di San Nicolò dei Mendicoli 26** (🕑 10am–noon Mon-Sat). Although it has been fiddled with over the centuries, the church still preserves elements of the 13th-century original. The portico attached to one side was used to shelter the poor. The whole area was fairly downtrodden and known for its *mendicoli*, or beggars. The church's tiny square, bound in by the canals and featuring a pylon bearing the winged lion of St Mark (one of the few not to have been destroyed under Napoleon), is at the heart of one of the oldest parishes in Venice. They say it was established in the 7th century.

Across the Rio delle Terese was the **Chiesa di Santa Teresa 27** and its attached former convent (now used occasionally as theatre space during the Biennale). A stroll up to Fondamenta Santa Marta and west into the quarter of the same name reveals a curious contrast to the Venice of monuments. It's a working-class district with orderly housing blocks and broad walkways. Just beyond, across the Canale Scomenzera, you can watch the desultory activity of Venice's commercial port, now much overshadowed by the monster of Marghera on the mainland.

You could then follow the suggested route back towards Campo Santa Margherita via Fondamenta delle Procuratie. Along here and the parallel Fondamenta dei Cereri, rental housing was built as early as the 16th century by the Procurators of St Mark for the less well off. It has remained largely unchanged since.

A short walk north from Campo Santa Margherita along Calle della Chiesa and over the bridge will bring you into Campo San Pantalon. Scaffolding covers the facade of the **Chiesa di San Pantalon 28** (p59), which is getting some much needed restoration work.

SESTIERI DI SAN POLO & SANTA CROCE

From Campo San Pantalon, follow the street around to the right of the church and head north over the next bridge. You will emerge in Campo San Rocco. In front of you rises the brooding Gothic apse of the **Chiesa di Santa Maria Gloriosa dei Frari 1** (p66), which you enter from the side. On your left, the **Scuola Grande di San Rocco 2** (p76) and the church of the same name face each other at an angle. Between them they contain a formidable concentration of Venetian art. A good ice cream stop here is Gelateria Millefoglie da Tarcisio (p126).

A brief detour towards the Grand Canal from the Campo San Rocco along Calle Larga Prima brings you to the charming little square of Campo San Tomà, closed off at the far end by the **Chiesa di San Tomà 3**, whose facade dates from 1742. On the San Rocco side of the square is the **Scuola dei Calegheri 4**, the shoemakers' confraternity. Across Rio di San Tomà is Palazzo Centani, now better known as the **Casa di Goldoni 5** (p64), the house of Venice's great playwright. From here you could head to Campo San Polo, but the route outlined here takes you back to the Frari. Next door to the great church spread the buildings and peaceful cloisters of the former Convento dei Frari,

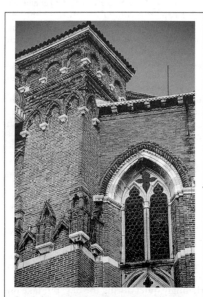

Detail of the Gothic Chiesa di Santa Maria Gloriosa dei Frari (p66)

Walk Facts

Start Campo San Pantalon (vaporetto San Tomà)
End Ponte di Rialto
Distance 5.5km (including detours)

Food for Thought

From Calle della Croce, you can make a detour to one of the rare strips of footpath actually on the Grand Canal. Turn left (north) up Calle Larga dei Bari, right along Lista dei Bari and left (north) along Ramo Zen then Calle Zen to the Riva de Biasio. A couple of the mansions here are interesting enough to behold and the views to the other side of the canal are more impressive still.

But the prize goes to a tale we all hope is taller than true. A sausage-maker by the name of Biagio (Biasio) Cargnio had a shop here in the 16th century. They say he was sent to the next world on charges of having sausages made of – wait for it – children.

suppressed in 1810 by Napoleon. Since 1815 it has housed the Archivio di Stato 6, the city's archives and treasure-trove of some 15 million documents covering the breadth of Venice's history from the 9th century on.

Cross the Rio dei Frari, turn left and cross the next bridge. Veer left around the block and you end up in the nondescript Campo San Stin. Take the western exit off the *campo* and turn right. Almost immediately on the left you will be struck by what seems like an iconostasis. Behind it, two impressive facades give onto a courtyard.

On the southern side is the Chiesa di San Giovanni Evangelista 7 (🕐 10am-noon & 3-5pm), raised in 970 but subsequently rebuilt several times. The heavy pillared building next door, once used as the church cemetery, now hosts temporary exhibitions. Opposite is one of the six major Venetian *scuole*, the Scuola Grande di San Giovanni Evangelista 8 (p76).

Back on Calle dell'Olio, proceed north to the canal and turn left. Cross the first bridge over Rio Marin and head along the bank to Calle della Croce. Head east down this lane, turn right then left into Campo San Nazario Sauro, and keep heading east down Ruga Bella, which takes you into Campo San Giacomo dell'Orio and the church 9 (p64) of the same name.

DETOUR FROM RIO MARIN TO PIAZZALE ROMA

Before heading for Campo San Giacomo dell'Orio, a few words on a possible detour and some minor but noteworthy items between Calle della Croce and the western end of the Sestiere di Santa Croce. Right across Rio Marin you are facing the Palazzo Soranzo-Cappello 10,

The Oldest Profession

Although prostitution in Venice was generally tolerated, and in some periods encouraged, attitudes towards the practice and its practitioners were always ambiguous.

In 1358 local authorities selected an area of Rialto to set aside for prostitution. Prostitutes and their matrons, who took care of the till and paid their workers a monthly wage, soon occupied a group of houses that came to be known as Il Castelletto (Little Castle), which was kept under surveillance by six guardians. Prostitutes were not allowed on the streets after a certain hour and were forbidden to work on religious holidays. The atmosphere must have been oppressive, for prostitutes began to spread out across the city, especially to the nearby Carampane area. At first, attempts were made to force them back into Il Castelletto, but in the end the authorities gave in to the situation and even proclaimed laws obliging the girls to display their wares to attract business.

By the 1640s, however, various regulations were in place to put a brake on prostitution. Prostitutes could not enter churches or potter around in two-oared boats (only 'ladies' could be taken about in such a manner). They were not to adorn themselves with gold or other jewellery. They could not testify in criminal court cases, nor could they prosecute when services rendered were not paid for (which was generally where pimps came in). Your average street whore was made to feel very much like a second-class citizen.

Different strokes for different folks: there was a whole other class of prostitution. In the 16th century the myth of *cortigiane* (courtesans) began to take shape. These were women of distinction, not simply better-paid, better-looking bimbos. Schooled in the arts, fluent in Latin, handy with a harpsichord, they were women of keen intellect and talent not fortunate enough to have been born into nobility. For such daughters of middle-class families, working for a high-class escort service seemed the only way to acquire independence and wellbeing.

In 1535, when the Venetian populace totalled about 120,000 and some 11,000 prostitutes were registered, a very handy tourist guide was published: *Questo si è il Catalogo de tutte le principal, et più honorate Cortigiane di Venetia* ('This is the Catalogue of the Main and Most Honoured Courtesans of Venice'). It contained names, rates and useful addresses. No wonder the city had such a lascivious reputation.

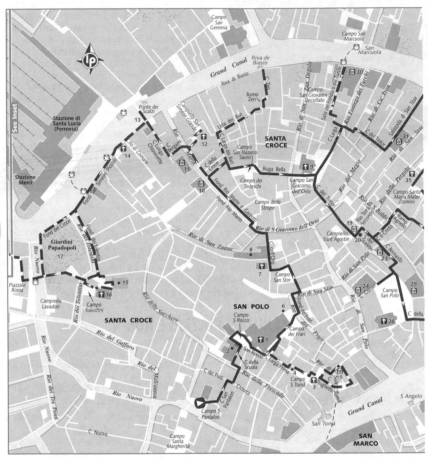

a 16th-century mansion graced with what must have been a beautiful (but now unruly) garden. From the same period is the **Palazzo Gradenigo 11**, further northwest, by the last bridge over the canal. Were you to walk up to that bridge and look to your right, you'd see the tiny **Chiesa di San Simeon Grande 12**. Of ancient origins, it was heavily restored in the 18th century. Inside you can see an *Ultima Cena* (Last Supper) by Tintoretto.

Across the bridge, you end up on Calle Bergami. Turn right at its end and head for the high-arched **Ponte dei Scalzi 13**. Built in 1934, it replaced an iron bridge built by the Austrians in 1858. Crossing over this bridge puts you onto the route through the Sestiere di Cannaregio (see p113).

If you turn left before the bridge and follow Fondamenta San Simeon Piccolo southwest, you'll pass the **church 14** of the same name. The present version was completed in 1738, and its outstanding feature is the bronze dome. At the next bridge, turn left down Fondamenta dei Tolentini. The modern facade on the bend is the entrance to the **Istituto Universitario di Architettura di Venezia 15**, designed by Carlo Scarpa. The institute is one the country's most prestigious architecture schools. Beside it, the late-16th-century **Chiesa di San Nicolò da Tolentino 16** houses works by Palma il Giovane.

The **Giardini Papadopoli 17** (⏲ 8am-dusk) across the canal seems almost an afterthought. The park was a deal more impressive until in 1932 the Rio Nuovo was slammed through. Beyond the park lies Piazzale Roma, home to the unlovely bus station and car parks.

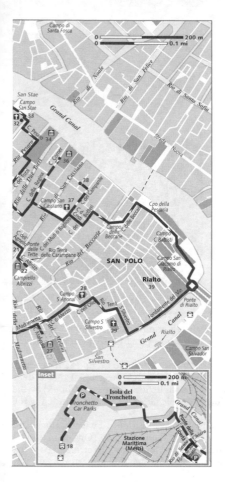

A wander around it and along Canale di Santa Chiara is a sobering reminder of how even the most beautiful of cities contain pockets of ugliness and neglect. By mid-2004 Santiago Calatrava's dazzling steel bridge will span the Grand Canal between Piazzale Roma and the train station.

Beyond the canal lies the now little-used merchant-shipping harbour and then the Isola del Tronchetto – a giant car park and home to the **PalaFenice 18** (p147), the big-top replacement for the Fenice theatre. The PalaFenice's future is uncertain, as the theatre it has substituted since 1996 was due to reopen at the end of 2003.

SAN GIACOMO DELL'ORIO TO RIALTO VIA CAMPO SAN POLO

From Campo San Giacomo dell'Orio, two separate routes suggest themselves to get you to the Ponte di Rialto. This first one follows a trail largely ignored by tourists. The other, via Campo San Stae (see the following section), is busier but still loaded with interest. You can also join them together into a circular route that would bring you right back into this square. From here you could then backtrack to Rio Marin and go on to the Ponte dei Scalzi to pick up the next route through Cannaregio (see p113).

From Campo San Giacomo dell'Orio, follow Calle del Tintor (Dyers' St) southeast, cross the bridge and continue until you hit a T-junction. As you turn left into Rio Terrà Secondo, note on the right-hand side, opposite the Gothic **Palazzo Soranzo-Pisani 19**, the building in which Aldo Manuzio got his **Aldine Press 20** started up and so revolutionised the world of European letters. His was an address much frequented by learned fellows from across the Continent.

Head northeast and turn right into Calle del Scaleter (Pastry-Makers' St). At Da Fiore (p127), Venice's only Michelin-star restaurant, turn left into Calle del Cristo, cross the bridge and take the second right (Ramo Agnello). Follow it straight over the bridge and stop at the second bridge.

It's hard to tell now, but this was long the centre of Venice's cheaper red-light zone. The bridge is known as **Ponte delle Tette** (Tits Bridge) **21** because a city ordinance stipulated that the whores who worked here should hang about in windows and doorways bare-breasted to encourage business. Pardon? Back in the 14th century, the city fathers had in fact tried to clamp down on prostitution (see the boxed text on p109), but by the late 15th century found it the only hope of reviving the ardour of Venetian men, who were apparently adopting imported Eastern habits of sodomising each other. La Serenissima took a far dimmer view of this than prostitution, so much so that anyone successfully prosecuted for sodomy, under a law of 1482, found themselves executed and incinerated between the columns on Piazzetta San Marco.

Beyond the bridge is Rio Terrà delle Carampane. The name originally came from a noble family's house in the area (Ca' Rampani), and at some point the ladies of the night working here came to be known as *carampane*. The word is now a colourful part of standard Italian and describes the mutton-dressed-up-as-lamb brand of loose woman.

From Ponte delle Tette, look south down Rio di San Cassiano and you will notice a high, wrought-iron walkway linking **Palazzo Albrizzi 22** to private gardens. Inside the 16th-century mansion, Isabella Teotochi Albrizzi held her literary salon around the end of the 18th century, with sculptor Antonio Canova and writer Ugo Foscolo among her guests.

Backtrack to Da Fiore. For a more modest lunch stop, try nearby Trattoria da Renato (p129). From here turn left (southeast) across the bridge and along Calle Bernardo (the fine Gothic **mansion 23** of the same name is best seen from the bridge), which brings you into the leafy expanse of Campo San Polo. Among the several mansions facing the square are **Palazzo Corner 24**, designed by Michele Sanmicheli in the 16th century, and the Gothic **Palazzi Soranzo 25**. Well worth visiting if you are a Tiepolo fan is the **Chiesa di San Polo 26** (p65).

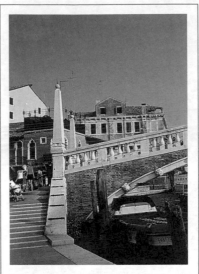

Ponte delle Guglie in Cannaregio (opposite)

A glance at the map will show that you have almost completed a circuit to the Frari. You could head down that way and beyond into Dorsoduro (see p105), or stroll eastwards towards Rialto and the Grand Canal.

From Campo San Polo, take Calle della Madonnetta and follow it to Campo Sant' Aponal. On the way, duck down Calle Malvasia to peer enviously through the gates at the gardens of the **Palazzo Papadopoli 27**. It seems almost unfair that such luxuriant greenery should be the preserve of the Istituto per lo Studio della Dinamica delle Grandi Masse (Institute for the Study of the Dynamics of Large Masses)!

The former **Chiesa di Sant'Aponal 28** has a simple Gothic facade topped by five statues, and its free-standing bell tower is Romanesque. From here, Calle dell'Olio (Oil St) takes you around the right side of the church. Turn right down Rio Terrà San Silvestro and pass the unremarkable early-20th-century facade of the **Chiesa di San Silvestro 29**. Turn onto the former wine docks on the Grand Canal, the Fondamenta del Vin, and the Ponte di Rialto is clearly in view ahead. The restaurants along here make a tempting spot for a break, but you'll pay €3 to €4 for a cup of coffee, and the food is not particularly recommended.

SAN GIACOMO DELL'ORIO TO RIALTO VIA CAMPO SAN STAE

Follow the signs north from the *campo* along Calle Larga (turning off at the canal) to reach the **Fondaco dei Turchi 30** (p66), home to a natural history museum due to reopen in 2004. From the *fondaco*, return to the canal, cross it and take Calle del Tintor east. Interesting shops line this route to Campo San Cassiano.

At Salizzada di San Stae, turn left (northeast). On the right is the **Palazzo Mocenigo 31** (p66), a patrician mansion containing 18th-century period furnishings. At the end of the street is the tiny canalside Campo San Stae (St Eustace Square), named after the baroque **church 32**. Next door to the left (No 1980) is the **Scuola dei Tiraoro e Battioro 33**, the former seat of the goldsmith confraternity.

From Campo San Stae, cross the bridge, turn right then left, cross another bridge and you reach the land entrance to **Ca' Pesaro 34** (p63), a fine, restored baroque mansion with important collections of modern art and Japanese Edo-period objects.

Walking southwest away from Ca' Pesaro, you could be forgiven for missing the **Chiesa di Santa Maria Mater Domini 35**. Sansovino supposedly had a hand in it and inside (if you happen to find it open) is an early work by Tintoretto, the *Invenzione della Croce* (Invention of the Cross).

Campo Santa Maria Mater Domini is an intriguing square, with well-preserved late-Byzantine and Gothic buildings. No 2174 dates from the 13th century. Cross the square and turn left (north) into Calle della Regina (Queen St). At the end of the street, looking onto the Grand Canal, is **Palazzo Corner della Regina 36**. The Corners, a powerful trading family, had mansions all over town. On this site lived Caterina Corner, who ended up on the throne of Venetian-controlled Cyprus in the late 15th century, only to be obliged later by the schemers of San Marco to abdicate. In exchange, she got Asolo and its lovely countryside (see the boxed text on p206). The building was remodelled in the early 18th century.

Tintoretto fans may want to stop at the **Chiesa di San Cassiano 37** (☼ 9am-noon Tue-Sat) in the *campo* of the same name. The sanctuary is decorated with three of his paintings, the *Crocifissione* (Crucifixion), the *Risurrezione* (Resurrection) and the *Discesa al Limbo* (Descent into Limbo). Make a quick detour towards the Grand Canal along Calle del Campanile and duck into **Corte de Ca' Michiel 38**. This was once known as Calle del Teatro, reputedly the site of one of the city's first theatres in 1580. It didn't last too long, as the Inquisition (not an overly popular institution in Venice) shut it down for what it claimed were lewd goings-on.

A couple of streets on from Chiesa di San Cassiano, you arrive at Campo delle Beccarie. Welcome to the nerve centre of Venice – **Rialto 39** (p75).

SESTIERE DI CANNAREGIO

Start Ponte dei Scalzi/Ferrovia (vaporetto Ferrovia)

Assume you have just stumbled over Ponte dei Scalzi after following the routes around Santa Croce and San Polo. Or you might have arrived at the train station. Either way, you are ready for an exploratory stroll through Cannaregio. The long thoroughfare connecting the train station and Piazza San Marco crawls with tourists heading from one to the other – few venture off it into the peaceful back lanes.

Walk Facts

Start Ponte dei Scalzi/Ferrovia (vaporetto Ferrovia)
End Fondaco dei Tedeschi or Campo SS Giovanni e Paolo
Distance 2.5km to Fondaco dei Tedeschi or 4.8km to Campo SS Giovanni e Paolo

The first sight of any significance you lay eyes on is the Carmelite **Chiesa dei Scalzi 1** (p77). At the northeastern end of bustling Rio Terrà Lista di Spagna is the **Chiesa di San Geremia 2** (p78), flanked by the **Palazzo Labia 3** (p80), known for its Tiepolo frescoes.

At **Ponte delle Guglie** (Needles Bridge) **4**, so called because of the obelisks at each end, the itinerary splits into two. The first option takes you to the Sestiere di San Marco via the Ghetto. The second is a more meandering stroll through many of the backstreets and canals of Cannaregio that brings you to Campo SS Giovanni e Paolo in Castello.

PONTE DELLE GUGLIE TO SESTIERE DI SAN MARCO

Cross Ponte delle Guglie and turn left. Just before you do, you may want to poke around the daily **fish and produce market 5** on Rio Terrà San Leonardo.

Turn off the Fondamenta di Cannaregio at Calle del Ghetto Vecchio (you'll recognise it by the Gam Gam kosher restaurant – see p130). On emerging into the small square, you will see two of the Ghetto's five synagogues, also known as *schole* (schools) because they were used for scripture studies. The existence of five places of worship within the Ghetto reflected in part the density of the Jewish population and also liturgical variations between the different communities. The **Schola Spagnola 6** is at the square's southern end (look for the plaque commemorating Italian Jewish victims of the Holocaust). It and the **Schola Levantina 7**, opposite, were erected by Jews from the Iberian Peninsula. You can visit the latter as part of a tour starting at the Museo Ebraico. The interior betrays a hefty rococo influence, best seen in the decor of the pulpit. The Schola Levantina is used for Saturday prayers in winter (it has heating) while the Schola Spagnola (which can't be visited) is used in summer.

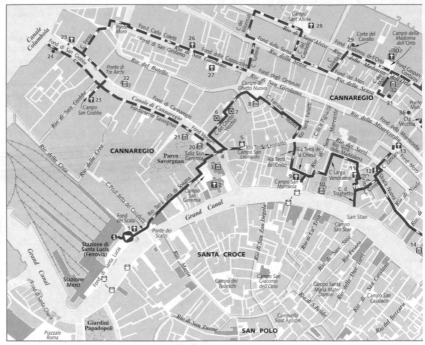

Calle del Ghetto Vecchio proceeds northeast over a bridge into the heart of Venice's Jewish community, Campo di Ghetto Nuovo, where you will find the **Museo Ebraico 8** (p80).

Leave the Ghetto by the portico that leads across the canal to Calle Farnese. This was one of the Ghetto gates that used to be locked at midnight. Proceed straight to Rio Terrà Farsetti and turn right, then duck down Rio Terrà del Cristo to look at the **Chiesa di San Marcuola 9** (p78). Heading east across Rio di San Marcuola, you will come up against the **Palazzo Vendramin-Calergi 10** (p80), where Wagner died and gamblers lose fortunes.

From here, return to the main drag (at this point called Rio Terrà della Maddalena – you'll know you've hit it when you are sucked up into the crowds again). Proceed a couple of blocks eastwards, then head off to the right (south). In a quiet little *campo* is the unique, circular **Chiesa della Maddalena 11**, the only round building in the city and a rare neoclassical presence. Inside, the walls are lined with some important paintings, including several Tiepolos. The pretty square around the church is flanked by houses with their upper parts poking over heavy timber barbicans. Notice anything yet? Like you are about the only one to have sufficient curiosity to get off the strip and have a quick look here? Try jumping back into the flood of passers-by and then jumping out again. Amazing, isn't it?

You could go around the back of the church and follow Calle del Forno around to a dead end right on the Grand Canal. It's a little mucky but it is always interesting to get another view of the canal. By backtracking and then taking Calle Correr, you end up back on the strip. The bronze statue on the square opposite you is of **Paolo Sarpi 12**, La Serenissima's greatest philosopher (some might suggest only). You could make a little detour at this point and scurry northeast across a couple of bridges to the **Chiesa di San Marziale 13**. If it's open, have a peek inside at the baroque baubles.

Otherwise skip it and head southeast along the main street. It's called Strada Nuova (New St) here and was bulldozed through the area some years after the rail link was opened in the 19th century. On your right you pass a veritable parade of Venetian mansions, but you'd never know it – they present their photogenic profile only to the Grand Canal. The

second of them after you cross Rio di San Felice (named after the church you pass on the left just before the bridge) is **Ca' d'Oro 14** (p77).

Strada Nuova then leads into the pleasing Campo dei SS Apostoli. The **church 15** of the same name (☺ 7.30-11.30am & 5-7pm Mon-Sat, 8.30am-noon & 4-6.30pm Sun) is worth visiting for a look at the 15th-century Cappella Corner by Mauro Codussi, which features a painting of Santa Lucia by Tiepolo.

Keep following the crowd over the next two bridges; on the left is the curious **Chiesa di San Giovanni Grisostomo 16** (p78). Around the back, Corte Prima del Milion leads into a chain of brief streets, *sotoporteghi* and squares. At No 5845 in Corte Seconda del Milion, you are supposedly looking at **Marco Polo's house 17**. That's one theory. Another suggests the Polo family house disappeared to make way for the **Teatro Malibran 18** (p147) in 1677. During restoration work on the theatre, which ended in 2001, traces of what might have been the Polo residence were unearthed.

Return to the Chiesa di San Giovanni Grisostomo and head south. The next canal marks the boundary between the *sestieri* of Cannaregio and San Marco. The building you are looking at on the right is the **Fondaco dei Tedeschi 19** (p53).

PONTE DELLE GUGLIE TO CASTELLO

For this second ramble, you don't cross Ponte delle Guglie, but instead head northwest along Fondamenta Venier, named after the late-18th-century neoclassical **mansion 20** of the same name. Further up, **Palazzo Savorgnan's 21** big draw is its garden, now a public park (☺ 8am-5.30pm Oct-Mar, 8am-7.30pm Apr-Sep) with slides and other amusements for the kiddies.

Beyond the palace, the character of the area changes quickly – it's clearly a working-class district. It was perhaps not always thus. Across the canal, just before you reach the last bridge (Ponte di Tre Archi), the 17th-century **Palazzo Surian 22** stands out. During the last century of the Republic, the French moved their embassy in here and Jean Jacques Rousseau managed to blag his way into a job as secretary to the ambassador.

To the left, down along Rio di San Giobbe, the rather ordinary **church 23** of the same name boasts a remarkable ceiling faced with multicoloured glazed terracotta.

Before crossing Ponte di Tre Archi, stroll to the end of Fondamenta di San Giobbe. The enormous complex at the end here was the **Macello Comunale 24**, the city's abattoir. Le Corbusier designed a hospital for the site, but (much to the annoyance of many citizens) it got the thumbs down in 1964. The Università Ca' Foscari has faculty buildings here, which has brought some student life to the area.

Across the bridge, towards the end of Fondamenta di Cannaregio, the former **Chiesa di Santa Maria delle Penitenti 25** was one of the seemingly abundant religious institutions set up to take in wayward women anxious to put their wicked past behind them.

The winding walk along Calle Ferau and through the Sacca di San Girolamo area, an unpretentious residential district, takes you past the barely noticeable **Chiesa delle Cappuccine 26** on the left and the ugly hulk of the **Chiesa di San Girolamo 27** on the right across the canal.

Apart from soaking up the peace and quiet of the area, your objective is to reach the **Chiesa di Sant'Alvise 28** (p78).

From there there is no choice but to make a detour across Rio di Sant'Alvise and then a little way along Fondamenta della Sensa and back up Calle Loredan to Fondamenta Madonna dell'Orto. The long courtyard on the left as you head east is called **Corte del Cavallo** (Horse Court) **29** because here the bronze was melted down for the great equestrian statue to Colleoni in Campo SS Giovanni e Paolo (see opposite page). A little way along to the east is the striking **Chiesa della Madonna dell'Orto 30** (p78).

If you cross the first bridge to the east of the church, you will end up in Calle dei Mori. Follow it to the next canal and turn left down Fondamenta dei Mori. Almost immediately you will see on your left a plaque noting that Tintoretto lived in this **house** (No 3399) **31**. The strange statue of a man with a huge turban that sticks out of the wall next door on **Palazzo Mastelli 32** is one of four spread out along here and around the corner on Corte dei Mori. The street names here (dei Mori) mean 'of the Moors' and refer to these statues, traditionally said to represent members of the Mastelli family (the one on the corner is known as Sior Rioba), 12th-century merchants from the Morea, one of La Serenissima's most important Greek possessions. The building on which they appear is also known as Palazzo del Cammello because of the distinctive bas-relief depicting this animal on the facade overlooking Rio della Madonna dell'Orto. The Mastelli family were said to be an unpleasant lot, forever on the lookout for a fast ducat and impoverishing local families. A tall tale says that one day they went too far and were turned to stone, later to be installed in their present positions.

Backtrack to the Chiesa della Madonna dell'Orto and continue southeast along Fondamenta Gasparo Contarini, named after **Palazzo Contarini del Zaffo 33**, which extends to the end of the street. A narrow **wooden quay 34** protrudes out into the little protected bay off the lagoon. Locals use it for sunbathing and from here you enjoy good views across to the islands of San Michele and Murano. Behind the *palazzo* spread luxuriant private gardens leading to an isolated building on the lagoon, the so-called **Casino degli Spiriti 35**, where in the 16th century students, literati and glitterati with the right contacts would gather for learned chitchat and a few drinks.

There is little choice here but to cross Rio della Madonna dell'Orto and follow Corte Vecchia southwest to Rio della Sensa. Before turning left to continue southeast, turn around to the right and you'll see a rare (and run-down) example of a **squero 36**, or gondola-building yard, complete with slipways into Rio dei Muti.

The next stop of importance is I Gesuiti, the massive hulk erected by the Jesuits. To get there, pass down Fondamenta dell'Abbazia under the portico of the **Scuola Vecchia della Misericordia 37**, once the seat of one of the city's grand religious confraternities. It later moved into the immense **Scuola Nuova della Misericordia 38**, designed by Sansovino in the 1530s, on the southern side of Rio della Sensa. Next to the Scuola Vecchia, on the pretty *campo* that overlooks the busy Canale della Misericordia, is the **Chiesa di Santa Maria della Misericordia 39**, established in the 10th century and altered in the 13th. The dead-end bridge leading to a private house is notable for the absence of any kind of barrier or railing on its sides, about the only one of its kind in Venice now. Once many of the city's bridges were like this – not good for stumbling home tipsy late at night!

A series of bridges takes you into Calle della Racchetta. To get to **I Gesuiti 40** (p80), follow this street northeast to Fondamenta Santa Caterina and head east until you reach Campo dei Gesuiti. Virtually across the *campo* from the grand Jesuit church is the tiny **Oratorio dei Crociferi 41** (p80).

Titian fans can find his **house 42** by walking up to the Fondamente Nuove, heading southeast as far as Calle delle Croci and penetrating the web of lanes in search of Corte della Carità. North of this square, a narrow, dead-end lane is your objective – at the end of it on the right is Titian's place.

From Corte della Carità, you can trace a path down along Calle del Fumo, past the 17th-century **Palazzo Widman 43** and down the narrow *calle* of the same name. You emerge on Campo Santa Maria Nova. Off to the right (northwest) is the **Chiesa di San Canciano 44**. Although here since the 9th century, what you see is the result of intervention by Massari and Gaspari. The real stunner is off to the left (southeast), the Renaissance **Chiesa di Santa Maria dei Miracoli 45** (p78). From the church, you can turn left (east) along Calle Castelli (which continues over the canal as Calle delle Erbe). Once over the next bridge, you are obliged to swing left and arrive in Campo SS Giovanni e Paolo. You are now in the city's easternmost *sestiere*, Castello.

SESTIERE DI CASTELLO

Presiding over Campo SS Giovanni e Paolo is the proud figure of the *condottiero* (professional mercenary commander) **Bartolomeo Colleoni 1**, who from 1448 commanded mercenary armies in the name of the Republic. It is one of only two equestrian statues in the city, a magnificent piece by the Florentine Verrocchio (1435–88). Although Colleoni

Walk Facts

Start Campo SS Giovanni e Paolo (vaporetto Ospedale)
End Piazzetta San Marco
Distance 9km

was of the school of mercenaries that tended to organise things so that they lived to fight another day, he remained faithful to La Serenissima. On his death in 1474, he bequeathed 216,000 gold and silver ducats and considerably more in property to Venice, on one condition – that the city erect a commemorative statue to him in Piazza San Marco. The Senato took the money but cheated, placing the grand statue here instead. Still, Colleoni can rest easy that the Republic didn't scrimp on the statue itself.

Around the mercenary commander rise the imposing edifice of the **Chiesa dei SS Giovanni e Paolo 2** (p82) and, next to it, the marble trompe l'oeil frontage of the **Scuola Grande di San Marco 3** (p87), now part of the city hospital. Just east of the church is the extraordinary baroque facade of the **Ospedaletto 4** (p86), with its *übermensch* statuary bulging out at you in the street. After a quiet stroll east along residential streets, you emerge in Campo San Francesco della Vigna, where the sudden appearance of the massive Palladian facade of the **church 5** of the same name (p83) comes as a bit of a shock.

Proceeding east around the south flank of Chiesa di San Francesco della Vigna, you'll end up in Campo della Celestia. Follow the only lane exiting off it across the canal and into Campo San Ternità. Calle Dona veers to the left (east) off this square. After the canal, turn right (southwest) and almost immediately on your left is **Casa Magno 6**, a unique example of Gothic housing. Now head straight down to and across Campo Do Pozzi. You'll end up on Calle degli Scudi (Shields St), at which point you turn right (northwest) and cross the canal into Campo delle Gatte (Cats Square). A quick dogleg and you will run into Rio di San Lorenzo. Just before the bridge, on the right, is the **Scuola di San Giorgio degli Schiavoni 7** (p87), the Dalmatian community's religious school.

After admiring Carpaccio's contributions to the school, proceed south along the canal and at the **Chiesa di Sant'Antonin 8** follow the main street south into Campo Bandiera e Moro. This quiet square is named after the Venetian brothers Bandiera, who lived in **Palazzo Soderini** (No 3611) **9**, and their companion Domenico Moro (who lived nearby), all of whom were executed by troops of the Bourbon Kingdom of the Two Sicilies after a hopelessly failed pro-unity insurrection in Cosenza (Calabria) in 1844 (all three are buried in the Chiesa di SS Giovanni e Paolo). The square is fronted in the southeastern corner by the **Chiesa di San Giovanni in Bragora 10** (p84).

From the Chiesa di San Giovanni in Bragora, follow Calle Crosera to the east. About the shortest route to what was once the military powerhouse of the Republic takes you up Calle Erizzo past the Renaissance **palazzo 11** of the same name and across the bridge to the **Chiesa di San Martino 12**. The church is a 16th-century Sansovino design on the site of a 7th-century predecessor that was built by mainland refugees fleeing Lombard invaders. Across the canal are the walls of the **Arsenale 13** (p81). To reach its entrance, walk along Fondamenta di Fronte until you reach the Rio dell'Arsenale. Continuing on a seafaring theme, the **Museo Storico Navale 14** (p85) is just a short hop south of the Arsenale.

Heading east, you enter very-few-tourists territory. Following the Arsenale walls past its entrances on Campo della Tana, cross the bridge and take Fondamenta della Tana, turning right down Calle di San Francesco di Paola – you'll soon hit the broad Via Giuseppe Garibaldi. The **Chiesa di San Francesco di Paola 15** is a fairly uninteresting 18th-century remake of the 16th-century original.

Walking Tours – Sestiere di Castello

117

Follow the road east and cross the last bridge northwards across the Rio di Sant'Anna (named after the ruined **church 16**, now encased in restorers' scaffolding, that looks out over the Canale di San Pietro). Proceed north across Campo di Ruga and take the last lane on the right (east). The bridge at the end of it takes you across to the Isola di San Pietro, where you may wish to visit what was long the city's official cathedral, the **Cattedrale di San Pietro di Castello 17** (p82).

There is no need to rush through. An aimless wander through the simple grid pattern of residential streets allows you to immerse yourself in the simple, gritty, everyday life of ordinary Venetians. No sights, just life.

The only other way off the Isola di San Pietro is by the more southerly of the two bridges, which brings you back to the ruins of Sant'Anna. Walk past them (heading west) and duck down Calle Correra. Cross the broad Secco Marina, keep on down Corte del Solda and cross the bridge. A stroll past the **Chiesa di San Giuseppe di Castello 18** will bring you into the somewhat tatty Giardini Pubblici (p84), one of the city's few public parks and home to the Biennale.

From here, wander over Rio dei Giardini to Sant'Elena, the quietest and leafiest residential corner of Venice. Housing construction began in 1925, before which there was little here but an abandoned pilgrims' hospice and the now closed **Chiesa di Sant'Elena 19**, a small Gothic number abandoned in 1806 (a great deal of housing was destroyed further west to make way for the Giardini Pubblici) and reopened for a while from 1928 when people started

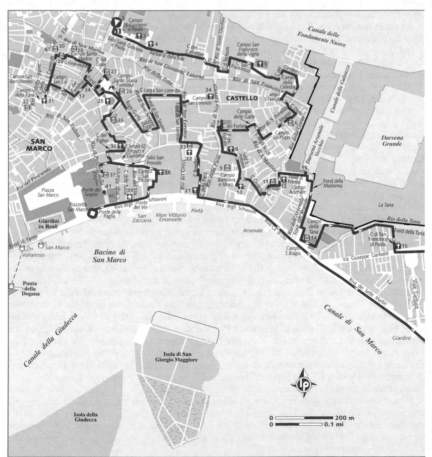

moving into the new residential district. The arrival of riot police and armies of football supporters occasionally snap it out of its usual (and not unpleasant) torpor. The crowds make for the **Stadio Penzo 20** to see the home side struggle.

TOWARDS SAN MARCO

At this point the weary could get the No 42 or No 52 circle line vaporetto from the Sant'Elena stop to San Zaccaria to continue this itinerary, or hop on to the No 1 and potter up the Grand Canal to do something else altogether. Otherwise, it's a pleasant and leafy walk from Sant'Elena through the Parco delle Rimembranze and then the Giardini Pubblici along the waterfront.

You will eventually find yourself on the waterfront boardwalk known as Riva degli Schiavoni (p87), just as busy now with tourists as it once was with all sorts. Just at the point where you turn inland is the **Chiesa di Santa Maria della Visitazione 21** (or more simply La Pietà; p84), associated with Vivaldi.

A short walk north brings you to the rear side of the **Chiesa di San Giorgio dei Greci 22** (p83). Walk around it to reach the main entrance alongside Rio dei Greci. Virtually next door is the Hellenic Institute's **Museo delle Icone 23** (p85).

As you leave San Giorgio and cross the bridge to the west, take Fondamenta di San Lorenzo north. At the second bridge across the canal is Campo San Lorenzo, dominated by the rather shaky-looking brick facade of the **church 24** of the same name. It is an odd structure, divided down the middle to form a section for the general public and another for members of a Benedictine nunnery that has long since ceased to exist. The church is closed for restoration.

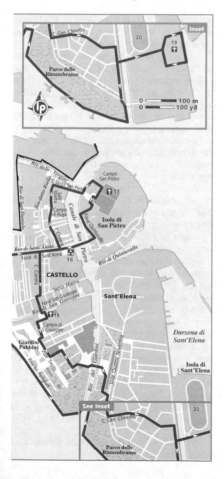

From here the objective is Campo Santa Maria Formosa, a winding walk to the west. It is one of the most appealing squares in Venice, full of local life, eateries, benches where you can take the weight off your feet and some interesting buildings. There was a time when all sorts of popular festivals were played out here (chasing bulls around the square was one of the less sensible activities). One of Venice's best-remembered courtesans, Veronica Franco, lived in a house on this *campo*. Poet, friend of Tintoretto and lover, however briefly, of France's King Henry III, Miss Franco was listed in the city's 16th-century guidebook to high-class escorts as: *Vero. Franco a Santa Mar. Formosa. Pieza so mare. Scudi 2*. The last bit is the base price for her services, which ranged from intelligent conversation to horizontal folk dancing. Perhaps there was always a little ribaldry in the air around here: the **Chiesa di Santa Maria Formosa 25** takes its name from a curiously saucy legend (see p84).

Among the ageing mansions facing the square, **Palazzo Vitturi 26** is a good example of the Veneto-Byzantine style, while the buildings making up the **Palazzi Donà 27** are a mix of Gothic and late Gothic. While you're here, a further quick circuit suggests itself.

Leave the square and head northwest. Don't cross the canal – veer right instead along Calle del Dose and then left along Calle Pindemonte. You end up in Campo Santa Marina, faced by the 13th-century **Palazzo Dolfin Bollani 28** and the Lombard-style **Palazzo Loredan 29**. A side lane off the square leads you to the 15th-century **Palazzo Bragadin-Carabba 30**, restored by Sanmicheli.

Coming out of the square to the west, head south along Calle Carminati, which brings you into Campo San Lio. A brief detour further south down Calle della Fava brings you to the square of the same name and the **Chiesa di Santa Maria della Fava 31**. It was begun by Gaspari and finished off in 1753 by Massari. Inside, the first painting on your right after you enter is Tiepolo's *Educazione della Vergine* (The Virgin's Education). Back outside, you can get a good view across Rio della Fava of the late Gothic **Palazzo Giustinian-Faccanon 32**, over in the Sestiere di San Marco.

Scurrying back to Campo San Lio, turn right (more or less east) down the busy Salizzada San Lio. The street retains some intriguing examples of Byzantine housing. More interesting still is **Calle del Paradiso** (Heaven St) **33**, which branches off it back in the direction of Campo Santa Maria Formosa. It is marked by the Gothic arch beneath which you enter, and gives you a pretty good idea of what a typical Gothic-period street in Venice looked like. On the ground floor were shops of various types. Jutting out above them on heavy timber barbicans are the upper storeys, which were offices and living quarters. At the end of the street is another arch, this one more elaborate. Known as the **Arco del Paradiso** (Heaven's Arch) **34**, it depicts the Virgin Mary and bears the standards of the families who financed its construction.

Once back in Campo Santa Maria Formosa, walk around the church. Behind it, a bridge leads you to **Palazzo Querini-Stampalia 35** (p86), a private mansion turned cultural foundation with a varied collection of period furniture, art and other odds and ends.

From Palazzo Querini-Stampalia, the route winds south past the former **Chiesa di San Giovanni Novo 36** (now used occasionally as exhibition space) and eventually across the Rio del Vin to the Chiesa di San Zaccaria. A quick detour to the **Museo Diocesano d'Arte Sacra 37** (p85), southwest of Campo SS Filippo e Giacomo, is worthwhile, especially for fans of Romanesque architecture. Back on the main street, instead of turning left (west) for Piazza San Marco, head in the opposite direction down Salizzada San Provolo. You are heading for the **Chiesa di San Zaccaria 38** (p84), and you'll know you've struck pay dirt when you pass under a Gothic arch depicting the Virgin Mary and Jesus, thought to have been crafted by a Tuscan sculptor around 1430. Beyond, you arrive in Campo San Zaccaria and stand before the Renaissance facade of the church.

When you exit the church, head south off the square and you emerge through a *sotoportego* onto Riva degli Schiavoni again, not far from where you left it earlier.

Turn right (west) to cross the Ponte del Vin (Wine Bridge); the building immediately on the right is Palazzo Dandolo, better known to most as the **Danieli 39** (p179), one Venice's most prestigious hotels. For a curious tale about the origins of the hideous Danieli extension on the other side of Calle delle Rasse, see the boxed text on p179.

Calle delle Rasse takes its name from the word *rascia* or *rassa*, a rough woollen material sold along this street for use as protective covers for gondolas. The material came from what is now Serbia, known to the Venetians centuries ago as Rascia. The next street, Calle degli Albanesi, was so named because an Albanian community lived on and around it. Interesting choice of address when you consider that prisons line its western side.

Walking past the **prisons 40**, which you may have visited while touring the Palazzo Ducale (see p55), you arrive at the bridge that marks the boundary between the *sestieri* of San Marco and Castello. Look north at the unassuming closed passage linking the Palazzo Ducale with the prisons. Yes folks, this is it, the bridge you've all been waiting for: the **Bridge of Sighs** (Ponte dei Sospiri) **41**, which you are looking at from Ponte della Paglia (Straw Bridge). Now you can breathe a sigh of relief that you've seen it. Some people walk away inconsolably despondent that the bridge in no way corresponds to all their romantic imaginings.

The pink and white walls of the Palazzo Ducale lead you back to the Piazzetta San Marco, the gateway to Venice, where you finally complete this long and tortuous circuit of the lagoon city that for more than 1000 years was the Most Serene Republic. Perhaps now is an opportune moment to again gaze out over the Bacino di San Marco and let your well-primed imagination do a little wandering.

On the other hand, maybe it's time for a drink. Why not loosen the old purse strings and pop across to Harry's Bar (p139) for a soothing (if costly) cocktail?

Eating

Eating

If you've enjoyed the cuisines of Tuscany and Emilia-Romagna, the 'down-home' style of a Roman meal or the Sicilians' gift for seasoned fantasies, you might find Venetian fare a trifle disappointing. Indeed, other Italians tend to be rather disparaging about La Serenissima's kitchen attempts, lamenting that *'si spende tanto e si mangia male'* ('you spend a lot and eat badly'), but then they are rather fastidious. For the rest of us, Venice isn't that bad. Even that august collective of self-appointed Italian foodies, Slow Food, has found about 20 places to stick into their annual *Osterie d'Italia* guide.

Search out the little eateries tucked away in the side alleys and squares, since many of the restaurants immediately around San Marco, near the train station and along main thoroughfares are tourist traps. If you don't find enough suggestions to keep you busy here, a fine local guide is Michela Scibilia's *A Guide to the Eateries of Venice*.

Opening Hours

Italians rarely eat a sit-down breakfast *(colazione)*. They tend to drink a cappuccino and eat a croissant *(cornetto)* or other type of pastry (generically known as *pastine*) at a bar.

For lunch *(pranzo)*, restaurants usually open from 12.30pm to 3pm. Few take orders after 2pm. Traditionally, lunch is the main meal of the day and many shops and businesses close for two or three hours to accommodate it.

A full meal will consist of a starter *(antipasto)*, which can vary from fried vegetables to a small seafood offering. Next comes the first course *(primo piatto)*, generally a pasta or risotto, followed by the second course *(secondo piatto)* of meat or fish. This does not usually come with vegetables and Italians will order a vegetable dish *(contorno)* to go with it. Salads *(insalate)* have a strange position in the order. They are usually ordered as separate dishes and, in some cases, serve as a replacement for the *primo piatto* – although there is nothing to stop you ordering a salad as a side order to a *secondo*.

Opening hours for dinner *(cena)* vary, but people start sitting down around 7.30pm. You'll be hard-pressed to find a place still serving after 10.30pm. The evening meal follows a similar pattern to lunch. It was once a simpler affair, but habits are changing because of the inconvenience of travelling home or going out for lunch every day.

Restaurants and bars are generally closed one day each week; the day varies depending on the establishment. In the reviews in this chapter, operating days are listed, but opening times are mentioned only where they vary substantially from the norm.

Cafés and bars that serve sandwiches and other snacks generally open from 7.30am to 8pm, although some stay open after 8pm and turn into pub-style drinking and meeting places.

Osteria 'Opping

Venice's *osterie* (aka *bacari*), long ago the preserve of men (women could wait outside to drag drunken husbands home!), are a cross between bars and trattorie (cheap restaurants). Here you can sample *cicheti* (small finger-food snacks such as stuffed olives, vegetables deep-fried in batter and an endless array of seafood items – basically the local version of Spanish *tapas*), washed down with an *ombra* (glass of wine). They say the name *ombra*, which means 'shade', comes from the days when people would go to stands set up in the shade in the local square for an afternoon tipple.

Locals often bar hop from *osteria* to *osteria*, munching *cicheti* as they go. It's a great way for visitors to experience a more down-to-earth side of Venice. Some *osterie* serve full meals and several are noted in the course of this chapter. The genre is experiencing a slow revival in Venice, although most locals will tell you that the real thing has all but died out. The reinventions, which often go to some lengths to serve carefully prepared meals, are sometimes wonderful, but few ooze the gritty history of Venice past. Like the many old London pubs that have been given the once-over and reconstituted as shiny chrome bars or mock throwbacks, the genuine article has often been lost.

Dining out beside a canal

How Much?

Venice is among the priciest of Italian cities for eating out. How much dosh you pay for your nosh clearly depends on just what you want. Many bars serve filling snacks with lunch-time and pre-dinner drinks. Most also have a wide range of *panini* (sandwiches or filled bread rolls) with every imaginable filling. *Tramezzi* (sandwich triangles) and huge bread rolls cost from €1 to €3.50 if you eat them standing up or take them away. You'll also find numerous outlets where you can buy pizza by the slice *(a taglio)* for not more than a couple of euros. Another option is to go to an *alimentari* (grocery shop) and ask them to make a *panino* with the filling of your choice. This can cost €3 to €5.

For a sit-down meal there are several options. Numerous restaurants offer a *menú turistico* or *menú a prezzo fisso*, a set-price lunch costing €12 to €18 excluding drinks. Generally, choice is limited and the food is breathtakingly unspectacular, if filling. Sometimes it's bloody awful. From your taste buds' point of view and as long as you are not overly hungry, you'd be better off settling for a plate of pasta, some salad and wine at a decent restaurant.

Prices throughout this guide are given for a full meal, by which we mean a *primo*, a *secondo*, a dessert and some house wine. You could also add an *antipasto* at the front end of your meal, but these are generally expensive and will simply help stunt your appetite. At modest restaurants a meal is unlikely to cost less than €25 per person. Any place where you have a good chance of paying €25 or less for a full meal, or places where you would mainly eat pizza, *cicheti* or sandwiches, have generally been classified as Cheap Eats. At good mid-range places expect to part with €35 to €60 per person. Much depends on your choice of dish and wine. You can easily hit €100 and more in the top-flight joints.

Many Italians are breaking with the habit of the full meal, preferring instead, say, a *secondo* with a side dish. Clearly your costs will decrease if you resist the pleasures of total gluttony, although the change in Italian habits is one reason cited by restaurateurs for the rise in prices over the past few years (not to mention the introduction of the euro).

Read the fine print if you want seafood, as most fish is sold by weight (prices are usually quoted per *etto*, ie 100g).

In many bars and eateries a two-tier system operates – one price for locals and another for all the *foresti* (out-of-towners). This is not something you can do much about. In restaurants locals often get a small discount at least. Just asking for the bill in Venetian ('podemo *haver el conto?'*) is enough to prompt most restaurateurs to chop a few euros off the bill in an attempt to win a regular local customer. It's not likely to work unless you can really manage to sound like a born and bred Castello kid!

Booking Tables

For much of the year, Venice heaves with visitors, so you should consider booking ahead. You can often get a table when you walk in off the street, but you can by no means bank on it.

Tipping

Most eating establishments have a cover charge ranging from €1 to €6. You also have to factor in the service charge of 10% to 15%. Since most places include this, further tipping is strictly optional. Most locals don't bother adding any more unless they have been particularly overwhelmed by service and quality. Remember this if you are presented a credit card receipt with space to add in the tip. In any case, it is always preferable to leave a tip in cash for the person who has waited on your table.

Self-catering

Making your own snacks is the cheapest way to keep body and soul together. The best markets take place on the San Polo side of the Ponte di Rialto (Map pp254-5).

For salami, cheese and wine, shop in *alimentari* or *salumerie*, which are a cross between grocery stores and delicatessens. Fresh bread is available at a *fornaio* or *panetteria*, a bakery that sells bread, pastries and sometimes groceries. You'll find a concentration of these around Campo Beccarie in the Rialto, which happens to lie next to the city's main fish market, or *pescaria*. See the boxed text in the Shopping chapter (p158). Supermarkets are listed in the Cheap Eats sections of the following reviews.

SESTIERE DI SAN MARCO

Entertainment p139; Sestieri p49; Shopping p152; Sleeping p164

A handful of classy restaurants and one or two more modestly priced hideaways ply their trade in the heart of Venice, surrounded by the serried ranks of mediocre tourist rip-off joints. Of the six *sestieri*, San Marco is in many respects the worst one when looking for dining options.

ACQUA PAZZA Map pp256-8   *Neapolitan*
☎ 041 277 06 88; Campo Sant'Angelo 3808; meal €50-60; ☺ Tue-Sun; vaporetto Sant'Angelo
Pull up an outdoor pew for an evening of southern Italian tastes and smells. A full meal can be a pricey experience so you may want to settle for an excellent (and still rather expensive) pizza (€14) – after all, Naples is the home of the edible flying saucer.

HARRY'S BAR Map pp254-5   *Venetian*
☎ 041 528 57 77; Calle Vallaresso 1323; meal €90-150; ☺ noon-11pm; vaporetto Vallaresso/San Marco
Arrigo (Harry to you) Cipriani's classic location is better thought of as a bar (see p139). The Cipriani family, who started the bar in 1931,

claims to have invented many Venetian specialities, including the Bellini cocktail. A meal is incredibly expensive and, given the fiscal effort, lacklustre, but many take comfort from knowing that the likes of Toscanini, Chaplin and Hemingway have preceded them.

OSTERIA AL BACARETO

Map pp256-8   *Venetian & Cicheti*
☎ 041 528 93 36; Calle Crosera 3447; meal €30-50; ☺ Mon-Fri; vaporetto San Samuele
The search for a good traditional trattoria in this corner of San Marco is over when you reach Al Bacareto. Since it doubles as an *osteria*, you can opt for a plateful of *cicheti* with a glass of wine. Some will tell you the fried sardines are the best in Venice. If you decide on a full sit-down meal you'll need to loosen the purse strings somewhat.

OSTERIA SAN MARCO

Map pp254-5   *Venetian*
☎ 041 528 52 42; Frezzeria 1610; meal €35-50; ☺ Mon-Sat; vaporetto Vallaresso/San Marco
A young enthusiastic team has turned this tired old *osteria* around and made of it a modern-looking, attractive eatery where considerable

store is placed in fine local cooking. Try the *faraona all'aceto balsamico* (guinea fowl cooked in balsamic vinegar).

RISTORANTE DA IVO Map pp254-5 *Meat*
☎ 041 528 50 04; Calle dei Fuseri 1809; meal €100-120; ☾ Mon-Sat; vaporetto Rialto

At the classic da Ivo you can choose from an array of mouth-watering meat dishes, such as *tagliata di manzo* (a juicy beef cut), or a limited selection of seafood, all washed down with a fine range of wines. The atmosphere is quietly elegant and your choice of dish and wine can easily send your bill into the deluxe category.

Cheap Eats

AI RUSTEGHI Map pp254-5 *Cicheti & Panini*
☎ 041 523 22 05; Campiello del Tentor 5513; snacks around €1.50-3; ☾ 8am-9.30pm Mon-Sat; vaporetto Rialto

For a great range of mini-*panini* with all sorts of fillings, pop in to this new version of a fine old institution (the historic address around the corner was abandoned in 2003). There's nothing better than an *ombra* or two and a couple of delicious *panini* as a quick lunch-time snack. In warmer weather you can hang about at tables on the tiny square.

ENOTECA IL VOLTO
Map pp254-5 *Cicheti & Wine*
☎ 041 522 89 45; Calle Cavalli 4081; snacks around €1.50-3; ☾ Mon-Sat; vaporetto Rialto

Near Campo San Luca, this long-time *osteria* (established 1936) has an excellent wine selection (more than 1000 labels according to one claim). Tipple in hand, proceed to choose from the tempting array of snacks, which no doubt will induce you to hang about for another glass. They will cook up a hot meal if you wish.

OSTERIA ALLA BOTTE
Map pp254-5 *Venetian & Cicheti*
☎ 041 520 97 75; Calle Bissa 5482; meal €30; ☾ Mon, Wed (lunch only), Fri, Sat, Sun (lunch only); vaporetto Rialto

Wander into this backstreet *bacaro* near the Ponte di Rialto for a great array of *cicheti* and a glass or two of *prosecco* (sparkling white wine). It's a youthful place, as you can tell from the racy music, rapid bar staff and crowds of young punters. You can sit out the

---

> ### Top Five Meat Eats
> In a city where just about everyone seems to 'specialise' in seafood, finding a place that offers a decent choice of non-seafood dishes is quite a challenge!
> - Ai Gondolieri (below)
> - Da Marisa (p130)
> - La Colombina (p130)
> - Osteria La Pergola (p136)
> - Ristorante La Bitta (p126)

back for no-nonsense Venetian meals washed down with some decent reds. Ask for a glass of sweet *fragolino* (strawberry-flavoured wine) to round off your meal.

SESTIERE DI DORSODURO
Entertainment pp140 & 143; Sestieri p58; Shopping p154; Sleeping p166

A handful of excellent restaurants are scattered about Dorsoduro, most of them not too far from the social hub of Campo Santa Margherita.

AI GONDOLIERI Map pp256-8 *Meat*
☎ 041 528 63 96; Fondamenta Ospedaleto 366; meal €40-60; ☾ Wed-Mon 12.30-3pm & 7.30-10pm; vaporetto Accademia

Surrounded by innumerable restaurants serving up seafood, Ai Gondolieri comes as a welcome change for red-blooded carnivores. All the mains are constituted from land-going critters, with such options as Angus steak, duck and liver. If you opt for all courses you will bust the €50 mark.

L'INCONTRO Map pp256-8 *Sardinian*
☎ 041 522 24 04; Rio Terrà Canal 3062; meal €25-30; ☾ 12.30-3pm & 7.30pm-1am Wed-Sun, Tue dinner; vaporetto Ca' Rezzonico

This is a long-standing favourite in the busy Campo Santa Margherita area and for once the food mostly isn't Venetian. Try the wonderful Sardinian specialities, like *culurgiones* (big potato- and mint-filled pasta pockets doused in a tomato sauce) and suckling pig.

OSTERIA AI QUATRO FERI
Map pp256-8 *Venetian Seafood*
☎ 041 520 69 78; Calle Lunga San Barnaba 2754/b; meal €30-35; ☾ Mon-Sat; vaporetto Ca' Rezzonico

Seafood only is the deal here, and they do it well. Tuna is a house speciality but you can

Top Five Gelato Stops

- **Alaska** (Da Pistacchi; Map pp250-2; ☎ 041 71 52 11; Calle Larga dei Bari, Santa Croce 1159; ⏰ 8am-1pm & 3-8pm; vaporetto Riva de Biasio) This is a great place tucked away in a quiet residential part of Santa Croce.
- **Boutique del Gelato** (Map pp254-5; ☎ 041 522 32 83; Salizzada San Lio, Castello 5727; ⏰ 10am-8.30pm daily; vaporetto Rialto) Rock up for some dreamy creamy ice cream at Silvio's place in Castello.
- **Gelateria Il Doge** (Map pp256-8; ☎ 041 524 40 49; Campo Santa Margherita, Dorsoduro 2604; ⏰ 8am-9pm; vaporetto Ca' Rezzonico) In among all the cafés, bars and restaurants in this lively section of Dorsoduro is this strategically placed *gelateria*. The serves are decent and flavours true.
- **Gelateria Millefoglie da Tarcisio** (Map pp256-8; ☎ 041 524 46 67; Salizzada San Rocco, San Polo 3033; ⏰ 8am-10pm; vaporetto San Tomà) This *gelateria*, behind the Chiesa di Santa Maria Gloriosa dei Frari, is an excellent ice cream stop where hordes queue up on hot sunny days.
- **Gelateria Nico** (Map pp256-8; ☎ 041 522 52 93; Fondamenta Zattere, Dorsoduro 922; ⏰ 6.45am-10pm Fri-Wed; vaporetto Zattere) Head here for some of the best ice cream in Venice, or just sit down for a juice or coffee. The locals take their evening stroll along the *fondamenta* while eating their heavily laden cones.

also tuck into some swordfish at your cosy oak table. Feel like a snack only? Head for the bar for a full array of *cicheti*, from *baccalà mantecato* (mashed cod with garlic and parsley) to octopus salad.

OSTERIA SAN PANTALON

Map pp256-8   *Venetian*
☎ 041 71 08 49; Calle del Scaleter 3958; meal €30-35; ⏰ Mon-Fri, Sat dinner; vaporetto San Tomà

This cosy place with its oak tables and down-home attitude is a favourite with students and puts on no-nonsense Venetian fare, including old favourites like *baccalà mantecato* and *sarde in saor* (sardines fried in an onion marinade). The same people also run the Osteria alla Patatina in San Polo (p128).

RISTORANTE LA BITTA Map pp256-8   *Meat*
☎ 041 523 05 31; Calle Lunga San Barnaba 2753/a; meal €30; ⏰ Tue-Sat; vaporetto Ca' Rezzonico
The short menu is dominated by meat dishes,

with veal, Angus steaks and similar carnivorous options leading the way. The bottle-lined dining room leads out to an attractive internal courtyard. At the bar you'll find a few *cicheti* too.

Cheap Eats

AL NUOVO PROFETA Map pp256-8   *Pizza*
☎ 041 523 74 66; Calle Lunga San Barnaba 2669; pizza €6-9; ⏰ Tue-Sun, Mon dinner; vaporetto San Basilio

With its cool garden out the back, this is a great spot to try a decent pizza before heading into Campo Santa Margherita for the evening's drinks. They also do a limited range of pasta and *secondi*.

BILLA Map pp256-8   *Supermarket*
Fondamenta Zattere al Ponte Lungo, Dorsoduro 1492; ⏰ 8.30am-8pm Mon-Sat, 9am-8pm Sun; vaporetto San Basilio

Near the Stazione Marittima, this is a big supermarket where you could stock up before hitting the high seas for Greece.

PUNTO SMA Map pp256-8   *Supermarket*
Rio Terrà della Scoazzera, Dorsoduro 3113; ⏰ 9am-12.50pm & 4.30-8pm Mon-Sat; vaporetto Ca' Rezzonico
This well-located supermarket is just off the Campo Santa Margherita, itself a good place to pick up fruit and veg at the market.

TRATTORIA DONA ONESTA

Map pp256-8   *Italian*
☎ 041 71 05 86; Calle Dona Onesta 3922; meal €20-25; ⏰ daily; vaporetto San Tomà
The Honest Woman hostelry is a straightforward, no-frills eatery that you might consider if money is tight but you wish to avoid overt tourist traps. The food is OK but no culinary dream – the main attraction is the modesty in price.

SESTIERI DI SAN POLO & SANTA CROCE

Entertainment p142; Sestieri p63; Shopping p155; Sleeping p167

Tucked away in the more unlikely places you'll stumble across cosy Venetian restaurants, the city's sole Indian redoubt, some of the oldest and most genuine of *osterie* and the city's lone Michelin-star splurge!

Gelateria Nico, a popular ice-cream stop along Fondamenta Zattere (opposite)

AL NONO RISORTO Map pp250-2   *Pizza*
☎ 041 524 11 69; Sotoportego de Siora Bettina, Santa Croce 2338; meal €30; ☽ Thu-Tue; vaporetto San Stae

Stop in if only to luxuriate in the leafy, wisteria-filled canalside garden in summertime. In the cooler months customers head inside the lofty, timber-lined dining area. Pizzas (€6 to €8) are the best bet, although locals say quality has declined. Service is friendly if a little scatty.

ANTICHE CARAMPANE
Map pp250-2   *Venetian*
☎ 041 524 01 65; Rio Terrà delle Carampane, San Polo 1911; meal €40-45; ☽ Tue-Sat; vaporetto San Stae

If you manage to navigate to this place in the heart of the one-time red-light district (the nearest bridge is Ponte delle Tette – Tits Bridge), you could be forgiven for hesitating to enter. The handwritten sign declaims: 'No lasagne, no pizza, no tourist menu'. A tad tetchy? Never mind: for good home-cooked fresh fish and vegetables, you have come to the right place.

CANTINA DO MORI
Map p253   *Cicheti & Other Snacks*
☎ 041 522 54 01; Sotoportego dei do Mori, San Polo 429; snacks €3-4; ☽ 8am-8.30pm Mon-Sat; vaporetto Rialto

Way back in 1642 they started selling wine in this dark tavern near the Ponte di Rialto. They haven't stopped since (except for a few years in the 16th century when fire and plague wrought havoc in the Rialto). In its present form it has operated as an *osteria*, offering a nice range of snacks to go with the wine, since the 1940s. Unfortunately, the local consensus is that the prices have gone up unreasonably (which is true). It's a shame, because it is an enticing place with its copper pots hanging from the ceiling, oozing history and still attracting a lot of local custom for such items as its *francobolli* ('stamps'), tiny stuffed sandwich snacks.

CANTINA DO SPADE Map pp250-2 *Venetian*
☎ 041 521 05 74; Calle do Spade, San Polo 860; meal about €35; ☽ Mon-Sat; vaporetto San Stae

Welcome to Venice's oldest eating house (c. 1400), where the emphasis is sadly more on full meals than on hanging about at the bar for snacks. Still, you can eat a range of bruschette (hardly a Venetian idea but tasty nonetheless). The place is slipping rapidly down the tourist slope but is at least worth a look-in, if only because of its venerable reputation.

DA FIORE Map pp250-2   *Refined Venetian*
☎ 041 72 13 08; Calle del Scaleter, San Polo 2202; meal €85-110; ☽ Tue-Sat; vaporetto San Stae

This is the city's only Michelin-star restaurant.

Chain Gang

Those on a tight budget may want to keep an eye out for chain eateries. Several Italian firms have taken the fast-food concept and put a local spin on it. The result is a cut way above the McDonald's of this world, but we have indicated one of the latter in Cannaregio (Map p253) for those who need a fix.

Brek (Map pp250-2; ☎ 041 244 01 58; Rio Terrà Lista di Spagna, Cannaregio 124; 1st/2nd courses about €4/6; ☉ 7.30am-10.30pm) If you have to do cheap fast food, you could do a lot worse than take a break here. For what you pay, the grub's not bad – light years from hamburgers and hotdogs! The restaurant area is open normal hours for lunch and dinner but you can get snacks at the bar all day. There is another branch in Mestre (Map p261; Via Carducci 54).

Spizzico (Map pp254-5; Campo San Luca, San Marco 4475-6; pizza slices around €3; ☉ 9am-11pm, sometimes closed Sun) For quick slices of pizza, this place isn't bad – the chain is quite popular across northern Italy. If you want burgers instead, a **Burger King** is located on the same premises.

Eating – Sestieri di San Polo & Santa Croce

The unprepossessing shopfront appearance belies an Art Deco interior and some traditional dishes, such as *risotto di scampi* (prawn risotto) and *bigoli in salsa* (thick pasta in tomato sauce), prepared with optimum care. Other dishes on the limited menu are home-grown inventions. While scrumptious and imaginative, portions can be stingy (what is all that *nouvelle* snobbery about anyway?). They have a predictably fine wine selection. Booking for dinner can be difficult; lunch is an easier proposition.

MIRAI Map pp250-2 *Japanese*
☎ 041 522 07 43; Rio Terrà Lista di Spagna 227; meal €40-50; ☉ Tue-Sun dinner only; vaporetto Ferrovia
What a surprise – halfway decent Japanese food finally arrives in Venice. After the demise of the poor imitation Sino-Japanese effort at Tokyo Sushi at the other end of town, this is a welcome development. Sure, the Venetians have their own way with fish, but sometimes sushi and sashimi is the way to go. Strange that it should be alone in a city renowned for its Oriental languages faculty!

OSTERIA ALLA PATATINA
Map pp256-8 *Venetian & Cicheti*
☎ 041 523 72 38; Calle dei Saoneri, San Polo 2741/a; meal €25-30; ☉ Mon-Fri, Sat lunch; vaporetto San Tomà
Pile in around the rough timber tables and benches for some *cicheti* (including *sarde in saor* and other classics) or simple pasta dishes, well washed down with a couple of glasses of robust red wine. The Potato Chip Inn (named after its scrummy fried potato slices), as it is called, makes no compromise with fickle trends and retains a traditional air that keeps regulars coming.

OSTERIA LA ZUCCA Map pp250-2 *Italian*
☎ 041 524 15 70; Calle del Tintor, Santa Croce 1762; meal €30-35; ☉ Mon-Sat; vaporetto San Stae
It seems like just another Venetian trattoria, but the menu (which changes daily) is an enticing mix of Mediterranean themes. The vegetable side orders (around €3.50) alone are inspired (try the *pepperonata alle melanzane*, a cool stew of capsicum and aubergine), while the mains (€12 to €15) are substantial. You won't need to order pasta as well.

OSTERIA VIVALDI Map pp256-8 *Venetian*
☎ 041 523 81 85; Calle della Madonnetta, San Polo 1457; meal €30-45; ☉ daily; vaporetto San Silvestro
You could easily rush past here in the crush of the San Polo shopping district, but if it's a food time of day, drop in to this traditional eatery, with its low timber beam ceiling and cosy dark wood tables. Some just like to sip on an *ombra*, but you should accompany the wine with a few *cicheti*. Alternatively, sit down to a full meal and try the *grigliata di pesce* (mixed fish grill).

TRATTORIA ALLA MADONNA
Map pp254-5 *Venetian*
☎ 041 522 38 24; Calle della Madonna, San Polo 594; meal €30-40; ☉ Thu-Tue; vaporetto Rialto
A few streets west of the Ponte di Rialto off Fondamenta del Vin, this place specialises in seafood but offers a decent range of meat dishes too. Housed at the base of a centuries-old mansion in a tight little lane, it's an old workhorse of the area and remains hugely popular.

TRATTORIA AL PONTE
Map pp250-2 *Venetian & Meat*
☎ 041 71 97 77; Ponte del Megio, Santa Croce 1666; meal €25-30; ☉ Mon-Fri, Sat lunch; vaporetto San Stae

Arrive early and try to grab a canalside table. This simple, down-home eatery tends to specialise in meat, but some fish options are available. The food quality is reliable and the prices reasonable.

VECIO FRITOLIN
Map pp250-2   *Inventive Venetian*
☎ 041 522 28 81; Calle della Regina, Santa Croce 2262; meal €35-45; ☼ Tue-Sat, Sun lunch; vaporetto San Stae

Traditionally, a *fritolin* was an eatery where diners sat at a common table and dug into fried seafood and polenta, or wrapped it up in paper and took it away, a tradition that goes back to the early 1800s. It was basically a chippie. At lunch time you can still pick up takeaway fried fish here, but things have changed greatly. The present owners regale you with fine meals based on local and national cooking. Pasta is home-made and all the ingredients purchased daily at the nearby Rialto markets. The quality shines through in every dish.

Cheap Eats

ALL'ANFORA Map pp250-2   *Pizza*
☎ 041 524 03 25; Lista dei Bari, Santa Croce 1223; pizza up to €8; ☼ Tue-Sun; vaporetto Riva de Biasio

Head out the back into the courtyard to indulge in an enormous choice of generous, tasty pizzas over a beer. Try the pizza all'Anfora, loaded up with various meats, artichokes and asparagus!

ALL'ARCO Map p253   *Cicheti*
☎ 041 520 56 66; Calle dell'Arco, San Polo 436; cicheti €1-2; ☼ Mon-Sat; vaporetto Rialto

For good value *cicheti* and a glass or two of wine, this is one of the most authentic *osterie* in San Polo. People gather around the bar or, on warmer days, cramp together on stools by tiny tables in among the hubbub of the cramped lanes outside.

IL REFOLO Map pp250-2   *Pizza*
☎ 041 524 00 16; Campo San Giacomo dell'Orio, Santa Croce 1459; pizzas €7-12, meal €25; ☼ Wed-Sun, Tue dinner; vaporetto Riva de Biasio

This place, hiding behind the mass of the Chiesa di San Giacomo dell'Orio, remains a firm favourite for pizza, especially in summer when you can take up a position along the peaceful canal. Now run by the son of the owners of Da Fiore (p127), the restaurant's other big plus is the divine home-made desserts. They do a limited selection of pasta, main courses and salads.

IN-COOP Map pp250-2   *Supermarket*
Campo San Giacomo dell'Orio, Santa Croce 1492; ☼ 9am-1pm & 4-7.30pm Mon-Sat; vaporetto Riva de Biasio

This supermarket is a handy option for self-caterers. There's another, bigger branch in Cannaregio (see p132).

SHRI GANESH Map pp250-2   *Indian*
☎ 041 71 90 84; Fondamenta Rio Marin, San Polo 2426; set menu €22.50; ☼ Thu-Tue; vaporetto Ferrovia

Fancy a quick curry? Forget it. But a good slow one can be had on the canalside terrace of this place. The charmingly chaotic staff serves up authentic dishes at reasonable prices – particularly pleased guests have scribbled their appreciation on the walls. This place even does takeaways.

TRATTORIA DA RENATO
Map pp250-2   *Italian*
☎ 041 524 19 22; Rio Terrà Secondo, San Polo 2245/a; meal €20; ☼ Fri-Wed; vaporetto San Stae

This place is affectionately known to local aficionados of reliable down-home cooking as Da Vittorio (a reference to the owner), or good-naturedly as Il Lento (the Slow One – some say service can be a little tardy). You are unlikely to eat as well for this price in too many other Venetian eateries. There is no pretence at gastronomic adventure, just tasty pasta dishes and decent second courses of meat or fish. The *fegato alla venexiana* (Venetian-style liver) is good.

SESTIERE DI CANNAREGIO
Entertainment pp142 & 144; Sestieri p77; Shopping p158; Sleeping p168

Numerous bars along the main thoroughfare between the train station and San Marco serve sandwiches and snacks. For restaurants, it is best to head for the side streets to look for trattorie and pizzerie. Fondamenta della Misericordia is something of a foodies' street where locals crowd into several *osterie* and bars.

A LA VECIA CAVANA
Map p253   *Inventive Venetian*
☎ 041 528 71 06; Rio Terrà dei SS Apostoli 4624/a; meal €35-45; ☼ Tue-Sun; vaporetto Fondamente Nuove

Exposed brick walls and backlit white timber beams create a soothing atmosphere in which to try a tempting mix of traditional Venetian seafood and a few gentle curve balls, such as raw tuna in teriyaki sauce.

ANICE STELLATO

Map pp250-2　　　　　　　　*Inventive Venetian*

☎ 041 72 07 44; Fondamenta della Sensa 3272; meal €30-35; 🕙 Wed-Sun; vaporetto Madonna dell'Orto

Awaiting you in the guise of doorman is a huge *damigiana* (glass wine cask) by the entrance. Inside, the heavy timber tables and wooden chairs invite you to a chatty, convivial meal. The pasta dishes are excellent and the mains imaginative, including the occasional use of curry and other spices not immediately associated with either local or national cuisine. The *filetto al Barolo con patate* (fillet steak cooked in a Barolo red wine with potatoes) is delicious.

BOCCADORO Map p253　　　　　*Seafood*

☎ 041 521 10 21; Campiello Widman 5405/a; meal €40-45; 🕙 Tue-Sun; vaporetto Fondamente Nuove

This is a new spot tucked away in one of the quieter parts of town but worth the extra walk. Seafood is the name of the game, ranging from fine oysters and raw tuna to *gnocchetti alle vongole* (little dumplings with clams), accompanied, oddly, by some fine Sardinian wines.

DA MARISA Map pp250-2　　　　　*Meat*

☎ 041 72 02 11; Fondamenta di San Giobbe 652/b; meal €25-30; 🕙 daily; vaporetto Tre Archi

They're not especially fond of tourists here so you may need to work up some Italian credentials to squeeze in, especially as local students have started to discover the place. If you do get in, expect robust, no-nonsense meat-based cooking (Da Marisa is near the former abattoir but seems to have taken no notice of its demise) in a simple, family-run place.

FIASCHETTERIA TOSCANA

Map p253　　　　　　　　　　*Venetian*

☎ 041 528 52 81; Salizzada San Giovanni Grisostomo 5719; meal €45-50; 🕙 Wed-Sun, Mon dinner; vaporetto Ca' d'Oro

A classic that has long maintained quality, the Fiaschetteria Toscana is about as Tuscan as a gondola. It serves up solid Venetian food, washed down with a choice of wines from an impressive list that includes tipples from around the country. The *frittura della Serenissima*, a mixed fried seafood platter, is memorable.

Seafood from the markets (p158) ends up in many Venetian restaurants

GAM GAM Map pp250-2　　*Mixed Med Kosher*

☎ 041 71 52 84; Calle del Ghetto Vecchio 1123; meal €25-30; 🕙 noon-10pm Sun-Thu, Fri lunch; vaporetto Guglie

Gam Gam is great for your taste buds if you like Israeli-style falafels and other Middle Eastern delicacies. This place is fully kosher and presents a diverse menu, from Red Sea spaghetti to couscous (with choice of meat, fish or vegetable sauce) and from hummus to that arch-Venetian side order of *fondi di carciofi* (artichoke hearts).

LA COLOMBINA Map pp250-2　　　　*Tuscan*

☎ 041 275 06 22; Campiello del Pegolotto 1828; meal €35-50; 🕙 Wed-Mon; vaporetto San Marcuola

An excellent wine list (including a few foreign drops) accompanies a delicious range of dishes and snacks, both Venetian and Tuscan. Although the restaurant is closed by standard Venetian times, you can hang about tasting wines (if there are enough customers to warrant the effort) as late as 2am. The culinary *pièce de résistance* is the *bistecca fiorentina*, a grand Tuscan steak.

OSTARIA AL PONTE Map p253　　　*Cicheti*

☎ 041 528 61 57; Calle Larga G Gallina 6378; cicheti

Eating – Sestiere di Cannaregio

€1.50-3 ☽ 8am-3.30pm & 4.30-8.30pm Mon-Sat;
vaporetto Ospedale Civile
On the 'frontier' with Sestiere di Castello is this
aptly named and highly recommended snack
joint. Enter the bright red doors and sidle up
to the bar to nibble on *cicheti* and indulge in
good wines. Or you could pull up a pew at one
of the couple of tables. Locals hang about in
here, chatting vociferously and sipping their
ombre.

OSTARIA DA RIOBA Map pp250-2 *Venetian*
☎ 041 524 43 79; Fondamenta della Misericordia 2553;
meal €35; ☽ Tue-Sun; vaporetto Madonna dell'Orto
Named after the Moorish-looking figure that
presides over the corner of the Palazzo Mastelli
(see p116), this relative newcomer to the area
presents a crisp, almost Spartan, interior and
a carefully prepared if limited menu. Unlike
some of the surrounding places, it concentrates largely on typical Venetian cuisine with
a briny bent.

OSTERIA ALLA FRASCA
Map p253   *Venetian*
☎ 041 528 54 33; Corte della Carità 5176; meal €40;
☽ Thu-Tue; vaporetto Fondamente Nuove
The dishes on offer are fairly standard, favour-
ing seafood, and are a smidge pricey for what
you get. However, the setting, with tables
spilling out into the charming *campiello* rarely
touched by tourist caravans, is a winner. The
locals like it too and you'll often see a few chatting over an *ombra*. They and their ancestors
have been doing so for more than 100 years.

OSTERIA DA ALBERTO
Map p253   *Seafood*
☎ 041 523 81 53; Calle Larga G Gallina 5401; meal
€25-30; ☽ Mon-Sat; vaporetto Fondamente Nuove
Another hidden Venetian jewel, this *osteria*

is run by Alberto, a well-known figure in the
business of serving up traditional food in Venice. Be aware that they close the kitchen by
about 9pm. The dried cod, a house speciality
prepared in various ways, is good. Dark wood
tables are spaced out nicely and surrounded
by huge *damigiane* and other odds and ends
on the walls.

OSTERIA DALLA VEDOVA
Map p253   *Venetian & Cicheti*
☎ 041 528 53 24; Calle del Pistor 3912; meal €30;
☽ Mon-Wed & Fri-Sat; vaporetto Ca' d'Oro
The 'Widow's Inn', off Strada Nuova, is also
called Trattoria Ca' d'Oro and is one of the oldest *osterie* in Venice. It was once a cheese store
and was taken over by a family from Puglia in
the 19th century. The food is good, whether
you nibble on the *cicheti* or settle in for a full
(mostly seafood) meal. The snacks are copious,
including battered vegetables and all sorts of
weird and wonderful sea creatures.

VINI DA GIGIO Map p253   *Venetian*
☎ 041 528 51 40; Fondamenta della Chiesa 3628/a;
meal €45-50; ☽ Tue-Sun; vaporetto Ca' d'Oro
Gigio stocks a fine selection of reds and whites
from the Veneto and beyond – come here to
taste good wines in the company of excellent
cooking. How about the *gnocchetti con scampi e
pesto* (little dumplings with prawns and pesto)?

Cheap Eats
IGUANA Map pp250-2   *Latin American*
☎ 041 71 35 61; Fondamenta della Misericordia
2515; burritos, tacos & fajitas €6.50-10.50; ☽ 6pm-
1am Tue-Sat; vaporetto Madonna dell'Orto
The low, wooden-beam ceiling makes for a
warm atmosphere at this Venetian excursion
into South American food. The burritos, tacos,

Where NOT to Eat

Feeding tourists second-rate meals is a Venetian sport. Places offering a set-price *menú turistico* (tourist menu) are
frequently a bit of a trap, as are those displaying a menu in multiple languages (although this is not always the case).
One fairly clear warning sign is tour groups chomping together on identical meals – usually a sorry-looking plate of
pasta with a tomato sauce, a side order of wilting salad and maybe even chips! Anyone who takes up a waiter/tout's
invitation to step inside and enjoy their food deserves everything they get.

   The worst areas are in Cannaregio – along the route from the train station towards San Marco – and in the San
Marco area itself. This is not to say you can't find good places in either of these areas – just that they have more than
their fair share of bad 'uns.

   There's something else to watch for. A new law allows most bars to serve food, but bear in mind that most bars do
not have proper kitchens, so many dishes are pre-prepared and possibly microwaved.

quesadillas and other Latin American specialities are OK and moderately priced. Some people just show up for tequila at the bar, especially at happy hour (6.30pm to 8pm) when you get three tipples for the price of two.

IN-COOP Map p253   *Supermarket*
Rio Terrà dei SS Apostoli, Cannaregio 4662; ☺ 9am-1pm & 4-7.30pm Mon-Sat; vaporetto Fondamente Nuove
This is a bigger branch of the Santa Croce store (see p129).

PARADISO PERDUTO
Map pp250-2   *Italian & Cicheti*
☎ 041 72 05 81; Fondamenta della Misericordia 2539; meal €25; ☺ Thu-Mon; vaporetto Madonna dell'Orto
Young people will enjoy this spot, which frequently proffers live music and has tables outside in summer. The *lasagna ai carciofi* (artichoke lasagne) is great and the long list of *cicheti* is equally enticing. It gets pretty packed and boisterous of an evening.

SAHARA Map pp250-2   *Middle Eastern*
☎ 041 72 10 77; Fondamenta della Misericordia 2520; meal €20; ☺ daily; vaporetto Madonna dell'Orto
At Sahara you can get a reasonable version of Syrian food, with old favourites such as falafel, hummus, kebab meat and other Oriental delights. The food is not bad and certainly makes a change. You may even get a display of bellydancing thrown in on Saturday night.

SESTIERE DI CASTELLO
Entertainment p143; Sestieri p80; Shopping p158; Sleeping p170
If you've wandered around the Castello area you'll have already realised that this part of the town, the tail of the fish that Venice resembles and the largest of the *sestieri*, is perhaps the most real.

AL COVO Map p259   *Seafood*
☎ 041 522 38 12; Campiello della Pescaria 3968; meal €40-45; ☺ Fri-Tue; vaporetto Arsenale
Cooking at Al Covo, a place that has earned the respect of many Venetians, is resolutely local and of a high quality. The atmosphere is hushed and unpretentious but some of the seafood dishes in particular are divine. Options include tempting fish soups and eel, and the desserts that follow are as sweet as the seafood is briny. Credit cards are not accepted.

ALLE TESTIERE Map pp254-5   *Seafood*
☎ 041 522 72 20; Calle Mondo Nuovo 5801; meal €55; ☺ Tue-Sat; vaporetto Rialto
In a cosy, nay, tiny dining area with black-and-white photos on the walls the chef may well come up for a chat as you sample the tasty offerings. Fish is the leitmotif. A handful of starters and pasta courses (all around €14 to €16) are followed by a couple of set main courses or fresh fish (whatever happens to have been caught that day). Round off your meal with quality wines.

Wine for Dining

Wine (*vino*) is an essential accompaniment to any Italian meal. Italians are justifiably proud of their wines and it would be surprising for dinner-time conversation not to touch on the subject, at least for a moment.

Wine is graded according to three main classifications – DOCG (*denominazione d'origine controllata e garantita*), DOC (*denominazione d'origine controllata*) and table wine (*vino da tavola*) – which are marked on the label. A DOC wine is produced subject to certain specifications, although the label does not certify quality. DOCG is tested by government inspectors for quality.

Your average trattoria will generally stock only a limited range of bottled wines, but quite a few of the better restaurants offer a carefully chosen selection of wines from around the country. Indeed, some places are better known for their wine lists than their grub. Ordering the house wine is generally safe if unexciting.

Although the Veneto is not one of Italy's prime wine-making regions, some good drops are produced around Verona, including **Soave** whites, **Valpolicella** reds and **Bardolino** reds and rosés. **Nosiola**, another white, is not bad. The Vicenza area is also dotted with wineries. Wines from the Friuli-Venezia Giulia area, Italy's easternmost region and for centuries part of Venice's mainland empire, are often good and readily available. Look out for **Pinot Grigio** whites and **Pinot Nero** reds.

A regional curiosity is the sweet *fragolino*. This strawberry-flavoured red isn't strictly wine and cannot be sold as such commercially, although you'll occasionally find it in bars in Venice and elsewhere in the Veneto. You sometimes come across a white version too. You can be fairly sure you are drinking the real thing if it is served in unlabelled bottles. Many stores have taken to selling a fizzy 'wine' they call *fragolino*. This is a travesty – it is little more than poor wine with strawberry flavouring added.

OSTERIA DI SANTA MARINA

Map pp254-5   *Inventive Venetian*
☎ 041 528 52 39; Campo Santa Marina 5911; meal
€45; ✆ Tue-Sat, Mon dinner; vaporetto Rialto
A relatively new arrival in this part of town, this
osteria offers a pleasant dining area and tables
on the square. The cuisine is largely a refined
take on Venetian seafood dishes. The best dishes
are without doubt the exquisite desserts, such as
the artfully presented chocolate mousse.

TRATTORIA CORTE SCONTA

Map p259   *Seafood*
☎ 041 522 70 24; Calle del Pestrin 3886; meal €45-
50; ✆ Tue-Sat; vaporetto Arsenale
A cosy eatery with the option of dining in the
rear vine-shaded courtyard, the Corte Sconta
is hidden well off even the unbeaten tourist
track, although good publicity has locals and
foresti beating a path to its door. The chefs prepare almost exclusively seafood classics, such
as their delicious *risotto ai scampi*. The owners
claim to use only the catch of the day. Who
can carp at such a policy?

TRATTORIA DA REMIGIO

Map p259   *Venetian*
☎ 041 523 00 89; Salizzada dei Greci 3416; meal €30-
35; ✆ Wed-Sun, Mon lunch; vaporetto San Zaccaria
It is not often you find a restaurant that in the
early evening can post a sign in the window
saying *completo* (full), as though it were a
hotel, but this place can. It has a mixed menu,
featuring Venetian fish dishes and a handful
of meat options. Service is fast and the results
reliable. It's clearly busy and you'll need to
book to be sure of a spot.

Cheap Eats

ALLA RIVETTA Map pp254-5   *Venetian*
☎ 041 528 73 02; Ponte San Provolo 4625; meal €20-
25; ✆ Tue-Sun; vaporetto San Zaccaria
This is one of the few restaurants near Piazza
San Marco that can be recommended. Surrounded by tourist traps, it has resisted the
temptation to abandon all quality and even
gets a few locals (including famished gondoliers) in for its no-nonsense dishes (especially
the fried seafood options).

AL PORTEGO

Map pp254-5   *Venetian & Cicheti*
☎ 041 522 90 38; San Lio 6015; cicheti €1.50-3;
✆ Mon-Sat; vaporetto Rialto

Top Five Pastry Shops

- **Antica Pasticceria Tonolo** (Map pp256-8;
  ☎ 041 523 72 09; Calle dei Preti, Dorsoduro
  3764; ✆ 7.45am-1pm & 3-8.30pm Tue-Sat,
  7.45am-1pm Sun; vaporetto San Tomà) This place
  has been turning out delicious pastries since
  1886. Stop by for a coffee or perhaps a midday
  prosecco and bar snacks.
- **Bucintoro** (Map pp250-2; ☎ 041 72 15 03;
  Calle del Scaleter, San Polo 2229; ✆ 7.15am-
  8pm Tue-Sun; vaporetto San Stae) The Venetian
  word for pastry-maker is *scaleter*, which comes
  from the step-shaped sign (the Italian word for
  stairs is *scale*) they once etched onto their sweets,
  which were known as *scalete*. Gino Zanin carries
  on antique Venetian traditions with his sweets
  and pastries, which come with such wonderful
  names as *bacingondola* (kiss in the gondola), a
  little meringue and chocolate number.
- **Gobbetti** (Map pp256-8; ☎ 041 528 90 14; Rio
  Terrà Canal, Dorsoduro 3108/b; ✆ 8am-1pm
  & 3.30-8pm Wed-Mon; vaporetto Ca' Rezzonico)
  This is another good place for sweet things, just
  off Campo Santa Margherita.
- **Pasticceria Da Bonifacio** (Map pp254-5;
  ☎ 041 522 75 07; Calle degli Albanesi, Castello
  4237; ✆ 7.30am-8.30pm; vaporetto San
  Zaccaria) This classic Venetian pastry shop has
  remained unspoiled by its proximity to Piazza
  San Marco. Alongside traditional local sweets and
  pastries you will occasionally encounter others
  sneaked in from surrounding provinces.
- **Pasticceria Puppa** (Map p253; ☎ 041 523 79
  47; Calle Spezier, Cannaregio 4800; ✆ 7am-
  1.30pm & 3-7.30pm Tue-Sun; vaporetto Fondamente Nuove) Sweeties for the kids, traditional
  pastries and cakes, and a range of good national
  items like Christmas panettone are on offer at
  this pastry shop that doubles as a café-bar along
  an otherwise quiet street in the north of town.

Situated beneath the portico that gives this *osteria* its name, Al Portego is an inviting stop for
cicheti and wine, along with some more robust
meals. It's all timber in here and very cosy. Try
the thick spaghetti-like pasta, *bigoli*, whatever
sauce it comes with, or perhaps a risotto.

AL VECIO PENASA

Map pp254-5   *Sandwiches*
☎ 041 523 72 02; Calle delle Rasse 4587; panini €2;
✆ 6.30am-11.30pm; vaporetto San Zaccaria
Between Riva degli Schiavoni and Campo SS
Filippo e Giacomo, this remains a good spot

Harry's Dolci on Giudecca (opposite) is famous for its desserts

for its excellent selection of sandwiches and snacks at reasonable prices.

LA MASCARETA Map pp254-5 *Cicheti & Wine*
☎ 041 523 07 44; Calle Lunga Santa Maria Formosa 5138; cheese & ham platter €15; ◷ Mon-Sat; vaporetto Rialto

A brief stroll off Campo Santa Maria Formosa is the 'Little Mask', a genial tavern for the sipping of wine accompanied by a limited but tempting range of *cicheti*. They take their tipples seriously here and the cold meats and cheeses served make the perfect accompaniment.

SUVE Map pp254-5 *Supermarket*
Salizzada San Lio, Castello 5817; ◷ 8.30am-7.45pm Mon-Tue & Thu-Sat, 8.30am-1pm Wed; vaporetto Rialto

A handy supermarket situated between Rialto and San Marco.

TRATTORIA DA PAMPO
Map p260 *Venetian & Cicheti*
☎ 041 520 84 19; Calle Gen Chinotto 3, Sant'Elena; meal €25; ◷ Wed-Mon; vaporetto Giardini

They say 'dal pampo non c'é scampo' ('there's no getting away from Pampo') and why would you want to? This is a real locals' place for *ombre* and *cicheti*, but you can sit down (inside or out) for a full, simple meal. It is set opposite a shady park in the quietest end of the city.

AROUND THE LAGOON
Entertainment p144; Sestieri p88; Shopping p159; Sleeping p180

Across the islands and down in Chioggia you'll find various enticing spots to sit down to eat – you need not go hungry anywhere in the lagoon!

AL GATTO NERO Map p264 *Buranese*
☎ 041 73 01 20; Fondamenta della Giudecca 88; meal €40; ◷ Tue-Sun; vaporetto Burano

Noisy Venetian families pile into this off-the-beaten-*calle* trattoria in Burano. Sure, you could join the crowds in the cheaper places along the island's main drag, but the food is generally not the greatest. Here you pay a premium but the quality is better.

ALLA MADDALENA
Map p264 *Seafood & Game*
☎ 041 73 01 51; Mazzorbo 7/c; meal €30; ◷ Fri-Wed; vaporetto Mazzorbo

On this peaceful, leafy island adjacent to Burano is a lively seafood oasis. Walk over the bridge from Burano to reach this soothing spot near the vaporetto stop. Relax by the canal or in the garden out the back. In the hunting season (autumn) you may encounter various birds on the menu – enough to make you feel a little like Hemingway!

BUSA LA TORRE Map p265   *Seafood*

☎ 041 73 96 62; Campo Santo Stefano 3; meal €40; ⏰ lunch only; vaporetto Murano Faro

Come here for lunch on your day out in Murano and try the seafood pastas, such as sea bass ravioli in a crab meat *(granseola)* sauce. On the subject of crabs, the place is also known for its fried *moeche*, little shore crabs.

HARRY'S DOLCI

Map pp262-3   *Inventive Venetian*

☎ 041 522 48 44; Fondamenta San Biagio, Giudecca 773; meal €90-110; ⏰ Wed-Mon Apr-Oct; vaporetto Palanca

This place is run by the Cipriani clan of Harry's Bar and has tables by the Canale della Giudecca looking across to Venice. The fantastic desserts are the main reason for stopping by. Should you want a full meal, they can also accommodate you – at elevated prices.

LOCANDA CIPRIANI

Map p264   *Inventive Venetian*

☎ 041 73 01 50; Piazza Santa Fosca 29, Torcello; meal €50-80; ⏰ lunch Wed-Mon & dinner Sat, closed Jan; vaporetto Torcello

This exclusive hideaway, another of the Ciprianis' eateries, was established in 1946. Ernest Hemingway set down his bags here in 1948 and wrote part of *Across the River and into the Trees*. The food is prepared with care and the leafy setting is magical. The internal dining areas, with low timber ceilings and exposed brick, are as enticing in cooler weather as the chirrupy garden is in summer.

MISTRÀ Map pp262-3   *Venetian & Ligurian*

☎ 041 522 07 43; Giudecca 212/a; meal €40-45; ⏰ Wed-Sun, Mon lunch; vaporetto Redentore

Grab a table at the back for views south over the lagoon. Located among the workshops of a major boatyard, this is a suitably maritime setting for great seafood, with a combination of local dishes and a few Ligurian imports (like pesto). At lunch time you can join the shipwrights for a cheaper midday meal. To get here, look for No 211 on Fondamenta di San Giacomo and pass down the narrow passage beside it. It opens out as you saunter through the shipyards to the rear end of the island.

OSTERIA PENZO   *Seafood*

☎ 041 40 09 92; Calle Larga Bersaglio 526, Chioggia; meal €30; ⏰ Wed-Mon; vaporetto Lido + bus 11

Once, all you would get here was wine and basic snacks, but nowadays staff prepare good local dishes based entirely on the fleet's catch.

RISTORANTE AL TRONO DI ATTILA

Map p264   *Venetian*

☎ 041 73 00 94; Fondamenta Borgognoni 7/a, Torcello; meal €25-30; ⏰ daily; vaporetto Torcello

Unless you plan to blow your budget at the Locanda Cipriani, try this place, between the vaporetto stop and the cathedral. The atmosphere is suitably bucolic and you will want to dine in the charming garden with pergola. Try the *gnocchetti con rucola e scampi* (little dumplings with rocket and shrimps). The restaurant generally opens for lunch only, unless you book ahead for dinner.

TRATTORIA DA SCARSO   *Venetian*

☎ 041 77 08 34; Piazzale Malamocco 4, Lido; meal €25-30; ⏰ Wed-Sun, Mon lunch; vaporetto Lido + bus No 11

This is a simple trattoria with a pleasant pergola. Set in the tiny old Venetian settlement of Malamocco (which was moved here when the original settlement further south was

---

Deciding on Dessert

For some, the question of what to have for *dolci* (dessert) poses a primordial prandial dilemma. What about a Venetian classic: tiramisu, a rich dessert with mascarpone? All sorts of light biscuits have also been dreamed up over the centuries in Venice – start looking in cake-shop windows. They come with such names as *baicoli*, *ossi da morto* ('dead man's bones') and *bigarani* and are supposed to be taken with dessert wine.

You may well be offered *sorbetto* (lemon sorbet) at the end of the main course. It is designed to clean your palate before dessert, but for many makes a good dessert on its own account. An alcoholic version with vodka and a dash of milk, called a *sgroppino*, will be more to the liking of some.

Speaking of alcohol, another classic way to round off a meal is with a *digestivo*, some strong liquor to aid digestion. You could try a shot of grappa, a strong, clear brew made from grapes whose name comes from a Veneto region (see Bassano del Grappa, p204). Or you could go for an *amaro*, a dark liqueur prepared from herbs. If you prefer a sweeter liqueur, try an almond-flavoured amaretto or the sweet aniseed *sambuca*.

Top Five Foreign Eats

- **Da Luca** (below) Mixed Japanese
- **Gam Gam** (p130) Mixed kosher
- **Iguana** (p131) Latin American
- **Sahara** (p132) Middle Eastern
- **Shri Ganesh** (p129) Indian

flooded out centuries ago), it isn't too heavily frequented by *foresti*. Local colour alone makes it an attractive stop.

Cheap Eats

AI TRE SCAINI Map pp262-3 *Venetian*
☎ 041 522 47 90; Calle Michelangelo 53/c, Giudecca; meal €25; ⌚ noon-2.30pm & 6pm-1am Fri-Sun, Tue-Wed & Mon lunch; vaporetto Zitelle
In this rambunctious and chaotic trattoria you can settle down with ebullient local families for copious pasta and seafood dishes (there are one or two meat options too). Throaty wine comes from a couple of small barrels set up inside. You can eat in the garden too.

RISTORANTE EL FONTEGO *Pizza*
☎ 041 550 09 53; Piazzetta XX Settembre 497; Chioggia; meal €25; ⌚ Tue-Sun; vaporetto Lido + bus No 11
The setting here is a little brassy but popular. The restaurant offers a broad range of vegetarian dishes and 'cream pizzas' with a Brie cheese base – they're not bad. Vegetarian pizzas cost around €7.

RISTORANTE VECIO FOGHERO
Seafood & Pizza
☎ 041 40 46 79; Calle Scopici 91, Chioggia; meals €20-25; ⌚ Tue-Sun; vaporetto Lido + bus No 11
This place has good pizzas and seafood. The *tagliolini al salmone* (ribbon pasta with salmon sauce) is tempting.

MESTRE
Entertainment p144; Shopping p160; Sleeping p182
The mainland half of Venice, by far the bigger and uglier brother, is unlikely to attract your attention for long, but if you happen to be here there are some good eating options to consider.

DA BEPI VENESIAN Map p261 *Venetian*
☎ 041 92 93 57; Via Sernaglia 27, Mestre; meal €30; ⌚ Mon-Sat, Sun lunch; train
A couple of blocks from the train station, Da Bepi Venesian has been serving traditional dishes for years. Some say it is past its prime, but you can still eat well here. The place is huge – with four dining areas – and specialises in fish. Try the *seppie con polenta* (cuttlefish with polenta).

DA LUCA Map p261 *International*
☎ 041 95 71 22; Via Monte Grappa 42, Mestre; meal €45-50; ⌚ Mon-Fri; train
Arguably the best restaurant in Mestre, this place takes you down a unique culinary path combining Venetian favourites with some good examples of Japanese cooking – clearly a fishy affair. The preparation is exquisite and the desserts better still.

Cheap Eats

OSTERIA LA PERGOLA Map p261 *Meat*
☎ 041 97 49 32; Via Fiume 42, Mestre; meal €20-25; ⌚ Mon-Fri, Sat dinner; train
As the name suggests, here you can sit under a pergola and enjoy some of the better value food in Mestre. What about a delicious plate of *pappardelle all'anatra* (a thick pasta with duck)? Venetians swear by this place, which, by the way, serves no seafood!

Eating – Mestre

Entertainment

Entertainment

When you consider that there are fewer than 65,000 permanent residents in Venice, the offerings for nocturnal diversion are quite broad. You can take in some theatre or an opera, go to the movies, prop up a bar or even lose a few euros at the roulette wheel. But this is not the big city and Venice is a rather staid sort of a place – not at all the licentious, hedonistic whirl it was in its twilight years before Napoleon and then the Austrians arrived to stamp out all the decadence.

A number of musical ensembles perform the music of Vivaldi and other baroque composers for visitors, often in period costume and in some of the otherwise largely disused monuments of the city. Although these performances can be a little cheesy, the musical quality is often not bad and it can make for a pleasant night out.

Venice is by no means a teetotal town. People like a drink and plenty of bars will oblige you on this front. Just don't expect long, crazy nights out!

Of course, Venice puts on various one-off parties. Carnevale in February is perhaps the best known, with masked balls in Piazza San Marco, parades, street theatre and all manner of diversions. Other big festivals (see City Calendar, pp9–11) also serve as an excuse for locals to let their hair down.

Information

For general listings on upcoming events and shows, see *Un Ospite di Venezia,* available from tourist offices, which also have brochures listing events and performances for the entire year. Keep your eyes on the monthly *VeNews*, available at newsstands.

DRINKING

Venetians have something of a reputation in Italy for being inveterate tipplers. Locals can often be seen propping up bars in the morning for a heart-starter, and the ever popular *prosecco*, the Veneto's lightly bubbly white wine, pours freely throughout the day. Just as Brits might pop down to the local for a pint, Venetians will nip down to the nearest bar or *osteria* for a quick *ombra* (small glass of wine) or *prosecco* and, maybe, a snack.

The colour of one's drink changes as the day progresses, and the early evening *aperitivo* (apéritif) favourite is the *spritz*. This is one part sparkling white wine, one part soda water and one part bitter (Campari, Amaro, Aperol or Select), topped with a slice of lemon and, if you wish, an olive. It's said this drink dates from the days of the Austrian occupation in the 19th century. In warm weather the bright red and orange versions of this tipple decorate the tables of outdoor terraces, while in the depths of winter you can see people crowded up against bars which are covered in all sorts of nibbles.

Cavatappi wine bar in San Marco (opposite)

While it may be true that Venetians like tippling, it can't be said that Venice rocks. There are basically two poles of interest. Campo Santa Margherita in Dorsoduro is a lively and bar-fronted square that attracts a mix of the young, the hip and the wannabes of town. Further away from the centre of things is the area around Fondamenta della Misericordia in Cannaregio, which is a more relaxed setting with a vaguely studenty feel.

There is more of course. A range of bars is scattered across the Sestiere di San Marco and a handful of other good ones are strung across Dorsoduro and San Polo. The old-time *bacari* (see the boxed text on p122 for more on these bars) are largely extinct, although a few soldier on.

About the latest you can hope for these places to remain open is 2am – you might manage to squeeze in one last drink on the hour and stretch things out a little. You could put on your dancing shoes but, as you will discover, the options for late nights out in Venice can be counted on one hand!

SESTIERE DI SAN MARCO

The San Marco area offers a disparate set of drinking options, from fine old taverns to UK-style pubs, and from trendy wine bars to slightly out-of-time piano bars. And of course, there's Harry's.

BACARO JAZZ Map pp254-5

☎ 041 528 52 49; Salizzada del Fondaco dei Tedeschi 5546; ☼ 11am-2am Thu-Tue, happy hour 2-7.30pm; vaporetto Rialto

The dark red interior and slightly brash feel, not to mention its location right on the main tourist thoroughfare, may not make it your favourite, but a drink's a drink in a town where bars aren't exactly in surplus.

CAVATAPPI Map pp254-5

☎ 041 296 02 52; Campo della Guerra 3805; ☼ 9am-midnight Mon-Sat Oct-Apr, 9am-midnight daily May-Sep; vaporetto Vallaresso/San Marco

This is a modern creamy-white bar with halogen lighting and wines from all over Italy. In a rather daring departure for what is in many ways a small town, this place will appeal to all who miss a slightly metropolitan touch. Try cheeses from all over Italy, with a few French and Swiss additions.

CLUB MALVASIA VECCHIA Map pp256-8

☎ 041 522 58 83; Calle della Malvasia 2586; ☼ 11pm-4am Fri & Sat; vaporetto Santa Maria del Giglio

You pay a small fee to become a member of this social club that functions as a late-night bar. Beloved of students and a hip artsy type of crowd, it takes a bit of finding.

DEVIL'S FOREST Map pp254-5

☎ 041 520 00 23; Calle dei Stagneri 5185; ☼ 10am-1pm & 5pm-12.30am Mon-Sat; vaporetto Rialto

This is a reasonable imitation of a UK pub, complete with old red telephone box, sports TV and Irish beers on tap (Kilkenny and Harp). It sometimes closes early if business is slow.

HARRY'S BAR Map pp254-5

☎ 041 528 57 77; Calle Vallaresso 1323; cocktails €10-12; ☼ noon-11pm; vaporetto Vallaresso/San Marco

Harry's is, of course, first and foremost a bar. Everyone who is anyone passing through Venice usually ends up in Harry's sooner or later. The Aga Khan lounged around here and

---

The Cocktail Circuit

Back in the 1950s, behind the bar at Harry's, a new sensation was born. It was deceptively simple: mix *prosecco* (sparkling white wine) with peach nectar, and you have a Bellini. Of course, they will tell you there is more to it than that – the quality of the ingredients and, more importantly, the proportions. Whatever – it is good.

You don't have to shell out the €12 for one at Harry's Bar, as Bellinis and other cocktails are popular at *aperitivo* time (that loose early-evening, predinner period) all over town. Still, if you can afford a drink or two at Harry's, it's worth it. Apart from the Bellini they do some other mean mixes. These guys have been practising the art of the Martini for as long as they have been open.

Truman Capote called a good Martini a Silver Bullet. What's in it? Good gin and a drop of Martini Dry. But of course the amount of the latter varies according to taste. For a strong, dry Martini, 'rinse' the glass with Martini and then pour in freezing-cold gin. Hemingway, who set part of his book *Across the River and into the Trees* at Harry's, had his own recipe – pour freezing-cold gin into a glass dipped in ice and sit it next to a bottle of Martini for a moment before drinking!

Top Five Cafés

- **Algiubagiò** (Map p253; ☎ 041 523 60 84; Fondamente Nuove, Cannaregio 5039; 7am-midnight; vaporetto Fondamente Nuove) There's nowhere better for a coffee (or something stronger) on the way to or from Murano and the northern lagoon islands. Join the vaporetto staff at the bar or take a lagoonside seat.
- **Caffè Florian** (Map pp254-5; ☎ 041 520 56 41; Piazza San Marco, San Marco 56/59; 9am-10pm Thu-Tue; vaporetto Vallaresso/San Marco) The plush interior of this, the city's best-known café, has seen the likes of Lord Byron and Henry James taking breakfast (separately!) before they crossed the piazza to Caffè Quadri for lunch. Venetians started paying exorbitant sums for the pleasure of drinking here in 1720.
- **Caffè Quadri** (Map pp254-5; ☎ 041 522 21 05; Piazza San Marco, San Marco 120; meal €80-100; 9am-midnight Tue-Sun; vaporetto Vallaresso/San Marco) Quadri is in much the same league as Florian, and equally steeped in history. Indeed, it opened its doors well before its better known competitor, in 1683. The 1st-floor dining area is a luxury trip, all dripping chandeliers, baroque mirrors and heavy wall-hangings.
- **Lavena** (Map pp254-5; ☎ 041 522 40 70; Piazza San Marco, San Marco 133; 9am-10pm daily Apr-Sep, Wed-Mon Oct-Mar; vaporetto Vallaresso/San Marco) Founded in 1750 and less renowned than its big brothers Florian and Quadri, Lavena is in the same vein. Wagner was among its more visible customers, but historically gondoliers and *codegas* (stout fellows who lighted the way home for people returning at night) also hung out here.
- **SuzieCafé** (Map pp256-8; ☎ 041 522 75 02; Campo San Basegio, Dorsoduro 1527/a; 7am-7pm Mon-Fri; vaporetto San Basilio) Students inhabit this cheerful spot, which makes a charming morning coffee stop just off the beaten track on a little Dorsoduro square.

other characters as diverse as Orson Welles, Ernest Hemingway and Truman Capote have all sipped on a cocktail or two at Harry's.

LE BISTROT DE VENISE Map pp254-5
☎ 041 523 66 51; Calle dei Fabbri 4685; 10am-1am; vaporetto Rialto
As much restaurant as bar, this bistro is an elegant setting for a little wine-tasting accompanied by nibbles, particularly Italian and French cheeses.

MARTINI SCALA Map pp254-5
☎ 041 522 41 21; Calle della Veste 1501; 9pm-3.30am Wed-Mon; vaporetto Santa Maria del Giglio
If you like the piano-bar scene, maybe this is for you. It's a little cheesy and very pricey, but then the options aren't bountiful (especially this late at night), are they?

TORINO@NOTTE Map pp254-5
☎ 041 522 39 14; Campo San Luca 459; 10pm-2am Tue-Sat; vaporetto Rialto
This unlikely-looking spot (during the day) livens up at night as a young student set, combined with carefree holidaying visitors, settles in for mixed drinks, music and the occasional live act.

VITAE (IL MURO) Map pp254-5
☎ 041 520 52 05; Calle San Antonio 4118; 7pm-2am; vaporetto Rialto
When things around this part of town start to look grim, people converge on this place. On a Friday or Saturday night it's a lively joint for a drink – and the only seriously decent option in the San Marco area. It's also busy by day – a popular brunch spot for local office workers and busy for after-work drinks too.

SESTIERE DI DORSODURO
Campo Santa Margherita is without doubt one of nocturnal Venice's major magnets. The long square is fronted on three sides by restaurants and bars, and attracts an eclectic crowd of students, hipsters, Biennale bods, local residents and, while the sun's still out, kids playing.

AI DO DRAGHI Map pp256-8
☎ 041 528 97 31; Calle della Chiesa 3665; 7.30am-2am Fri-Wed; vaporetto Ca' Rezzonico
Long neglected by the student and arts crowd that fills the bars further down on Campo Santa Margherita, this tiny but historic *bacaro* has become flavour of the month with many. Prices are a little lower and it seems punters have rediscovered the atmosphere of this timber-lined relic.

AI VINI PADOVANI Map pp256-8
☎ 041 523 63 70; Calle dei Cerchieri 1280; 10am-10pm Mon-Fri; vaporetto Ca' Rezzonico
At this real old-time *bacaro*, hunch at the red marble-top bar for wine and *cicheti* (snacks) or try to get one of the five tables for a full

Confused Over Coffee

Coffee in Italy is complex. An espresso is a small cup of strong black coffee. A *doppio espresso* is a double. A *caffè lungo* is more watery, and an approximation of bland filter coffee is a *caffè americano*.

Enter the milk. A *caffè latte* is coffee with milk. Cappuccino is a frothy version. Both are breakfast drinks to Italians. *Caffè macchiato* is an espresso with a dash of frothy milk. In summer you can opt for a *caffè freddo*, a long glass of cold coffee with ice cubes. Good on winter afternoons is a *corretto* – an espresso 'corrected' with grappa or other hard liquor.

An espresso at a regular bar costs €0.80 to €0.90. It costs €4.50 at Caffè Florian and more still if you sit outside! An Irish coffee can cost €13! At Caffè Quadri prices are similar.

If you can cope with these sorts of prices, spend an hour or so sitting at an outdoor table at Florian, Quadri or Lavena, soaking up the atmosphere in Piazza San Marco. In summer they have quartets playing under awnings on the square. These compete with one another for attention, one striking up some stirring Vivaldi and the other countering with a little modern stuff. Usually they have the courtesy to play in turns, but if you stand in the middle of the square when they aren't being so gentlemanly, the effect is more cacophonous than melodious. Which is reassuring – even when trying to outdo itself in refined elegance, Venice can occasionally be humanly lacking in finesse. But not in business acumen – listening to the music over your coffee involves a €4.50 surcharge!

In all three cafés you can pay less extravagant prices for a coffee or a drink taken on your feet at the bar inside and still enjoy the elegant surroundings.

meal. Before WWII the bar got its wine supplies from the Colli area around Padua, hence the name.

AL BOTTEGON (CANTINA DI VINI GIÀ SCHIAVI) Map pp256-8

☎ 041 523 00 34; Fondamenta Maravegie 992;
☼ Mon-Sat; vaporetto Zattere

This is a fusty old wine bar across from the Chiesa di San Trovaso. Wander in for a glass of *prosecco* beneath the bar's low-slung rafters and in the wavering light provided by dodgy bulbs. Alternatively, buy a bottle of whatever takes your fancy and take it away.

AL CHIOSCHETTO Map pp256-8

☎ 338 117 40 77; Fondemente Zattere 1406/a;
☼ 7.30am-8pm Oct-Apr, 7.30am-1am May-Sep;
vaporetto San Basilio

Live music is no longer allowed here, so they occasionally hire a boat with musicians – come aboard and groove around the Canale della Giudecca. It's a strictly summertime scene with tables sprawled out around a tiny bar in the kind of kiosk where you'd normally expect to buy the paper.

CAFÉ NOIR Map pp256-8

☎ 041 71 09 25; Calle dei Preti 3805; ☼ 7am-2am
Mon-Sat; vaporetto San Tomà

You can start the day with breakfast in here or hang out into the night with a mixed crowd of Italian students and foreigners. The place has a laid-back, underground feel about it. A cocktail costs around €4 to €5.

CAFFÈ Map pp256-8

☎ 041 528 79 98; Campo Santa Margherita 2693;
☼ Mon-Sat; vaporetto Ca' Rezzonico

A lively student bar with snacks, this place is known to locals affectionately as the *caffè rosso* because of the red sign. It is something of a classic and on warmer nights the animated bustle at the outside tables is hard to pass up.

CAFFÈ BLUE Map pp256-8

☎ 041 523 72 27; Calle dei Preti 3778; ☼ 8am-2pm
& 5pm-2am Mon-Sat; vaporetto San Tomà

This is a coolish student bar with live music on some evenings. When it's on, the place packs to the rafters and punters spill out on to the street. It can be a little quiet on midweek evenings.

Caffè Florian on Piazza San Marco (opposite)

Top Five Drinking Establishments

- **Al Bottegon** (p141) Classic old wine cellar.
- **Al Chioschetto** (p141) For a summer breeze buzz on the Zattere.
- **Café Noir** (p141) Lively student hangout.
- **Harry's Bar** (p139) Ready for *the* Bellini?
- **Margaret Duchamp** (below) A hip place to hang out.

IMAGINA Map pp256-8

☎ 041 241 06 25; Rio Terrà Canal 3126; ☻ 8am-2am Mon-Sat; vaporetto Ca' Rezzonico

A new kid on the block, this one-time art gallery is now also a bar. Sit on fat white lounges around timber-top tables over a wine and then wander around the latest exhibition. Alternatively, head outside for a table on the street.

MARGARET DUCHAMP Map pp256-8

☎ 041 528 62 55; Campo Santa Margherita 3019; ☻ 9am-2am Wed-Mon; vaporetto Ca' Rezzonico

Across the square from Caffè, this is a highly popular spot for a *spritz* and chat until the early hours. It attracts a hip mix of young wannabes and Biennale types with shades – you can't blame them as you get the afternoon sun shining straight through your cocktail glass.

ORANGE Map pp256-8

☎ 041 523 47 40; Campo Santa Margherita 3054/a; ☻ 8am-2am daily; vaporetto Ca' Rezzonico

Huge sheet glass windows now dominate the southern end of the *campo* (square). This newcomer, the colour of an Aperol *spritz* inside, appeals to fashionistas and other narcissists. Skip the lurid bar and head out the back to the pleasant garden. They do some food too.

SUZIECAFÉ Map pp256-8

☎ 041 522 75 02; Campo San Basegio 1527/a; ☻ 7am-7pm Mon-Thu, 7am-1am Fri & concerts; vaporetto San Basilio

This happy student bar picks up in buzz in the summer months as punters crowd the outdoor tables and occasional live music is staged. Together with the nearby Al Chioschetto (see p141), it creates a lively summertime corner in Dorsoduro.

TAVERNA DA BAFFO Map pp250-2

☎ 041 520 88 62; Campiello Sant'Agostin 2346; ☻ 7am-2am Mon-Sat; vaporetto San Tomà

Named after Casanova's licentious poet pal, Giorgio Baffo, and lined with his rhymes in praise of 'the round arse' and other parts of the female body, this bar has a young, chirpy feel. In summer the tables outside are an especially pleasant spot to sip on a *spritz* or two, and the beers are good too.

VINUS VENEZIA Map pp256-8

☎ 041 71 50 04; Calle del Scaleter 3961; ☻ 10am-midnight; vaporetto San Tomà

This is a classy new spot for tasting wines in an area better known for its more ebullient student bars. The clean crisp lines of this timber-bedecked bar create a pleasing ambience for wine-hopping across Italy and beyond.

SESTIERI DI SAN POLO & SANTA CROCE

The options around these parts are limited but a couple of places are worth seeking out.

AI POSTALI Map pp250-2

☎ 041 71 51 76; Fondamenta Rio Marin 821; ☻ 6pm-2am, sometimes later, Mon-Sat; vaporetto Ferrovia

This is a buzzy locals' bar along the Rio Marin. Roberto gave up flying for Alitalia to pilot this place, which in years gone by served as an early opener for dawn posties.

BAGOLO Map pp250-2

☎ 041 277 08 50; Campo San Giacomo dell'Orio, Santa Croce 1584; ☻ 7am-2am; vaporetto Riva de Biasio

This place, with its timber floors and low lighting inside and candlelit tables outside on the *campo*, has added a little nocturnal adrenalin to this pretty square, aided and abetted by a couple of busy spots round the corner on Calle del Tintor.

SESTIERE DI CANNAREGIO

There are some noisy (and noisome) bar-restaurants along the main drag leading away from the train station that fill with day-trippers tanking up on huge beakers of amber fluid after a hard day's sight-seeing. You may well be inclined to leave this lot to the fast-drinking, unsteady newbies and proceed instead to a more pleasant local scene around Fondamente della Misericordia.

LA FONDAMENTA Map pp250-2

☎ 041 71 73 15; Fondamenta della Misericordia

Entertainment – Drinking

2578; 🕐 11am-3pm & 5pm-2am Fri-Wed; vaporetto Madonna dell'Orto

This cheap and cheerful restaurant is nothing special, but people tend to use it as a bar as well later in the evening.

OSTERIA AGLI ORMESINI Map pp250-2
☎ 041 71 38 34; Fondamenta degli Ormesini 2710; 🕐 7pm-2am Mon-Sat; vaporetto Madonna dell'Orto

Oodles of wine and 120 types of bottled beer in one knockabout little place? Perhaps you should get along to this *osteria*. It's something of a student haunt and tipplers spill out onto the *fondamenta* to enjoy their grog.

PARADISO PERDUTO Map pp250-2
☎ 041 72 05 81; Fondamenta della Misericordia 2539; 🕐 Thu-Sat & Mon-Tue; vaporetto Madonna dell'Orto

This hip eatery (see p132) also serves quite handsomely as a bar, and they occasionally organise a little live music.

THE FIDDLER'S ELBOW Map p253
☎ 041 523 99 30; Corte dei Pali 3847; 🕐 5pm-1am Thu-Tue; vaporetto Ca' d'Oro

On the Irish scene, this place is representative of the genre. It's warm, fusty and cosy, and in summer they set up a few tables on the street.

ZENEVIA Map p253
☎ 041 520 62 22; Salizzada San Canciano 5548; 🕐 5pm-2am Wed-Mon; vaporetto Ca d'Oro

A rambunctious place with blaring music and a reasonable selection of beers, this bar gets noisy with a young, largely Italian crowd. Some pile in for the live music on Thursdays while others want to see the live Italian football on TV.

SESTIERE DI CASTELLO

There's not a helluva lot happening in Castello at night but there is at least one bright exception.

ZANZIBAR Map pp254-5
☎ 339 200 68 31; Fondamenta Santa Maria Formosa 5840; 🕐 9am-1am; vaporetto Rialto

This is a crooked little kiosk that looks set to crumble into the canal provides some great life-theatre entertainment. Pull up a seat on the square, settle in for a few people-watching drinks to the thumping music emanating from the kiosk bar, and enjoy.

CLUBBING

The club and dancing scene (locals call a club a *discoteca*) in Venice is virtually zero. One or two possibilities are available, but if you are looking for serious clubbing action you are in the wrong place! Things look up a little in summer, when a handful of places open on the Lido, but the real action then is out at Jesolo (see p144), on the coast to the northeast of Venice.

> ## Gay & Lesbian Options
>
> The pickings in Venice are extremely slim. Specifically gay or lesbian bars are conspicuous by their absence. A couple of gay spots lurk on the mainland (they're listed here under Clubbing). Otherwise, you'll have to travel to Padua to broaden your options a little.

In Italy, clubs for the young, student-age set tend to be placed well out of the way, in the countryside or small towns. Generally, the only way to get to them is to drive, and you need to be right up to date with what's in and what's out. The same is true around Venice. Get hold of *VeNews* for some specific ideas.

The national right-wing government was looking at passing a law in 2003 that would oblige all clubs to shut at 3am. The aim is to reduce the frightening road toll among youngsters but has club owners and night owls alike up in arms.

Expect to pay anything from €5 to €20 to get into a club. This may include the first drink.

SESTIERE DI DORSODURO

PICCOLO MONDO Map pp256-8
☎ 041 520 03 71; Calle Corfu 1506; 🕐 midnight-4am Tue-Sun; vaporetto Accademia

This teensy little disco and bar is a bit on the slimy side, but perfectly all right in its own wide-lapel fashion. It pulls a 30-plus crowd and the uncared-for retro décor (can we call it that?) harks to the 1970s.

ROUND MIDNIGHT Map pp256-8
☎ 041 523 20 56; Fondamenta dello Squero 3102; 🕐 7pm-4am Mon-Sat Sep-May; vaporetto Ca' Rezzonico

After you're through hanging about on Campo Santa Margherita, head around to this drink-and-dance cove on a nearby back canal. You can sip on all sorts of cocktails and even get a snack. The music tends towards acid jazz and Latin. Although open quite early, you'll be lucky to see a soul in here before midnight.

SESTIERE DI CANNAREGIO

CASANOVA Map pp250-2
☎ 041 524 06 64; Rio Terrà Lista di Spagna 158/a; ☽ 6pm-4am Tue & Thu-Sat; vaporetto Ferrovia
A quick stumble from the train station, this is it, about the only place in Venice that can vaguely call itself a disco (and it really is more disco than club). Each night has its own musical theme, from rock revival on Thursday to Latin on Friday and thumping techno on Saturday.

LIDO DI VENEZIA

PACHUKA Map p248
☎ 041 242 00 20; Spiaggia San Nicolò; ☽ 8.30am-4am Wed-Mon Oct-May, 8.30am-4am daily Jun-Sep; vaporetto Lido + taxi
The most reliable of the Lido's summertime dance spots, this place right on the beach works year round as a snack bar and pizzeria but at night, especially on summer weekends, cranks up as a bit of a beachside dance club.

MESTRE & AROUND

Mestre and a couple of small towns on the mainland have a handful of clubs, a couple of them gay, and host basically a local crowd of mainlanders (who far outnumber those living in Venice itself). If you have your own transport they are all accessible. If you have the patience for night buses from Mestre, a couple are also possible. Otherwise it's a taxi.

GOSSIP DISCO
☎ 347 580 81 52; Via San Marco 106, Ponte di Brenta; ☽ 11pm-4am; taxi
This is one of the few gay clubs operating in the hinterland of Venice. You might be able to get a bus here from Piazzale Roma but to get back you'll be reliant on taxis, which can be scarce.

INSOMNIA
☎ 0421 30 97 80; Via dell'Armi 31, San Donà di Piave; ☽ 11pm-4am Thu-Sun; taxi

On the edge of this small town is one of the few busy gay clubs in the whole area. Go-go boys animate the mood, which is also given a fillip with the occasional live show. It's near the Billa supermarket on the edge of town.

MAGIC BUS
☎ 041 595 21 51; www.magicbus.it; Via delle Industrie 118, Marcon; ☽ Fri & Sat; taxi
Here you can expect the unexpected – anything from rock nights to more experimental electronic stuff.

METRÒ VENEZIA Map p261
☎ 041 538 42 99; Via Cappuccina 82/b, Mestre; admission €14; ☽ 2pm-2am daily; train or N2 night bus
This is basically a gay sauna, with various sauna and massage rooms but also a bar. Rather than a dark room they have a dark labyrinth!

T.A.G. CLUB Map p261
☎ 041 92 19 70; Via Giustizia 19, Mestre; ☽ 10pm-5am Wed, Fri & Sat; train or N1 night bus
A mix of local live bands followed by DJs pumping out a predictable but enjoyable mix of house and rock keeps this small club busy.

ZOO URBAN DANCE Map p248
☎ 041 541 51 00; Via Ca' Zorzi 2, Tessera; admission up to €20; ☽ 11pm-4am Fri & Sat; bus Nos 5 & 55 or taxi
The best club offering in the Mestre area is this venue, near Marco Polo airport. In four dance spaces you can weave from house to Latin rhythms or mainstream pop.

LIDO DI JESOLO

About one hour's drive from Venice, this seaside resort is where the nightlife really is from June to September, with more than half a dozen places to chose from. ATVO bus No 10a from Piazzale Roma takes about 70 minutes and costs €3.80 (€6.20 return). The problem is getting back: buses don't run particularly late. If you find a taxi, you are looking at €80 or more, depending on traffic.

IL MURETTO
☎ 348 410 11 20; www.ilmuretto.net (Italian only); Via Roma Destra 120/d; admission up to €25; ☽ 10pm-5am Sat; bus or taxi

This is one of the hippest nocturnal dance locales. An army of DJs spin mostly house. Flyers for this place can be seen floating around as far away as bars in Padua. A couple of other spots are located on the same road.

SOUND GARDEN
☎ 0421 97 19 02; Via Aleardi/Piazza Mazzini;
🕑 10pm-4am Tue-Sat; bus or taxi
Sound Garden concentrates on rock (sometimes of the hard variety) and features live

bands on Friday. It is one of the old stalwarts of Jesolo.

TERRAZZAMARE
☎ 041 37 00 12; www.terrazzamare.com; Vicolo Faro 1;
🕑 10pm-4am Tue-Sat; bus or taxi
Sitting on a beach at the southern end of Lido di Jesolo is this classic self-described 'theatre-bar'. Music thumps into the night and punters often groove in the sand. Theme nights dot the summer calendar.

LIVE MUSIC

Tickets & Reservations

Tickets for the classical and baroque music performances staged by several groups in various churches and *scuole* (religious confraternities) around Venice can generally be purchased on the spot, from touts around town (hard to miss as they generally dress in 18th-century kit) or from travel agents like **Agenzia Kele & Teo** (Map pp254-5; ☎ 041 520 87 22; Ponte dei Baratteri, San Marco). For jazz and other live music gigs, you generally pay at the door.

CLASSICAL & BAROQUE

Musical ensembles dressed in billowing 18th-century costume regularly perform concerts of baroque and light classical music from about Easter to the end of September. These shows are clearly aimed at tourists and can be cheesy but the musical quality is not necessarily bad. Those listed here (there are still others) change venues, so check when purchasing tickets.

CONCERTI DELLA VENEZIA MUSICA
Map p259
☎ 041 523 10 96, 041 520 87 67; www.vivaldi.it; La Pietà, Riva degli Schiavoni, Castello 4149; tickets adult/student €25/13; 🕑 Apr-Sep; vaporetto San Zaccaria
This group, divided into several different ensembles such as the five-member Putte di Vivaldi (Vivaldi's Girls) and the grander I Virtuosi dell'Ensemble (Virtuosos Ensemble), performs a range of Venetian baroque music, usually at the church where Vivaldi himself often worked, the Chiesa di Santa Maria della Visitazione (La Pietà) in Castello. At the time of writing, the group was temporarily based at Ca'Papafava in Cannaregio.

I MUSICI VENEZIANI Map pp254-5
☎ 041 521 02 94; www.imusicivveneziani.com; Scuola Grande di San Teodoro, Campo San Salvador, San Marco 4811; tickets €16-31; 🕑 Apr-Sep; vaporetto Rialto
Resplendent in 18th-century garb, these musicians offer a fairly broad repertory that ventures into a little opera, although some shows can be

strictly instrumental. Performances can range from morsels of Mozart to bits of Offenbach.

ORCHESTRA DI VENEZIA Map pp256-8
☎ 041 522 81 25; www.orchestra.venezia.it; Chiesa di San Samuele, San Marco 3202; tickets €17-25;
🕑 Apr-Sep; vaporetto San Samuele
The Orchestra di Venezia includes dance in its programme and is decidedly Venetian in its approach, sticking with Vivaldi, Albinoni and company.

JAZZ, ROCK & CONTEMPORARY

A handful of eateries and bars such as **Paradiso Perduto** (p143) and **Caffè Blue** (p141) intermittently put on live music, usually jazz, blues and mild pop.

Very occasionally you can see bands play in Venice. Otherwise you'll need to go to Mestre or even Padua.

In summer, occasional concerts are organised in Jesolo – watch the local press. A big rock event is **Jesolo Beach Bum** (the Italian rendering of the English 'boom'), usually held over a weekend at the beginning of July. In Mestre's Forte Marghera area, the big annual event is **Marghera Estate Village** (the name changes from one year to the next), a programme of nightly live music, from rock to ethnic, that runs from late June right through the summer.

AL VAPORE Map p261
☎ 041 93 07 96; Via Fratelli Bandiera 8, Marghera;

admission varies; ⊙ 7pm-2am Tue-Sun; train or bus Nos 6, 6B, 66 & N2

About the best place for a consistent programme of jazz, blues and other music is this spot in the rather dispiriting Marghera, on the mainland. Concerts start at 9.30pm and finish at midnight.

JAM CLUB Map p261

☎ 339 413 89 65; www.jamclubvenice.com; Via della Crusca 34; ⊙ 11pm-5am Wed & Fri-Sun; taxi

A dirt road leads to this house of alternative rock, dark wave and various other waves of underground music. Bands and DJs from Europe, the USA and even Australia make their way here.

FILM

The city doesn't have an English-language cinema. The time to see foreign cinema in the original language is during the Venice International Film Festival in September (see p11).

CINEMA DANTE D'ESSAI Map p261

☎ 041 538 16 55; Via Sernaglia 12, Mestre; train or bus No 1

This is the best bet in Mestre for good flicks.

CINEMA GIORGIONE MOVIE D'ESSAI
Map p253

☎ 041 522 62 98; Rio Terrà di Franceschi, Cannaregio 4612; vaporetto Fondamente Nuove

This modern cinema also frequently presents quality movies.

MULTISALA ASTRA Map pp262-3

☎ 041 526 57 36; Via Corfu 9; vaporetto Lido

This new cinema shows a broad range of art-house movies and mainstream releases.

SUMMER ARENA Map pp256-8
Campo San Polo; ⊙ Jul-Aug; vaporetto San Silvestro

This cinema under the stars is set up in Campo San Polo in the hot months of summer – local residents can watch the movie from their windows!

VIDEOTECA PASINETTI Map pp250-2

☎ 041 524 13 20; Palazzo Carminati, Santa Croce 1882; vaporetto San Stae

This film archive and research centre occasionally puts on film nights featuring classics.

THEATRE, OPERA & DANCE

Although some fine opera comes to Venice, dramatic theatre and ballet are a little more limited. Local theatre-lovers dream of liberation from what seems to them an endless diet of Shakespeare and Goldoni, although the scene is not as restricted as that. A smattering of fringe stuff surfaces from time to time.

Tickets & Reservations

Tickets are available directly from the theatre concerned, usually one hour before the show. To book in advance you can call or go online as indicated under individual entries.

A national centralised ticket office with local outlets is **Box Office** (☎ 041 94 02 00; www.boxoffice.it), which has a few agents in Venice, including the travel agency **Gran Canal Viaggi** (Map pp254-5; ☎ 041 271 21 11; Ponte dell'Ovo, San Marco 4759/4760). You can also book tickets with credit cards over the phone or online.

For some events, you can get tickets at **Vela** outlets (Map pp250-2 & 254-5; ☎ 041 24 24; www.velaspa.com), which are part of the ACTV. Vela has kiosks in front of the train station, at Piazzale Roma, at the San Marco ACTV office and at the Venice Pavilion Infopoint.

CENTRO CULTURALE BOLDÙ Map p253

☎ 041 529 48 12; www.sumonline.it (Italian only); Campiello Santa Maria Nova, Cannaregio 6000; vaporetto Rialto

This association organises all sorts of events, from poetry readings to impromptu theatre by budding local wordsmiths. It's not always grand quality but provides a lively alternative to mainstream stuff.

KAIRÓS Map pp256-8

☎ 041 241 35 30; Calle delle Botteghe, Dorsoduro 3170; vaporetto Ca' Rezzonico

This local theatrical association stages intimate performances of local theatre, sometimes in Venetian dialect, and usually followed by a drop of wine and snacks. The centre runs courses in everything from theatre for kids to shiatsu.

Faltering Phoenix

From as far off as the Ponte della Libertà, the flames could be seen shooting into the night sky as the pride of the city, the Teatro La Fenice, burned to the ground on 29 January 1996. Built in 1792, the theatre was a tangible link with the final days of the Republic. The horseshoe-shaped auditorium created exquisite acoustics. Before a fire in 1836, various opera greats, including Rossini, Bellini and Donizetti, had made their mark here. Rebuilt within two years, the theatre's halcyon days came with the years of close association with Giuseppe Verdi. As the 20th century dawned, a more international flavour dominated, with works by composers such as Britten and Prokofiev staged. All the greats have graced its stage, from Callas to Pavarotti.

If the manner of the theatre's demise was lamentable, the story of its return to brilliance is perhaps even more so. The then mayor, Massimo Cacciari, vowed to have it back in action by 2000. But the mysterious circumstances of the fire and subsequent irregularities in the awarding of contracts brought things to a halt. Cacciari's successor, Paolo Costa, sacked the building companies and started again, awarding the contract to a local firm that would work 16 hours a day to have the theatre ready for a big reopening with Riccardo Muti in December 2003. At the time of writing work was on schedule and fingers crossed.

TEATRINO GROGGIA Map p249
☎ 041 524 46 65; Parco Villa Groggia, Cannaregio 3161; vaporetto Sant'Alvise
In this tiny space performances ranging from contemporary theatre through to classical music recitals dot the calendar, generally on Friday and Saturday nights only.

TEATRO A L'AVOGARIA Map pp256-8
☎ 041 520 92 70; Corte de l'Avogaria, Dorsoduro 1617; vaporetto San Basilio
A tiny brass plate on the door of what looks like just another shuttered house tells you that you've reached this modest avant-garde theatre, which has been experimenting with unknown and new playwrights since the late 1960s.

TEATRO GOLDONI Map pp254-5
☎ 041 240 20 11; www.teatrogoldonive.it (Italian only); Calle Teatro Goldoni, San Marco 4650/b; tickets €15-42; vaporetto Rialto
Named after Venice's greatest playwright, this is the city's main drama theatre. It's not unusual for Goldoni's plays to be performed here – after all, what better location? But all sorts of events, including music concerts, also take place.

TEATRO LA FENICE Map pp256-8
☎ 041 78 65 11; www.teatrolafenice.it; Campo San Fantin, San Marco 1970; tickets €10-95; vaporetto Santa Maria del Giglio
It's hoped that this phoenix *(fenice)* will rise by the end of 2003 (see the boxed text above). Its replacement since 1996 has been the **PalaFenice** (Map p249; Isola del Tronchetto), but what the fate of this big-top theatre will be when the Fenice comes back to life is anyone's guess. Until then it continues to host most of the city's operas, sharing the load with the **Teatro Malibran** (Map p253; Calle del Teatro, San Marco 5870).

TEATRO TONIOLO Map p261
☎ 041 97 16 66; Piazzetta C Battisti 1, Mestre; admission up to €20; train or bus No 1
This busy theatre in the centre of Mestre puts on eclectic programmes ranging from Shakespeare to local drama, occasionally in dialect.

TEATRO VERDE Map pp262-3
Isola di San Giorgio Maggiore; vaporetto San Giorgio
This open-air theatre belonging to the Fondazione Cini comes to life in summer for performances tied in with the Biennale.

CASINOS

People under 18 are not allowed in to the following gambling dens.

CASINÒ DI VENEZIA Map pp250-2
☎ 041 529 71 11; www.casinovenezia.it; Palazzo Vendramin-Calergi, Cannaregio 2040; admission €5; ☼ 3pm-3am daily; vaporetto San Marcuola
There's something distinguished about stepping off a water taxi at the Grand Canal entrance to this mansion and going in for a night on the tables. This is old-world class – it's no surprise there's a dress code (jacket and tie).

VENICE CASINO Map p248
☎ 041 529 71 11; www.casinovenezia.it; Ca' Noghera, Via Triestina 002, Tessera; admission €5; ☼ 11am-4.45am Sun-Fri, 11am-6am Sat; free shuttle bus from Piazzale Roma
If quantity is more important to you than ambience, then this might be the casino for you. It's Italy's premier mainland gambling house and is near the airport. The dress code is casual.

SPORTS, HEALTH & FITNESS

Tickets & Reservations

Tickets to see the local football side, **AC Venezia** (☎ 041 238 07 11; www.veneziacalcio.it – Italian only), are available at the stadium itself (see Football, below) and from Vela outlets (see Theatre, Opera & Dance, p146). They can cost around €15 to €20 depending on the seat. Getting a ticket on the day is rarely a problem.

FOOTBALL

As elsewhere in Italy, *il calcio* (football) reigns supreme in the hearts and minds of many Venetians. Venezia, or the *arancioneroverde* (orange, black and greens), is a middling team hovering at the bottom of Serie B (2nd division). Since it was founded in 1907 it has all too rarely played in the top division.

The team plays at the **Stadio Penzo** (Map p249), on Isola di Sant'Elena at the far eastern end of the lagoon city. The uniqueness of the team's home town makes for some interesting logistics when the side plays at home. Special ferry services are laid on between Tronchetto car park and Sant'Elena. All buses arriving in Venice on a match day are diverted first to Tronchetto to disgorge their loads of fans before reaching Piazzale Roma.

GYM

Tucked away in hidden corners of Venice are a handful of gyms where you can get a work-out if walking around from one end of the city to the other is not enough.

PALESTRA BODY WORLD Map pp250-2

☎ 041 71 56 36; Calle del Ravano, Santa Croce 2196/a; ☾ 9am-10pm Mon-Fri, 9am-1pm Sat-Sun Sep-May; 9am-10pm Mon-Fri Jun-Aug; vaporetto San Stae
Here in a tiny lane is a decent gym with the usual options for cardiovascular exercise and body building. The emphasis is on the latter. Ten entries (valid for 60 days) cost €65.

PALESTRA CLUB DELFINO Map pp256-8

☎ 041 523 27 63; www.palestraclubdelfino.com; Fondamenta Zattere au Gesuati, Dorsoduro 788/a; ☾ 9am-10pm Mon-Fri, 9am-noon Sat; vaporetto Zattere
You could do a little jogging along the Fondamenta Zattere before wandering into this compact health club. You can sign up for a day (€13), but better value are the one-week (€44) and two-week (€69) passes.

ROWING

It comes as little surprise that Venetians are keen rowers. Venice and the lagoon count nine rowing clubs, all of which usually line up to participate in the many regattas held during the year.

REALE SOCIETÀ CANOTTIERI BUCINTORO Map pp254-5

☎ 041 522 20 55; www.bucintoro.org; Punta della Dogana, Dorsoduro 10; vaporetto Salute
The oldest rowing club in Venice was established in 1882. Inspired by the Oxbridge rowing clubs, it went on to furnish Italy with Olympic champions (the entire gold medal team at the 1952 Olympics were Bucintoro members). Nowadays the club boasts about 300 members. Outsiders are welcome to join. You can sign up for lessons in *voga alla veneta* (Venetian-style rowing, done standing up); eight lessons cost €80 and can be organised any time. It's also possible to join courses in *vela al terzo*, sailing with traditional lagoon vessels. These tend to take place late in spring or in September and require a minimum of five people.

SWIMMING POOLS

Opening hours are limited and complicated at both of the following pools – go along and pick up a copy of the latest timetable.

PISCINA COMUNALE A CHIMISSO Map p249

☎ 041 528 54 30; Sacca S Biagio, Giudecca; swim €4.50; ☾ Sep-Jun; vaporetto Sacca Fisola
This pool is often crowded but some semblance of lane discipline is maintained.

PISCINA COMUNALE DI SANT'ALVISE Map p249

☎ 041 71 35 67; Campo Sant'Alvise, Cannaregio 3161; swim €4.50; ☾ mid-Sep–mid-Jul; vaporetto Sant'Alvise
A slightly more modern pool, this one gets just as full and can be a little chaotic.

Shopping

Shopping

A city best seen on foot, Venice is a honeytrap for shopaholics. You will find it hard to resist wandering into an endless array of stores, purveying everything from Italian high fashion to exquisite Carnevale masks, from model gondolas to Murano glass, from antiques to old lace.

What to Buy

Carnevale masks make beautiful souvenirs, but quality and price are uneven. You can find people selling masks on just about every canal corner, but for serious craftsmanship you have to look a little closer. The cheap touristy rubbish is manufactured industrially in Padua, for instance, and worthless. The genuine articles are carefully crafted objects in papier-mâché *(cartapesta)* or leather (although you can find some nice decorative porcelain versions). Several fine stores are listed here. Some of them double as grand costume stores too – these are the places to pick up your 18th-century clobber, powdered wig and tricorner hat to join in the grand masked balls of Carnevale.

The other two obvious objects of your retail desire will be Murano glass and Burano lace. The latter is clearly easier to take home but often just as pricey. Glass comes in all conceivable shapes and sizes, from elegant tableware to the most outlandish glass statuary – the sky is the limit in terms of price, size, imagination and…taste.

Occasionally you'll see ceramics shops. Although ceramics can't really be said to be at the forefront of traditional Venetian crafts (Gubbio, in Umbria, and several towns in Sicily are Italy's most renowned pottery producers), some pieces are particularly arresting.

One much less cumbersome way to remember a visit to Venice is by taking home images of the city. Several shops produce high-quality prints and etchings, and plenty of street stalls churn out cheap material. As long as you don't bend them on the way home, they can be a good, lightweight souvenir or gift. The serious art collector can also wallow in the splendours of a range of galleries.

Elegant glassware on display at L'Isola in San Marco (p153)

Venice is noted for its marbled paper *(carta marmorizzata)*, often made to traditional and evocatively named designs. It has become something of a hit with visitors and is used for all sorts of things, from expensive giftwrap to book covers.

Shopping Areas

The greatest concentration of Italian fashion brands is west of Piazza San Marco on and around Calle Larga XXII Marzo, Calle dei Fabbri, Calle Vallaresso and Frezzeria (Map pp254-5). If you can't make it to Milan, you'll find a good selection right here, with everything from Armani to Valentino. We haven't mentioned individual stores in this chapter because they are all bunched together in the same area.

For less high-flying clothes, shoes, accessories and jewellery, hunt around the narrow streets between San Marco and the Rialto, particularly the Mercerie and around Campo San Luca (Map pp254-5).

There is no shortage of workshops and showrooms full of Murano glass, particularly between San Marco and Castello (Map pp254-5) and, of course, on Murano itself – here you can also see glass-blowing. Shop around as quality and prices vary dramatically. Similarly, you can find Burano lace on the island and in stores scattered across the city centre.

Art-lovers should make for Dorsoduro. The city's single biggest concentration of galleries, containing all kinds of stuff, is on the streets between the Gallerie dell'Accademia and the Peggy Guggenheim Collection (Map pp256-8). A few stragglers line Calle del Bastion on the approach to the former Chiesa di San Gregorio just east of the Guggenheim. The area around Campo San Fantin in San Marco is replete with galleries and another area to look is Calle delle Carrozze, close to Palazzo Grassi in San Marco (Map pp256-8). Anyone looking for innovative, cutting-edge, contemporary art will be sorely disappointed in Venice, as most galleries peddle safer goods likely to appeal to a broad, passing tourist trade. Some galleries are one-person shows, where the artist has their own work for sale.

For arts and crafts, including Carnevale masks and costumes, ceramics and model gondolas, San Polo (Map pp256-8) is the place to look. You'll encounter some mouth-watering delicatessens and speciality food shops in the area too.

Top Five Shopping Areas

- **High Fashion** West of Piazza San Marco (Map pp254-5)
- **Carnevale Masks & Other Crafts** Sestiere di San Polo (Map pp256-8)
- **Art Galleries** Between Gallerie dell'Accademia and Peggy Guggenheim Collection in Dorsoduro (Map pp256-8)
- **Books** Sestiere di San Marco (Map pp254-5)
- **Glass** Murano (Map p265)

How to Shop

Venice bulges with shops and stands hoping to sell you anything they can, from extreme kitsch to serious art. Traps abound. One basic rule applies to all purchases – shop around.

Some people love cheap kitsch souvenirs (pencil sharpeners in the shape of the Campanile in Piazza San Marco, gondoliers' hats, cheap little masks and so on). That's fine and you'll find plenty of this all over the more frequented parts of town (like along Rio Terrà Lista di Spagna on the way from the train station to Piazza San Marco, Map pp250-2). Know that it's basically rubbish and try to haggle the price down.

Haggling is not an option in most straightforward stores (supermarkets, clothing stores and the like) but can be a useful skill in certain shops retailing higher-quality souvenirs. Murano glass is a good example. Shop around carefully and when you find something you like, see if you can get the price down.

As a rule, heavy, cumbersome and fragile items (this especially means glass, ceramics and some antiques) need to be shipped home. Many stores will take care of this for you and include the costs of shipping in the price. Ask before you buy, as shipping it yourself can be a pain. If you do find yourself with something that you need to ship, head for the main post office (Map pp254-5).

Opening Hours

In general, shops are open 9am to 1pm and 3.30pm to 7.30pm (or 4pm to 8pm) Monday to Saturday. They may remain closed on Monday morning or Wednesday and/or Saturday afternoon. Laws on opening hours are fairly flexible so shopkeepers have a large degree of discretion. Many shops whose customers are mostly tourists will also open on Sunday. On the other hand, some shops close for the holidays for all or part of August. Department stores such as Coin and most supermarkets are open 9.30am to 7.30pm Monday to Saturday. Some even open 9am to 1pm on Sunday.

In the following reviews, opening hours are given only if they differ from general opening hours by more than half an hour.

SESTIERE DI SAN MARCO

Eating p124; Entertainment p139; Sestieri p49; Sleeping p164

This is the core of old Venice, its most venerable face and predictably where the highest class of city shopping is concentrated. Prices are high and there's loads of tourist tat too.

A+A Map pp256-8   *Art Gallery*
☎ 041 277 04 66; Calle Malipiero 3073; vaporetto San Samuele

Slovenia runs this curious exhibition space dedicated to contemporary artists, mostly but not exclusively Slovenian.

ANTIQUUS Map pp256-8   *Antiques*
☎ 041 520 63 95; Calle Crosera 3131; vaporetto San Samuele

This inviting shop along Calle delle Botteghe, where several antiques stores reside, boasts a solid collection of old masters, silver and antique jewellery. In among the few items of furniture sit grand tea sets and other aristocratic bric-a-brac.

BUGNO ART GALLERY
Map pp254-5   *Art Gallery*
☎ 041 523 13 05; Campo San Fantin 1996/a; vaporetto Vallaresso/San Marco

This gallery has some works by contemporary artists on permanent display, although money is the object. While you might not be able to afford a Miró or De Chirico, there's plenty of other material for the modern art collector. Needless to say, this is not a hobby for anybody short of Rockefeller status.

CODOGNATO Map pp254-5   *Jewellery*
☎ 041 522 50 42; Calle Seconda dell'Ascensione 1295; vaporetto Vallaresso/San Marco

Possibly the city's best-known jeweller, Codognato sells classic pieces that attracted the likes of Jackie Onassis in their time.

FIORELLA GALLERY Map pp256-8   *Fashion*
☎ 041 520 92 28; Campo Santo Stefano 2806; vaporetto Accademia

All sorts of odd, billowing and fantastical clothing items adorn the transsexual doge mannequins scattered about the inside and in the windows of this unique store. High fashion it ain't, but definitely a source of curiosity.

GALLERIA MARINA BAROVIER
Map pp256-8   *Glass*
☎ 041 522 61 02; Calle delle Carrozze 3216; vaporetto San Samuele

Marina Barovier is one of the key names in quality Murano glass, and this store is a handy outlet for assessing just how expensively exquisite pieces can be.

GALLERIA TRAGHETTO
Map pp256-8   *Art Gallery*
☎ 041 522 11 88; Calle di Piovan 2543; vaporetto Santa Maria del Giglio

A stalwart on the Venetian art scene, this is one of the most respected of the few Venetian galleries dealing in contemporary art, most of it Italian but open to international flavours.

IL PAPIRO
Map pp256-8   *Marbled Paper & Stationery*
☎ 041 522 30 55; Calle del Piovan 2764; ☾ Mon-Sun; vaporetto Santa Maria del Giglio

A bright, spacious stationer's, Il Papiro doesn't pretend to compete with the handful of traditional marbled paper shops around town. Among a modest selection of such items you will also find anything from elegant envelopes to letter openers and quills.

JESURUM Map pp254-5   *Lace*
☎ 041 520 60 85; Merceria del Capitello 4856; vaporetto Rialto

Jesurum has been in business since 1860 and remains one of the big names in lace – and the prices are commensurate. There's a smaller branch on Piazza San Marco too.

LEGATORIA PIAZZESI

Map pp256-8   *Marbled Paper*
☎ 041 522 12 02; Campiello della Feltrina 2551/c; vaporetto Santa Maria del Giglio

At the Legatoria Piazzesi, the oldest purveyor of quality paper products in Venice, time-honoured methods are employed to turn out high-class (and high-priced) items. It is a dark but tempting treasure trove.

LIBRERIA GOLDONI Map pp254-5   *Books*
☎ 041 522 23 84; Calle dei Fabbri 4742; vaporetto Rialto

One of the city's establishment bookshops, the Libreria Goldoni has an impressive range of material on Venice in Italian, English and French, as well as a broad selection of books covering most subjects in Italian.

LIBRERIA AL PONTE Map pp254-5   *Books*
☎ 041 522 40 30; Calle Cortesia 3717/d; vaporetto Rialto

This small but useful shop offers a solid range of guides and other books on Venice, as well as children's books, many in English. It stocks a good assortment of Donna Leon's mystery detective yarns.

L'ISOLA Map pp254-5   *Glass*
☎ 041 523 19 73; Salizzada San Moisè 1468; vaporetto Vallaresso/San Marco

L'Isola has glass objects by Carlo Moretti, much appreciated for their elegance and finesse. The prices aren't exactly low.

LIVIO DE MARCHI Map pp256-8   *Crafts*
☎ 041 528 56 94; Salizzada San Samuele 3157/a; vaporetto San Samuele

This place, with wooden sculptures of under-pants, socks and shirts, is rather strange but endearing all the same. Just what you might do with a fine carving of an unironed shirt in your living room is another question.

MARTINUZZI Map pp254-5   *Lace*
☎ 041 522 50 68; Piazza San Marco 67/a; vaporetto Vallaresso/San Marco

This is one of the city's oldest sellers of Burano lace products. The work is of a high standard.

SAN MARCO STUDIUM Map pp254-5 *Books*
☎ 041 522 23 82; Calle Canonica 337/a; vaporetto San Zaccaria

Just off Piazza San Marco, this shop has books piled high on every available square centimetre of space. You'll find a broad offering of English-language guides and books on Venice.

SCHOLA SAN ZACCARIA

Map pp256-8   *Prints & Posters*
☎ 041 523 43 43; Campo San Maurizio, San Marco 2664; vaporetto Santa Maria del Giglio

In this intriguing place you will find only works depicting characters of the commedia dell'arte, such as Arlecchino (Harlequin). The movement and colour in some of the paintings and prints make them stand out from much of the standard Venetian fare.

THE DISNEY STORE Map pp254-5   *Toys*
☎ 041 522 39 80; Campo San Bartolomeo 5257; vaporetto Rialto

Saved by Lace

Perhaps it helped stave off boredom when their men were out fishing. Burano's business of lace-making goes back at least to the 14th century, when the Duchess Morosina Morosini, wife of Doge Morosini, set up a lace workshop on the island employing 130 people. The workshop closed at her death, but a habit had been formed and Venetian lace was already winning a name for itself.

By the 16th century it was in big demand throughout the courts of Europe and produced in various locations around the lagoon, including Burano and Pellestrina. They say the Sun King of France, Louis XIV, wore a black collar of Burano lace that had taken two years to make! The French eventually enticed some Burano lace-workers to Paris, and by the end of the 17th century France was producing it on an industrial scale. It was, however, Napoleon's march into Venice and the collapse of the Republic in 1797 that finally killed off the industry.

The rebirth of lace-making on Burano came when the Countess Adriana Marcello opened a lace-making school there in 1872. All seem to agree that the idea of reviving the industry came in part as a response to the extreme hardship the island's fishing families were experiencing. By the end of the 19th century Burano lace had again attained its worldwide reputation. The school was closed in 1970, and today the number of island women who still know and practise this delicate art is dwindling fast.

All right, perhaps you'll think it's as bad as mentioning McDonald's. Fact is, kids love Disney toys and this place may well save a failing parental relationship with loved little ones.

VALESE
Map pp254-5   *Crafts*
☎ 041 522 72 82; Calle Fiubera 793; vaporetto Vallaresso/San Marco

Since 1918 the Valese family has cast figures in bronze, copper and other metals here. Their reputation is unequalled in the city. Some items, such as the ornamental horses that adorn the flanks of the city's gondolas, suggest themselves more readily as souvenirs than others.

VIVALDI STORE
Map pp254-5   *CDs*
☎ 041 522 13 43; Salizzada del Fontego dei Tedeschi 5537; vaporetto Rialto

Can't get the sounds of Vivaldi out of your mind? If you need a CD of music related to Venice, pop by here. Cristiano Nalesso specialises in all things Venetian, ranging from the Renaissance through to Baroque and including recordings by some of the better baroque groups that perform in Venice, notably Rondó Veneziano.

SESTIERE DI DORSODURO
Eating p125; Entertainment p140 & 143; Sestieri p58; Sleeping p166

Art is the word to sum up shopping here. You can inspect the many galleries on and near the short route separating Peggy Guggenheim's modern collection from the classics of the Gallerie dell'Accademia. Can't afford the real thing? You'll find some good print shops too.

BAC ART STUDIO
Map pp256-8   *Prints & Posters*
☎ 041 522 81 71; Campo San Vio 862; vaporetto Accademia

This studio has paintings, aquatints and engravings signed by two local artists, Cadore and Paolo Baruffaldi, that make fine gifts. Cadore concentrates his commercial efforts on Venetian scenes, while Baruffaldi depicts masked people. The store is a good place for quality postcards too.

CA' MACANA
Map pp256-8   *Carnevale Masks & Costumes*
☎ 041 520 32 29; Calle delle Botteghe 5176; vaporetto Ca' Rezzonico

Top Five Craft Shops

- **Jesurum** (p152) Exquisite lace
- **Ca' Macana** (below) Carnevale masks
- **Galleria Marina Barovier** (p152) High-class glass
- **Atelier Pietro Longhi** (p156) Gala costumes
- **Arca** (opposite) Ceramics

Wander in and watch the artists at work on the raw papier-mâché of future masks. Apparently Stanley Kubrick was impressed – he made a rather large order for his last picture, *Eyes Wide Shut*. Along black walls the finished products gaze down at you, beckoning to be donned.

CARTOLERIA ACCADEMIA
Map pp256-8   *Art Supplies*
☎ 042 520 70 86; Campo Santa Margherita 2928; vaporetto Ca' Rezzonico

This store has been selling artists' supplies since 1810, so it must have some idea! The place looks a little like no renovations have been done since it first opened but it offers a decent range of materials.

GALLERIA FERRUZZI
Map pp256-8   *Prints & Posters*
☎ 041 520 59 96; Fondamenta Ospedaleto 523; vaporetto Accademia

Ferruzzi's images of Venice are an engaging, almost naive distortion of what we see. With fat brushstrokes and primary colours, the artist creates a kind of children's gingerbread Venice. On sale are screen prints, paintings and postcards.

IL BAULE BLU
Map pp256-8   *Toys*
☎ 041 71 94 48; Campo San Tomà 2916/a; vaporetto San Tomà

Come here for a luxury bear. The owners of this shop have turned cuddly bears into a business for aficionados. If you really can't live without your bear and have brought it along to Venice, be assured that the shop also operates a Teddy Hospital.

IL GRIFONE
Map pp256-8   *Leather*
☎ 041 522 94 52; Fondamenta del Gaffaro 3516; vaporetto Ferrovia

A virtually décor-free shopfront disguises this one-man leather workshop where you can get to grips with quality handmade bags, belts, wallets and other leather objects for quite reasonable prices.

IL PAVONE Map pp256-8 *Marbled Paper*
☎ 041 523 45 17; Fondamenta Venier dai Leoni 721;
vaporetto Accademia

The dominant colours (blues, reds or yellows)
and motifs (floral shapes, cherubs and others)
at Il Pavone change from one day to another.
The templates are applied to hand-printed
paper as well as ties and other objects. You
can have T-shirts made here too.

LE FORCOLE DI SAVERIO PASTOR
Map pp256-8 *Forcole & Oars*
☎ 041 522 56 99; Fondamenta Soranzo detta Fornace
341; vaporetto Salute

In need of an oar or, more importantly, a *forcola* to sit it on? These unique timber contrap-
tions could make a quirky decorative item, or
you might want one of the handful of souvenir
items Saverio makes on the side.

LEGNO E DINTORNI Map pp256-8 *Crafts*
☎ 041 522 63 67; Fondamenta Gherardini 2840;
vaporetto Ca' Rezzonico

Wonderful little wooden models of various
monuments and facades, akin to simple
3-D puzzles, are sold here. They make rather
refined gifts for kids, but wouldn't go amiss
with many an adult.

LORIS MARAZZI Map pp256-8 *Crafts*
☎ 041 523 90 01; Campo Santa Margherita 2903;
vaporetto Ca' Rezzonico

Like Livio de Marchi (see p153), Loris Marazzi
presents sculptures on a weird wooden
theme. The ideas are remarkably similar, suggesting there must be a customer base for this
kind of thing!

PEGGY GUGGENHEIM MUSEUM
SHOP Map pp256-8 *Books*
☎ 041 240 54 24; Dorsoduro 701; vaporetto Accademia

Located in the same building as the gallery of
the same name (but with a different entrance),
this shop offers a select array of coffee-table
books and souvenirs related to the gallery's
modern-art collections.

SESTIERI DI SAN POLO & SANTA CROCE

*Eating p126; Entertainment p142; Sestieri
p63; Sleeping p167*

These *sestieri* seem somehow more labyrinthine than the rest. In many of their

almost maddening nooks and crannies
lurk all sorts of surprises, from speciality
food stores to a series of quality mask and
costume workshops.

ALIANI Map p253 *Food & Drink*
☎ 041 522 49 13; Ruga Vecchia San Giovanni, San
Polo 654; vaporetto San Silvestro

For an outstanding collection of cheeses and
other delicatessen products, Aliani has long
been a favoured gastronomic stop in the
Rialto area.

A MANO Map pp256-8 *Crafts*
☎ 041 71 57 42; Rio Terrà, San Polo 2616; vaporetto
San Tomà

This shop is full of all sorts of decorative items,
all handmade. Quirky lampshades, mirrors and
a host of other gewgaws certainly make it an
interesting stop for some window-shopping.

ARCA Map pp250-2 *Ceramics*
☎ 041 71 04 27; Calle del Tintor, Santa Croce 1811;
vaporetto San Stae

The designs in this eye-catching shop are
powerful and, for some, the colours are possibly a little strong. Teresa della Valentina
paints her tiles and other ceramic objects in
bold, bright, deep colours.

*Colourful marbled paper, such as this collection at
Legatoria Piazzesi (p153), is a Venetian speciality*

Fill 'Er Up

Yes, it's all very fine sitting about posturing in fine restaurants, but sometimes you just want some plonk to have at home. And there's the question of cost – not everyone can afford to go out and invest in great-name labels.

Fortunately, apart from the wonderful option of sipping wines in a local *osteria* or *bacaro* (restaurant/bar), a fine take-home tradition persists in Venice. Every now and then you will stumble across a wine shop. You'll know you've hit one if you find it crammed with huge glass containers (the kind of 'bottle' even Hercules would have trouble slugging from) known as *damigiane*. From these monsters, each containing a sea of simple and quite acceptable Veneto table wine, you make a choice and have it poured into whatever you bring – used wine or mineral-water bottles, it's up to you. You will be charged, on average, €2 per litre.

A chain called **Nave de Oro** has at least five branches in Venice (listed below) and one each on the Lido and Murano. A handful of other places along the same lines can also be found. None opens on Sunday.

Cantina del Baffo (Map pp250-2; Fondamenta degli Ormesini, Cannaregio 2678; 🕙 8.30am-1pm & 4.30-7.30pm, afternoon only Wed)

Casa Mattiazi (Map pp256-8; Calle dell'Avogaria, Dorsoduro 1614; 🕙 8.30am-1pm & 4.30-7.30pm, morning only Wed)

Nave de Oro (Map pp250-2; Rio Terrà San Leonardo, Cannaregio 1370; 🕙 8am-1pm & 4.30-7.30pm, afternoon only Wed)

Nave de Oro (Map p253; Rio Terrà dei SS Apostoli 4657; 🕙 9am-1pm & 4-7.45pm, morning only Wed)

Nave de Oro (Map pp254-5; Calle Mondo Nuovo, Castello 5786/b; 🕙 9am-1pm & 5-7.45pm, morning only Wed)

Nave de Oro (Map pp256-8; Campo Santa Margherita, Dorsoduro 3664; 🕙 9am-1pm & 5-7.30pm, morning only Wed)

Nave de Oro (Map p259; Calle Santa Maria Formosa 5179; 🕙 9am-1pm & 5-7.45pm, morning only Wed)

Wine Shop (Nameless; Map pp250-2; Fondamenta di Cannaregio 1116; 🕙 8.30am-12.30pm & 4.30-7.30pm, morning only Wed)

ARTEMISIA Map pp256-8 *Art Supplies*
☎ 041 244 02 90; Campiello Zen, San Polo 972; vaporetto San Tomà

This well-stocked shop has just about everything imaginable for painting, restoration, sculpture and so on – perfect for the artist inspired by the lagoon city. Students get a 20% discount.

ATELIER PIETRO LONGHI
Map pp256-8 *Carnevale Masks & Costumes*
☎ 041 71 44 78; Rio Terrà, San Polo 2604/b; vaporetto San Tomà

This is the place to come if you've ever fancied buying a helmet and sword to go with your tailor-made Carnevale costume. Or indeed just about any kind of costume item from a Harlequin outfit through to 18th-century gala wear.

BAC ART STUDIO
Map pp256-8 *Prints & Posters*
☎ 041 523 11 08; Ruga Rialto, San Polo 1069; vaporetto San Silvestro

Another branch of the fine prints and posters store located in Dorsoduro (see p154).

CENERENTOLA Map pp256-8 *Lampshades*
☎ 041 527 44 55; Calle dei Saoneri, San Polo 2718; vaporetto San Tomà

Every conceivable kind of lampshade is on display here, but the tendency is towards classic pieces, often made of old embroidered cloth with a 19th-century feel – nothing slick and modern here. It also sells antique lace.

DROGHERIA MASCARI
Map p253 *Food & Drink*
☎ 041 522 97 62; Ruga degli Spezieri, San Polo 381; vaporetto Rialto

Not far from Aliani (p155), this is another foodies' classic. All sorts of goods in jars, salty and sweet, are accompanied by a mouth-watering range of sweets, including slabs of chocolate and nougat (especially around Christmas).

GILBERTO PENZO Map pp256-8 *Crafts*
☎ 041 71 93 72; Calle 2 dei Saoneri, San Polo 2681; vaporetto San Tomà

Here you can buy exquisite, hand-built wooden models of various Venetian vessels. Mr Penzo also takes in old ones for restoration. For the kids, you can fork out €25 for gondola model kits or buy them ready-made and painted. And round the corner, you can have a peek at his workshop. See the boxed text opposite.

JALLITS Map pp250-2 *Toys & Bric-a-brac*
☎ 041 71 37 51; Ramo Santa Maria Mater Domini, Santa Croce 2268/a; vaporetto San Stae

This is a fun and original shop with items that might interest adults and kids, like pencils topped with little animals, decorative pandas and rabbits that look more like brushes, and old-fashioned wooden toy trains, as well as general bric-a-brac.

L'ARLECCHINO
Map pp250-2   *Carnevale Masks & Costumes*
☎ 041 71 65 91; Calle dei Cristi, San Polo 1722-29; vaporetto San Silvestro
The folks at L'Arlecchino claim the masks are made only with papier-mâché to their own designs. To prove it you can inspect the workshop and see production from the earliest phases to the final touches. The quality of masks is evident and reflected in the price tags. There is another **branch** (Map pp254-5; ☎ 041 520 82 20; Ruga del Ravano, San Polo 789) nearby.

LA MARGHERITA CERAMICHE
Map pp250-2   *Ceramics*
☎ 041 72 31 20; Sotoportego de Siora Bettina, Santa Croce 2345; vaporetto San Stae
The contrast between this place and Arca (see p155) couldn't be greater. Margherita Rossetto's kitchen pots, clocks and other hand-painted items are all tranquil designs in soft blues and yellows – an altogether sunnier look.

LEGATORIA POLLIERO
Map pp256-8   *Marbled Paper*
☎ 041 528 51 30; Campo dei Frari, San Polo 2995; vaporetto San Tomà
Here is a traditional exponent of the art of Venetian bookbinding with (and without) marbled paper. You barely have room to stand when you penetrate this den, with piles of leather-bound books, paper-bound folders and all sorts of other stationery piled higgledy-piggledy to the rafters.

MANUELA CALZATURE Map pp256-8 *Shoes*
☎ 041 522 66 52; Ruga Rialto, San Polo 1046; vaporetto San Silvestro
This is a small family business with a nice range of shoes, including more expensive footwear that the family makes under its own name. Don't judge it by the cheap junk outside.

MAZZON LE BORSE
Map pp256-8   *Leather Goods*
☎ 041 520 34 21; Campiello San Tomà, San Polo 2807; vaporetto San Tomà

An unassuming store and workshop, Mazzon le Borse is a good place to shop for handmade leather bags and accessories. The goods are top class and often better than many of the big names (with their commensurately bigger prices).

MILLE E UNA NOTA
Map pp256-8   *Musical Instruments*
☎ 041 523 18 22; Calle di Mezzo, San Polo 1235; vaporetto San Silvestro
If during your stay in Venice you require strings for your guitar, or would like to acquire some new panpipes, a shiny new mouth organ or perhaps even a harp, this is the place.

PETER PAN Map pp250-2 *Masks*
☎ 041 71 64 20; Campo Santa Maria Mater Domini, Santa Croce 2118; vaporetto San Stae
Valentina Franceschini runs this delightful little mask shop, producing some nice stuff in both papier-mâché and porcelain.

TRAGICOMICA
Map pp256-8   *Carnevale Masks & Costumes*
☎ 041 72 11 02; Calle Nomboli, San Polo 2800; vaporetto San Tomà
This is one of the city's bigger mask and costume merchants, and is quite overwhelming at first sight. It also organises costume parties during Carnevale.

The Boat Man
Gilberto Penzo doesn't just make nice model boats. A Chioggia man, his life passion has been to painstakingly gather all the material he can on Venetian vessels past and present. His research has led him to write several books on the many kinds of traditional Venetian and lagoon vessels, many now extinct. It has also allowed him to construct detailed replicas. An engineer, Penzo comes from a shipbuilding family. His grandfather and earlier forebears built the classic Chioggia vessel, the *bragozzo*. Penzo found that one way to pay for his almost obsessive studies was to make models – which he does with equal love and attention. His best efforts wind up in museums and although scale models, he tries to get the details of construction as close to the real thing as he can. As the last of the great gondola-builders disappear (the death of master Giovanni Giuponi, aged 92, in 2002 caused quite a commotion in Venice), Penzo is fast becoming a last living repository of information on Venice's maritime history and traditions. As he points out, there were boats in Venice before there were palaces.

SESTIERE DI CANNAREGIO

Eating p129; Entertainment pp142 & 144; Sestieri p72; Sleeping p168

For the great majority of first arrivals in Venice, the train station is point A and one inevitably marches down the Lista di Spagna and its prolongation towards Piazza San Marco. The shopping around here is nothing to get the blood rushing but a few interesting exceptions stand out.

CAFFÈ COSTARICA

Map pp250-2   *Food & Drink*
☎ 041 71 63 71; Rio Terrà San Leonardo 1337; vaporetto San Marcuola

Since 1930 the Marchi family has been importing coffee from Costa Rica and other coffee-producing countries. They toast it up daily for your delectation. If you don't want to take any away, sip on your favourite mix at the bar.

COIN Map p253   *Department Store*
☎ 041 520 35 81; Salizzada San Giovanni Grisostomo 5790; 9.30am-7.30 Mon-Sat, 11am-7.30pm Sun; vaporetto Rialto

This is a rarity in Venice. Although not gargantuan, the store brings a bit of department-store action to canalside shoppers, with this branch specialising in affordable men's and women's clothes and accessories. Another branch on Campo San Luca (Map pp254-5) specialises in beauty products and accessories.

LABORATORIO BLU Map pp250-2   *Books*
☎ 041 71 58 19; Campo del Ghetto Vecchio 1224; vaporetto Guglie

A handy little children's bookshop, with a good selection in English as well as Italian for a range of ages.

LA STAMPERIA DEL GHETTO

Map pp250-2   *Prints*
☎ 041 275 02 00; Calle del Ghetto Vecchio 1185/a; vaporetto Guglie

Here you will encounter a pleasing collection of prints with general scenes of Venice as well as Ghetto and Jewish themes.

LIBRERIA DEMETRA Map pp250-2   *Books*
☎ 041 275 01 52; Campo San Geremia 282; 9am-midnight Mon-Sat,10am-midnight Sun; vaporetto Guglie

A limited range of paperbacks in several languages and some material on Venice, ranging from maps to cuisine guides, are sold in this handy store, a kind of book supermarket that stays open later than many restaurants!

MOLIN GIOCATTOLI Map p253   *Toys*
☎ 041 523 52 85; Salizzada San Canciano 5899; vaporetto Rialto

---

To Market, To Market

Hanging about Venice's handful of markets is in many ways more interesting than browsing shops. Here are the locals are out in force, searching for the perfect artichoke or halibut. Every now and then the local citizenry get the chance to potter about antique markets too.

Cannaregio Produce Market (Map pp250-2; Rio Terrà San Leonardo, Cannaregio) This bustling market stretched out along the main route from the train station to San Marco makes a handy stop for picking up some fruit and veg.

Dorsoduro Produce Market (Map pp256-8; Campo Santa Margherita, Dorsoduro) In the mornings you can stock up at this limited farm-produce market held in one of the city's most likable squares.

Pescaria (Fish Market; Map p253; Rialto, San Polo) Underneath the neo-Gothic roof built at the beginning of the 20th century, the fish market gets a mixed clientele of housewives and restaurateurs in search of ingredients for the day's menu. They have been selling fish here for 700 years.

Rialto Produce Markets (Map p253; Rialto, San Polo) The raucous cries of vendors rise above the general hubbub of canny shoppers rubbing shoulders with unsuspecting tourists wandering into the area for the first time. A favourite local item is the artichoke.

Mercatino Dei Miracoli (Map pp253 & 260; ☎ 041 274 73 15; Cannaregio/Castello) On the second or third weekend of each month a bric-a-brac fair is held either in the Campo San Canciano and the adjacent Campo Santa Maria Nova or along Via Giuseppe Garibaldi. You can turn up all sorts of odds and ends at this market and the atmosphere is always fun.

Mercatino dell'Antiquariato (Map pp256-8; ☎ 041 45 41 76; Campo San Maurizio, San Marco) Three times a year this antiques market sets up to the delight of collectors far and wide. It's a little hard to plan a visit around the market since it happens so infrequently (generally in April, September and December).

Shopping in the Ghetto

The Ghetto's tiny Jewish community is still busy and you'll discover a few curious shops around Ghetto Nuovo and along Calle del Ghetto Vecchio. They generally sell an odd mixture of Jewish art, souvenirs, books on Venice's ghetto and religious stuff. One such place is **Arte Ebraica** (Map pp250-2; ☎ 041 72 00 92; www.shalomvenice.com; Calle del Ghetto Vecchio 1218-1219). Ghetto shops are likely to be closed on Saturdays.

Nestled up along the bridge (locally known as Ponte dei Giocattoli – Toys Bridge), this shop will attract kids with a yearning for something more titillating than Tintoretto. Want a model Ferrari, or for that matter a model vaporetto?

SESTIERE DI CASTELLO

Eating p132; Entertainment p143; Sestieri p80; Sleeping p170

Castello backs on to the Sestiere di San Marco and so takes some of its overflow, whether you understand that to be grand monuments or the tourists who visit them. But as you head east things quickly quieten down into about the closest one comes to Venetian suburbia – fascinating to wander around in but a little short on retail stimulation.

CA' DEL SOLE

Map p259 *Carnevale Masks & Costumes*
☎ 041 528 55 49; Fondamenta dell'Osmarin 4964; vaporetto San Zaccaria
Although much of what is on sale here is aimed at the theatre business, anyone can purchase a fantasy in this 'House of the Sun'. The masks are of a high standard.

EDITORE FILIPPI Map pp254-5 *Books*
☎ 041 523 56 35; Calle Casselleria 5763; vaporetto San Zaccaria
Don't let the unremarkable appearance fool you. This is a den of books on all manner of subjects related to Venice, many published and on sale only here. The Filippis have been in the book business for nearly a century, and scholars search them out for their tomes and encyclopaedic knowledge.

LABORATORIO DEL GERVASUTI

Map p259 *Antiques*
☎ 041 523 67 77; Campo Bandiera e Moro, Castello 3725; vaporetto Arsenale

In a higgledy-piggledy workshop, enough goods are stacked to whet the appetite of any antiques collector. If you are a serious purchaser, ask about the warehouse, which you can arrange to see by appointment. Michele Gervasuti is continuing the work of his father, Eugenio, a master craftsman who opened the shop here in 1959.

LIBRAIRIE FRANÇAISE Map p259 *Books*
☎ 041 522 96 59; Barbaria delle Tole 6358; vaporetto Ospedale Civile
Voulez-vous vos livres en français? Here you will kind everything from the latest bestsellers of Gallic literature through to a plethora of tomes on all subjects Venetian – all of it in French.

AROUND THE LAGOON

Eating p134; Entertainment p144; Sestieri p88; Sleeping p180

There's not an awful lot to buy on most of the islands, but two stand out for their specialities. Murano has for centuries been the centre of Venetian glass production. Further away, the art of lace-making is associated with the little pastel-hued island of Burano. You can of course shop for glass and lace in Venice itself but there is something more 'real' about coming to the source. With a little luck, you'll see people making the stuff too!

On Murano, the bulk of the glass-sellers are congregated, as they should be, along and near Fondamenta dei Vetrai. Ever since the *vetrai*, or glass-makers, were transferred to the island at the close of the 13th century, this is where they have practised their art. You can see glass being blown in workrooms attached to some of the glass shops: look for the sign *'fornace'* (furnace).

Over on Burano, local ladies can occasionally be seen hunched on the front step or sitting in the shade near the vaporetto stop, busily plucking away at some new lace creation. The island's main drag, Via Galuppi,

Top Five Shops for Kids
- **Gilberto Penzo** (p156) Model gondolas
- **Il Baule Blu** (p154) Teddy bears
- **Legno e Dintorni** (p155) All sorts of gewgaws and toys in wood
- **Molin Giocattoli** (opposite) Toys and models
- **The Disney Store** (p153) An old favourite

The Noble Art of Glass-Blowing

Sparks fly off the glowing orange ball of flame inside the furnace. Twisted and twirled on the end of a long iron pole, the glob of glass is heated and shaped, heated and shaped. It is fascinating to watch the glass-makers of Murano at work.

It is thought the first glass-makers were ancient Phoenicians, who discovered that exposing sand to extreme temperatures caused it to melt and form a glassy paste. The blowpipe used for glass-blowing came into use in Palestine in the 1st century BC.

The Romans imported glass objects from the East. One of the first centres of glass production in Roman Italy seems to have been Aquileia, northeast of Venice. By the 11th century, Venetian glass-makers had learned the art from Aquileian refugees and colleagues in the East.

By 1291 all the glass-making kilns had been obliged to move to Murano for safety reasons (fires were common), but possibly also to better preserve the secrets of the glass-makers. Their work had achieved Europe-wide renown and was a valuable export product. It was long considered treason for a glass-worker to leave Venice. Most didn't try and some of the great glass dynasties that began in the Middle Ages are still at work today.

As Islamic glass production faded, Venetian artisans moved away from strictly utilitarian production to more artistic objects in the course of the 15th century. Enamels were increasingly used to decorate the glass. Meanwhile, Venetian crystal, obtained by using soda ash in the melting stage, became increasingly popular. The following century saw the development of diamond-edge engraving of clear glass. Floral motifs dominated. Only towards the end of the century did enamel decoration, by now more sophisticated, come back into vogue.

Things started to go downhill in the 17th century. Competition from France and later Bohemia made itself felt, and tough conditions imposed by the Republic on its Murano glass-workers pushed many of them to seek a living elsewhere. They left the lagoon and sought a better life in capitals across Europe. Some even ended up in the Americas. With Bohemian crystal dominating the European markets in the 1700s, Murano glass-makers began to imitate their products, with uneven success. One hit, however, were the heavy framed Murano glass mirrors. The 20th century has breathed new life into the glass business, with production ranging from the practical to the strictly fanciful, with all tastes catered for.

is, well, laced with lace shops. Inspect the wares closely – the stuff on sale is sometimes of uneven quality and/or imported from Asia. The reason? It's a lot cheaper to import imitations than to make the real thing, and most tourists aren't prepared to spend money on the genuine article.

BAROVIER & TOSO Map p265 *Glass*
☎ 041 527 43 85; www.barovier.com; Fondamenta dei Vetrai 28; vaporetto Murano Colonna
Your chequebook will tremble as you enter this temple of artistic glassware, connected with the **Galleria Marina Barovier** in San Marco (p152). But no-one is obliging you to buy and the displays let you appreciate top-flight glass creations.

BERENGO Map p265 *Glass*
☎ 041 527 63 64; www.berengo.com; Fondamenta dei Vetrai 109/a; vaporetto Murano Colonna
Here is a purveyor of glass that has long abandoned any pretence of functionality in its products. This is glass for art's sake.

VENINI Map p265 *Glass*
☎ 041 73 99 55; www.venini.it; Fondamenta dei Vetrai 47-50; vaporetto Murano Colonna
Venini is yet another location for browsing the

top-shelf stuff before wandering off to poke your nose into less exalted glass factories and shops. Independent wealth comes in handy.

MESTRE
Eating p136; Entertainment p144; Sleeping p182
About the only reason for coming across here to the mainland is if you have shopping cabin fever and feel the need for major department stores.

LE BARCHE Map p261 *Shopping Centre*
☎ 041 97 78 82; Piazza XXVII Ottobre; ☼ 9am-8.30pm Tue-Sat, 2-8.30pm Mon; train
There are no serious department stores in Venice itself. For this kind of thing you will need to head to this shopping complex, just off Piazza XXII Marzo in the centre of Mestre. The complex is home to several of the country's leading stores, including **Feltrinelli**, the bookshop chain, **Ricordi Mediastore**, for CDs and music, **Coin**, a leading budget department store and **PAM**, particularly noted for its value-for-money food department. For clothes shopping you could try **Belfe & Belfe**, on the ground floor.

Sleeping

Sleeping

Styles of Accommodation

The APT office has a list of houses and apartments offering bed and breakfast accommodation – this is an option rapidly growing in popularity, with more opening up all the time. In general they offer only a couple of rooms and so none has been listed here. They can, however, be a pleasant and cheaper alternative to hotels, with a more 'at home' feeling. Try **Bed & Breakfast Italia** (www.bbitalia.it), a nationwide network that has several listings for Venice. The more traditional version is the *affittacamere* (room rental), basically the same deal in private houses but without the breakfast.

Hotels go by various names. An *albergo* is a hotel. A *pensione* or *locanda* is generally a smaller, simpler, family-run establishment, although frequently there is little to distinguish them from lower-end hotels. The great majority of these places are housed within buildings that date back several centuries and often have no more than a dozen rooms.

Budget travellers have the choice of the youth hostel on Giudecca or a handful of other dormitory-style possibilities, some of them religious institutions. They are mostly open in summer only.

Most of the top hotels are around the San Marco area and along the Grand Canal, but it is still possible to find 'bargains' (the concept is, of course, relative) tucked away in tiny streets and on side canals in the heart of the city. There are lots of hotels near the train station, especially in the budget to mid-range bracket, but it is a good 30-minute walk from there to Piazza San Marco. The Dorsoduro area is tranquil and offers a smattering of interesting accommodation options.

Price Ranges

Sleeping in Venice can be an expensive business; the first piece of advice is try to bargain. Rates in this guide represent the high-season maximum, but when business is slow many hotels will offer more competitive deals. In recent years there has been a bit of an accommodation boom in Venice, with many small hotels opening up and the B&B phenomenon taking hold. Tourism in Venice, as elsewhere, has been hit by fears over terrorism, SARS and the economic slowdown, so the chances of bargaining successfully have increased greatly.

Even in the depths of the low season, you're unlikely to pay less than €45 for a single (or €70 for a double) without private bathroom. In the high season, only a handful of cheapies offer such prices. Expect to pay €80 to €130 for a budget double, sometimes with bathroom (which often means shower, washbasin and toilet). For good mid-range places you can be looking at €150 or more for singles (€200 or more for doubles). We have included some 'cheap sleeps' in this chapter, by which we mean places where you pay less than €80 for a single or less than €120 for a double. Some of these places have more expensive doubles with private bathroom.

Lone travellers are particularly penalised. Most hotels have few, if any, single rooms. When they do, such rooms are usually rather poky. You will generally be offered a double at two-thirds to three-quarters of the price two people would pay.

Most hotel proprietors pad out the bill by including a compulsory breakfast. The (in)famous continental breakfast in these cases generally consists of a lavishly laid-out stale bread roll, accompanied by little packets of butter and jam and a pot of weak instant coffee. If you have the cash, you may as well view this as an optional arrangement and get a proper cup of coffee in a bar.

Hotel rates vary wildly for a range of reasons, although the year-on-year tendency is always upwards. Some hotels have the same prices year round, while others drop them when things are slow. 'Low season' for the average Venetian hotelier means November, early December and January (after the New Year rush). *Lowish* season for some hotels comes in the July–August period, when Italian tourists tend to head for the seaside and leave the cities to the foreigners.

The prices that follow should be regarded as a high-season guide. Rooms come with private bathroom (which often means a shower and not a full bathtub) unless otherwise stated. Where prices are mentioned 'with bathroom', the hotel also has cheaper rooms with communal facilities in the hall.

Checking In & Out

Hotels do not hold rooms for you indefinitely. Always confirm your arrival, especially if it's going to be late in the afternoon or evening. Generally there is no problem if you have paid a deposit or left a credit card number. While you can check in at any time of the morning, you may not get access to your room until after noon, when it has been vacated and cleaned. Most of the time you will be able to leave your luggage with the reception and go for a wander until the room is ready.

Checkout time is generally noon, although some places can be a little draconian and set a leaving time of 11am or even 10am (rare)! Technically, if you overstay you can be charged for another night.

An important point to note in Venice: turning up at night (anything from 10pm on) and searching for your hotel can be a daunting experience, especially if you are staying in a small *pensione* hidden away up some small *calle* (street). The city is dark and mostly quiet at night and the streets deadly confusing to the newcomer. Depending on where you are staying, you may find no-one to ask for directions. The first suggestion is try not to arrive late at night. If you have no choice, get hold of good directions and a detailed map before you leave for Venice.

Reservations

It is advisable to book in advance in Venice, particularly for Christmas, Easter and Carnevale, in May, June and September and on weekends. Unless you pay a deposit, many hotels won't feel obliged to hold a room for you all day unless you call to confirm on the day. Some hoteliers overbook in the way airlines do.

The **Associazione Veneziana Albergatori** (Venice Hoteliers Association; Map pp250-2; ☎ 041 71 52 88; www.veniceinfo.it; ☽ 8am-10pm Easter-Oct, 8am-9pm Nov-Easter) has offices at the train station, in Piazzale Roma and at the Tronchetto car park. Staff will book you a room but you must leave a small deposit and pay a minimal booking fee. It has 'last-minute' booking numbers: from within Italy, the number is freephone ☎ 800 843 006; from abroad dial ☎ 39 041 522 22 64.

The **Consorzio Alberghi della Terraferma Veneziana** (Hotels' Association of Venice Mainland; Map p261; ☎ 041 93 01 33; www.venicemainland.com; ☽ 8.30am-7.30pm Mon-Sat, sometimes noon-5pm Sun) is a separate organisation based in Mestre train station (platform 1). If you arrive in Mestre and are worried Venice may be full, these people can put you up in a hotel in Mestre – be warned, though, that they have been known to be a little less than frank about the situation in Venice. They have about 40 Mestre hotels on their books. The booking fee is €2.05.

Long-term Rentals

Few of us can afford to hang around even the cheapest hotel indefinitely. You could try cutting a deal for cheaper long-term accommodation in a B&B or *affittacamere*.

A cheaper option, but not an easy one to set up, is to share an apartment. In Italy, only students tend to do this, so start by heading to the Università Ca' Foscari notice boards at Calle Larga Foscari in San Polo and next to Chiesa di San Sebastian in Dorsoduro (both Map pp256-8). You can put up your own ad here. You could also try for an apartment to rent alone. It's possible to get a room in a shared place for about €300 to €400 a month. To rent even a studio for yourself, you are looking at €1000 to €1500. Another approach is to ask small-hotel owners if they know of anything – sometimes they can quickly find a place for you to rent.

Venetian Apartments (☎ 020-8878 1130; www.venice-rentals.com; 403 Parkway House, Sheen Lane, London SW14 8LS), a UK-based organisation, arranges accommodation in flats, often of a luxurious nature. It has about 100 places on the books. Two- to three-person apartments cost from around UK£700 per week.

You can find many other such dealers on the Web. **Wotspot** (www.wotspot.com) has a series of apartments in Venice that generally go for around US$1000 to $1500 per week, sleeping two to four people. **Euroflats** (www.ccrsrl.com) has flats sleeping up to six from €500 to €1400 per week. Another online agency is **Guest in Italy** (www.guestinitaly.com), with apartments ranging in price from about €1000 to €1500 per week. They let on a daily rate too, starting from about €170. With all of these you must add in a little more for booking and cleaning fees.

SESTIERE DI SAN MARCO

Eating p124; Entertainment p139; Sestieri p49; Shopping p152

The San Marco area, especially along the Grand Canal, is home to some of the city's grander hotels. It is, however, not so hot for good value mid-range or budget deals. A few exceptions prove the rule. Given the tourist throngs in the area, there is a case to be made for opting for something of better quality in a less congested part of town – after all, you are never really far away from anything.

AL GAMBERO Map pp254-5

☎ 041 522 43 84; hotgambero@tin.it; Calle dei Fabbri 4687; s/d with bathroom up to €130/170; vaporetto Rialto 🔀

Recently renovated, this hotel is in a great location north of Piazza San Marco. Clean and comfortable, if not overly large, rooms come with tapestries, satellite TV, phone and that very Italian consideration, a hairdryer in the sparkling bathroom. They have a few smaller and cheaper rooms without private bathroom.

BAUER Map pp254-5

☎ 041 520 70 22; www.bauervenezia.it; Campo San Moisè 1459; s/d €440/517; vaporetto Vallaresso/San Marco 🔀

Don't mind the awful 1949 Soviet-style entrance – the canalside neo-Gothic frontage of the palazzo is sufficiently elegant. From some rooms you have views across the Grand Canal to Chiesa di Santa Maria della Salute (the most expensive are hard to beat), and you're a stone's throw from Piazza San Marco. The elegant rooms on the 2nd floor drip Carrara marble and Murano glass.

CA' DEL CAMPO Map pp254-5

☎ 041 241 16 60; www.cadelcampo.it; Campo della Guerra 511; s/d up to €175/260; vaporetto Vallaresso/San Marco 🔀 🖵

Located on a busy little *campo* just 100m north of Piazza San Marco, this refurbished mansion offers tastefully presented and generous rooms. They come in a variety of shapes and sizes, are mostly very sunny and look onto the square or a small courtyard. Don't bump your head on the beams in the lovely attic rooms.

GRITTI PALACE Map pp256-8

☎ 041 79 46 11; www.starwood.com/grittipalace; Campo Traghetto 2467; s/d up to €587/1155; vaporetto Santa Maria del Giglio 🔀

A luxury property fronting the Grand Canal, the Gritti is one of the most famous hotels in Venice. If you can afford it, you'll mix with celebs and royalty. Of the 90 rooms, the most enticing look out over the Grand Canal. All are stuffed with antique furnishings, and staff provide all sorts of little touches, including bathrobes and slippers. A good portion of Hemingway's *Across the River and into the Trees* is set here. Hotel guests have access to a range of sporting options on the Lido, including golf, tennis and horse riding.

HOTEL GRASPO DE UA Map pp254-5

☎ 041 520 56 44; www.graspodeua.com; Rialto 5094; s €73-190, d €95-237; vaporetto Rialto 🔀

Rooms here are straightforward, with tasteful furnishings and en suite bathroom. The position couldn't be more central, right by the hustle and bustle of the Ponte di Rialto. You could feel a little hemmed in by all the tight

---

Top Five Small Hotels with Charm

- Hotel San Cassiano (p168)
- Locanda Antico Fiore (opposite)
- Locanda Ca' del Console (p179)
- Locanda Leon Bianco (p169)
- Locanda San Barnaba (p167)

lanes, but the hotel is good value, especially when they put on midweek offers. The attached restaurant is a posh affair especially popular with office workers from the nearby town hall in Ca' Farsetti.

HOTEL LOCANDA FIORITA Map pp256-8
☎ 041 523 47 54; www.locandafiorita.com; Campiello Nuovo 3457/a; s €80-130, d €100-145; vaporetto Accademia 🍴

Set on a wonderful little square a spit away from the broad Campo Santo Stefano, the Locanda Fiorita is a gem. The rooms, some of which look onto the square, are simple but well maintained and it is hard to complain about the prices. With its greenery, timber beams and friendly service, it feels like home. They set up a few breakfast tables outside.

HOTEL SERENISSIMA Map pp254-5
☎ 041 520 00 11; www.hotelserenissima.it; Calle Goldoni 4486; s/d up to €102/170; vaporetto Rialto 🍴 🖵

Bright, white rooms with parquet floors and simple, elegant furnishings, satellite TV and en suite bathrooms make this a safe choice, tucked away between San Marco and the Ponte di Rialto.

LOCANDA ANTICO FIORE Map pp256-8
☎ 041 522 79 41; www.anticofiore.com; Corte Lucatello 3486; s/d up to €125/145; vaporetto San Samuele 🍴 🖵

Located in an 18th-century *palazzo* (palace), this completely restored hotel is a charmer. The front door is on a narrow canal just in from the Grand Canal, so you can arrive in style by water taxi. Inside you will find cosy lodgings over a couple of floors. All rooms are tastefully decorated (tapestries, timber furniture), each with a different colour scheme.

LOCANDA ART DECO Map pp256-8
☎ 041 277 05 58; www.locandaartdeco.com; Calle delle Botteghe 2966; d up to €135; vaporetto Accademia 🍴 🖵

Bright, whitewashed rooms with timber beam ceilings in this cheerful and immaculately kept hotel are especially enticing. Iron bedsteads are attached to particularly comfy beds with orthopaedic mattresses – no chance of backache here!

LOCANDA BARBARIGO Map pp256-8
☎ 041 241 36 39; www.locandabarbarigo.com; Fondamenta Barbarigo 2503/a; s/d up to €160/181; vaporetto Santa Maria del Giglio 🍴

Housed in part of a grand Venetian noble family's house, the Palazzo Barbarigo, this new hotel has a handful of nicely decorated (typical Venetian 18th-century-style painted furnishings) rooms, some with exposed timber beams and views over a side canal. A couple of the rooms have a full bath; others have showers.

PALAZZO DEL GIGLIO Map pp256-8
☎ 041 271 91 11; www.hotelgiglio.com; Campo Traghetto 2462; s/d €160/205, ste up to €440; vaporetto Santa Maria del Giglio 🍴

This refurbished mansion just off the Grand Canal has a variety of rooms and suites, all furnished with antiques and equipped with sparkling modern bathrooms in Carrara marble, kitchenettes and small dining areas. You can be served breakfast in your room.

PALAZZO LA SCALA Map pp254-5
☎ 041 522 25 02; www.palazzolascala.com; Calle dei Fabbri 4737l; d €240-400; vaporetto Rialto 🍴

A fine central address, this *palazzo* offers a range of opulently decorated rooms, a truly enchanting suite (€500) and good service. Prices vary enormously according to room position, size (some are smallish) and season (in winter prices can more than halve). In high season the prices are on the swingeing side.

Gritti Palace in San Marco (opposite)

Cheap Sleeps

HOTEL AI DO MORI Map pp254-5

☎ 041 520 48 17; www.hotelaidomori.com; Calle Larga San Marco 658; d without/with bathroom up to €90/135; vaporetto San Zaccaria ✦

Just off Piazza San Marco, this higgledy-piggledy hotel has pleasant rooms, some of which offer close-up views of the Basilica. The pick of the crop is without doubt the cosy double at the top that comes with a terrace.

LOCANDA CASA PETRARCA Map pp254-5

☎ /fax 041 520 04 30; Calle Schiavone 4386; s/d without bathroom up to €60/93, d with toilet & shower up to €120; vaporetto Rialto

A family-run place in an ancient apartment building, this is one of the nicest budget places in the San Marco area. The cheerful owner speaks English. To get here, find Campo San Luca, follow Calle dei Fuseri, take the second left and then turn right into Calle Schiavone.

SESTIERE DI DORSODURO

Eating p125; Entertainment pp140 & 143; Sestieri p58; Shopping p154

This area offers some interesting choices, often a good deal quieter than in San Marco and frequently better quality. Some wonderful deals could have you in a room overlooking either the Grand Canal of the Canale della Giudecca. Perhaps you'd like something along a tranquil side canal or near the bustling Campo Santa Margherita?

ALBERGO AGLI ALBORETTI Map pp256-8

☎ 041 523 00 58; www.aglialboretti.com; Rio Terrà Antonio Foscarini 884; s/d €104/180; vaporetto Accademia ✦ ▯

This charming hotel almost feels like an inviting mountain chalet when you step inside. In its category, it is one of Venice's star choices. The management is friendly and the rooms tastefully arranged and mostly of a good size. The restaurant is also of a high standard.

CA' PISANI HOTEL Map pp256-8

☎ 041 240 14 11; www.capisanihotel.it; Rio Terrà Antonio Foscarini 979/a; r from €204 to €330; vaporetto Accademia ✦

Named after the hero of the siege of Chioggia in 1310, this centuries-old building houses a curious departure in the Venetian lodging scene – a self-conscious design hotel, filled with 1930s and 1940s furnishings, as well as items specially

Top Five Hotel Gardens

- Boscolo Grand Hotel Dei Dogi (p168)
- Il Lato Azzurro (p182)
- Hotel Pausania (below)
- Locanda Cipriani (p181)
- Pensione Accademia Villa Maravege (opposite)

made for the hotel. The rooms, some with exposed beams, are elegant, well equipped and full of pleasing decorative touches. There are great views from the small roof terrace.

CA' SAN TROVASO Map pp256-8

☎ 041 277 11 46; www.locandasantrovaso.com; Fondamenta delle Eremite 1350; s/d €90/125; vaporetto Zattere ✦

With its traditional *terrazzo alla Veneziana* floors and elegant Venetian décor, this little hotel is a pleasant surprise packet set just a few steps from Canale della Giudecca. The rooms are spacious, and in summer you can sun yourself on the hotel's *altana*, the traditional Venetian timber roof terrace.

HOTEL ALLA SALUTE DA CICI Map pp256-8

☎ 041 523 54 04; www.hotelsalute.com; Fondamenta di Ca' Balà 002; s/d up to €115/135; vaporetto Salute ✦

This is a comfortable hotel in a well-kept old Venetian house on a quiet canal just a stone's throw away from Chiesa di Santa Maria della Salute. Some rooms look onto the canal and all are nicely decorated with timber furnishings and rugs. The owners also have a couple of cheaper rooms without private bathroom.

HOTEL GALLERIA Map pp256-8

☎ 041 523 24 89; www.hotelgalleria.it; Accademia 878/a; s/d up to €88/145; vaporetto Accademia

The Hotel Galleria is the only one-star hotel right on the Grand Canal, near the Ponte dell'Accademia. The place was a 17th-century private mansion before being converted into the modest and cosy hotel it is now. Space is a little tight, but the 18th-century décor in the bright rooms is welcoming. If you can snag one of the rooms on the canal, how can you possibly complain?

HOTEL PAUSANIA Map pp256-8

☎ 041 522 20 83; fax 041 522 29 89; Fondamenta Gherardini 2824; s/d up to €160/250; vaporetto Ca' Rezzonico ✦

A wonderful Gothic residence preceded by a courtyard with an internal staircase creates a romantic setting for your Venice trip. Just a stone's throw from Campo Santa Margherita but nice and quiet, the hotel boasts comfortable if smallish rooms, a grand salon and a verdant rear garden where you can take breakfast.

LA CALCINA Map pp256-8

☎ 041 520 64 66; www.lacalcina.com; Fondamenta Zattere ai Gesuati 780; s/d up to €106/182; vaporetto Zattere

John Ruskin wrote *The Stones of Venice* here in 1876. The hotel has a smidgen of garden and looks across to the Giudecca. Its immaculate rooms, with parquet floors and timber furnishings, are sober but charming. Some have small terraces and others views over Canale della Giudecca. One has both views *and* terrace. Less expensive rooms come without the view and a few cheaper ones still without private bathroom. You can dine inside or canalside.

LOCANDA SAN BARNABA Map pp256-8

☎ 041 241 12 33; www.italian-shop.com/lsb; Calle del Traghetto 2785-6; s/d up to €110/170; vaporetto Ca' Rezzonico 🎫

This 13-room hotel has been elegantly carved out of a fine mansion. Rooms are well equipped and some face onto the canal. A small terrace graces the top of the building, and there's a canalside garden for breakfast or evening drinks.

PENSIONE ACCADEMIA VILLA MARAVEGE Map pp256-8

☎ 041 521 01 88; www.pensioneaccademia.it; Fondamenta Bollani 1058; s/d up to €122/180; vaporetto Accademia 🎫

Set in its own lovely gardens right by the Grand Canal and just a few steps away from the Gallerie dell'Accademia, this fine 17th-century villa is understandably popular. Grand sitting and dining rooms, capped by splendid timber ceilings and oozing a past grandeur, will tempt you to just stay inside. Rooms are simple but elegant, some with four-poster beds and timber floors. Most look onto the gardens and some have canal glimpses.

PENSIONE SEGUSO Map pp256-8

☎ 041 528 68 58; fax 041 522 23 40; Fondamenta Zattere ai Gesuati 779; s/d with bathroom up to €145/168; ⏳ Mar-Nov; vaporetto Zattere 🎫

This typically Venetian russet-red *pensione* is in a lovely, quiet position facing the Canale della Giudecca. Rooms are all nicely furnished and many enjoy canal views. There are also some cheaper rooms without private bathroom.

Cheap Sleeps

ALBERGO ANTICO CAPON Map pp256-8

☎ 041 528 52 92; hotelanticocapon@hotmail.com; Campo Santa Margherita 3004/b; r up to €90; vaporetto Ca' Rezzonico 🖳

This place is right on the liveliest square in Dorsoduro and has seven widely varying rooms. The beds are wide and firm; the rooms in which they stand bright and airy. Bear in mind that the square can be pretty noisy at night.

ANTICA LOCANDA MONTIN Map pp256-8

☎ 041 522 71 51; locandamontin@libero.it; Fondamenta di Borgo 1147; s/d without bathroom €70/110, d with bathroom up to €135; vaporetto Accademia

Ezra Pound and Modigliani favoured this small, comfortable place, located on a quiet back canal a few minutes' walk from the Gallerie dell'Accademia and busy Campo Santa Margherita. It's been in business since the 1800s and the cosy rooms look onto either the canal or the rear garden. There's a popular (but pricey) restaurant – the rear pergola-covered garden dining area is enticing.

SESTIERI DI SAN POLO & SANTA CROCE

Eating p126; Entertainment p142; Sestieri p63; Shopping p155

A few hotels cluster close to the train station end of the Sestiere di Santa Croce. Further away the pickings thin out a little, but various modestly priced, attractive lodgings are scattered about, along with some Grand Canal classics.

ANTICA LOCANDA STURION Map pp254-5

☎ 041 523 62 43; www.locandasturion.com; Calle Sturion, San Polo 679; s/d up to €150/250; vaporetto San Silvestro 🎫

This *locanda* is two minutes from the Ponte di Rialto and has been a hotel on and off since the 13th century (when it was the Hospitium Sturionis). The best of its 11 rooms are the two generous suites overlooking the canal. All rooms come with mod cons and are a deep wine-red colour harking to the 18th century.

One downside is the long stairway up to the hotel. When things are going slow prices can more than halve.

HOTEL CANAL Map pp250-2
☎ 041 523 84 80; www.hotelcanal.com; Fondamenta San Simeon Piccolo, Santa Croce 553; s/d up to €150/ 180; vaporetto Ferrovia 🔾

Although this area is not the most picturesque in Venice, the hotel, a few minutes' walk from Piazzale Roma, overlooks the Grand Canal. Rooms are fairly neutral in terms of décor, incorporating the fairly typical 18th-century style furnishings on offer in many hotels. The owners also run the **Hotel Walter**, around the corner. Chop off one-third of the rates here in the low season.

HOTEL SAN CASSIANO Map pp250-2
☎ 041 524 17 68; www.sancassiano.it; Calle della Rosa, Santa Croce 2232; s/d up to €228/335; vaporetto San Stae 🔾 🔲

The 14th-century Ca' Favretto houses a mixed selection of rooms (and an incredibly mixed range of prices), the better ones doubles with high-ceilings overlooking the Grand Canal. The building is a wonderful old pile (which the managers continue to slowly refurbish), with stone doorways along the staircases. If you're up early, grab one of a couple of tables for breakfast on the balcony overlooking the Grand Canal.

LOCANDA SANT'AGOSTIN Map pp250-2
☎ 041 275 94 14; www.locandasantagostin.it; Campo Sant'Agostin, San Polo 2344; s/d up to €155/175; vaporetto San Stae 🔾

In this cosy residence you'll find a variety of rooms, the best of them a couple of spacious doubles looking over the square of the same name. All are decorated with taste, from the antique furniture picked up in various stores around the city, to the deep blue bedding and curtains, and the Murano glass lamps. The marble bathrooms shine.

PENSIONE GUERRATO Map p253
☎ 041 528 59 27; web.tiscali.it/pensioneguerrato/; Ruga due Mori, San Polo 240/a; d without/with bathroom €95/120; vaporetto Rialto

Amid the Rialto markets, this *pensione* is a gem, a one-star place that has spacious, light rooms with glimpses of the Grand Canal. It is housed in a former convent, which before (so they say) had served as a hostel for knights heading off on the Third Crusade. The friendly managers

Top Five for Sheer Bloody Luxury
- Excelsior (p180)
- Gritti Palace (p164)
- Hotel Cipriani (p181)
- Hotel Danieli (p179)
- San Clemente Palace (p181)

run a tight ship, so book early. Up on the 4th floor they also run **Guerratino**, where some of the five rooms (which cost a smidgin more than those downstairs) look out on to the Rialto markets. The managers have an apartment for rent near Piazza San Marco too.

Cheap Sleeps
ALBERGO CASA PERON Map pp256-8
☎ 041 71 00 21; fax 041 71 10 38; Salizzada San Pantalon, Santa Croce 85; s/d with shower €48/75, with toilet & shower €85/95; vaporetto San Tomà 🔾

This is a small but characterful place, family-run and with immaculately maintained rooms tucked around corners and up stairs. It's well placed, not too far from the train station and close to the Frari church. You will be greeted by the resident parrot on the way in!

HOTEL DALLA MORA Map pp256-8
☎ 041 71 07 03; hoteldallamora@libero.it; Salizzada San Pantalon, Santa Croce 42/a; s/d with bathroom up to €61/88; vaporetto Ferrovia 🔾

Located on a small canal just off Salizzada San Pantalon, this hotel has clean, airy rooms, some with lovely canal views, and a terrace. Some rooms are equipped with own shower and sink. It's a popular choice.

SESTIERE DI CANNAREGIO
Eating p129; Entertainment pp142 & 144; Sestieri p77; Shopping p158

This is the world of cheap and sometimes cheerful accommodation just a few steps from the train station. Few of these places have anything remarkable to recommend them but they are handy for quick getaways. You'll find more enticing choices in the side *calli* and further away from the station.

BOSCOLO GRAND HOTEL DEI DOGI
Map pp250-2
☎ 041 220 81 11; www.deidogi.boscolohotels.com;

Fondamenta Madonna dell'Orto 3500; s/d up to €390/530; vaporetto Madonna dell'Orto ✇

Once an embassy, this haughty hotel stands in splendid isolation in the northwest of the city. The airy rooms are well appointed in 18th-century style and the presidential suite enjoys magnificent views out to the island of Murano. Others look onto tranquil private gardens. Private hotel boats will shuttle you to Piazza San Marco.

HOTEL ABBAZIA Map pp250-2
☎ 041 71 73 33; www.abbaziahotel.com; Calle Priuli detta dei Cavalletti 68; s/d up to €180/200; vaporetto Ferrovia ✇

This hotel is in a restored abbey, a few minutes' walk from the train station. Many of the lovely rooms in this seemingly endless, rambling hotel face onto a blooming central garden. The better ones all have a different primary colour scheme, with yellows, reds and blues. The buffet breakfast is good.

HOTEL GIORGIONE Map p253
☎ 041 522 58 10; www.hotelgiorgione.com; Calle Larga dei Proverbi 4587; s/d up to €173/400; vaporetto Ca' d'Oro ✇

In this welcoming hotel you will find comfortable, if in some cases rather small, rooms mostly in a 15th-century mansion (part of the building is modern). At the centre of the hotel is a peaceful courtyard. You can take breakfast outside and sip drinks on the 1st-floor terrace. Some of the best top-floor rooms have little terraces.

HOTEL SAN GEREMIA Map pp250-2
☎ 041 71 62 45; fax 041 524 23 42; Campo San Geremia 290/a; s/d €118/129; vaporetto Ferrovia ✇

This is a friendly establishment. The rooms are standard, with phone and TV. Some have views of the square and a couple up top have little terrace arrangements, although these are usually rented as triples. The prices are inflated in comparison with neighbouring places, but it's a reasonable option for people travelling in pairs.

HOTEL TRE ARCHI Map pp250-2
☎ 041 524 43 56; www.hoteltrearchi.com; Fondamenta di Cannaregio 923; s/d €210/240; vaporetto Tre Archi ✇

Set away from the tourist rush, this attractive hotel of 24 rooms is in a bit of the 'real Venice'. The place is furnished and decorated in classical Venetian style. Some rooms (a couple with small terraces) look over the Canale di Cannaregio, while others are set around the internal garden, where you can take breakfast in summer. In slow periods the rooms can go for less than half price.

LOCANDA LEON BIANCO Map p253
☎ 041 523 35 72; www.leonbianco.it; Corte Leon Bianco 5629; d with Grand Canal view €165; vaporetto Ca' d'Oro

To find this wonderful old *locanda*, cross Rio dei SS Apostoli (heading towards San Marco) and turn right. Pass the high staircase on your left and head straight into the dead-end courtyard. Go up two flights of stairs in which medieval-style flaming torches would be at home and you are there. The best three rooms (of eight) look onto the Grand Canal (the others are cheaper). The undulating *terrazzo alla Veneziana* floors (see the boxed text on p86) and heavy timber doors with their original locks lend the rooms real medieval charm. Breakfast is served in the rooms. The house next door is the 12th-century Ca' da Mosto, which from the 16th to the 18th centuries housed Venice's first and most famed hotel, Del Leon Bianco.

Cheap Sleeps
ALLOGGI CALDERAN & CASA GEROTTO Map pp250-2
☎ 041 71 53 61; Campo San Geremia 283; dm €25, s/d with bathroom up to €80/150; vaporetto Ferrovia

These twin family places are the pick of the crop on this square for a simple, budget deal. They have combined to offer a whole range of rooms with a commensurately bewildering battery of prices depending on size, views and whether there is a private bathroom. The handful of bright singles are hard to come by as they are generally occupied by long-term residents. The dorms are single sex. Triples are also available and most rooms have pleasing views over the square.

HOTEL ROSSI Map pp250-2
☎ 041 71 51 64; Calle delle Procuratie 262; s/d without bathroom up to €52/75; d with bathroom €90; vaporetto Ferrovia ✇

Set in a tiny lane off the Rio Terrà Lista di Spagna, this hotel's rooms are pleasant enough, with wood panelling, fans and heating. The location is quiet and handy for the train station.

HOTEL SILVA & ARIEL Map pp250-2
☎ 041 71 47 73; fax 041 72 03 26; Calle della Masena

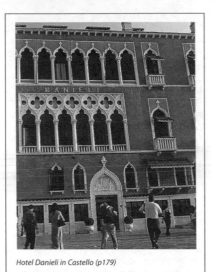
Hotel Danieli in Castello (p179)

Secreted away on a square with a real local flavour, this hotel is a good option. Sure, there is a passing trade in tourists, but here you feel you have moved away from the glitz and into a grittier side of Venice. However, there's nothing particularly gritty about the rooms, which are elegantly furnished and equipped with shower, TV and phone, but no air-con in summer. Loners get a rough deal.

ALBERGO PAGANELLI Map p259
☎ 041 522 43 24; www.hotelpaganelli.com; Riva degli Schiavoni 4182; s/d up to €150/200; vaporetto San Zaccaria ☒
Guests have been staying here since the mid-19th century. Aim for one of the three spacious waterfront rooms with sweeping views across the lagoon. Other rooms, which look onto Campo San Zaccaria or a small garden can be almost half the price and are quieter.

ALLOGGI BARBARIA Map p259
☎ 041 522 27 50; www.alloggibarbaria.it; Calle delle Cappuccine 6573; s/d up to €120/150; vaporetto Ospedale Civile ☒
The six rooms in this bright new *pensione* are white, bright and roomy, with tiled floors and attractive, functional furniture. It's a little out of the way up near the Fondamente Nuove but that is part of its charm – you don't feel any of the mass tourist pressure around here.

HOTEL BRIDGE Map pp254-5
☎ 041 520 52 87; www.hotelbridge.com; Calle Sagrestia 4498; s/d up to €150/212; vaporetto San Zaccaria ☒
The better rooms here are furnished in typical period Venetian style (creamy painted woodwork with floral decorations). All is modern and clean but space is a bit of a problem. Prices halve in low season.

HOTEL DA BRUNO Map pp254-5
☎ 041 523 04 52; www.hoteldabruno.it; Salizzada San Lio 5726/a; s/d up to €160/215; vaporetto Rialto
This hotel is just west of Campo Santa Maria Formosa. The rooms are a reasonable size, bright and decorated in the almost standard Venetian style with painted headboards and matching furniture. The flowers are a nice touch. In slower periods (such as March–April and July–August) prices can drop to €90 for singles and €120 for doubles.

1391/a; d without/with bathroom €78/100; vaporetto San Marcuola ☒
Hidden away in a narrow lane leading into the Ghetto, this is not a bad spot, and you can sit in a diminutive back garden. The owners also have some apartments that could be handy for groups of up to six. Rooms are about €20 less if taken as singles.

HOTEL VILLA ROSA Map pp250-2
☎ 041 71 89 76; villarosa@ve.nettuno.it; Calle della Misericordia 389; s/d €92/110; vaporetto Ferrovia ☒
This hotel has comfortable rooms; some on the top floor (of three) have pleasant terraces. Out the back is a quiet courtyard where you can take your compulsory breakfast. You can frequently get singles for about €60 and doubles for about €80.

SESTIERE DI CASTELLO
Eating p135; Entertainment p143; Sestieri p80; Shopping p159
This area to the east of San Marco, although close to the piazza, is less touristy. From the train station, catch a vaporetto and get off at San Zaccaria. Castello offers a broad palette on the accommodation front, with a couple of gems and some worthy runners-up.

ALBERGO AL NUOVO TESON Map p259
☎ 041 520 55 55; fax 041 528 53 35; Ramo Pescaria 3980; s/d €136/153; vaporetto Arsenale

(Continued on p179)

1 *View over rooftops from the top of the Campanile (p53)* 2 *Peate, the workhorses of the canals (p13)* 3 *View across the Bacino di San Marco from the bell tower of Chiesa di San Giorgio Maggiore (p90)* 4 *Chiesa di Santa Maria della Salute (p60)*

1 Seafood figures large on Venetian menus (p15) *2* Grappa, produced in the Veneto (p204) *3* Butchers' shops offer an alternative for self-caterers (p124) *4* Caffè Florian on Piazza San Marco (p140)

1 Fresh fruit for sale *2* Seahorses at the Pescaria (fish market) in Rialto (p75) *3* Tourists enjoying a toast at one of the city's many bars (p138) *4* Alfresco dining is popular in summer

1 Wine for sale on Rio Terrà Lista di Spagna (p151) 2 Harry's Bar (p139) 3 Piano bar Martini Scala (p140) 4 There are plenty of spots to enjoy a drink (p138)

1 Flag of Venezia, the local football team (p148) 2 Casinò de Venezia (p147) 3 Costumed party-goers at Carnevale (p9)

1 Carnevale masks (p150) *2* Glass sculpture from Berengo (p160)
3 Finely crafted glass from Berengo (p160)

1 Model gondolas make popular souvenirs (p151) 2 Burano lace for sale at Martinuzzi (p153)
3 Venice's oldest paper merchant, Legatoria Piazzesi (p153)

1 *Basilica Palladiana, Vicenza (p196)* 2 *Fishing fleet in Chioggia (p95)* 3 *Colourful houses in Caorle (p207)* 4 *Roman Arena, Verona (p187)*

(Continued from p170)

HOTEL DANIELI Map pp254-5

☎ 041 522 64 80; www.starwood.com/luxury; Riva degli Schiavoni 4196; s/d up to €500/1050; vaporetto San Zaccaria 🎦

Most of the rooms in this Venetian classic look across the water towards Chiesa di Santa Maria della Salute and Chiesa di San Giorgio Maggiore. It opened as a hotel in 1822 in the 14th-century Palazzo Dandolo. Just wandering into the grand foyer – all arches, sweeping staircases and balconies – is a trip through centuries of splendour. Dining in the Terrazza Danieli rooftop restaurant is a feast for the eyes and palate. See the boxed text below.

HOTEL SCANDINAVIA Map pp254-5

☎ 041 522 35 07; www.scandinaviahotel.com; Campo Santa Maria Formosa 5240; s/d up to €260/310; vaporetto Rialto 🎦

This 15th-century converted mansion is not a bad choice. The heavy timber beams and period furnishings give the rooms a cosy touch – the best (and most expensive) ones look onto the wonderfully busy square, one of the prettiest in Venice. There are also a few not-so-inspiring singles.

LA RESIDENZA Map p259

☎ 041 528 53 15; www.venicelaresidenza.com; Campo Bandiera e Moro 3608; s/d up to €95/155; vaporetto Arsenale 🎦

If you can live without watery views, head inland to this delightful 15th-century mansion. It is also known as Palazzo Gritti-Badoer, after two of the families who have owned it. The main hall upstairs makes quite an impression with its candelabras, elaborate decoration and distinguished furniture. The rooms are rather more restrained, but fine value. The narrow street that wraps around the *palazzo* from the left side, Calle de la Morte (Street of Death), is so named because the Consiglio dei Dieci regularly had people considered a nuisance to the Republic executed here.

LOCANDA AL PIAVE Map pp254-5

☎ 041 528 51 74; hotel.alpiave@iol.it; Ruga Giuffa 4838-40; s/d up to €92/155; vaporetto San Zaccaria

This *locanda* has fine and, in most cases, spacious rooms, furnished with a muted elegance. All have shower and TV and are spotlessly clean. Some rooms give onto a quieter side courtyard.

LOCANDA CA' DEL CONSOLE Map pp254-5

☎ 041 523 31 64; www.locandacadelconsole.com; Calle Trevisana 6217-40; s/d €100/130; vaporetto Rialto

Ambling down this narrow side lane, you would never guess that the Austrian consul lived here in the early 19th century. The front door of the building tells you little of what lies inside: eight tastefully restored rooms with period furniture from the consul's days, exposed beams, stucco work and frescoes. All the rooms (there is only one single) are quite different. The managers also have apartments for rent.

LOCANDA REMEDIO Map pp254-5

☎ 041 520 62 32; fax 041 521 04 85; Calle del Rimedio 4412; s/d up to €180/220; vaporetto San Zaccaria 🎦

A Dogey Death

When Doge Vitale Michiel returned to Venice with the sorry remains of his fleet in May 1172, he must have known things weren't going to go well for him. He had set off in the previous September with a war fleet of 120 vessels to avenge assaults on Venetians carried out in Constantinople. Unfortunately, he decided to agree to talks.

While his negotiators got bogged down in ultimately fruitless chitchat, his idle fleet at the Greek island of Chios collapsed as plague broke out. By the time it had become clear that Constantinople had no intention of continuing serious negotiations, the fleet was in no condition to fight. And so Michiel had little alternative but to go home – taking the plague with him.

As he gave his sorry report in the Palazzo Ducale, he realised from the mounting anger that he would have to flee. He didn't get far. Scampering east along the Riva degli Schiavoni, he was met by the mob and killed. (A conflicting version of events says Michiel was on his way to the Chiesa di San Zaccaria for Mass when he was struck down.)

When things had settled, the city's leaders searched for, tried and executed the assassin. If anyone was going to do the killing around here, it was the State. The man's house was found to be at Calle delle Rasse, virtually next to the spot where Michiel met his end, and was flattened. It was decreed that no building of stone should be raised on the site.

The decree was respected until 1948. When it was finally repealed, the silent vacuum of reproach was filled with the rather Mussolini-esque expansion of the Hotel Danieli, an ugly sister that sits rather uncomfortably beside Palazzo Dandolo, the hotel's main home.

This is indeed a remedy after the streaming, screaming masses thronging nearby Piazza San Marco. It's hard to imagine them so close to the tranquil courtyard in which this inn hides. The building dates from the 16th century and belonged to the Rimedio family. In the same courtyard was a *malvasia*, a tavern where wine of the same name (ie malmsey), imported from the Venetian-controlled Greek islands, could be had. In a nice play on words, the building came to be known as *remedio* (remedy) towards the end of the 16th century – the medicinal qualities of *malvasia* were thought to ward off the plague. Try for the front double, the ceiling of which is graced with a mid-16th-century fresco.

LONDRA PALACE Map p259
☎ 041 520 05 33; www.hotelondra.it; Riva degli Schiavoni 4171; s/d up to €275/585; vaporetto San Zaccaria 🔀

Most rooms in this four-star property have views over the water. They feature 19th-century period furniture, spa baths and marble bathrooms. The colour of the brocades and other decorative touches varies from one room to the next. The most expensive double is a spacious junior suite. The cheaper rooms have views over the city rather than the lagoon.

Cheap Sleeps
FORESTERIA VALDESE Map p259
☎ /fax 041 528 67 97; www.diaconiavaldese.org/venezia; Castello 5170; dm €21, d €56-74; vaporetto Ospedale Civile

This is in a rambling old mansion near Campo Santa Maria Formosa. Head east from the square on Calle Lunga Santa Maria Formosa, cross the small bridge and the Foresteria is in front of you. Double rates depend on the room and whether or not it has a bathroom. Breakfast is included. Book well ahead.

LOCANDA SANT'ANNA Map p260
☎ /fax 041 528 64 66; hsantanna@tin.it; Corte del Bianco 269; s/d without bathroom up to €75/90; d with bathroom €130; vaporetto San Pietro 🔀

Hidden away right in the east of Castello, you can't get much farther away from the heart of Venice and still be there! This is a real residential quarter and may appeal to some for that reason alone. Rooms are modest but comfortable.

LOCANDA SILVA Map pp254-5
☎ 041 522 76 43; www.locandasilva.it; Fondamenta

del Rimedio 4423; s/d without bathroom €48/80, s/d with shower & toilet €70/105; vaporetto San Zaccaria

A few of the rooms here south of Campo Santa Maria Formosa look onto a narrow canal. They are modest but well maintained and a reasonable deal in the price range.

PENSIONE BUCINTORO Map p259
☎ 041 522 32 40; pensionebucintoro@tin.it; Riva San Biagio 2135; s/d without bathroom €73/137, s/d with bathroom €93/167; vaporetto Arsenale 🔀

The big advantage of this *pensione* is that all the good-sized rooms look onto the lagoon and are well kept. They shave off about €10 per person in slack periods.

AROUND THE LAGOON
Eating p134; Entertainment p144; Sestieri p88; Shopping p159

From the luxury villas of the Lido and the Giudecca's Cipriani to a modest Burano *pensione* and rural hideaway on the little visited island of Sant'Erasmo, there are plenty of options outside Venice that will give you a very different take on the city and its lagoon setting.

ALBERGO BELVEDERE Map pp262-3
☎ 041 526 01 15; www.belvedere-venezia.com; Piazzale Santa Maria Elisabetta 4, Lido; s/d up to €157/229; vaporetto Lido 🅿 🔀

People have been staying here since 1857. Rooms are comfortable, if a little standard, but most have views across the lagoon to Venice and you couldn't be closer to the vaporetto stop. The hotel has a private stretch of beach and offers a baby-sitting service.

ALBERGO QUATTRO FONTANE
Map pp262-3
☎ 041526 02 27; www.quattrofontane.com; Via Quattro Fontane 16, Lido; s/d up to €250/370; vaporetto Lido 🅿 🔀

With some of the feel of an Alpine chalet, this grand country house set in luxuriant gardens is a wonderful place to call home. Rooms of varying types and sizes are graced with iron bedsteads and in some cases balconies. You can dine indoors or in the hotel gardens.

EXCELSIOR Map pp262-3
☎ 041 526 02 01; www.starwood.com/westin; Lungomare Guglielmo Marconi 41, Lido; d €450-775; vaporetto Lido 🅿 🔀 🛥

A fanciful Moorish-style property, the Excelsior has long been the top address on the Lido. The Oriental theme continues in its luxurious rooms, many of which look out to sea or across the lagoon to Venice. Lounge about the outdoor and heated pools if the beach seems too far away! The hotel boasts a range of spacious suites too.

HOTEL CIPRIANI Map pp262-3
☎ 041 520 77 44; www.hotelcipriani.it; Giudecca 10; s €335-825, d €570-1370, ste €900-7000; vaporetto Zitelle 🔲 🔲
This deluxe place is set in the one-time villa of the Mocenigo family and is surrounded by lavish grounds and pools, with unbeatable views across to Piazza San Marco. It occupies virtually the whole eastern chunk of the island and one UK newspaper declared recently that it 'may fairly lay claim to be the world's best hotel'. Suites are spread out across several grand *palazzi*, some with gardens, others directly on the Canale della Giudecca.

HOTEL DES BAINS Map pp262-3
☎ 041 526 59 21; fax 041 526 01 13; www.starwood.com/sheraton; Lungomare Guglielmo Marconi 17, Lido; s/d up to €500/700; 🕐 May-Sep; vaporetto Lido 🅿 🔲 🔲
This is the top address for Thomas Mann fans. Take a room at the tail end of the season to enjoy the fully melancholic effect. The hotel is graced with Palladian terraces and a turn-of-the-19th-century feel. Rooms look out to sea or over private parkland. Mann's character Aschenbach probably was not into the sporty activities on offer here, which range from tennis to horse riding. If you aren't either, you can relax by the tree-lined pool.

HOTEL VILLA CIPRO Map pp262-3
☎ 041 73 15 38; www.hotelvillacipro.com; Via Zara 2, Lido; s/d up to €160/230; vaporetto Lido 🅿 🔲
A charming villa set in lush gardens and a short walk from the vaporetto stop, the Villa Cipro offers spacious, elegantly decorated rooms, some with balconies. You can take breakfast in the leafy courtyard. Like many of the better Lido hotels, it offers a baby-sitting service.

LOCANDA CIPRIANI Map p264
☎ 041 73 01 50; Piazza Santa Fosca 29, Torcello; r per person €115, half board per person €160; 🕐 closed January; vaporetto Torcello

Feel like following in Papa's footsteps? You too can stay over for a night or two in one of the six spacious, tranquil rooms at this country-lagoon getaway that found favour with Hemingway. The food here is excellent so half board is a recommended way to go. The rooms have high ceilings and feel more like studio apartments; they have recently been renovated. Booking is essential.

SAN CLEMENTE PALACE Map p248
☎ 041 244 50 01; www.sanclemente.thi.it; Isola San Clemente; s/d/ste €330/360/930 🔲 🔲 🔲
The rose-coloured buildings of the restored one-time monastery and madhouse of San Clemente make a unique setting. The hotel has 205 rooms and suites, two swimming pools, tennis courts, a golf course, conference space and wonderful gardens. The views out over the lagoon towards southern Venice and the Lido are truly romantic. Opened in 2003, its starting prices are remarkable given the nature of the place. Perhaps the depressed tourism market will keep them under control! A private shuttle boat runs to the hotel from the Alilaguna airport boat stop at San Zaccaria.

SOFITEL VENEZIA IN ISOLA Map p248
☎ 041 520 43 88; www.sofitel.com; Isola di Sacca Sessola; r & ste €325-3000 🔲 🔲 🔲
The Sofitel group has long run a hotel near Piazzale Roma, but with the purchase of this lagoon island south of Giudecca it has really gone to town. With its lush gardens and small olive grove (some say it's the only one north of the much warmer Tuscany), the island makes a wonderful setting for a hotel. The long-abandoned former sanatorium buildings have been converted into a luxury hotel with two restaurants, all due to open in 2004.

VILLA MABAPA Map pp262-3
☎ 041 526 05 90; www.villamabapa.com; Riviera San Nicolò 16, Lido; s/d up to €182/315; vaporetto Lido 🅿 🔲
This is a pleasant Lido hideaway handy for the vaporetto stop. A grand old residence dating from the 1930s with a couple of annexes, it is worth making the effort for. You need to book months in advance in summer and for the cinema festival in September. Rooms are elegantly appointed in period furniture and look back across the lagoon to Venice. You can dine well in the garden.

Cheap Sleeps

IL LATO AZZURO Map p248
☎ 041 244 49 00; Via Forti 13, Sant'Erasmo; s/d €40/60; vaporetto Sant'Erasmo Capannone
This is a unique and rather un-Venetian experience. Sleep on the island that was traditionally Venice's garden, Sant'Erasmo. Pleasant, spacious rooms give on to a veranda. The island still lives mostly from small-scale agriculture and if you choose to eat here you will be presented with a largely vegetarian menu of home-grown products. They will also make you a packed lunch for your excursions on the island or into Venice. The place has a very alternative bent and organises everything from bike rides to gay and lesbian holidays in August. Bring your mosquito repellent.

ISTITUTO CANOSSIANO Map pp262-3
☎/fax 041 522 21 57; Fondamenta di Ponte Piccolo 428, Giudecca; dm €15; 🕒 Jun-Sep; vaporetto Palanca
Near the Ostello Venezia, this place takes in women only and is a handy, quiet option. It also has a few more-expensive doubles.

LOCANDA AL RASPO DE UA Map p264
☎/fax 041 73 00 95; Via Galuppi 560, Burano; s/d €40/75; vaporetto Burano ⬚
This modest *locanda* on the island's main drag is the only place to stay here and could make your Venetian visit a quite different experience. After the last of the tourists head back to Venice at night, it's just you and the locals on this pretty pastel islet. The singles are without private bathroom.

OSTELLO VENEZIA Map pp262-3
☎ 041 523 82 11; fax 041 523 56 89; Fondamenta della Croce 86, Giudecca; B&B dm €16.50; 🕒 7-9.30am & 2-11.30pm; vaporetto Redentore
This Hostelling International (HI) property is open to members only but you can buy a card there. Evening meals are available for €8. The hostel, which is a reasonable example of the genre and a good place to meet other budget travellers, is on HI's computerised International Booking Network, so you can book online (www.hostelbooking.com).

PENSIONE LA PERGOLA Map pp262-3
☎ 041 526 07 84; Via Cipro 15, Lido; s/d €42/83; vaporetto Lido ⬚
This homey little *pensione*, just off Gran Viale Santa Maria Elisabetta, is a good budget deal if you want to base yourself near the beach

and commute into Venice when it suits you. Prices can be halved in the low season and there are some cheaper rooms without private bathroom.

MESTRE

Eating p136; Entertainment p144; Shopping p160
Only 10 to 15 minutes away on city bus Nos 2 and 7 (the former passes Mestre train station) or by train, Mestre is a drab, if sometimes necessary, alternative to staying in Venice. There are a number of good hotels, as well as plenty of cafés and places to eat around the main square.

HOTEL TRITONE Map p261
☎ 041 538 31 25; www.httritone.com; Viale Stazione 16; s/d up to €110/160; train ⬚ Ⓟ
This three-star property is quite comfortable (the rooms were all renovated in 2001) and has the obvious advantage of being right by the station – ideal for quick getaways to the lagoon.

HOTEL VIVIT Map p261
☎ 041 95 13 85; www.hotelvivit.com; Piazza Ferretto 75; s/d €76.50/102.50; bus Nos 2 & 7 ⬚ Ⓟ
Set in the heart of Mestre's central and lively pedestrianised square, this hotel is housed in a somewhat cumbersome looking *palazzo* dating to the early 1900s. Comfortable rooms with parquet floors and crisp, clean bathrooms are pleasant enough, and the buffet breakfast isn't bad.

Cheap Sleeps

HOTEL GIOVANNINA Map p261
☎ 041 92 63 96; www.hotelgiovannina.it; Via Dante 113; s/d without bathroom €36/62, d with bathroom up to €72; train ⬚
This is a perfectly comfortable cheapy, with bright if somewhat bare rooms not far from the train station. Downstairs you can chow down at a couple of no-nonsense restaurants.

HOTEL MONTE PIANA Map p261
☎ 041 92 62 42; www.hotelmontepiana.it; Via Monte San Michele 17; d €65-88; train ⬚ Ⓟ
This hotel is similar in quality to the Giovannina and is also close to the station, but in a quiet residential street. For what you pay the rooms are surprisingly sparkling and spacious after recent renovation.

Excursions

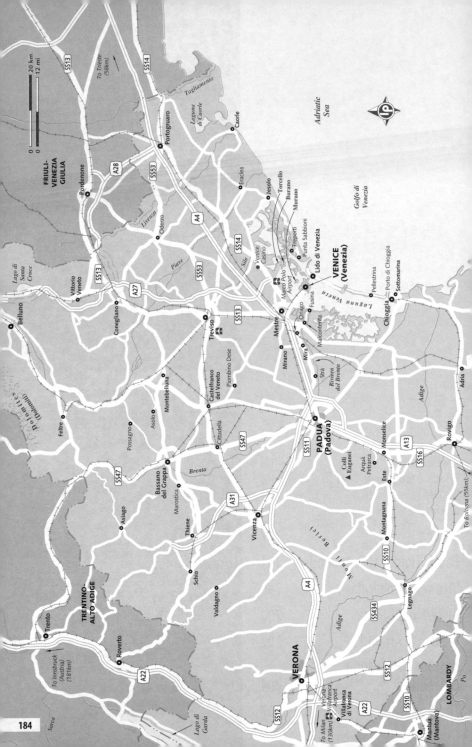

Excursions

For centuries the proud flag of the Lion of St Mark fluttered over the cities and towns of most of northeastern Italy. At its core is the region today known as the Veneto, a land of plains country in the south and mountains (great walking territory) on its northern boundary.

Water, as always in the story of Venice, also plays its part. The western extremity of the region is shut off by one of Italy's great northern lakes, Lago di Garda, while to the north and south of La Serenissima stretch the beaches of the Adriatic. The region's southern boundary is marked by the country's mightiest river, the Po, which empties into the Adriatic here after its long passage across northern Italy.

Long before Venice swallowed up the territory in the early 15th century, it was divided into a series of competing city-states, the most important of which were Padua (Padova), Vicenza and Verona. The mark of the lion is unmistakable in all, but each has retained its own distinct character.

An abundance of other towns, rarely more than a couple of hours away from Venice, will also draw the curious traveller, from the riverside medieval core of Treviso to the heart of grappa country, Bassano, and the hilltop eyrie of Asolo.

In between the towns rise the proud mansions and villas of Venice's once wealthy noble families, particularly along the River Brenta and around Vicenza.

Your own vehicle makes it easier to get around the more out-of-the-way towns and villas in the region, but the more important centres are all easily reached by train and never more than three hours away, making day trips a cinch from Venice. If you change your mind and want to stick around, you'll find plenty of nice places to spend a night outside Venice. High-season prices are given for the sleeping options listed in this chapter, and rooms come with private bathroom unless otherwise stated. For eating options, meal prices are based on a first course, second course, dessert and house wine for one person, and opening hours are given only where they differ from standard meal times (see p122).

THE BIG CITIES

The most striking attractions beyond Venice lie conveniently strung out along the main east–west railway line. First stop is Padua (p191), a busy university town 37km away and still partly protected by its old city walls. Known to some as the city of St Anthony and to others as a fine-arts shrine because of Giotto's remarkable frescoes, it is a dynamic place with a surprisingly extensive medieval core. Dedicate time to the central market squares and their fine Gothic palaces, as well as to the area around Piazza del Santo, where the church dedicated to St Anthony proudly stands. Foodies won't be disappointed either.

Next up on the trail is Vicenza (p196), a quieter town 32km northwest of Padua. Its compact old centre is a veritable showground of Palladian wonders, ranging from the grand Basilica Palladiana through numerous private mansions (including the much aped La Rotonda) to the delightful Teatro Olimpico.

Another 51km brings you to Verona (p187), the prettiest of the trio. The star attraction is the grand Roman arena, but romantics also come on a Shakespearean quest to seek out reminders of his heart-breaking heroes, Romeo and Juliet. Beautifully sited on the River Adige, the city has much to offer and although only about two hours out of Venice by train, might tempt you to stay longer than a day.

PALLADIO & THE VENETIAN VILLAS

As wealthy Venetian families turned their sights away from the sea and towards the land, so by the age of Palladio they had come to invest in fine country residences.

These Venetian villas, in particular those clustered along the River Brenta (p200) and around Vicenza (p196), provide a remarkable insight into the lives of the lagoon city's aristocrats in a bygone era. Many remain private property but throw open their doors to the masses at certain times. Some are more worth your while than others. While you could spend a day or two touring the villas of the Brenta, you can also be choosy. Keep an eye out for Palladio's Villa Foscari (p200) and the sprawling gardens of the magnificent Villa Pisani (p201).

Part Two of the Venetian Villa escapade takes you to Vicenza (p196). The city itself boasts several mansions by Palladio and others, but those with a passion for villas and a set of wheels can tour the surrounding countryside in search of still more. Several important ones are open to the public, while many others sit in reserved stony silence on their country estates or in small, otherwise unremarkable towns.

One of the towers in the defensive walls that surround Montagnana (p193)

FORTIFIED TOWNS &...DRINK

In between the grand medieval cities are scattered all sorts of minor gems that are perfect for a day or two's exploration. And for many of them you don't need your own wheels either. Several possible circuits suggest themselves.

Just 30km north of Venice is a gem often overlooked even by those whose Ryanair flights take them to within a whisker of the place – Treviso (p202). The 'City of Water', as locals like to think of the place, is a surprisingly charming stop whose old centre nestles in between the River Sile and Canal Cagnan, featuring old water mills and leafy corners. To the north and northeast of Treviso is a trio of delightful little towns: Oderzo (a miniature version of Treviso, p203), Conegliano (the wine capital of the Veneto, p203) and Vittorio Veneto (p203). You could pop into the last two on your way north to Belluno (see p203).

West of Treviso, a railway line proceeds to the curious walled town of Castelfranco del Veneto (p206) and on to its more impressive neighbour, Cittadella (p205), before heading to the home of grappa, Bassano (p204). Every attempt should be made to reach the nearby hill town of Asolo (p205).

South of Padua is another string of engaging fortified towns: Monselice, Este and the most striking of all, Montagnana (p193).

BEACHES

Although the Adriatic is not the most splendid of Mediterranean coastlines, it does provide a viable summertime escape from the humidity of the Venetian lagoon. Of course, you could always head for the beaches of the Lido di Venezia, but for better beaches you need to head further out of town. One option is Sottomarina, at Chioggia, to the south (see p96). To the northeast of Venice lie the beaches of Lido di Jesolo (p207). You can reach their southern strips by taking the ferry to Punta Sabbioni, or drive around to Lido di Jesolo itself. This is the most popular of the Veneto's summertime spots, with sandy beaches, reasonably clear water and a fairly busy summer clubbing scene. Further to the northeast, Caorle (p207) is a pleasant seaside fishing town with a good deal more history than its brasher neighbour.

VERONA

Wander the quiet streets of Verona (population 257,500) on a winter's night and you might almost be forgiven for believing the tragic love story of Romeo and Juliet to be true. Past the Shakespearean hyperbole, however, you'll find plenty to keep you occupied in one of Italy's most beautiful cities (the whole place is a Unesco World Heritage site). Known as *piccola Roma* (little Rome) for its importance in the days of the Roman Empire, its truly golden era came during the 13th and 14th centuries under the Della Scala family (aka the Scaligeri). The period was noted for the savage family feuding to which Shakespeare alluded in his play.

Old Verona is small and easy to find your way around. Buses leave for the centre from outside the train station; otherwise, walk to the right, past the bus station, cross the river and head along Corso Porta Nuova to Piazza Brà, about 1km away.

Remember that on Monday a lot of sights are closed, or open in the afternoon only. A combined sights ticket, the **Verona Card** (€8/12 per adult for one/three days, available from the sights and tobacco outlets), gains you admission to all the main monuments and churches and reduced admission to a few places of lesser importance. The card also gives you unlimited use of the town's buses.

For many, the heart of Verona is its pink marble 1st-century-AD **Roman Arena** in the bustling Piazza Brà. Once the scene of gladiatorial spectacles, it now stages a rather less blood-curdling annual open-air opera season. The third-largest Roman amphitheatre in existence, it could seat around 20,000 people. It is remarkably well preserved, despite a 12th-century earthquake that destroyed most of its outer wall. See Entertainment (p190) for information about opera and plays at the arena.

Just off Via Giuseppe Mazzini, central Verona's main shopping street, is the **Casa di Giulietta** (Juliet's House). Romeo and Juliet may have been fictional, but here you can swoon beneath what popular myth says was her balcony or, if in need of a new lover, approach a bronze statue of Juliet and rub her right breast for good luck. Others have made their eternal mark by adding to the slew of scribbled love graffiti on the courtyard walls. It is, by the way, doubtful there ever was a feud between the Cappello and Montecchi families, on whom Shakespeare based the play. If the theme excites you sufficiently, you could also search out the **Tomba di Giulietta** (Juliet's Tomb).

On the site of the Roman forum, Piazza delle Erbe remains the lively heart of the city. Although the permanent market stalls in its centre detract from its beauty, the square is lined with some of Verona's most sumptuous buildings, including the baroque **Palazzo Maffei**, at the northern end, with the adjoining 14th-century **Torre del Gardello**. On the eastern side the fresco-adorned facade of **Casa Mazzanti**, a former Della Scala family residence, stands out.

Separating Piazza delle Erbe from Piazza dei Signori is the **Arco della Costa**, beneath which is suspended a whale's rib. Legend says it will fall on the first 'just' person to walk beneath it. In several centuries, it has never fallen, not even on the various popes who have paraded beneath it. Ascend the nearby 12th-century **Torre dei Lamberti** for a great view of the city.

Occupying the northern side of Piazza dei Signori is the 15th-century **Loggia del Consiglio**, the former city council building and Verona's finest Renaissance structure. It is attached to the **Palazzo degli Scaligeri**, once the

Transport

Distance from Venice 120km

Direction West

Air Verona-Villafranca airport (☎ 045 809 56 66) is 16km outside town and accessible by regular bus from the train station. Flights arrive here from all over Italy and some European cities, including Amsterdam, Barcelona, Berlin, Brussels, London and Paris.

Bus The main intercity bus station is in front of the train station, in an area known as Porta Nuova. Buses are generally useful only for provincial localities not served by train. The AMT city transport company's bus Nos 11, 12, 13 and 72 (bus No 91 or 98 on Sunday and holidays) connect the train station with Piazza Brà, and bus No 70 goes to Piazza delle Erbe.

Car Verona is at the intersection of the Serenissima A4 (Milan–Venice) and Brennero A22 autostrade. From Venice you can be there in not much more than an hour.

Train The trip from Venice is easiest by train (up to €12.65; one to 1½ hours). Note that slow regional trains take 2½ hours.

main residence of the Della Scala clan. Through the archway at the far end of the piazza are the **Arche Scaligere**, the elaborate family tombs of what was Verona's most illustrious, although often blood-thirsty, ruling family, prior to Verona's submission to Venice's more sober (and more peaceful) rule. You can see the tombs quite well from the outside, but a combined ticket for these and the Torre dei Lamberti allows you to wander in and have a closer inspection.

North from the Arche Scaligere stands the Gothic **Chiesa di Sant'Anastasia**, started in 1290 but not completed until the late 15th century. A long parade of fine canvases is capped by a Pisanello fresco, in the sacristy, of *San Giorgio che Parte per Liberare la Donzella dal Drago* (St George Setting out to Free the Princess from the Dragon).

The 12th-century **Duomo** (cathedral) combines Romanesque (lower half) and Gothic (upper half) styles and has some intriguing features. Look for the sculpture of Jonah and the Whale on the south porch and the statues of two of Charlemagne's paladins, Roland and Oliver, on the west porch. In the first chapel of the left aisle is an *Assunta* (Assumption) by Titian.

At the river end of Via Leoni, **Chiesa di San Fermo** is actually two churches in one. The Gothic church was built in the 13th century over the original 11th-century Romanesque structure. On the way southwest from Piazza delle Erbe towards the Castelvecchio is the **Chiesa di San Lorenzo**, a Romanesque church raised in the early 12th century but much altered with Gothic and Renaissance additions.

On the banks of the Adige, the 14th-century **Castelvecchio** fortress was raised by Cangrande II (of the Scaligeri family), little loved by the townspeople and anxious to protect himself against threats from home and abroad. Ironically, he was stabbed to death by his brother Canfrancesco inside the fortress walls. Restored in the 1960s after suffering bomb damage during WWII, the fortress now houses a museum with a diverse collection of paintings, frescoes, jewellery and medieval artefacts. Among the paintings are works by Pisanello, Giovanni Bellini, Tiepolo, Carpaccio and Veronese. Also of note is a 14th-century equestrian statue of Cangrande I, the fortress-builder's ancestor and most illustrious of the Della Scala clan. The **Ponte Scaligero** spanning the Adige was also rebuilt after being destroyed by WWII bombing.

A masterpiece of Romanesque architecture, the **Basilica di San Zeno Maggiore** in honour of the city's patron saint was built mainly in the 12th century, although its apse was rebuilt in the 14th century and its bell tower, a relic of an earlier structure on the site, was started in 1045. The basilica's magnificent rose window depicts the Wheel of Fortune, which had a habit of turning good and bad for Verona's ruler with dizzying rapidity. The main doors are decorated with bronze reliefs of biblical subjects. The highlight inside is Mantegna's triptych of the *Madonna col Bambino tra Angeli e Santi* (Madonna and Child with Angels and Saints), above the high altar.

Across Ponte Pietra, north of the city centre, is a **Roman theatre**, built in the 1st century AD and still used today for concerts and plays. Take the lift at the back of the theatre to the convent above, which houses an interesting collection of Greek and Roman pieces in the **Museo Archeologico**. On a hill high behind the theatre and museum is the **Castel San Pietro**, built by the Austrians on the site of an earlier castle.

Sights & Information

Arche Scaligere (Via Arche Scaligere; combined admission with Torre dei Lamberti by lift/on foot €2.50/2.10; ☼ 9.30am-7.30pm Tue-Sun, 1.30pm-7.30pm Mon)

Basilica di San Zeno Maggiore (Piazza San Zeno; admission €2, or combined ticket for all churches €5; ☼ 8.30am-6pm Mon-Sat, 1-6pm Sun)

Casa di Giulietta (Juliet's House; ☎ 045 803 43 03; Via Cappello 23; admission adult/child €3.10/2.10; ☼ 8.30am-7.30pm Tue-Sun, 1.30-7.30pm Mon)

Castelvecchio (☎ 045 59 47 34; Corso Castelvecchio 2; admission adult/student €3.10/2.10; ☼ 9am-6.30pm Tue-Sun)

Chiesa di San Fermo (Stradone San Fermo; admission €2, or combined ticket for all churches €5; ☼ 10am-6pm Mon-Sat, 1-6pm Sun)

Chiesa di San Lorenzo (Corso Cavour; admission €2, or combined ticket for all churches €5; ☼ 10am-6pm Mon-Sat, 1-6pm Sun)

Chiesa di Sant'Anastasia (Piazza di Sant'Anastasia; admission €2, or combined ticket for all churches €5; ☼ 9am-6pm Mon-Sat, 1-6pm Sun)

Duomo (Cathedral; Piazza Duomo; admission €2, or combined ticket for all churches €5; ☼ 10am-5.30pm Mon-Sat, 1.30-5.30pm Sun)

Guardia Medica (☎ 045 807 56 27; ☼ 8pm-8am) A locum doctor service – they usually come to you.

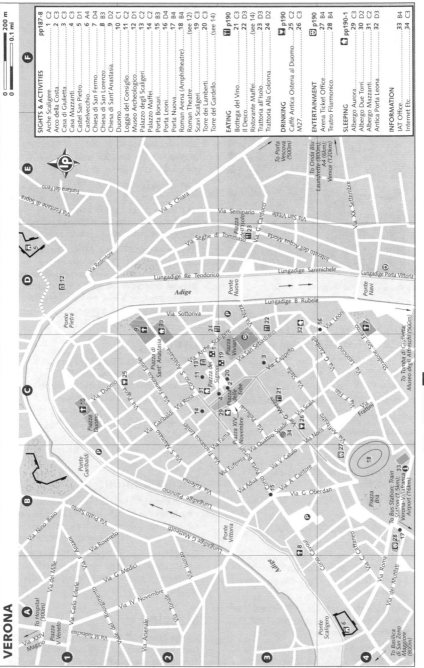

VERONA

SIGHTS & ACTIVITIES		pp187-8
Arche Scaligere	1	C2
Arco della Costa	2	C3
Casa di Giulietta	3	C3
Casa Mazzanti	4	C3
Castel San Pietro	5	D1
Castelvecchio	6	A4
Chiesa di San Fermo	7	D4
Chiesa di San Lorenzo	8	B3
Chiesa di Sant'Anastasia	9	D2
Duomo	10	C1
Loggia del Consiglio	11	C2
Museo Archeologico	12	D1
Palazzo degli Scaligeri	13	C2
Palazzo Maffei	14	C2
Porta Borsari	15	B3
Porta Leoni	16	D4
Porta Nuova	17	B4
Roman Arena (Amphitheatre)	18	B4
Roman Theatre	(see 12)	
Scavi Scaligeri	19	C2
Torre dei Lamberti	20	C3
Torre del Gardello	(see 14)	
EATING		🍴 p190
Bottega del Vino	21	C3
Il Desco	22	D3
Ristorante Maffei	(see 14)	
Trattoria all'Isolo	23	D3
Trattoria Alla Colonna	24	D2
DRINKING		🍷 p190
Caffè Antica Osteria al Duomo	25	C2
M27	26	C3
ENTERTAINMENT		🎭 p190
Arena Ticket Office	27	B4
Teatro Filarmonico	28	B4
SLEEPING		pp190-1
Albergo Aurora	29	C3
Albergo Due Torri	30	D2
Albergo Mazzanti	31	C2
Antica Porta Leona	32	D3
INFORMATION		
IAT Office	33	B4
Internet Etc	34	C3

Excursions – Verona

189

Eating

Bottega del Vino (☎ 045 800 45 35; Vicolo Scudo di Francia 3/a; meal €45-55; ✆ Wed-Mon) At least wander into this age-old wine cellar for the frescoes and atmosphere. Better still, sit down to fine food, an endless wine list and exquisite service.

Il Desco (☎ 045 801 00 15; Via Dietro San Sebastiano 7; meal €80-100; ✆ Tue-Sat, Sun lunch) Rated one of the best restaurants in Italy and a Michelin star winner, this is a quietly elegant stop for high-class local cuisine.

Ristorante Maffei (☎ 045 801 00 15; Piazza delle Erbe 38; meal €60; ✆ daily) Dine in the magnificent setting of the grand Palazzo Maffei's central courtyard.

Trattoria Alla Colonna (☎ 045 59 67 18; Via Pescheria Vecchia 4; meal €25-30; ✆ Mon-Sat) Pop in to this family-run place for a genuine local food experience. The 'column' in the name is a red Verona marble job smack in the middle of the restaurant, around which huddle the tables.

Trattoria all'Isolo (☎ 045 59 42 91; Piazza dell'Isolo 5/a; meal €25-30; ✆ Thu-Tue) Scoot across the river to find yourself in what feels like a more genuine Verona. Much the same can be said of this tiny eatery. Just about anything they do with *bigoli*, the Veneto version of a thick, rough spaghetti, is bound to please.

Drinking

Caffè Antica Osteria al Duomo (Via Duomo 7; ✆ noon-2pm & 7-10pm Mon-Sat) This is a cosy tavern with mandolins and other stringed instruments hanging on the wall. Pop in for a drop of *fragolino* (the local sweet strawberry wine).

M27 (☎ 045 803 42 42; Via Giuseppe Mazzini 27/a; ✆ 10am-2am Tue-Sun) Get down to this angular, modern bar to hang with a young, hip, Veronese crowd.

Entertainment

Roman Arena (☎ 045 800 51 51; www.arena.it; ticket office (Ente Lirico Arena di Verona) Via Dietro Anfiteatro 6/b; tickets €15-150; opera season Jul-Sep) Tickets are available online and at travel agents around the country.

Teatro Filarmonico (☎ 045 800 28 80 information, 045 800 51 51 bookings; Via dei Mutilati 4; tickets €8.50-36.50) The theatre's season of opera, ballet and classical music runs from October to May.

Sleeping

Albergo Aurora (☎ 045 59 47 17; fax 045 801 08 60; Piazza XIV Novembre 2; s/d with bathroom up to €104/117) The better rooms in this sprawling, central hotel are spacious and comfortable, although time is beginning to take its toll.

Verona's well-preserved Roman Arena (p187)

IAT office (☎ 045 806 86 80; www.tourism.verona.it; Via degli Alpini 9; ✆ 9am-7pm Mon-Sat, 9am-3pm Sun)

IAT office (☎ 045 800 08 61; train station; ✆ 9am-6pm Mon-Sat, 9am-3pm Sun)

IAT office (☎ 045 861 91 63; Verona-Villafranca airport; ✆ to meet flights)

Internet Etc (☎ 045 800 02 22; Via Quattro Spade 3/b)

Main post office (Piazza Viviani 7; ✆ 8am-7pm Mon-Sat)

Museo Archeologico (☎ 045 800 03 60; Regaste Redentore 2; admission adult/child €2.60/1.50; ✆ 8.30am-7.30pm Tue-Sun, 1.30-7.30pm Mon)

Onda Blu laundrette (Via XX Settembre 62/a; ✆ 8am-10pm)

Ospedale Civile Maggiore (Hospital; ☎ 045 807 11 11; Piazza A Stefani 1)

Questura (Police Station; ☎ 045 809 04 11; Lungadige Porta Vittoria)

Roman Arena (☎ 045 800 32 04; Piazza Brà; admission adult/child €3.10/2.10; ✆ 9am-7pm Tue-Sun, 1.45-7.30pm Mon Oct-Jun; 8am-3.30pm daily during opera season Jul-Sep)

Tomba di Giulietta (Juliet's Tomb; ☎ 045 800 03 61; Via del Pontiere 35; admission adult/child €2.60/1.50; ✆ 8.30am-7.30pm Tue-Sun, 1.45-7.30pm Mon)

Torre dei Lamberti (☎ 045 803 27 26; Piazza dei Signori; admission by lift/on foot €2.10/1.50, combined admission with Arche Scaligere €2.50/2.10; ✆ 9am-6pm Tue-Sun)

Albergo Mazzanti (☎ 045 800 68 13; fax 045 801 12 62; Via Mazzanti 6; s/d up to €72/104) Just off Piazza dei Signori, this place has some nice rooms but some pokey singles.

Antica Porta Leona (☎ 045 59 54 99; fax 045 59 52 14; Corticella Leoni 3; s/d up to €104/150) Located close to Juliet's supposed house, this is a reasonable three-star place with rooms full of faded character.

Hotel Due Torri (☎ 045 59 50 44;www.baglionihotels .com; Piazza di Sant'Anastasia 4; s/d up to €385/550) The Hotel Due Torri is Verona's top address: a grand old mansion where the ambience takes you back to a long-abandoned era of slightly stuffy, studied elegance. You'll find that antique wooden furniture dominates the rooms.

PADUA (PADOVA) & AROUND

The dynamic student city of Padua (population 209,600) is known to many as the city of St Anthony, considered by the faithful to be a kind of heavenly lost-and-found agent. Padua is also the site of some of the most exquisite of Giotto's frescoes. They alone warrant the effort to get here, but the old city core repays a leisurely visit, with its arcaded streets and grand squares.

As long ago as the 6th century BC the Veneti tribe had an important centre here, later known as Patavium under the Romans. The Lombards made short shrift of the place in AD 602, virtually razing it to the ground. The comeback was slow, but by the 13th century, when it was controlled by the querulous counts of Carrara, Padua was a burgeoning independent city-state. The Carrara encouraged cultural and artistic pursuits (when they weren't busy warring with all and sundry), and established the Studium, the forerunner of the university, in 1222. The foundation of the Basilica del Santo, dedicated to St Anthony, followed 10 years later. Venice put an end to the Carrara counts' passion for conquest when the Republic incorporated Padua into its growing land empire in 1405. The city largely prospered in peace until the demise of La Serenissima.

Just a five-minute walk south along Corso del Popolo (which later becomes Corso di Garibaldi and leads into the city centre) from the train station brings you to the **Cappella degli Scrovegni** in the Giardini dell'Arena. Enrico Scrovegni commissioned its construction in 1303 as a resting place for his father, who was denied a Christian burial because of his money-lending practices. Giotto's remarkable fresco cycle, probably completed between 1304 and 1306, illustrates the lives of Mary and Christ and is arranged in three bands. Among the most famous scenes in the cycle is the *Bacio di Giuda* (Kiss of Judas). The series ends with the *Ultima Cena* (Last Supper) on the entrance wall, and the Vices and Virtues are depicted around the lower parts of the walls. Keep in mind when the frescoes were painted – Giotto was moving well away from the two-dimensional figures of his medieval contemporaries. Giotto effectively was on the cusp between Gothic art and the remarkable explosion of new creativity that was still decades away – the Renaissance. Booking ahead is obligatory – see Sights & Information (p193). The admission ticket is also valid for the adjacent **Musei Civici agli Eremitani**, whose collection of 14th- to 18th-century Veneto art and largely forgettable archaeological artefacts includes a remarkable crucifix by Giotto.

A few steps from the Cappella degli Scrovegni stands the early-14th-century **Chiesa degli Eremitani**, an Augustinian church painstakingly rebuilt after being almost totally demolished by bombing in WWII. The remains of frescoes done by Andrea Mantegna during his 20s are displayed in a chapel to the left of the apse. Most were wiped out in the bombing, the greatest single loss to Italian art during the war. The *Martirio di San Jacopo* (Martyrdom of St James), on the left, was pieced together from fragments found in the rubble, while the *Martirio di San Cristoforo* (Martyrdom of St Christopher), opposite, was saved because it had been removed before the war.

Corso di Garibaldi spills into the like-named piazza, the first of a series of interlocking squares in the heart of Padua. You might want to stop for a coffee in **Caffè Pedrocchi**, just off Via VIII Febbraio on a little square adjoining Piazza Cavour. Restored a few years ago, it has long been *the* central café in Padua. During the day you can visit the *piano nobile*, the grand 1st floor. The succession of rooms created in the first half of the 19th century sweep in style from ancient Egyptian to Imperial.

About 100m down Via VIII Febbraio is the **university**, the main part of which is housed in Palazzo Bò ('ox' in Veneto dialect – it's named after an inn that previously occupied the site).

Transport

Distance from Venice Padua 37km; Arquà Petrarca 59km; Monselice 59km; Este 68km; Montagnana 83.5km

Direction West

Bus Regular SITA buses (☎ 049 820 68 11) from Venice (€2.90, 45 to 60 minutes) arrive at Padua's Piazzale Boschetti, 400m south of the train station. Local ACAP bus No 10 will get you to Piazza Cavour from the train station, while No 12 goes to Prato della Valle. Buy tickets (€0.85) at tobacconists and stamp them in the machines on the bus. To get to Arquà Petrarca you can take one of up to three daily buses (€2.35, 55 minutes) that run through here between Padua and Este.

Car The A4 connects Venice and Padua. The A13, which connects Padua with Bologna, starts at the southern edge of Padua. The two autostrade are connected by a ring road. Follow the SS16 south of Padua for Monselice and Arquà Petrarca, then branch west on the SS10 for Este and Montagnana.

Train The easiest way to Padua from Venice is by train (up to €4.44, 20 to 40 minutes). Trains run from Padua to Montagnana (€2.90, 50 minutes) via Monselice and Este.

Established in 1222, the university is Italy's oldest after the one in Bologna. Europe's first anatomy theatre opened here in 1594, and Galileo Galilei taught at the university from 1592 to 1610. The main courtyard and its halls are plastered with coats of arms of the great and learned from across Europe. Ask at the IAT office in Vicolo Pedrocchi about joining a guided visit.

Turn back about 100m to the west and you wander into the contiguous Piazza delle Erbe and Piazza della Frutta. These 'herbs' and 'fruit' squares still live very much up to their names, with boisterous produce markets setting up daily. The squares are also lined by a cornucopia of little shops selling all sorts of delicacies, interrupted by the occasional little bar where shoppers and market workers can take a liquid break from the buying and selling.

The two squares are separated by the majestic hulk of the **Palazzo della Ragione**, also known as the Salone for the grand hall that occupies its upper floor. Built in the 13th and 14th centuries, the building features frescoes by Giusto de' Menabuoi and Nicolò Mireto depicting the astrological theories of Pietro d'Abano. It is frequently the scene of temporary exhibitions.

West from here is the Piazza dei Signori, dominated by the 14th-century **Palazzo del Capitanio**, the former residence of the city's Venetian ruler. South is the **cathedral**, built from a much-altered design by Michelangelo. Its 13th-century Romanesque **baptistry** features a series of frescoes of Old and New Testament scenes by Giusto de' Menabuoi, influenced by Giotto.

From Piazza del Duomo return to Piazza delle Erbe and head east along Via San Francesco. When you hit Via del Santo, turn south (right) and you will soon emerge in the grand square of the same name, dominated by the city's most celebrated monument, the **Basilica del Santo** (or Basilica di Sant'Antonio), which houses the corpse of the town's patron saint and is an important place of pilgrimage. Construction of what is known to the people of Padua as Il Santo began in 1232. The saint's tomb, bedecked by requests for his intercession to cure illness or thanks for having done so, is in the Cappella del Santo, in the left transept. There was a time when the area surrounding the tomb was awash with crutches and other prosthetic devices of the grateful cured – these have been reduced to a symbolic few. Look out for the saint's relics in the apse. The sculptures and reliefs of the high altar are by Donatello, the master sculptor of the Florentine Renaissance.

Donatello remained in town long enough to carry out another assignment, the **Gattamelata equestrian statue** that presides over the centre of Piazza del Santo. This magnificent representation of the 15th-century Venetian *condottiero* (mercenary leader) Erasmos da Narni (whose nickname, Gattamelata, translates as 'Honeyed Cat'), was done in 1453 and is considered the first great bronze of the Italian Renaissance. Donatello made a lasting impression on Padua, leaving behind a whole school of sculptors that followed in his footsteps. They would come to specialise in *bronzetti* (bronze miniatures) coveted across Europe.

On the southern side of the piazza is the **Oratorio di San Giorgio**, the burial chapel of the Lupi di Soranga family, with 14th-century frescoes. Next door is the **Scoletta del Santo**, with works believed to be by Titian.

Just south of Piazza del Santo, the **Orto Botanico** is purportedly the oldest botanical garden in Europe and a Unesco World Heritage site. It was first laid out in 1545.

Southwest of Padua, along the A13 or the SS16, the **Colli Euganei** (Euganean Hills) are dotted with vineyards and good walking trails – ask at the Padua IAT office for information. If you are driving (which you pretty much have to, as public transport is abysmal), follow the signposted Strada dei Vini dei Colli Euganei (Euganean Hills Wine Road), which will take you on a road tour of many vineyards. Pick up a map and itinerary from the IAT office in Padua. Most of the vineyards are open to the public and some offer accommodation. The area is also famous for its hot springs, or *terme*. The two main centres in this respect are Abano Terme and Montegrotto Terme.

The quiet, hilly, medieval village of **Arquà Petrarca** in the southern Colli Euganei was where Italy's great poet Petrarch (Petrarca) chose to spend the last five years of his life. You can visit his **house**, which is set in cheerful gardens and contains various bits and bobs that purportedly had something to do with the scribe. Buses run here from Este and Monselice, both a short distance to the south.

Monselice, on the train line south from Padua, was once wrapped in no less than five protective layers of fortifications. Only bits of the old walls remain, along with the tower of the Rocca, or hilltop fort. The main point of interest here is the 11th-century **castle**, actually a complex collection of buildings raised over several centuries. The oldest part of the site, the Castelletto, is what remains of the original fort. The grand Torre di Ezzelino is a 13th-century tower. By the time the 15th-century Palazzo Marcello was built, the castle had lost its defensive character. Under Venetian rule it was further converted into a noble residence, but in later centuries decayed. It was in poor shape after WWI but restored in the 1930s.

West of Monselice along the road to Mantua (Mantova), **Este** is another in the chain of fortified strongholds in the area. Padua's Carrara clan were assiduous fortress builders – it seems they had a good number of enemies to keep at bay. Although the walls of their castle are in reasonable condition, the inside is pretty much a ruin. On the bumpy lane that climbs northwards behind the castle is the **Villa Kunkler**, where Byron settled in for a year or so in 1817. Shelley also stayed here.

About 12km west of Este rise the magnificent defensive perimeter walls, dating to the 13th and 14th centuries, of the fortified plains town of **Montagnana**. Of all the Veneto's walled towns, this is the most impressive – from the outside. Two kilometres of crenellated walls, studded by 24 defensive towers and four gates, still protect this rural centre. Once inside, however, there's not an awful lot to see.

Sights & Information

Baptistry (☎ 049 65 69 14; Piazza del Duomo, Padua; admission adult/child €2.50/1; ⏱ 10am-6pm)

Basilica del Santo (☎ 049 824 28 11; Piazza del Santo, Padua; ⏱ 7.30am-7pm)

Cappella degli Scrovegni (☎ 049 201 00 20; www.capp elladegliscrovegni.it; Giardini dell'Arena, Padua; admission adult/child €11/4, Mon €7.50/4; ⏱ 9am-7pm, extended to 10pm at times) The higher admission price includes admission to the Musei Civici agli Eremitani (which is closed on Monday). Booking by phone or online at least 24 hours before your visit is obligatory, and you are given a maximum of 15 minutes inside the chapel.

Cathedral (☎ 049 66 28 14; Piazza del Duomo, Padua; ⏱ 7.30am-noon & 3.30-7.30pm Mon-Sat, 7.45am-1pm & 3.45-8.30pm Sun & holidays)

Chiesa degli Eremitani (Giardini dell'Arena, Padua; ⏱ 8am-12.30pm & 4-6pm Mon-Sat, 9.30am-noon & 4-6pm Sun)

Complesso Clinico Ospedaliero (Hospital; ☎ 049 821 11 11; Via Giustiniani 1, Padua)

IAT office (☎ 049 875 20 77; www.apt.padova.it; Padua

train station; ⏱ 9am-7pm Mon-Sat, 8.30am-12.30pm Sun Apr-Oct; 9.20am-5.45pm Mon-Sat, 9am-noon Sun Nov-Mar)

IAT office (☎ 049 876 79 27; Vicolo Pedrocchi, Padua; ⏱ 9am-12.30pm & 3-7pm Mon-Sat)

From Portugal to Padua

St Anthony of Padua (1193–1232) was actually St Anthony of Portugal, where he was born (in Lisbon) and spent most of his life. At the age of 25, his wanderings began when he joined the Franciscans and headed for Morocco to preach among the Muslims. This could easily have proven little more than a suicide mission, but before he had the chance to become a martyr, poor health brought him back to Europe, where he spent the ensuing years travelling and teaching in France and northern Italy. He earned great respect for his erudition and his capacity to preach to the learned as convincingly as to more simple folk. St Anthony died in Padua and the shrine built to him became a prime centre of pilgrimage. To this day countless miracles are attributed to him, as well as a knack for being the finder of lost articles.

PADUA (PADOVA)

0   400 m
0   0.2 mi

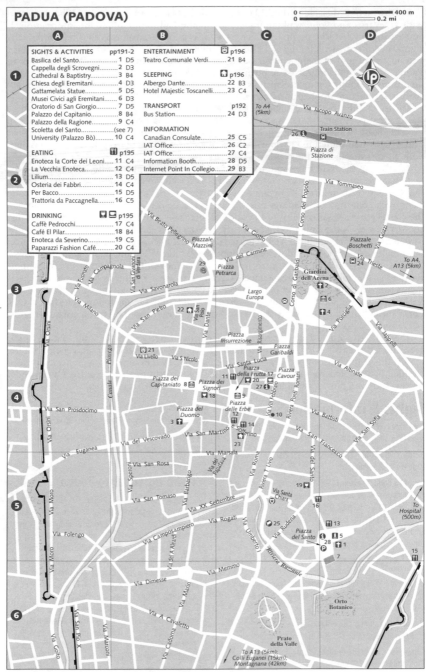

SIGHTS & ACTIVITIES	pp191-2
Basilica del Santo	1 D5
Cappella degli Scrovegni	2 D3
Cathedral & Baptistry	3 B4
Chiesa degli Eremitani	4 D3
Gattamelata Statue	5 D5
Musei Civici agli Eremitani	6 D3
Oratorio di San Giorgio	7 D5
Palazzo del Capitanio	8 B4
Palazzo della Ragione	9 C4
Scoletta del Santo	(see 7)
University (Palazzo Bò)	10 C4

EATING	p195
Enoteca la Corte dei Leoni	11 C4
La Vecchia Enoteca	12 C4
Lilium	13 D5
Osteria dei Fabbri	14 C4
Per Bacco	15 C5
Trattoria da Paccagnella	16 C5

DRINKING	p195
Caffè Pedrocchi	17 C4
Café El Pilar	18 B4
Enoteca da Severino	19 C5
Paparazzi Fashion Café	20 C4

ENTERTAINMENT	p196
Teatro Comunale Verdi	21 B4

SLEEPING	p196
Albergo Dante	22 B3
Hotel Majestic Toscanelli	23 C4

TRANSPORT	p192
Bus Station	24 D3

INFORMATION	
Canadian Consulate	25 C5
IAT Office	26 C2
IAT Office	27 C4
Information Booth	28 D5
Internet Point In Collegio	29 B3

Information booth (☎ 049 875 30 87; Piazza del Santo, Padua; ☼ peak season, variable timetable)

Internet Point In Collegio (☎ 049 65 84 84; Via Petrarca 9, Padua; membership €1.60, first hour €6, subsequent hours €3; ☼ 9am-2am)

Monselice Castle (☎ 0429 7 29 31; Monselice; one-hour guided tour adult/child €5.50/3; ☼ 9am-11am & 3-5pm Apr–mid-Nov) Admission by guided tour only.

Musei Civici agli Eremitani (☎ 049 820 45 50; Piazza Eremitani 8, Padua; admission adult/child €9/4, €11/4 including Cappella degli Scrovegni; ☼ 9am-7pm Tue-Sun Feb-Oct, 9am-6pm Tue-Sun Nov-Jan)

Oratorio di San Giorgio (Piazza del Santo, Padua; admission €2 with Scoletta del Santo; ☼ 9am-12.30pm & 2.30-6pm Mar-Oct, 9am-12.30pm & 2.30-5pm Nov-Feb)

Orto Botanico (☎ 049 827 21 19; Padua; admission adult/child €2.58/1.55; ☼ 9am-1pm & 3-6pm Apr-Oct, 9am-1pm Nov-Mar)

Padova Card (€13; valid 48 hours) A pass that allows you to visit the Cappella degli Scrovegni, Musei Civici agli Eremitani, Palazzo della Ragione, the first floor of Caffè Pedrocchi, a couple of minor chapels and Petrarch's House in Arquà Petrarca. It's available from tourist offices and the sights concerned.

Palazzo della Ragione (Piazza delle Erbe, Padua; admission adult/child €6/3, more during exhibitions; ☼ 9am-7pm Tue-Sun Feb-Oct, 9am-6pm Tue-Sun Nov-Jan)

Petrarch's House (☎ 0429 71 82 94; Via Valleselle 4, Arquà Petrarca; admission adult/child €5/3; ☼ 9am-12.30pm & 3-7pm Tue-Sun Mar-Oct, 9am-12.30pm & 2.30-5.30pm Tue-Sun Nov-Feb)

Piano Nobile Caffè Pedrocchi (☎ 049 820 50 07; Galleria Pedrocchi, Via VIII Febbraio 15, Padua; admission adult/child €3/2; ☼ 9.30am-12.30pm & 3.30-6pm Tue-Sun)

Post office (Corso Garibaldi 33, Padua; ☼ 8.15am-7pm Mon-Sat, 8.30am-6.30pm Sun)

Questura (Police Station; ☎ 049 83 31 11; Riviera Ruzzante 11, Padua)

Scoletta del Santo (Piazza del Santo, Padua; admission €2 with Oratorio di San Giorgio; ☼ 9am-12.30pm & 2.30-7pm Mar-Oct, 9am-12.30pm & 2.30-5pm Nov-Feb)

University (Palazzo Bò; ☎ 049 876 79 27; Via VIII Febbraio, Padua) Guided tours are offered three times per day from Monday to Saturday – ask at the IAT office on Vicolo Pedrocchi.

Eating

Caffè Pedrocchi (☎ 049 878 12 31; Via VIII Febbraio 15, Padua) A spruced up neoclassical facade fronts this classic café, which has been in business since the 19th century.

It was one of Stendhal's favourite haunts in a town that left him otherwise indifferent.

Enoteca la Corte dei Leoni (☎ 049 875 00 83; Via Pietro d'Abano 1, Padua; meal €45; ☼ Tue-Sat, Sun lunch) This modern temple of wine (you can taste from a broad list by the glass at the bar) in the heart of old Padua is also the site of a fine dining experience. In summer especially, book a table in the courtyard, where jazz concerts are occasionally staged. The food is good if a little *nouvelle* in terms of portions.

La Vecchia Enoteca (☎ 049 875 28 56; Via San Martino e Solferino 32, Padua; meal €40-45; ☼ Tue-Sat, Mon eve) This is a more traditional fine dining location. They do a nice *filetto di manzo alla salsa bernese* (steak fillet in a Béarnaise sauce).

Lilium (☎ 049 875 11 07; Via del Santo 181, Padua; ☼ 7.30am-8pm Tue-Sun winter, 7.30am-10pm Tue-Sun summer) This traditional pastry shop offers wonderful *gelato* and delicious sweet things.

Osteria dei Fabbri (☎ 049 65 03 36; Via dei Fabbri 13, Padua; meal €20-25; ☼ Mon-Sat) This lively spot is full of atmosphere. Try the *ravioloni di magro*, exquisite, light ravioli done in a butter and sage sauce.

Per Bacco (☎ 049 875 46 64; Piazzale Pontecorvo 10, Padua; meal €30-35; ☼ Tue-Sun) Try the *tagliatelle alla norcina con tartufo nero* (pasta with black truffles), a classic of Umbrian cuisine and a long-standing favourite here.

Trattoria da Paccagnella (☎ 049 875 05 49; Via del Santo 113, Padua; meal €30; ☼ Mon-Sat) This trattoria is a comfortably elegant setting for fine Veneto cuisine – try the *arrosto di coniglio disossato alle erbe* (boneless roast rabbit in herbs).

Drinking

Café El Pilar (☎ 049 65 75 65; Piazza dei Signori 8, Padua; ☼ 11am-3pm & 6pm-midnight) This is a classic example, where a mix of beautiful souls and others converge for the evening *spritz*. Often by 10pm people have scarpered, but nearby on Piazza del Duomo a crowd of pretty people, students and others hang about sipping cocktails later on in the evening.

Enoteca da Severino (☎ 049 65 06 97; Via del Santo 44, Padua; ☼ 11am-9pm) Come by to taste wines from around the region and beyond in this tiny wine bar. The walls of the bar are lined with bottles, and appreciative wine-lovers spill out into the street during the warmer months.

Paparazzi Fashion Café (☎ 049 875 93 06; Via Marsilio da Padova 17, Padua; ☼ 6pm-1am Tue-Sun) With its low red lights and dark drinking corners, this place attracts a young, cool crowd, all sunglasses at night and designer stubble.

Entertainment

Teatro Comunale Verdi (☎ 049 877 70 11; www.teatroverdipd.it, Italian only; Via Livello 32, Padua) For theatrical classics and the occasional opera.

Sleeping

Albergo Dante (☎ 049 876 04 08; Via San Polo 5, Padua; s/d €26/37 **P**) The bathroom is in the corridor and the rooms are a little bare but the prices are tough to argue with.

Hotel Majestic Toscanelli (☎ 049 66 32 44; www2.goldgate.it/hoteltoscanelli; Via dell'Arco 2, Padua; s/d up to €124/161 **⊠** **P**) Hidden away in a leafy corner of one of the lanes that twist away from Piazza delle Erbe, this

hotel boasts classy, newly renovated rooms, all in various styles (ranging from Imperial to what the owners call '19th-century English') and complete with all the usual mod cons.

Koko Nor Association (☎ 049 864 33 94; www.bandb-veneto.it/kokonor; Via Selva 5, Padua) This association can help you to find B&B-style accommodation in family homes as well as furnished apartments (they have 15 places on the books) starting from around €36 for a single or €55 for a double. The tourist office has a list of about 30 B&Bs.

Ostello Rocca degli Alberi (☎ /fax 0429 8 10 76; fax 049 807 02 66; Castello degli Alberi, Montagnana; per person €9.50; ⊗ Apr–mid-Oct) This unique HI youth hostel is in a former watchtower of Montagnana's extraordinary walls and close to the town's train station.

VICENZA & THE VILLAS

Vicenza (population 110,500) is the centre for Italian textile manufacturing and a leader in the development and production of computer components, making it one of the country's wealthiest cities. Indeed, this rather self-satisfied provincial centre has always done OK. It flourished as Roman Vicentia and after being swallowed up by the Venetian Republic in 1404 had no apparent qualms about adapting itself to the new situation. It appears that many locals rather liked being part of the Venetian mini-empire, reflected in their predilection for Venetian-style Gothic mansions.

Wedged in between Padua and Verona, Vicenza is a comparatively neglected stop on the Venetian tourist trail. And yet it has plenty to offer the day-tripper in its compact centre and beyond. The single great theme is Palladio, who left his mark all over the place. Unesco decided this was enough to include the city (along with Palladio's villas spread out across the Veneto region) in its list of World Heritage sites.

From the train station, in the gardens of Campo Marzo, walk straight ahead along Via Roma into Piazzale de Gasperi. From here Corso Andrea Palladio leads through the grand city gates into Piazza Castello. The square is lined with several grand edifices, including the oddly truncated **Palazzo Porto-Breganze** on the southern side, designed by Palladio and built by Scamozzi (one of the city's leading 16th-century architects). Its couple of outsize columns look strange now, but had the building been completed it would have been one of the city's most imposing structures. Corso Andrea Palladio continues northeast from the square and is the old town's central artery. Off it to either side is a host of striking architecture.

The Church has its main square in Piazza del Duomo but the **cathedral** here is of comparatively little interest. Allied bombs destroyed it during WWII and only a few artworks could be saved.

In nearby Piazza dei Signori rises the immense **Basilica Palladiana**, which Palladio began in 1549 on top of an earlier Gothic building – the slender 12th-century bell tower is all that remains of the original structure. Palladio's **Loggia del Capitaniato**, at the northwestern side of the piazza on the corner of Via del Monte, was left unfinished at his death.

Contrà Porti, which runs north off Corso Andrea Palladio, is one of the city's most majestic streets. The **Palazzo Thiene** (No 12), by Lorenzo da Bologna, was originally intended to occupy the entire block. Palladio's **Palazzo Barbaran da Porto** (No 11) features a double row of columns. A World Heritage–listed building, it is the richly decorated home to a museum and study centre devoted to Palladio, and frequently hosts architecture exhibitions. Palladio also built the **Palazzo Isoppo da Porto** (No 21), which remains unfinished. **Palazzo Valmarana** (Corso Antonio Fogazzaro 18) is considered one of his more eccentric creations.

Heading north along Corso Andrea Palladio and left into Contrà di Santa Corona, you reach the **Chiesa di Santa Corona**, established in 1261 by the Dominicans to house a relic from Christ's crown of thorns. Inside are the *Battesimo di Gesù* (Baptism of Christ) by Giovanni Bellini and *Adorazione dei Magi* (Adoration of the Magi) by Veronese.

Corso Andrea Palladio ends at the **Teatro Olimpico**, started by Palladio in 1580 and completed by Scamozzi after the former's death. Considered one of the purest creations of Renaissance architecture, the theatre design was based on Palladio's studies of Roman structures. Scamozzi's remarkable street scene, stretching back from the main facade of the stage, is modelled on the ancient Greek city of Thebes. He created an impressive illusion of depth and perspective by slanting the street up towards the rear of the set. The theatre was inaugurated in 1585 with a performance of *Oedipus Rex*, but soon fell into disuse – the ceiling caved in and it remained abandoned for centuries until 1934, when it was restored and reopened. Since then, the theatre has become a prized performance space for opera and drama – it is one of the few working theatres where the performers and audience are eyeball to eyeball.

The nearby **Museo Civico**, in the Palladian Palazzo Chiericati, contains works by local artists as well as by the Tiepolos and Veronese. The **Museo Naturalistico e Archeologico** has a modest collection of local ancient artefacts.

The sober baroque facades of the **Gallerie di Palazzo Leoni Montanari** belie a more extravagant interior. Long a private mansion and seat of a bank, it now contains a collection of more than 400 Russian icons (top floor) and mostly 18th-century Venetian paintings (1st floor). Among the outstanding works on show are some by Canaletto and Pietro Longhi. There are frequent temporary exhibitions too.

South of the city, the **Basilica di Monte Berico**, set on top of a hill, presents magnificent views. The basilica was built in the 18th century to replace a Gothic structure, itself raised on the supposed site of two appearances by the Virgin Mary in 1426. An impressive 18th-century colonnade runs most of the way up Viale X Giugno to the church – handy when it's pouring with rain. Walk or catch city bus No 9.

A 20-minute walk, back down Viale X Giugno and then east along Via San Bastiano, will take you to the **Villa Valmarana 'ai Nani'**. The villa features brilliant frescoes by Giambattista and Giandomenico Tiepolo. The 'ai Nani' (dwarves) refers to the statues perched on top of the gates surrounding the property.

A path leads on about 500m to Palladio's Villa Capra, better known as **La Rotonda**. It is one of the architect's most admired – and most copied – creations, having served as a model for buildings across Europe and the USA. The name comes from the low dome that caps this square-based structure, each side fronted by the columns of a classical facade. Bus No 8 stops nearby.

Villa hunters don't need to stop here. As Venetian patricians studded the Riviera del Brenta with their sumptuous summer palaces (see p200), so the countryside around Vicenza began to mushroom with country residences as early as the 15th century. One reason for this is that the Venetian Senate forbade the high and mighty of Vicenza, or any other of the mainland cities under Venetian control, from building castles. Venice feared a landscape dotted with well-defended forts occupied by potentially independent-minded individuals. And so Vicenza's great and good cottoned on to the villa construction fad. Many of the thousands that were built still remain, although most are inaccessible to the public.

The APT in Vicenza can provide reams of information about the villas most worth visiting, including an illustrated map entitled *Ville dal 1400 al 1800*.

Drivers should have little trouble planning an itinerary. One would see you taking the SS11 south of Vicenza to Montecchio Maggiore and then on to Lonigo and Pojana Maggiore. From there head north for Longare and back to Vicenza. A round trip of 100km, the route takes in about a dozen villas.

If you don't have a car, take the FTV bus north from Vicenza to Thiene, passing through Caldogno and Villaverla, and then

Transport

Distance from Venice 69km

Direction West

Bus Regular FTV buses (☎ 0444 22 31 15) leave from the bus station, just near the train station, for Thiene, Asiago (in the hilly north of the province), Bassano and towns throughout the nearby Monti Berici (Berici Hills).

Car Vicenza is on the A4 tollway connecting Venice with Milan. The slower (but cheaper!) SS11 also connects Vicenza with Venice (via Padua) and Verona. There is a large car park near Piazza Castello and the train station.

Train Regular trains arrive from Venice (up to €5.58, 55 minutes) and Padua (up to €4.44, 20 to 30 minutes). You can reduce the cost by getting slower *regionali* or *interregionali* trains. Other trains connect Vicenza with Milan, Verona, Treviso and smaller towns in the north.

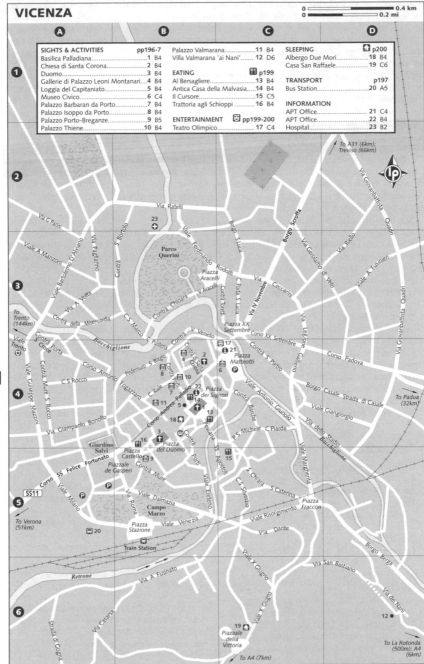

VICENZA

0 — 0.4 km
0 — 0.2 mi

SIGHTS & ACTIVITIES pp196-7
Basilica Palladiana.............................1 B4
Chiesa di Santa Corona.....................2 B4
Duomo..3 B4
Gallerie di Palazzo Leoni Montanari...4 B4
Loggia del Capitaniato.......................5 B4
Museo Civico.....................................6 C4
Palazzo Barbaran da Porto.................7 B4
Palazzo Isoppo da Porto.....................8 B4
Palazzo Porto-Breganze......................9 B5
Palazzo Thiene..................................10 B4

Palazzo Valmarana.............................11 B4
Villa Valmarana 'ai Nani'......12 D6

EATING p199
Al Bersagliere...................................13 B4
Antica Casa della Malvasia.....14 B4
Il Cursore..15 C5
Trattoria agli Schioppi 16 B4

ENTERTAINMENT pp199-200
Teatro Olimpico..................17 C4

SLEEPING p200
Albergo Due Mori.................18 B4
Casa San Raffaele.................19 C6

TRANSPORT p197
Bus Station........................20 A5

INFORMATION
APT Office..............................21 C4
APT Office..............................22 B4
Hospital.................................23 B2

continue on to Lugo. The Villa Godi-Valmarana, now known as the **Malinverni**, at Lonedo di Lugo, was Palladio's first villa.

Check with the tourist office in Vicenza for details of the Concerti in Villa Estate, a series of classical concerts held in villas around Vicenza each summer (usually July). You can also ask about accommodation, which is available in some villas.

Sights & Information

APT office (☎ 0444 54 41 22; www.vicenzae.org; Piazza dei Signori 8, Vicenza; ☒ 10am-12.30pm & 3-6.30pm) The office organises free guided tours of the city.

APT office (☎ 0444 32 08 54; Piazza Matteotti 12, Vicenza; ☒ 9am-1pm & 2-6pm)

Basilica di Monte Berico (☎ 0444 32 09 98; Piazzale della Vittoria, Vicenza; ☒ 6.15am-12.30pm & 2.30-6pm Mon-Sat, 6.15am-12.30pm & 2.30-7pm Sun & holidays)

Basilica Palladiana (☎ 0444 32 36 81; Piazza dei Signori, Vicenza; ☒ 9am-5pm Tue-Sun)

Chiesa di Santa Corona (Contrà di Santa Corona, Vicenza; admission free; ☒ 8.30am-noon & 3-6pm Tue-Sun, 4-6pm Mon)

Combined sights ticket Several combined ticket options are available. The Card Musei costs €7 (valid for three days) and gives you entry to the Teatro Olimpico, Museo Civico (Palazzo Chiericati) and the Museo Naturalistico e Archeologico. For €8 you can also visit the obscure Museo del Risorgimento e della Resistenza, dedicated to Italian reunification and the Resistance in the latter stages of WWII. It's located southeast of the train station at Viale X Giugno 115. The Card Musei e Palazzi (€11) gets you entry to all of these, plus the Gallerie di Palazzo Leoni Montanari and Palazzo Barbaran da Porto. The Card Vicenza e Ville (€22) adds La Rotonda and Villa Valmarana to the list.

Gallerie di Palazzo Leoni Montanari (☎ 800 57 88 75; www.palazzomontanari.com; Contrà di Santa Corona 25, Vicenza; admission adult/student €3.50/2.50, or combined sights ticket; ☒ 10am-6pm Fri-Sun, 10am-6pm Wed-Sun during temporary exhibitions)

La Rotonda (☎ 0444 32 17 93; Via Rotonda 29, Vicenza; admission to gardens only €3, admission to villa €6, or combined sights ticket; ☒ gardens 10am-noon & 3-6pm Tue-Sun Mar-Nov, villa 10am-noon & 3-6pm Wed Mar-Nov) Groups can book ahead to visit outside the normal opening hours – the price is hiked up to €8 per person in this case.

Main post office (Contrà Garibaldi, Vicenza)

Museo Civico (☎ 0444 32 13 48; Palazzo Chiericati, Piazza Matteotti 37/39, Vicenza; admission by combined sights ticket; ☒ 9am-5pm Tue-Sun Sep-Jun, 9am-7pm Tue-Sun Jul-Aug)

Museo Naturalistico e Archeologico (☎ 0444 32 04 40; Contrà di Santa Corona 4, Vicenza; admission by combined sights ticket; ☒ 9am-5pm Tue-Sun Sep-Jun, 9am-7pm Tue-Sun Jul-Aug)

Ospedale Civile (Hospital; ☎ 0444 99 31 11; Viale Ferdinando Rodolfi 37, Vicenza)

Palazzo Barbaran da Porto (☎ 0444 32 30 14; Contrà Porti 11, Vicenza; admission adult/student €5.50/3.50, or combined sights ticket; ☒ 10am-6pm Tue-Sun)

Palazzo Thiene (☎ 0444 54 21 31; entrance Contrà San Gaetano Thiene, Vicenza; admission free; ☒ 9am-noon & 3-6pm Tue-Wed Oct-Apr; 9am-noon & 3-6pm Wed & Fri, 9am-noon Sat May-Sep) Bookings are required.

Palladio website (www.cisapalladio.org/veneto) Information on just about every one of Palladio's Veneto buildings.

Questura (Police Station; ☎ 0444 33 75 11; Viale Giuseppe Mazzini 24, Vicenza)

Teatro Olimpico (☎ 0444 22 28 00; Corso Andrea Palladio, Vicenza; admission by combined sights ticket; ☒ 9am-5pm Tue-Sun Sep-Jun, 9am-7pm Tue-Sun Jul-Aug)

Villa Valmarana 'ai Nani' (☎ 0444 54 39 76; Via dei Nani 2/8, Vicenza; admission €6, or combined sights ticket; ☒ 10am-noon & 3-6pm Wed-Thu & Sat-Sun, 3-6pm Tue & Fri mid-Mar–early Nov)

Eating

Al Bersagliere (☎ 0444 32 35 07; Contrà Pescheria 11, Vicenza; meal €30; ☒ Mon-Sat) This is a traditional *osteria* (restaurant/bar) where you can eat *cicheti* (snacks) at the bar or proceed to the cosy little tables for seasonal cooking (watch for the mushrooms in autumn).

Antica Casa della Malvasia (☎ 0444 54 37 04; Contrà delle Morette 5, Vicenza; meal €20; ☒ daily) This den has been around since 1200. Drinking is still a primary occupation in a locale that has changed little in all those centuries – on offer is an array of 80 types of wine (especially Malvasia varieties) and around 100 types of grappa!

Il Cursore (☎ 0444 32 35 04; Stradella Pozzetto 10, Vicenza; meal €20-25; ☒ Wed-Mon) They've been serving up food in here since the 19th century and although it's been given a facelift, it's a great little spot for some local dishes, such as *spaghetti col baccalà mantecato* (spaghetti with cod prepared in parsley and garlic).

Entertainment

Teatro Olimpico (☎ 800 323 285, 0444 22 28 01; www.olimpico.vicenza.it; Corso Andrea Palladio, Vicenza) For theatre, classical music and other performances.

Vicenza Jazz A popular annual jazz festival held in various venues around town in May.

Villa Valmarana 'ai Nani' Ask the tourist office for details of summer concerts.

Sleeping

Albergo Due Mori (☎ 0444 32 18 86; fax 0444 32 61 27; Contrà do Rode 26, Vicenza; s/d up to €48/85) The rooms at this central cheapy are basic but it's clean and reliable.

Casa San Raffaele (☎ 0444 54 57 67; fax 0444 55 22 59; Viale X Giugno 10, Vicenza; d with bathroom up to €65 P) Located in a former convent behind the colonnade leading to Monte Berico, this is a charming spot to spend the night.

RIVIERA DEL BRENTA

Dotted along the River Brenta, which passes through Padua and spills into the Venetian lagoon, are more than 100 villas built over the centuries by wealthy Venetian families as summer homes. Many are dilapidated and closed, a sorry reflection of the fall from grace of many a grand Venetian family in the Republic's twilight years before it finally fell with a whimper to that upstart Corsican, Napoleon. Mind you, some prospered and a number of the villas date only to the 19th century, by which time Venice was under Austrian control (until 1866). Today, a handful of the most outstanding villas may be visited. Among them are Villa Foscari (1571), built by Palladio at Malcontenta, and Villa Pisani, also known as Villa Nazionale, at Strà.

No sooner do you roll out of the nightmare industry-scape of Marghera than you find yourself heading for **Malcontenta**. Here the Foscari family commissioned Palladio to construct a pleasure dome on the River Brenta. The result was a Palladian trademark – the riverside facade, with its ionic columns and classical tympanum, echoes the ancients that inspired him. The **Villa Foscari** is also known as La Malcontenta (the Malcontent), supposedly because a female family member was exiled here for fooling around with people other than hubby. Its interior is remarkable only for the frescoes with which it is covered. They mostly depict scenes from classical literature.

Next up is an early 18th-century rococo caprice just west of **Oriago**, the **Villa Widmann Foscari**. Built by a trading family, the Serriman (of Persian origin), it was later taken over by the Widmann clan and given the French rococo flavour it exudes today. Inside, the most impressive element is the grand Ballroom (Sala delle Feste), sumptuously decorated and ringed halfway up by an ornate gallery. The garden is littered with 18th-century statuettes of nymphs and cherubs.

Across the Brenta from Villa Widmann Foscari is the **Villa Barchessa Valmarana**, which was built a century later and is noteworthy mainly for its frescoes. Similarly alluring are the frescoes in the **Villa Barchessa Alessandri**, a little further along in Mira.

Transport

Distance from Venice Villa Foscari 12km; Villa Widmann Foscari 16km; Villa Barchessa Valmarana 16km; Villa Pisani 26km; Oriago 14km; Mira 18.5km; Strà 28.7km

Direction West

Boat The luxurious *Burchiello* barge plied the River Brenta from Venice to Padua in the 17th and 18th centuries. Today's rather more modern version (☎ 049 877 47 12; www.ilburchiello.it; adult/child €62/36 one way; operates Mar-Oct) cruises up and down the river between Venice and Strà (price includes tours of Villa Foscari and Villa Barchessa Valmarana; lunch is extra). Departures from Venice (Riva degli Schiavoni) are on Tuesday, Thursday and Saturday; those from Strà are Wednesday, Friday and Sunday. Shuttle buses connect the docking point in Strà with Padua's main bus station. Call for information, or try travel agents in Venice. Other companies also operate tours along the Brenta, including I Batelli del Brenta (☎ 049 876 02 33; www.antoniana.it), offering similar tours at similar prices. Ask at the Venice or Padua tourist offices for more details.

Bus Regular ACTV buses running between Venice and Padua (via Mestre, Marghera, Oriago, Mira, Dolo and Strà) stop at or near the villas. Take the No 53 bus from Mestre headed for Padua via Malcontenta to visit the Villa Foscari and then proceed west. You'll need some patience if you intend to do this excursion by bus.

Car From Venice follow the signs out of Mestre through Marghera to Malcontenta. From there follow the SS11 for Strà.

Villa Pisani is by far the most magnificent of the lot. It is set in extensive gardens just short of **Strà** and was completed in 1760 for Doge Alvise Pisani. In a later incarnation the villa was used by Napoleon as a temporary residence, and in more recent times hosted Hitler's first meeting with Mussolini. It is quite an exercise in family trumpet-blowing. From the outsize statues at the main entrance to Tiepolo's ceiling fresco (a pictorial eulogy to the Pisani clan), it is a flashy display of wealth. Outside, a close-cropped lawn and pond separate the main house from a lesser mansion. On either side, privacy is maintained by heavily wooded gardens.

In Strà itself is the imposing **Villa Foscarini Rossi**, dating to the 17th century and constructed for one of Venice's senior families. Among the many architects involved was Vincenzo Scamozzi (who worked from designs by Palladio), although the present look results partly from a later neoclassical reworking. The restored mansion, surrounded by carefully manicured grounds, hosts a couple of permanent displays, one dedicated to Rossimoda, which for decades has produced footwear for the biggest names in fashion (from Yves Saint Laurent to Fendi), and the other a private art collection of Luigino Rossi, who happens to be behind the shoes and now owns the villa. A separate and more modest building, the **Foresteria** (once used for distinguished guests), is now used for high-flying conventions.

A couple of other noteworthy villas are **Villa Sagredo** in Vigonovo and **Villa Gradenigo** in Oriago.

On Sundays and holidays in June, September and October, guided visits are sometimes organised to further villas in the area as part of the Ville Aperte (Open Villas) initiative.

For the latest information on all the villas open to the public, including some not mentioned here, ask at the APT main office in Venice. Bear in mind that their information may not always be accurate – since most of the villas are privately owned, opening times and prices can vary capriciously. See Vicenza & The Villas (p196) for more grand mansions.

Sights & Information

APT office (Map pp254-5; ☎ 041 529 87 11; fax 041 523 03 99; Piazza San Marco 71/f, Venice; 🕙 9am-3.30pm Mon-Sat)

IAT office (Map p194; ☎ 049 875 20 77; www.apt .padova.it; train station, Padua; 🕙 9am-7pm Mon-Sat, 8.30am-12.30pm Sun Apr-Oct; 9.20am-5.45pm Mon-Sat, 9am-noon Sun Nov-Mar)

Infopoint (Map pp254-5; Venice Pavilion, Venice; 🕙 10am-6pm daily)

Villa Barchessa Alessandri (☎ 041 41 57 29; Via Nazionale 64, Mira; admission €10 combined with Villa Barchessa Valmarana and Foresteria in Villa Foscarini Rossi; 🕙 10am-12.30pm & 2.30-6pm Tue-Sun May-Sep; 2-5pm Sat, 10.30am-12.30pm & 2-5pm Sun Feb-Apr)

Villa Barchessa Valmarana (☎ 041 426 63 87; admission adult/child €5.16/4.13; 🕙 9am-12.30pm & 2.30-6pm Tue-Sun, Apr-Oct; groups by appointment only)

Villa Foscari (Map p248; ☎ 041 520 39 66; Via dei Turisti 9; admission €7; 🕙 9am-noon Tue & Sat Mar-Oct) Groups of 12 or more can book ahead for other times at €8 per person.

Villa Foscarini Rossi (☎ 049 980 10 91; Via Doge Pisani 1/2, Strà; admission adults/12-18/under 12 €5/2.50/free; 🕙 9am-12.30pm & 2.30-6pm Mon-Fri, 9.30am-12.30pm & 2-6pm Sat, 10am-6.45pm Sun, closed weekends Nov-Jan)

Villa Gradenigo (☎ 049 876 02 33; Oriago di Mira; admission €3; 🕙 only by appointment for groups)

Villa Pisani (☎ 049 50 20 74; Via Alvise Pisani 7, Strà; admission adult/EU citizens 18-25/under 18 €5/2/free; grounds only €2.50/1.20/free; 🕙 9am-6pm Apr-Sep, 9am-4pm Oct-Mar)

Villa Sagredo (☎ 049 50 31 74; Vigonovo; admission free; 🕙 5-10pm Tue-Fri, 1-10pm Sat-Sun)

Villa Widmann Foscari (☎ 041 42 49 73; Mira Porte; admission €5; 🕙 10am-5pm Tue-Sun Apr, 10am-6pm Tue-Sun May-Sep)

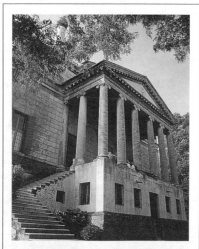

Palladio's Villa Foscari in Malcontenta

TREVISO & AROUND

A small, pleasant city (population 82,500) with historical importance as a Roman centre, Treviso is well worth a day trip from Venice, easily accomplished by train.

Treviso claims Luciano Benetton, the fashion king with the outrageous advertising campaigns, as its favourite and easily most controversial son. You will find a huge Benetton shop in the centre of town, but factory outlets around the outskirts of town are the strict preserve of Benetton employees.

The local tourist office likes to promote Treviso as the Città d'Acqua (City of Water) and compare it with Venice. While the River Sile, which weaves through the centre, is quite beautiful in parts, the comparisons are more touching than realistic.

That said, the city is a delight to wander. From the train station, head north along Via Roma (over the canal), past the bus station and across the bridge (the nicely placed McDonald's on the river is an unmistakable landmark), and keep walking straight ahead along Corso del Popolo. At Piazza della Borsa, veer left down Via XX Settembre and you arrive in the heart of the city, **Piazza dei Signori**.

Transport

Distance from Venice Treviso 30km; Oderzo 55km; Conegliano 58km; Vittorio Veneto 73.5km
Direction North
Bus The Treviso bus station is on Lungosile Mattei, near the train station in Piazzale Duca d'Aosta. ACTV buses connect Venice with Treviso, and La Marca buses link Treviso with other towns in the province. Buses travel to Conegliano (45 minutes) and Vittorio Veneto (one hour five minutes).
Car Take the SS13 from Venice (Mestre) to Treviso and on to Conegliano and Vittorio Veneto. The A27 autostrada is faster but bypasses all three. For Oderzo, take the SS53 northeast from Treviso.
Train Trains from Venice to Treviso (€1.95, 25 to 30 minutes) make better sense than the bus. Other trains link the town with Belluno (via Conegliano and Vittorio Veneto), Padua and major cities to the south and west.

Piazza dei Signori is dominated by the fine brick **Palazzo dei Trecento**, the one-time seat of city government. Beneath the vaults you can now stop for coffee and a bite. Also under the vaults is the worn 16th-century Fontana delle Tette (Tit Fountain), from whose breasts red and white wine flowed for three days each year on the appointment of a new town governor. The practice ended with the fall of Venice in 1797. The medieval main street is the porticoed Via Calmaggiore, which leads to the **cathedral**, a massive structure whose main source of interest lies in the frescoes inside by Il Pordenone (1484–1539).

Backtrack to Piazza dei Signori and head east (around and behind the Palazzo dei Trecento), and you will soon find yourself in a little warren of lanes that leads to five delightful bridges across the Canal Cagnan, which runs roughly north–south and spills into the River Sile. Treviso is a comparatively leafy town and this is particularly the case at some points along the canal. You can also see the occasional mill wheel (the one by Vicolo Molinetto still turns).

While on the right bank of the canal you might pop into the deconsecrated **Chiesa di Santa Caterina**. The church and its attached convent and cloisters are being developed as a museum to house the city's art treasures. In the church itself are remarkable frescoes attributed to Gentile da Fabriano (who worked in the early 15th century). The beautiful Cappella degli

Benetton's Burgeoning Business

Back in 1965 a young Treviso lad by the name of Luciano Benetton and his younger siblings, Giuliana, Gilberto and Carlo, decided to set up a clothing business. They could not have known that less than 40 years later they would have more than 5000 stores set up across 120 countries, €150 million in annual profit and a brand name that sticks in the mind. Concentrating on attractive, young fashion (with a children's line thrown in) their two brands, the United Colors of Benetton and Sisley, have established themselves worldwide. This is in part due to the daring advertising campaigns nowadays cooked up at Fabrica, a modern complex not far from the Benetton headquarters north of Treviso. Many would argue that Benetton has often breached the bounds of good taste, but whatever you think of their controversial publicity, it has always managed to attract attention. The business is still in the family and an outstanding success story of the Veneto economic miracle, which has seen a largely poor, agricultural economy transform itself into a dynamic small-business oriented dynamo since the 1960s.

Innocenti contains frescoes by other artists of the same period, depicting the lives of Christ and the Virgin Mary. To these have been added the extraordinary fresco cycle by Tommaso da Modena (1326–79) on the life and martyrdom of St Ursula (Santa Orsola or Orseola), recovered late in the 19th century from an already partly demolished church. You may have seen Carpaccio's depictions of the same subject in Venice's Gallerie dell'Accademia.

Tommaso also left frescoes in the imposing **Chiesa di San Nicolò**, on the other side of town. Also at the other end of town is the **Museo Civico Luigo Bailo**, named after the friar who in the late 19th century made it his life work to collect ancient artefacts and artworks to preserve the memory of Treviso's past. At the time most townsfolk thought him an eccentric. Today they owe him a debt of thanks. The museum hosts an archaeological section and a collection of mostly Veneto artists, including works by Tintoretto, Lorenzo Lotto, Titian and Cima da Conegliano. They are followed by local art of the early 20th century.

Where the Canal Cagnan empties into the Sile is a particularly pleasant corner with part of the city walls still intact. In summer, you can take a **boat cruise** on the *Silis* or *Altino* down the Sile to the Venetian lagoon and back. The tours are by reservation only – call or ask at the tourist office.

Oderzo, 25km northeast of Treviso, is a microcosm of its grander neighbour. The central Piazza Grande is flanked by the 15th-century cathedral and a fine clock tower, and is frequently the scene of classical music recitals in summer. The town's handful of peaceful canals, crisscrossed by little bridges bearing pretty flower boxes, is inevitably reminiscent of Treviso.

North of Treviso, on the road to Belluno, you could call in at **Conegliano**, wine capital of the Veneto region (Treviso province provides a lot of the region's *prosecco*, a sparkling white wine) and dominated by a castle (which you can reach on foot or by car). The centre of town, a few minutes' walk straight ahead down Via Carducci from the train station, is notable for the long Scuola dei Battuti on Via XX Settembre, decorated inside and out with frescoes. The cathedral, which you enter from the Scuola, is noteworthy for an altarpiece painted by local painter Cima da Conegliano in 1492–93.

The train from Venice via Treviso stops at Conegliano then proceeds to the strange animal that is **Vittorio Veneto**. Actually a composite of two towns (Ceneda and Serravalle), Vittorio Veneto is most comfortably visited with your own transport. As you arrive from the south, do not follow signs for the *centro* (as you normally would). These take you to the modern part of the conglomerate, which lacks any real interest. Instead, follow signs for **Ceneda**, whose main attractions are the sweeping Piazza Giovanni Paolo I and **Castello di San Martino**, about a 1km hike up into the leafy hills. To reach the picturesque huddle of houses that is **Serravalle**, you need to follow signs for Belluno. These apparently lead you out of Vittorio Veneto, but just as you get that leaving feeling you stumble on this northernmost, and prettiest, part of the sprawling municipality.

Sights & Information

APT office (☎ 0422 54 76 32; Piazzetta Monte di Pietà 8, adjacent to Piazza dei Signori, Treviso; ☼ 9am-12.30pm & 2-6pm Tue-Fri, 9.30am-12.30pm & 3-6pm Sat-Sun, 9am-12.30pm Mon) From October to March, the afternoon hours shorten a little. The office sometimes organises free guided tours of the city.

APT office (☎ 0422 81 52 51; Piazza Castello 1, Oderzo)

APT office (☎ 0438 2 12 30; Via XX Settembre 61, Conegliano)

APT office (☎ 0438 5 72 43; Piazza del Popolo 18, Vittorio Veneto)

Boat Cruises (☎ 0422 78 86 63, 0422 78 86 71) For cruises along the River Sile.

Cathedral (Piazza del Duomo, Treviso; ☼ 7.30am-noon & 3.30-7pm Mon-Fri, 7.30am-1pm & 3.30-8pm Sat & Sun)

Chiesa di San Nicolò (Via San Nicolò, Treviso; ☼ 7am-noon & 3.30-7pm)

Chiesa di Santa Caterina (☎ 0422 54 48 64; Via di Santa Caterina, Treviso; admission €3; ☼ 9am-12.30pm & 2.30-6pm Tue-Sun)

Museo Civico Luigi Bailo (☎ 0422 65 84 42; Borgo Cavour 24, Treviso; admission €3; ☼ 9am-12.30pm & 2.30-5pm Tue-Sat, 9am-noon Sun)

Eating

Piola (☎ 0422 54 02 87; Via Carlo Alberto 11, Treviso; pizzas from €5-7; ☼ Tue-Sun) This is a hip bar-cum-pizzeria, where you can sit outside on a little terrace or bury yourself in the dimly lit innards of the bar with Treviso's night crowd.

Ristorante al Dante (☎ 0422 59 18 97; Piazza Garibaldi 6, Treviso; meal €20-25; ☼ Mon-Sat) This is

Detour: Belluno & the Dolomites

Belluno is an attractive town (population 35,000) at the foot of the Dolomites. You could come on a long day trip via Treviso, but much better would be to take a couple of days and use it as a base to explore the mountains. The heart of the old town is formed by Piazza del Duomo, dominated on one side by the early-16th-century Renaissance Cattedrale di San Martino, the Palazzo Rosso, from about the same period, and the Palazzo dei Vescovi.

About two hours' drive north of Venice on the A27 tollway, the town is a starting point for activities in the mountains, from summertime hiking to skiing in winter. Stretching away to the northwest is the Parco Nazionale Dolomiti Bellunesi, a beautiful national park laden with opportunities for those who want some mountain air.

Six Alte Vie delle Dolomiti (high altitude walking trails) pass through the territory surrounding Belluno, and along them you will find *rifugi* (mountain huts), on route No 1 in particular, where you can stay at the end of a day's hiking. Route No 1 stretches between Belluno and Lago di Braies in the region of Trentino-Alto Adige. The huts are generally open from late June to late September.

About 50km north of Belluno and connected by bus is the chic ski resort of Cortina d'Ampezzo, for wintertime visitors to Venice with an urge to rip down a few fashionable Italian slopes.

The **IAT office** (☎ 0437 94 00 83; Piazza dei Martiri 8, Belluno; 9am-12.30pm & 3.30-6.30pm daily) has further information.

an excellent budget option where you can sidle up to the bar for a host of *cicheti*, or dine at one of the teeny tables. In the summer months you can sit outside and gaze across to the river. Typically, people pop in to this restaurant for *cicheti* and *prosecco*, or perhaps a crisp Friuli white.

Ristorante Alle Becchiere (☎ 0422 54 08 71; Piazza Ancilotto 10, Treviso; meal €20-25; Tue-Sat, Sun lunch) This historic central eatery offers a local menu with a few curve balls thrown in (such as *trenette al pesto* from Liguria). The products are fresh and the end results are pleasing. The owners claim that tiramisu was invented here!

Shopping

Benetton (☎ 0422 55 99 11; Piazza dell' Indipendenza 5, Treviso; 9.15am-12.30pm & 3.30-7.30pm Tue-Sat, 3.30pm-7.30pm Sun-Mon) Shopaholics will be unable to resist a trip to the store where the Benetton story began.

Sleeping

Albergo Campeol (☎ 0422 5 66 01;www.albergocampeol .it; Piazza Ancilotto 4, Treviso; s/d €52/83) This is a nicely maintained place in a restored building just off Piazza dei Signori. It's about the only decent central choice and three of the doubles have canal views.

BASSANO DEL GRAPPA & AROUND

Known above all for its firewater, grappa, and to a lesser degree for its ceramics, Bassano del Grappa (population 40,300) sits astride the River Brenta just south of the first line of hills that are a prelude to the Dolomites. To art-lovers, the name will ring another bell. The Da Ponte family of Renaissance painters, known to us now as the Bassano, came from here. The pretty, old centre of town and a chance to get inside the grappa story are enough incentive to come here (easily done by train from Venice), but around Bassano radiate half a dozen curious objectives, from the charming hill village of Asolo to the fortified plains towns of Cittadella and Castelfranco del Veneto.

From Bassano train station it's about a five-minute walk west to the edge of the old town and the APT office. Buses halt a couple of hundred metres south of the tourist office at Piazzale Trento; from there another five-minute walk west takes you to the heart of the old centre. The River Brenta, crossed by the Ponte degli Alpini, flows to the west of the centre.

The centre of Bassano is composed of two sloping and interlinking squares, Piazza Garibaldi and Piazza Libertà. In the latter, the winged lion of St Mark stands guard on a pedestal to remind you of who was long in charge here.

In the **Museo Civico**, attached to the Chiesa di San Francesco on Piazza Garibaldi, you can see an assortment of items, including paintings by members of the Bassano clan and archaeological finds such as ancient Greek ceramics and bronze figurines. Among the Bassano collection, which takes up a whole floor, are 17 canvases by Jacopo. Also on display is a section devoted to the sculptor Canova, with his letters, books, drawings and plaster casts. A separate ceramics collection with more than 1000 porcelain pieces, the **Museo della Ceramica**, is housed in Palazzo Sturm on the banks of the Brenta and can be visited on the same ticket.

Follow Via Matteotti north off Piazza Libertà towards the remains of **Castello Ezzelini**, the stronghold that belonged to the medieval warlords of the same name.

Via Gamba slithers downhill from Via Matteotti to the River Brenta and the covered bridge designed by Palladio and known as the **Ponte degli Alpini**. It is nicknamed after the mountain troops who rebuilt it in 1948 after retreating German soldiers seriously damaged it at the tail end of WWII. Via Gamba and the bridge are lined with ceramics shops and a few grappa outlets. Throw in some bars and snack joints and it makes a pleasant stroll. The views across to old Bassano from the far riverbank alone make the walk from the centre worthwhile.

While by the bridge, pop into the Poli grappa shop with its **Poli Museo della Grappa**, which briefly outlines the history of the production of the drink. You'll have trouble resisting the chance to buy an elegant bottle or two of the clear, high-octane liquid (which comes in a surprising array of styles and varieties). A short walk south along Via Ferracina brings you to the above-mentioned Museo della Ceramica.

Transport

Distance from Venice Bassano del Grappa 77km; Asolo 64.5km; Possagno 74.7km; Cittadella 54.5km; Castelfranco del Veneto 42km

Direction West

Bus Regular buses linking Bassano with Padua call in at Cittadella (20 minutes from Bassano). Buses (up to six per day) between Bassano and Montebelluna stop below Asolo. You need to get the little orange shuttle bus from there to reach the centre, otherwise it's a long walk. About 10 buses a day run from Bassano to Possagno (one hour).

Car The most direct route from Venice is the Castelfranco del Veneto road leading northwest out of Mestre. You could also combine tours and head first to Treviso, then arc northwest towards Montebelluna to make for Asolo (and maybe Possagno) before proceeding further west to Bassano del Grappa and then returning to Venice via Cittadella and Castelfranco. It's a slightly exhausting itinerary but possible.

Train The easiest way to Bassano from Venice is by train on the Venice–Trento line (€3.70, 1¼ hours). A train from Padua (€2.90, one hour) is another option. Castelfranco is on the Venice–Bassano line (€2.90, 50 minutes from Venice).

East of Bassano, **Asolo's** position high in the hills, surrounded by fields, farms and woods, makes it an enchanting village. Caterina Corner, the ill-fated Venetian queen of Cyprus, was given the town and surrounding county towards the end of the 15th century in exchange for her abdication (see the boxed text on p206). The writer Pietro Bembo attended Caterina's salons and, perhaps in search of a hint of that same atmosphere, Robert Browning also spent time in Asolo.

Piazza Garibaldi forms the town centre, from where streets wind up in all directions between the tight ranks of golden-hued houses that lend this place so much of its charm. The **cathedral** lies below and just to the south of the square. It contains a few paintings by Jacopo Bassano and Lorenzo Lotto. Caterina Corner lived in the **castle**, now used as a theatre. An arduous climb up Via Collegio from Piazza Brugnoli will get you to the **rocca**, the town's medieval fortress. The walk north out of town to the **Cimitero di Sant'Anna** is rewarding for the views over the lush, green countryside. Eleonora Duse, a whirlwind actress romantically involved with poet Gabriele d'Annunzio, was buried here in 1924.

Birth and resting place of Antonio Canova, Italy's master of neoclassical sculpture, **Possagno** (population 2035) is a good place to get an idea of how Canova worked. The **Gipsoteca** is home to a long series of clay models and other preparatory pieces for his finished work (you can see some statues and reliefs by Canova in Venice's Museo Correr).

Before you reach the Gipsoteca, you'll have been astonished by the rather outsize **Tempio**, to all intents and purposes the parish church, that Canova was considerate enough to leave to his town. Finished in 1832, it could be described as neo-mongrel-classical, as it is an amalgam of Greek and Roman models.

Southeast of Bassano lie a couple of fortified plains towns worth a quick stop. **Cittadella** (population 18,700), a 12km bus ride south of Bassano on the busy SS47 to Padua, is enclosed by 1.5km of towering red-brick walls and a moat. Of the four gates, the northern Porta Bassano is the most elaborate. Padua raised the fort in the 13th century to face off the one built by Treviso at **Castelfranco del Veneto** (population 31,500), 10km east, towards the end of the 12th century.

Castelfranco ('Free Fort') could not have been an overly sought-after address, as the rulers of Treviso exempted from all taxes anyone prepared to move in. From its construction until 1339, when it was absorbed into Venice's mainland empire, Castelfranco del Veneto remained a hotly contested site and frequently changed hands. Padua laid siege to it barely 10 years after its construction. More than 60 years after Venice took control of Castelfranco, the lion of St Mark was finally raised over Cittadella in 1405.

The square-based walls of Castelfranco are less impressive than the circular version at Cittadella, but the town has an extra claim to fame as the birthplace of the mysterious painter Giorgione. Little is known about his life and only half a dozen works can be definitely attributed to him. One of them, the *Madonna col Bambino in Trono e Santi Francesco e Liberale* (Madonna and Child Enthroned with Saints Francis and Liberale), is in the **cathedral**.

A Queen Cornered

In 1468, as 14-year-old Caterina Corner was escorted in pomp out of the family mansion in San Polo to the Palazzo Ducale, she must have wondered what was coming next. *'Niente di buono'* ('nothing good') would have been the response of wise onlookers. Betrothed to 28-year-old James, the usurper king of Cyprus, Caterina found herself four years later pregnant, widowed and surrounded by enemies in her new island home.

James' untimely (and suspicious) death convinced Venice that it must act to protect its growing interest in the island. Captain General Pietro Mocenigo was dispatched first to fortify Venetian forts and then later to reverse a coup against the queen. The Cypriots were none too enamoured of de facto Venetian rule on their island, but after the coup attempt, government was effectively in the hands of two Venetian *consiglieri* (councillors), ostensibly in the service of the queen.

After the death of her infant son in 1474, Caterina's problems only increased. Plots against her from Cypriot nobles came thick and fast, and her protectors, the Venetians, virtually held her prisoner. In 1488, Venice decided enough was enough. Cyprus was threatened by Turkish invasion and the latest plots against Caterina were proving insufferable. It was decided to absorb the island into the Venetian Empire. For this, Caterina had to be convinced to abdicate.

This she did with some reluctance but she had little choice. For her trouble she was compensated with a mainland fief centred on Asolo and a generous life pension. She returned to her Venetian home only in 1509, where she died the following year. She kept her title of queen until the end. Less than a century later Venice would lose Cyprus to the Turks anyway.

Sights & Information

APT office (☎ 0424 52 43 51; Largo Corona d'Italia 35, Bassano; ☻ 9am-1pm & 2-6pm)

Cathedral (Castelfranco del Veneto; admission free; ☻ 8am-noon & 3.30-7pm)

Gipsoteca (☎ 0423 54 43 23; Possagno; admission adult/student €4/3; ☻ 9am-noon & 3-6pm Tue-Sun)

Museo Civico (☎ 0424 52 22 35; Via del Museo 12, Bassano; admission adult/student €4.50/3; includes Museo della Ceramica; ☻ 9am-6.30pm Tue-Sat, 3.30-6.30pm Sun)

Museo della Ceramica (☎ 0424 52 49 33; Palazzo Sturm, Via Schiavonetti, Bassano; admission see Museo Civico; ☻ 9am-12.30pm & 3.30-6.30pm Tue-Sat, 3.30-6.30pm Sun Apr-Oct; 9am-12.30pm Fri, 3.30-6.30pm Sat-Sun Nov-Mar)

Poli Museo della Grappa (☎ 0424 52 44 26; www.poligrappa.com; Ponte Vecchio, Bassano; admission free; ☻ 9am-1pm & 2.30-7.30pm)

Tempio (Possagno; admission free; ☻ 9am-noon & 3-6pm)

Eating

Ca' Derton (☎ 0423 52 96 48; Piazza d' Annunzio 11, Asolo; meal €40; ☻ Tue-Sat) They do a tempting *capretto alle erbe aromatiche* (kid meat in herbs) and have a fine wine list and dessert menu.

Nardini (Ponte degli Alpini, Bassano; ☻ 9am-8pm) Sit down among the grand old wine barrels and sip grappa at this wonderful old bar right on the old city centre side of the bridge.

Ostaria al Borgo (☎ 0424 52 21 55; Via Margnan 7, Bassano; meal €25-30; ☻ Thu-Fri, Sun-Tue, Sat dinner) Hearty cuisine, such as skewers of lamb and pasta dishes with porcini mushrooms, is on the menu.

Sleeping

Hotel Castello (☎ /fax 0424 22 86 65; Via Bonamigo 19, Bassano; s/d up to €52/82) In the shadow of the old castle walls, this is the only hotel within the old town. It's a fairly small and simple affair but perfectly acceptable.

Hotel Duse (☎ 0423 5 52 41; fax 0423 95 04 04; Via Browning 190, Asolo; s/d up to €52/120) The hotel has lovely rooms and they would certainly want to be at this price. Bear in mind that the Duse is the cheapest option in town.

Hotel Victoria (☎ 0424 50 36 20; www.hotelvictoria -bassano.com; Viale Diaz 33, Bassano; s/d up to €52/82) The whitewashed and carpeted rooms are well kept and boast TV, minibar and all the usual bits and bobs. The location is nothing great but otherwise it's not a bad deal.

Detour: Marostica's Life-Size Chess Match

For the most colourful game of chess you are ever likely to see, you need to be in the quiet medieval town of **Marostica** (population 12,800) on the second weekend of September in even-numbered years (2004, 2006 and so on). You know you have almost arrived (if coming from nearby Bassano) when you see the jagged line of battlements that climbs the hill from Marostica's town centre to the upper castle.

Pretty enough to warrant a brief stop in its own right, Marostica comes into its own for the biennial **Partita a Scacchi** (Chess Match). Back in 1454, they say, two knights challenged each other to a duel for the hand of the fair Lionora, elder daughter of the town's ruler, Taddeo Parisio. The latter, not wanting to lose either warrior, banned the duel and ordered them to 'fight' it out in a grand game of chess using real people on a huge 'board' at the gates of the lower castle. The two knights ordered the moves and the winner got Lionora. The loser didn't come off too badly, since he wed Parisio's younger daughter, apparently just as radiant.

The event today is as colourful as the original must have been, with an assembly of players and other characters in period costume. The game is choreographed in advance, using one of the classic matches between chess champions as the basis. If you can't be here for the match, you can admire the costumes in the lower castle (Castello da Basso). Marostica is a 15-minute bus ride from Bassano.

More information can be found at the **tourist office** (☎ 0424 7 21 27; www.marosticascacchi.it; Piazza Castello 1, Marostica).

THE ADRIATIC COAST

The Adriatic coast, spreading east and gradually north away from Venice, is lined with popular local beach resorts. They tend to be crowded on summer weekends but not quite so bad during the week. Quite a few foreigners flock to them too, using the resorts as the core of their summer holiday and chucking in the odd excursion to Venice as a diversion. These places are pleasant enough, but the northern Adriatic is not the place to plan a classic Mediterranean beach holiday.

Lido di Jesolo, the strand a couple of kilometres away from the main town of Jesolo, is far and away the Venetians' preferred beach. The sand is fine and clean, the water is OK and the place hops in summer with several dance clubs grooving through the night.

Jesolo (population 23,000) marks the northern end of a long peninsula that becomes Litorale del Cavallino as you head south and culminates in Punta Sabbioni, which together with the northern end of the Lido di Venezia forms the first of the three entrances into the Venetian lagoon from the Adriatic.

The beaches tend to be covered in umbrellas, recliners and the people using them. The area also has camping grounds and plenty of hotels of all classes. The whole lot is predictably short on character but can make a fun diversion from heavy-duty sightseeing in Venice; sort of a sunny Blackpool-near-Venice.

Nothing is left to remind you of the ancient roots of **Eraclea**, now a small agricultural town on the way from Jesolo to Caorle, itself 30km east around the coast from Jesolo.

In the 1st century BC **Caorle** (population 11,500) was a Roman port, and it remains a

Transport

Distance from Venice Lido di Jesolo 44.5km; Caorle 68.5km

Direction Northeast

Boat In summer (roughly June to September), ferry services to Venice are sometimes available, but cannot be guaranteed from one year to the next.

Bus ATVO buses run from Piazzale Roma in Venice to Jesolo (one way/return €3.80/6.20, 70 minutes) and Caorle (one way/return €4.40/7.80, 1½ hours).

Car Driving up this way can be a nightmare on mid-summer weekends and holidays, and even midweek is sometimes fraught because of the intense traffic. Take the SS14 from Mestre.

Excursions – The Adriatic Coast

busy fishing centre today. Small but proud, it dropped resistance to Venetian pressure and passed under the paws of St Mark's lion only in the 15th century. The centre of the medieval town is watched over by the extraordinary cylindrical bell tower of the 11th-century **cathedral**. The cheerful streets present a pastel pageant. Although they haven't gone to quite the lengths of the people of Burano, the townsfolk take a special pride in keeping their houses gleaming with a fresh coat of paint in an array of bright colours.

The beaches are busy but OK and the whole place has a restrained vibe that sets it apart from the more soulless Jesolo. It is quite popular with Germans. If you want to stay, the old town centre is blessed with a handful of places to lay down your weary head. The surrounding area and beachside waterfront are lined with phalanxes of hotels. There is no shortage of restaurants in which to enjoy the local seafood, although quality tends to be a little mediocre.

For Adriatic Coast information, try the **Palazzo del Turismo** (☎ 041 37 06 88) in Piazza Brescia, Jesolo, or the **Ufficio Turismo** (☎ 0421 21 92 53) in Caorle.

Directory

Directory

The information in this chapter is divided into two parts, Transport and Practicalities. Within each section information is presented in alphabetical order.

TRANSPORT

AIR

Venice is one of Italy's smaller air traffic centres. Direct flights from major European centres and sometimes from New York are available, alongside internal flights from the rest of Italy, but for most intercontinental air travel you will have to change flights at least once, either in Rome or Milan or at another major European hub.

Flights

Look out for budget airline deals. EasyJet in particular occasionally puts on very cheap flights from the United Kingdom to Venice's Marco Polo airport, while Ryanair has good deals from London Stansted and Brussels to Treviso's San Giuseppe airport. Ryanair also flys to Brescia airport, which can be handy for those wanting to get to or leave from Verona. Italy's Volare does similar deals. These budget airlines work on a first-come, first-served basis: the earlier you book on a flight the less you pay. As flights fill, the price of a ticket rises. These no-frills airlines skip extras such as in-flight meals (although you can buy snacks).

Within Italy, air travel is expensive. In the northern half of the country it makes more sense to go by train, as the time saving by air is rarely that great and the economic savings are considerable. Alitalia and Meridiana are the main airlines serving Venice. Most direct flights into Venice come from Rome and Milan, with a handful from Naples, Olbia and Palermo.

Most airlines, especially the budget ones, encourage you to search for and book fares on their websites. Useful general sites to search for competitive fares are www.planesimple.co.uk, www.opodo.co.uk and www.expedia.co.uk.

Airlines

Airlines don't bother with shopfront offices in Venice, so you'll need to go online, call the following numbers or try a travel agent. Most airlines have desks at the airports they serve.

Air Dolomiti (EN; ☎ 01803 869 900 in Germany, 800 013 366 in Italy; www.airdolomiti.it) Flights from Berlin and Munich.

Air Littoral (FU; ☎ 0825 834 834 in France, 035 23 30 04 in Italy; www.airlittoral.com) Flights from Nice (and other French cities via Nice).

Air One (AP; ☎ 800 900 966; www.flyairone.it) Flights from throughout Italy.

Alitalia (A2; ☎ 848 865 641/2/3; www.alitalia.it) Flights from Rome, Milan and other Italian centres, as well as from many European hubs.

Alpi Eagles (E8; ☎ 041 599 77 88; www.alpieagles.com) Flights from several Italian and Greek cities, as well as Barcelona (Spain).

British Airways (BA; ☎ 0870 850 9850 in UK, 199 712 266 in Italy; www.britishairways.com) Flights from the UK.

Delta (DL; ☎ 1-800 221 1212 in USA; www.delta.com) Flights from New York.

EasyJet (U2; ☎ 0871 750 0100 in UK, 848 887 766 in Italy; www.easyjet.com) Flights from London Stansted, Bristol and East Midlands.

Meridiana (IG; ☎ 899 199 001; www.meridiana.it) Flights from Barcelona and several Italian cities.

Ryanair (FR; ☎ 0871 246 0000 in UK; 899 89 98 44 in Italy; www.ryanair.com) Flights from London Stansted and Brussels to Treviso.

Qantas Airways (QF; ☎ 13 13 13 in Australia, 06 524 82 725 or 800 785 361 in Italy; www.qantas.com.au) Flights from Australia.

Volare (8D; ☎ 899 700 007; w3.volareweb.com) Flights to Venice from London Gatwick, Madrid and various Italian cities. Buy online or contact a travel agent (in Italy).

Airports

Venice's **Marco Polo airport** (VCE; ☎ 041 260 92 60 for flight information; www.veniceairport.it) is 12km outside Venice and just east of Mestre. Some flights, notably Ryanair's budget services from London and Brussels, use Treviso's minuscule **San Giuseppe airport** (TSF; ☎ 0422 31 53 31), about 5km southwest of Treviso and

30km (about an hour's drive through traffic) from Venice.

A new terminal was opened at Marco Polo airport in 2002. Arrivals (arrivi) is on the ground floor, where will you also find an Azienda di Promozione Turistica (APT) office, numerous car rental outlets, hotel booking agencies, bureaux de change, left luggage (deposito bagagli) and lost luggage (bagagli smarriti). Check-in and departures are on the 1st floor. You'll find banks, ATMs, cafés and shops on both floors.

At Treviso's San Giuseppe airport, the arrivals hall boasts a small, thinly stocked regional tourist information booth, a lost-luggage office next to it, a bureau de change and several car-hire outlets. Next door in departures you'll find an ATM and a couple of tour and airline offices (including Ryanair). There is no left luggage service.

There are several options for getting to Venice from Marco Polo airport, from the superexpensive water taxi to the cheap and relatively straightforward bus. The main problem is with night flights that arrive late. Some people have found themselves at the airport faced with a long wait for public transport and no taxis. All this will change radically in the coming years. A daring €250 million project to build a sublagoon rail link from the airport via Murano to the Arsenale in Venice will put the city just 12 minutes from its airport! Work is due to start in 2004 and the link should be running in 2010. Meanwhile…

BUS

ATVO (Azienda Trasporti Veneto Orientale; ☎ 041 520 55 30) buses run from Marco Polo airport to Piazzale Roma via Mestre train station – they're also known as Fly buses. The journey takes 20 minutes and costs €3 (€2.50 from the airport to Mestre train station). There are regular departures throughout the day (around 28 to 30 per day).

The **ACTV** (Azienda Consorzio Trasporti Veneziano; ☎ 041 528 78 86; www.actv.it) city bus No 5 also runs between Marco Polo airport and Piazzale Roma (€1.50). It makes more stops and takes closer to 30 minutes. The No 15 operates between the airport and Mestre train station.

Eurobus (☎ 041 541 51 80) buses connect with Ryanair's flights at Treviso's San Giuseppe airport. The trip to/from Piazzale Roma takes 65 minutes and costs €4.40 (€7.80 return, but the ticket is valid for one week only). Alternatively, local Treviso bus No 6 stops right outside the terminal gates and goes to the main train station in Treviso. From there you can proceed to Venice by train.

BOAT

Alilaguna fast ferries from Marco Polo airport to Venice or the Lido (€10) and Murano (€5) operate approximately once an hour. There are two lines, the red (rosso) and blue (blu). The main difference between them is that the blue line stops at Fondamente Nuove and Stazione Marittima but not at Zattere. Travelling to the airport, you can pick up the red ferry at several stops, including Zattere (Map pp256-8), San Marco (Map pp254-5), San Zaccaria (Map pp254-5) and Arsenale (Map p259). A free shuttle bus connects the embarkation point at the airport with the new terminal building. Note that, coming from the airport, the red ferry runs to Murano (Museo), the Lido, Arsenale, San Zaccaria, Piazza San Marco and Zattere in that order. The trip to Piazza San Marco takes one hour and 10 minutes (a few minutes longer on the blue line).

A **water taxi** (☎ 041 522 23 03, 800 066 315) is sheer luxury. The rate for the ride between Piazzetta di San Marco and Marco Polo airport is €44.95.

See also Venice Card (p219).

TAXI

Normal land taxis cost around €25 to €30 one way from Marco Polo airport to Piazzale Roma (15 to 20 minutes). From Treviso's San Giuseppe airport (€60 or more) can take an hour in heavy traffic.

BICYCLE

Cycling (which is hardly feasible anyway) is banned in Venice. On the Lido and Pellestrina, however, it can be a mighty pleasant option. A couple of bicycle hire places are clustered around the vaporetto stop on Gran Viale Santa Maria Elisabetta (Map pp262-3). You'll pay €8.50 per day.

BOAT

You probably know already that, aside from your feet, boats are the only way around Venice. You may not realise that you can also arrive by boat. Apart from Mediterranean cruise ships that call in, a couple of companies run regular ferries to Venice from Greece. Contact **Minoan Lines** (www.minoan.gr) and **Blue Star Ferries** (www.bluestarferries.com). **Venezia Lines** (www.venezialines.com) runs high-speed catamarans between Venice and six destinations, including pretty Pola, along the Istrian coast (once part of La Serenissima's merchant empire) in Croatia.

Vaporetto

The most common form of transport around Venice, after your own two feet, are the vaporetti, the city's ferries. Actually, there are at least three kinds of ferry: the standard, ponderous vaporetto (as in line No 1 down the Grand Canal), the sleeker *motoscafo*, which also runs local routes, and the *motonave* – big inter-island boats that head for Torcello and other more distant destinations. Just to complicate things a little, locals tend to call any public transport boat a *batello*.

The **ACTV** (☎ 041 528 78 86) runs public transport in the Comune di Venezia (the municipality), covering mainland buses and all the waterborne public transport around Venice. You can pick up timetables and route maps for the vaporetti and buses from the ACTV information office on Piazzale Roma (Map pp250-2).

Something to remember: the vaporetti get crowded and visitors have a habit of gathering by exits. If you are standing near one, it is common practice on reaching a stop to get off and let passengers behind you disembark before you get back on.

A night vaporetto service (the N line) does a slow circuit around Venice and the Lido (see Routes below).

ROUTES

From Piazzale Roma, vaporetto No 1 zigzags up the Grand Canal to San Marco and then on to the Lido. If you aren't in a rush, it's a great introduction to Venice. Vaporetto No 17 carries vehicles from Tronchetto, near Piazzale Roma, to the Lido.

A route map can be found on p266. Routes and route numbers change regularly, so the following list should be taken as a guide only. Not all routes go both ways.

DM (Diretto Murano) Tronchetto–Piazzale Roma–Ferrovia–Murano and back.

LN (Laguna Nord) San Zaccaria–Lido–Litorale del Cavallino (Punta Sabbioni)–Burano and back OR Fondamente Nuove–Murano–Burano–Punta Sabbioni and back.

T Torcello–Burano (half-hourly service) and back.

No 1 Piazzale Roma–Ferrovia–Grand Canal (all stops)–Lido and back.

No 3 Fast circular line: Tronchetto–Ferrovia–San Samuele–Accademia–San Marco–San Basilio–Tronchetto (summer only).

No 4 Fast circular line in reverse direction to No 3 (summer only).

No 5 San Zaccaria–Murano and back (summer only).

No 11 Lido–Pellestrina and back.

No 13 Fondamente Nuove–Murano–Vignole–Sant'Erasmo–Treporti and back.

No 17 Car ferry: Tronchetto–Lido and back (extends to Punta Sabbioni in summer).

No 18 Murano–Vignole–Sant'Erasmo–Lido and back (summer only).

No 20 San Zaccaria–San Servolo–San Lazzaro and back.

No 24 Fondamente Nuove–San Giuliano.

No 31 Pellestrina–Chioggia and back.

No 41 Circular line: Piazzale Roma–Sacca Fisola–Giudecca–San Zaccaria–San Pietro–Fondamente Nuove–Murano–Ferrovia.

No 42 Circular line in reverse direction to No 41.

No 51 Circular line: Piazzale Roma–Zattere–San Zaccaria–Lido–San Pietro–Fondamente Nuove–Ferrovia.

No 52 Circular line in reverse direction to No 51.

No 61 Limited-stops circular line: Ferrovia–Piazzale Roma–San Basilio–Zattere–Arsenale–Sant'Elena–Lido.

No 62 Limited-stops circular line, reverse direction to No 61.

No 82 San Zaccaria–San Marco–Grand Canal (all stops)–Ferrovia–Piazzale Roma–Tronchetto–Zattere–Giudecca–San Giorgio. A Limitato San Marco or Limitato Piazzale Roma sign means it will not go beyond those stops. Sometimes it goes only as far as Rialto. In summer the line extends from San Zaccaria to the Lido.

N All-stops night circuit: Lido–Giardini–San Zaccaria–Grand Canal (all stops)–Ferrovia–Piazzale Roma–Tronchetto–Giudecca–San Giorgio–San Zaccaria (starts around 11.30pm; last service around 5am).

NMU (Notturno Murano) A night service from Fondamente Nuove – three or four runs from midnight.

NLN (Notturno Laguna Nord) A night version of the Laguna Nord service – a handful of services between Fondamente Nuove and Burano, Mazzorbo, Torcello, Sant'Erasmo and Treporti.

TICKETS

Tickets can be purchased from the ticket booths at most stops. Generally they are validated when sold to you, which means they are for immediate use. If they are not validated, or if

Directory

you request them not to be (so you can use them later), you are supposed to validate them in the machines at each stop before you get on the vaporetto. You can also buy tickets when boarding (at a slightly higher price). You may be charged double if you have lots of luggage. If you are caught without a ticket you must buy one and pay a €23 fine.

The following tickets are poor value and should only be used if you rarely catch a vaporetto:

Corsa semplice (one-way trip; valid one hour) €3.50

Andata e ritorno (round trip; valid 24 hours) €6

Grand Canal (valid 90 minutes) €5

Line 11 (boat and bus, Lido to Chioggia) €5

Return trip using Grand Canal one way (lines 3 & 4) €7

Better value is a *biglietto a tempo* (€10.50), a ticket valid on all transport (except the Alilaguna, Fusina, LineaBlù and Clodia services) for unlimited travel during 24 hours from the first validation (*convalida*). The *biglietto tre giorni* is a three-day version (€22, or €15 if you have a Rolling Venice card). See also Venice Card (p219).

OTHER SERVICES

Linea Clodia (Venice–Chioggia) €9.30 same-day return from Venice (Pietà); operates June to September only.

Linea Fusina (No 16; Zattere–Fusina) €5/9 one way/return.

WARNING

Vaporetto stops can be confusing, especially at the bigger and busier stops like Piazzale Roma, Ferrovia, San Marco and San Zaccaria. At these and some others you will see several stops, each catering to a line and direction. Study the signs at the various quays carefully, otherwise you might find yourself on a vaporetto with the right number but going the wrong way!

Vessels making for the Piazza San Marco area in particular can cause anguish, as most stop at one of a string of stops along Riva degli Schiavoni (Map pp254-5 & p259). Always keep an eye out for San Zaccaria. If your boat stops here, it is unlikely to make another San Marco stop before heading off elsewhere.

Traghetto

The poor man's gondola, *traghetti* are used by locals to cross the Grand Canal where there is no nearby bridge. There is no limit (except

common sense) on the number of passengers, who stand. The ride costs €0.40.

Traghetti operate from about 9am to 6pm between Campo Traghetto (near Santa Maria del Giglio) and Calle de Lanza (Map pp256-8); Campo San Samuele, north of the Ponte dell'Accademia, and Calle del Traghetto (Map pp256-8); Calle Mocenigo Casa Vecchia, further north, and Calle Traghetto (Map pp256-8); and Campo Santa Sofia and Campo della Pescaria (Map p253), near the produce market.

Several other *traghetto* routes operate from 9am to noon only. They include Stazione di Santa Lucia to Fondamenta San Simeon Piccolo (Map pp250-2); Campo San Marcuola to Salizzada del Fondaco dei Turchi (Map pp250-2); Fondamenta del Vin to Riva del Carbon, near the Ponte di Rialto (Map pp254-5); and Calle Vallaresso to Punta della Dogana (Map pp254-5). Some of these may on occasion not operate at all.

Water Taxi

Venetian water taxis are prohibitively expensive, with a set €13.95 charge for a maximum of seven minutes, an extra €4.15 if you order one by telephone, and various surcharges that make a gondola ride begin to seem affordable. The town hall promised in 2003 that a meter system would eventually be introduced, with the aim of reducing fares and also speed (and so the damage caused by waves).

Rogue Taxis

A particular problem on the Isola del Tronchetto is illegitimate water-taxi drivers. These people may wear official-looking caps and badges and approach the freshly parked tourist with stories of having the only vessel available to transfer people from Tronchetto to destinations elsewhere in Venice. This is rubbish, as vaporetti call here regularly. Unwitting victims are transported (often to places they did not want to go) for outrageous sums of money. Some have been whisked away to Murano to look at someone's cousin's glass shop!

Ignore all approaches from boat captains or illegal 'taxis'. This is a racket that has gone on for years and its practitioners can become menacing – thankfully some of them do occasionally end up behind bars. The vaporetto line 82 will get you safely to most parts of Venice.

Gondola

A gondola ride is the quintessence of romantic Venice, but few people use them for practical transport purposes (like getting from the train station to your hotel). And at €62 for 50 minutes (€77.50 after 8pm) the official price is a rather hefty return from the clouds to reality. The rates are for a maximum of six people – less romantic but more affordable. After the first 50 minutes you pay in 25-minute increments (€31, or €38.75 after 8pm). Several travellers have reported successfully negotiating below the official rates (definitely possible if business is slow), so get your haggling skills in order! And don't let them haggle you above the official rates, which haven't changed since 1997.

Gondolas are available near main canals all over the city, or can be booked in San Marco (☎ 041 520 06 85), Rialto (☎ 041 522 49 04) and Piazzale Roma (☎ 041 522 11 51), and at the train station (☎ 041 71 85 43).

Rental

The truly freewheeling tripper with nerves of steel might want to rent a boat to get around Venice with more panache than your average tourist. Try **Brussa** (Map pp250-2; ☎ 041 71 57 87; www.brussaisboat.it, Italian only; Fondamenta Labia, Cannaregio 331; ⏱ 7am-5.30pm Mon-Fri, 7am-1pm Sat). You can hire a boat for an hour (€20.66) or a day (€131), or make an arrangement for a longer period. Prices include petrol (if you need to fill up there are only four boat petrol stations around Venice). Although you don't need a boat licence, you will be taken on a test run to see if you can manoeuvre and park – if you have no experience, they won't rent you a vessel.

BUS

All buses serving Venice use Piazzale Roma as their terminus. **Eurolines** (www.eurolines.com), in conjunction with local bus companies across Europe, is the main international carrier. Eurolines' website provides links to the sites of all the national operators. In Venice, Eurolines tickets can be bought from **Agenzia Brusutti** (Map pp250-2; ☎ 041 522 97 73; Piazzale Roma 497/e). Buses run several times a week from London, Paris, Barcelona and other European centres.

ACTV (☎ 041 528 78 86) buses serve the area immediately surrounding Venice, including Mestre and Chioggia, while **ATVO** (☎ 041 520 55 30) operates buses to destinations all over the eastern part of the Veneto. Numerous other companies go further west in the Veneto, across into Friuli-Venezia Giulia (Italy's easternmost region) and elsewhere throughout the country. Tickets and information are available at the ticket office in Piazzale Roma (Map pp250-2). As a rule, most main destinations (Padua, Vicenza, Verona and Treviso in the Veneto; Bologna, Florence, Milan, Rome and Trieste beyond) are more conveniently reached by train.

You can't take buses anywhere around Venice itself, but buses (including night buses) run across the bridge to Mestre and up and down the Lido. Tickets cost €1 and are valid for one hour from the time you validate them in the machine on the bus. A carnet of 10 tickets costs €9.

You can buy tickets at the main bus station in Piazzale Roma, and from many newsstands and tobacconists (tabaccherie). See also Vaporetto (p212).

CAR & MOTORCYCLE
Driving to Venice

To give you an idea of how many clicks you'll put behind you if travelling with your own wheels, Venice is 279km from Milan, 529km from Rome, 579km from Geneva, 1112km from Paris, 1135km from Berlin, 1515km from London and 1820km from Madrid.

The main points of entry to Italy are the Mont Blanc tunnel from France at Chamonix, which connects with the A5 for Turin and Milan; the Grand St Bernard tunnel from Switzerland, which also connects with the A5; and the Brenner Pass from Austria, which connects with the A22 to Bologna. Mountain passes in the Alps are often closed in winter and sometimes in autumn and spring, making the tunnels a less picturesque but more reliable way to arrive in Italy. Make sure you have snow chains in winter.

Once in Italy, the A4 is the quickest way to reach Venice from east or west. It connects Turin with Trieste, passing through Milan and Mestre. Take the Venezia exit and follow the signs for the city. Coming from the Brenner Pass, the A22 connects with the A4 near Verona. From the south, take the A13 from Bologna, which connects with the A4 at Padua. A more interesting route is the SS11 from Padua to Venice.

Directory

Many of Italy's autostrade (four- to six-lane motorways) are toll roads and the tolls tend to be expensive. You sometimes have the choice of the toll road or busy *strada statale* (represented on maps as 'S' or 'SS'). These tend to pass through towns and can as much as double your travel time. The SS11 from Padua to Venice is an example. Smaller roads are known as *strade provinciali* (represented on maps as 'P' or 'SP'). You can pay tolls by credit card (including Visa, MasterCard, Amex and Diners Club) on most autostrade in northern Italy.

Vehicles must be roadworthy, registered and insured (third party at least). Ask your insurer for a European Accident Statement form, which can simplify matters in the event of an accident. A European breakdown assistance policy, such as the AA Five Star Service or the RAC Eurocover Motoring Assistance in the UK, is a good investment.

You can pay for petrol with most credit cards at most service stations. Those on the autostrade are open 24 hours. Otherwise, opening hours are generally around 7am to 12.30pm and 3.30pm to 7.30pm (7pm in winter). Up to 75% of service stations are closed on Sundays and public holidays; others close on Mondays. Don't assume you can't get petrol if you pass a station that is closed: quite a few have self-service pumps that accept banknotes.

Parking

Visitors to Venice who insist on driving their cars right into the city pay a hefty price for the pleasure, and not necessarily just in parking fees. On busy days (especially holiday weekends), day-trippers who drive into the city frequently find themselves stuck on the Ponte della Libertà making little forward progress and unable to go back. It is not unknown for traffic to get so jammed that the police shut the city off from the mainland. Why risk it?

Driving in Venice is, of course, impossible. Once over the Ponte della Libertà from Mestre, cars must be left at one of the huge car parks in Piazzale Roma or on the island of Tronchetto. There is a small area in Piazzale Roma where you can drop a car for 30 minutes free of charge (in practice, people tend to leave their cars longer). Queuing to get into one of these few spaces can be supremely frustrating, but locals generally observe the first come, first served rule. Otherwise, you

can pay to tie up your metallic steed at the following places.

Autopark Doge (Map pp256-8; Piazzale Roma; €2.50 per hr; 7am-1am)

Garage Comunale (Map pp250-2; Piazzale Roma; €19 per day; 24 hr)

Parking San Marco (Map pp256-8; Piazzale Roma; €19 for 12 hr or €26 for 24 hr; 24 hr) Guests of certain hotels get discounts.

Parking Stazione (Map p261; Viale Stazione 10, Mestre; €1.50 per hour, €4.50 per day; 24 hr) This is one of several car parks in Mestre, which all tend to be much cheaper than those in Venice. Nearly all street parking is metered in Mestre.

Tronchetto (Map p249; Isola di Tronchetto; €18 for 24 hr; 24 hr)

ILLEGAL PARKING

If you return to your car to find that it's no longer there, call the *vigili urbani* (local police) on ☎ 041 274 70 70. They dump towed cars in one of three depots. It'll cost you upwards of €130 to recover the car and pay the parking fine.

WARNING

Thieves haunt some of the car parks, particularly in Mestre. Do not leave anything of even remote value in a parked car.

Rental

Avis (☎ 041 523 73 77) has an office in Piazzale Roma, as do **Europcar** (☎ 041 523 86 16), **Hertz** (☎ 041 528 35 24) and **Expressway** (☎ 041 522 58 25). They all have reps at Marco Polo airport too.

PORTERS

Getting from the vaporetto stop to your hotel can be difficult if you are heavily laden with luggage. There are several stands around the city where porters (*portabagagli*) can be engaged to escort you to your hotel. They charge €15.50 for one item and roughly €5 for each extra one. Prices virtually double to transport bags to any of the other islands, including Giudecca.

Points where porters can be found include the Ponte dell'Accademia (☎ 041 522 48 91), the train station (☎ 041 71 52 72), Piazzale Roma (☎ 041 522 35 90), the Ponte di Rialto (☎ 041 520 53 08) and Piazza San Marco (☎ 041 523 23 85).

TAXI

Land taxis operate from a rank in Piazzale Roma. Call ☎ 041 523 77 74 or ☎ 041 93 62 22.

TRAIN

Train is the most convenient overland option for reaching Venice from other Italian cities or abroad. For information on travelling from the UK contact the **Rail Europe Travel Centre** (☎ 0870 5848848; www.raileurope.co.uk; 178 Piccadilly, London W1V 0BA). For travel within Italy you can get information at your nearest train station or travel agent. Alternatively, contact **Trenitalia** (☎ 892021; www.trenitalia.it).

A wide variety of trains run on the Italian rail network. They start with all-stops *locali*, which generally don't travel much beyond their main city of origin or province. Next come the *regionali*, which also tend to be slow, but cover greater distances. *Interregionali* cover greater distances still and don't necessarily stop at every station.

On InterCity (IC) trains, fast services that operate between major cities, you generally have to pay a supplement on top of the normal cost of a ticket. EuroCity (EC) trains are the international version.

High-speed *pendolini* and other top-of-the-range services, which on high-speed track can zip along at more than 300km/h, are collectively known as Eurostar Italia (ES).

Almost every train leaving Santa Lucia station stops in Mestre (€0.93, 10 minutes). Get tickets from station tobacconists.

Apart from the standard division between 1st and 2nd class (*prima classe* and *seconda classe* – generally you can get 2nd-class seats only on *locali* and *regionali*), you usually have to pay a supplement for taking a fast train. You can pay the supplement separately from the ticket. Thus, if you have a 2nd-class return ticket from Venice to Milan, you might decide to avoid the supplement one way and take a slower train, but pay it on the way back to speed things up a little. You need to pay the supplement *before* boarding the train. If you know exactly which train you want, the supplement will be included in your ticket.

You can buy rail tickets (for major destinations on fast trains at least) at the station (often crowded) and from most travel agents. If you choose to buy them at the station, there are automatic machines that accept credit cards and cash.

Validate your ticket in the orange machines on station platforms. Failure to do so will almost certainly result in embarrassment and a hefty on-the-spot fine when the ticket inspector comes around.

Orient Express

The Venice Simplon Orient Express (www .orient-express.com) runs between London and Venice via Paris, Zürich and Verona on Thursday and Sunday (late April to November), taking about 30 hours. The one-way fare (most people take a plane for the return trip) costs a staggering UK£1270. You can extend the journey with add-ons to Florence and Rome or do the trip between Venice and Istanbul via Budapest and Bucarest.

Venice Train Stations

Inside Venice's main **Santa Lucia station** (Map pp250-2) there's a rail-travel information office (☼ 7am-9pm) opposite the APT office (see p228). Next door to the APT office is an Associazione Veneziana Albergatori hotel booking service (☼ 8am-10pm).

The left-luggage office (☼ 6am-midnight daily; €3 per piece of luggage per 12 hours) is opposite platform 14 and there are lockers on platform 1.

Mestre station (Map p261) has similar services, including rail information, a hotel booking office, phones (including a credit-card phone) and a left-luggage office (☼ 6am-midnight).

TRAVEL AGENTS

Venice is not awash with good-value travel agents but you could try the following.

Centro Turistico Studentesco e Giovanile (CTS; Map pp256-8; ☎ 041 520 56 60; www.cts.it; Calle Foscari, Dorsoduro 3252) The main Italian student and youth travel organisation.

CTS (Map p261; ☎ 041 96 11 25; Via Ca' Savorgnan 8, Mestre)

Gran Canal Viaggi (Map pp254-5; ☎ 041 271 21 11; Ponte dell'Ovo, San Marco 4759/4760)

PRACTICALITIES
ACCOMMODATION

Sleeping options in Venice range from the official HI youth hostel and a handful of other dorm-style options through to some of the grandest old hotels in the world, with prices to match. See the Sleeping chapter (pp161–182) for recommendations. The emphasis is on mid-range accommodation but we have slipped in some of the city's great top-end hotels too. Each section ends with a Cheap Sleeps list for those travelling on a tighter budget.

High season is most of the year for most hotels, which means that you should be prepared to pay their top rates. Many hotels do not alter their rates significantly during the year. That said, there are slower times. The depths of winter (late November to December, except Christmas, and mid-January to March) are quieter in Venice and hoteliers sometimes chop more than half off their top asking price.

BUSINESS
Opening Hours
In general, shops are open from 9am to 1pm and 3.30pm to 7.30pm (or 4pm to 8pm) Monday to Saturday. They may remain closed on Monday morning, or on Wednesday and/or Saturday afternoon. Laws on opening hours are fairly flexible so shopkeepers have a large degree of discretion.

Big department stores, such as Coin, and most supermarkets are open from around 9am to 7.30pm Monday to Saturday. Some open on Sunday.

Banks tend to open from 8.30am to 1.30pm and 3.30pm to 4.30pm Monday to Friday, but often vary their hours a little. A few may open on Saturday morning.

Bars (in the Italian sense, ie coffee-and-sandwich places) and cafés generally open from 7.30am to 8pm, although some stay open after 8pm and turn into pub-style drinking and meeting places. Pubs and bars in the nocturnal sense are mostly shut by 1am; a few soldier on until around 2am or 3am.

For lunch (pranzo), restaurants usually open from 12.30pm to 3pm, but many are not keen to take orders after 2pm. In the evening, opening hours for dinner (cena) vary, but people start sitting down to dine at around 7.30pm. You'll be hard-pressed to find a place still serving after 10.30pm.

Doing Business in Venice
People wishing to make the first moves towards expanding their business into Italy should contact their own country's trade department. The commercial department of the Italian embassy in your own country should also have information – at least on red tape.

In Italy, the trade office of your embassy can provide tips and contacts.

A GSM mobile phone and a good laptop computer will probably be all you need to do business in Venice. Some of the better hotels have secretarial assistance for guests. Other companies that might be of help are listed in the Yellow Pages (Pagine Gialle) under Uffici Arredati e Servizi. Translators/interpreters are listed under Traduzioni Servizio. For organising business conventions in Venice, getting temporary accommodation for clients, secretarial services and so on contact the following.

ENDAR (Veneto Congressi; Map p259; ☎ 041 523 84 40; www.endar.it; Castello 4966)

Venezia Congressi (Map pp256-8; ☎ 041 522 84 00; www.veneziacongressi.com; Dorsoduro 1056)

CHILDREN
Venice isn't just for art-lovers and hopeless romantics. Its uniqueness alone makes it fascinating for children of most ages. Make it an adventure and they'll soon start wondering as much as you just what lies around the next corner.

The kids will certainly enjoy a trip down the Grand Canal on vaporetto No 1. If you can't afford a gondola ride, at least treat them to a short trip across the canal on a traghetto. They are bound to appreciate a trip to the islands, particularly to see the glass-making demonstrations on Murano. Older kids might enjoy watching the big ships pass along the Canale della Giudecca, so take them to Gelateria Nico (p126) on the Fondamenta Zattere (Map pp256-8) for a relaxing waterside gelato.

Children of all ages will get a kick out of watching the Mori strike the hour at the Torre dell'Orologio on Piazza San Marco (p99).

Understandably, most of the museums and galleries will leave the little 'uns cold, but some may work. Kids with a nautical interest should be drawn by the boats and model ships at the Museo Storico Navale (p85). The sculpture garden at the Peggy Guggenheim Museum (p62) may prove an educational distraction while you indulge your modern art needs.

Climbing towers is usually a winner. Try the Campanile in Piazza San Marco (p53) or the bell towers of San Giorgio Maggiore (p90) and Santa Maria Assunta in Torcello (p92).

Parco Savorgnan (part of Palazzo Savorgnan, Map pp250-2) and the Giardini Pubblici (Map p260) have playgrounds.

In summer, a trip to the beach – the Lido di Venezia, Sottomarina (Chioggia) or Lido di Jesolo – should win points with children. If you are using your own transport, remember to leave early to beat the horrible traffic jams. And forget it at weekends (except on the Lido di Venezia) – whether you drive or catch buses, you'll be stuck on the roads for an eternity.

Discounts are available for children (usually aged under 12) on public transport and at museums, galleries and other sights.

A couple of handy books are *Viva Venice*, by Paola Scibilia and Paolo Zoffoli, and *Venice for Kids*, by Elisabetta Pasqualin. These books are richly illustrated and bursting with games, legends, anecdotes and suggestions on what to do.

Baby-sitting

Some of the major hotels, especially those on the Lido di Venezia, offer a baby-sitting service.

CLIMATE

Midsummer is the worst time of year to be in Venice – average daytime temperatures hover around 27°C but can go considerably higher. Humidity is high, the canals can get a little on the nose and prevailing southern winds (the sirocco) are hot.

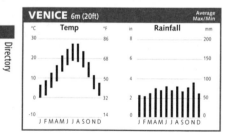

In spring the weather is often crisp and clear and the temperatures pleasant. That said, quite a lot of rain falls in May and into June. In July and August the humidity can bring cracking storms in the evening.

The first half of winter sees heavy rainfall, with flooding most likely in November and December. On bad days, the city and lagoon are enveloped in mist (which some find enchanting), but every now and then you get lucky and the sky clears.

January and February are the coldest months, with average temperatures hovering between 0°C and 7°C, and often clear skies.

Because of the city's position on the lagoon, snow is a rarity.

COURSES

The **Istituto Italiano di Cultura** (IIC; Italian Cultural Institute), a government-sponsored organisation with the aim of promoting Italian culture and language, is a good place to research courses in Italy. The institute has branches all over the world, including Australia (Sydney), Canada (Montreal), the UK (London) and the USA (Los Angeles, New York and Washington). There is a full list of contact details at www.esteri.it/polestera/dgpcc/03/0302rete.htm.

Some suggestions for Italian language and other courses in Venice:

Fondazione Cini (Map pp262-3; ☎ 041 528 99 00 , 041 271 02 29; www.cini.it; Isola di San Giorgio Maggiore) Organises seminars on subjects relating to the city and its culture, in particular music and art.

Istituto Venezia (Map pp256-8; ☎ 041 522 43 31; www.istitutovenezia.com; Campo Santa Margherita, Dorsoduro 3116/a) Offers language and one- and two-week cooking courses. It also has a course in Venetian history and art, involving 12 guided tours of the city. Four weeks (80 hours) of intensive language classes cost €540.

Società Dante Alighieri (Map p259; ☎ 041 528 91 27; venicedantealighieri@libero.it; Istituto Paolo Sarpi, Fondamenta di Santa Giustina, Castello 2821) Offers courses in Italian at all levels.

Università Internazionale dell'Arte (Map pp262-3; ☎ 041 528 70 90; uiave@tin.it; Calle Michelangelo 54/p, Giudecca) Runs full courses on art history.

CUSTOMS

Travellers entering Italy from outside the EU are allowed to bring in duty-free one bottle of spirits, one bottle of wine, 50ml of perfume and 200 cigarettes.

Duty-free allowances for travel between EU countries were abolished in 1999. For duty-paid items bought at normal shops in one EU country and taken into another, the allowances are 90L of wine, 10L of spirits, unlimited quantities of perfume and 800 cigarettes. VAT-free shopping is available in the duty-free shops at airports for people travelling between EU countries.

DISABLED TRAVELLERS

People with disabilities have not been completely left out of what is, after all, a fairly unfriendly environment for wheelchair users or those with other mobility problems.

A map available from APT offices (p228) has areas of the city shaded in yellow to indicate that they can be negotiated without running into one of Venice's many bridges. Some of the bridges are equipped with lifts (montascale), which are marked on the map. You can get hold of a key to operate these lifts from the tourist offices.

Most of the important vaporetto lines allow wheelchair access. Those that don't are Nos 13, 20, 51 and 52.

Five bus lines are adapted for wheelchair users: No 2 (Piazzale Roma to Mestre train station), No 4 (Piazzale Roma to Corso del Popolo in Mestre), No 5 (Piazzale Roma to Marco Polo airport), No 6/ (Tronchetto and Piazzale Roma to the mainland) and No 15 (a mainland service running between Marco Polo airport and Mestre).

Organisations

Accessible Travel & Leisure (☎ 01452-729739; www.accessibletravel.co.uk; Avionics House, Naas Lane, Gloucester GL2 4SN) Claims to be the biggest UK travel agent dealing with travel for the disabled. The company encourages the disabled to travel independently.

Holiday Care (☎ 0845 124 9971; ww.holidaycare.org.uk; 2nd floor, Imperial Bldgs, Victoria Rd, Horley, Surrey RH6 7PZ) Information on hotels with disabled access, where to hire equipment and tour operators dealing with the disabled.

Informahandicap (☎ 041 534 17 00; informahandicap@ comune.venezia.it; Villa Franchin, Via Garibaldi 155, Mestre)

Informahandicap (Map pp254-5; ☎ 041 274 80 80; Ca' Farsetti, San Marco 4136)

Royal Association for Disability & Rehabilitation (RADAR; ☎ 020-7250 3222; www.radar.org.uk; Unit 12, City Forum, 250 City Rd, London EC1V 8AS) Publishes European Holidays & Travel Abroad: A Guide for Disabled People, which provides a good overview of facilities available to disabled travellers throughout Europe.

DISCOUNT CARDS

An ISIC (International Student Identity Card) can get you discounted admission prices at some sights and help with cheap flights out of Italy. Similar cards are available to teachers (ITIC) and non-students (IYTC). The cards also carry a travel insurance component. They are issued by student unions, hostelling organisations and some youth travel agencies.

In Venice the concrete benefits of an ISIC are limited. A couple of restaurants and half a dozen bars give discounts, along with a couple of cinemas and some shops. As for sights, the card will only come in handy at the Palazzo Querini-Stampaglia, the Scuola Grande di San Rocco and a couple of minor sights. It may get you discounted travel at the CTS student travel agency. For full details see www.isic.org.

Rolling Venice

If you are aged between 14 and 29, take your passport and a colour photograph to the **Assessorato alla Gioventù** (Map pp254-5; ☎ 041 274 76 50; fax 041 274 76 42; Corte Contarina, San Marco 1529; ☼ 9.30am-1pm Mon, Wed & Fri, 9.30am-1pm & 3-5pm Tue & Thu), and pick up the Rolling Venice card (€2.60), which offers significant discounts on food, accommodation, entertainment, public transport, museums and galleries.

You can also pick up the card at the **Agenzia Arte e Storia** (Map pp250-2; ☎ 041 524 02 32; Corte Canal, Santa Croce 659) or from the ACTV office in Piazzale Roma (Map pp250-2) and outlets of the ACTV subsidiary, Vela. Two of these are located in front of the train station (Map pp250-2); there are two more in San Marco (Map pp254-5). The Rolling Venice map lists all the hotels, restaurants, shops, museums, cinemas and theatres where the card entitles you to reductions.

Venice Card

Since late 2001 a new all-inclusive transport and sights card, Venice Card (☎ 041 24 24; www.venicecard.it), has been in operation. It does not represent a financial saving over alternatives (indeed it can work out more costly), but with added potential discounts at certain restaurants, hotels and the like could prove handy. Having the card also removes some of the hassle of procuring individual museum tickets and vaporetto passes.

There are two types of Venice Card. The blue card gives you unlimited use of ferries and buses throughout the Venice municipality for one, three or seven days. It also gives you free access to the public toilets (otherwise €0.50) scattered around town.

The orange version throws in the Musei Civici (City Museums) for free (see Special Tickets, p48).

The junior (those aged under 29) blue card costs €9/22/49 for one/three/seven days, while

Directory

the senior version costs €14/29/51. The junior orange card costs €18/35/61 and the senior version €28/47/68.

Check out the website for full details.

ELECTRICITY

The electric current in Venice is 220V, 50Hz, as in the rest of continental Europe. Several countries outside Europe (such as the USA and Canada) use 110V, 60Hz, which means that some appliances from those countries may perform poorly. It is always safest to use a transformer. Plugs have two round pins, as in the rest of continental Europe.

EMBASSIES & CONSULATES

Most countries have an embassy in Rome. Look them up under Ambasciate in that city's Yellow Pages (Pagine Gialle). A limited number of countries maintain consulates in Venice:

Austria (Map pp256–8; ☎ 041 524 05 56; Fondamenta Condulmer, Santa Croce 251)

France (Map pp254–5; ☎ 041 522 43 19; Ramo del Pestrin, Castello 6140)

Germany (Map pp256–8; ☎ 041 523 76 75; Campo Sant'Angelo, San Marco 3816)

Netherlands (Map pp256–8; ☎ 041 528 34 16; Ramo Giustinian, San Marco 2888)

Switzerland (Map pp256–8; ☎ 041 520 39 44; Campo di Sant'Agnese, Dorsoduro 810)

UK (Map pp256–8; ☎ 041 522 72 07; Palazzo Querini, Campo della Carità, Dorsoduro 1051)

The nearest **Australian consulate** (☎ 02 77 70 41) is in Milan, at Via Borgogna 2. The nearest **US consulate** (☎ 02 29 03 51) is also in Milan, at Via Principe Amedeo 2/10. The **Canadian consulate** (Map p194; ☎ 049 876 48 33) is in Padua, at Riviera Ruzzante 25.

EMERGENCIES

The **main police station** (Map p259; ☎ 041 271 55 11; Fondamenta di San Lorenzo, Castello 5053), or *questura*, is a little far from the centre but there is a handy station at Piazza San Marco 67 (Map pp254–5).

Military Police *(carabinieri)*	☎	112
Police *(polizia)*	☎	113
Fire Brigade *(vigili del fuoco)*	☎	115
Ambulance *(ambulanza)*	☎	118

GAY & LESBIAN TRAVELLERS

Homosexuality is legal in Italy and well tolerated in Venice and the north in general. However, the city offers precious little in the way of gay bars and the like. Indeed, most gays living in Venice agree that the place is rather dead from their point of view.

ArciGay (www.arcigay.it), the national gay organisation, has general information on the gay and lesbian scene in Italy, while the companion **Gay.It** website (http://it.gay.com; Italian only) provides listings for everything from bars and discos to gay beaches and beauty centres. The pickings in Venice are slim, as you'll see.

Venice's rather low-key gay association, **ArciGay Dedalo** (Map p261; ☎ 041 753 84 15; Via A Costa 38/a), is in Mestre.

HOLIDAYS

For Venetians as most Italians, the main holiday periods remain summer (July and especially August), the Christmas–New Year period and Easter. August is a peculiar time as all Italy grinds to a halt, especially around Ferragosto (Feast of the Assumption; 15 August), when just about everything closes. Restaurants, however, stay open as they do a roaring trade! Travelling to and around Venice in this high holiday period is far from ideal. For information on the city's many festivals and other events, see pp9–11. National public holidays are as follows.

New Year's Day (Anno Nuovo) 1 January

Epiphany (Befana) 6 January

Good Friday (Venerdì Santo) March/April

Easter Monday (Pasquetta/Giorno dopo Pasqua) March/April

Liberation Day (Giorno della Liberazione) April 25 – marks the Allied Victory in Italy, and the end of the German presence and Mussolini, in 1945

Labour Day (Giorno del Lavoro) 1 May

Feast of the Assumption (Ferragosto) 15 August

All Saints' Day (Ognissanti) 1 November

Feast of the Immaculate Conception (Concezione Immaculata) 8 December

Christmas Day (Natale) 25 December

Boxing Day (Festa di Santo Stefano) 26 December

INTERNET ACCESS

Travelling with a portable computer is a great way to stay in touch with life back home, but unless you know what you're

Directory

doing it's fraught with potential problems. Make sure you have a universal AC adaptor, a two-pin plug adaptor for Europe and a reputable 'global' modem. Italian telephone sockets are mostly the US RJ-11 type (if you find yourself confronted with the old-style Italian three-prong socket, most electrical stores can sell you an adaptor). Some of the better hotels are set up with Internet connections and sometimes just plugging into the hotel room's phone socket will be sufficient (although frequently this will not work as you have to go through a switchboard). For more information on travelling with a portable computer, see www.teleadapt.com or http://igo.ententeweb.com.

Major Internet service providers (ISPs) like CompuServe (www.compuserve.com) have dial-in nodes in Italy; download a list of the dial-in numbers before you leave home.

Some Italian servers can provide short-term accounts for local Internet access. **Agora** (☎ 800 304 999; www.agoratelematica.it) is one of them. Several Italian ISPs offer free Internet connections: check out the websites (in Italian only) of **Tiscali** (www.tiscali.it), **Kataweb** (www.kataweb.it) and **Libero** (www.libero.it).

If you intend to rely on cybercafés, you'll need to carry three pieces of information: your incoming (POP or IMAP) mail server name, your account name and your password.

Internet Cafés

Some of the following places offer student rates and also have deals on cards for several hours' use at much reduced rates.

Casanova (Map pp250-2; ☎ 041 524 06 64; Rio Terrà Lista di Spagna, Cannaregio 158/a; ☽ 9am-11.30pm; €7 per hr) Clubbing by night, online by day.

EasyContact (Map pp250-2; ☎ 041 71 10 97; www.easy-contact.it, Italian only; Campo San Nazario Sauro, Santa Croce 1005/a; ☽ 10am-1.30pm & 3.30-8.30pm; from €7.20 per hr)

Internet Point (Map pp256-8; ☎ 041 71 46 66; Calle dei Preti, Dorsoduro 3812/a; ☽ 9.15am-8pm Mon-Sat; €9 per hr)

Net House (Map pp256-8; ☎ 041 277 11 90; Campo Santo Stefano, San Marco 2958-67; ☽ 8am-2am Mon-Thu, 24 hr Fri-Sun May-Sep; 8am-2am daily Oct-Apr; €9 per hr) Sip cocktails, eat sandwiches, slug Irish beers and/or go online.

Planet Internet (Map pp250-2; ☎ 041 524 41 88; Rio Terrà San Leonardo, Cannaregio 1519; ☽ 9am-midnight; €8 per hr)

Venice Internet Point (Map pp250-2; ☎ 041 275 82 17; Rio Terrà Lista di Spagna, Cannaregio 149; ☽ 9am-11pm; €8 per hr)

World House (Map pp254-5; ☎ 041 528 48 71; www.world-house.org; Calle della Chiesa, Castello 4502; ☽ 10am-11pm; €8 per hr)

LAUNDRY

Self-service laundries are finally beginning to appear in Venice.

Bea Vita Lavanderia (Map pp250-2; Calle Chioverette, Santa Croce 665/b; 8kg wash €3.50, dry €2; ☽ 7am-10pm)

Laundromat (Map pp254-5; Ruga Giuffa, Castello 4826; 8kg wash €4.50, dry €6, or reductions on €20 card; ☽ 9am-10pm)

Laundry (Map p261; Via Piave 41, Mestre; 7.5kg wash €3, dry €3; ☽ 7.30am-11.30pm)

Speedy Wash (Map pp250-2; Rio Terrà San Leonardo, Cannaregio 1520; 8kg wash €4.50, dry €3; ☽ 9am-11pm)

LOST PROPERTY

If you lose stuff in Venice it may well be gone forever, but check with the local police *(vigili urbani)* office on Piazzale Roma (Map pp250-2; ☎ 041 522 45 76). Otherwise, the following numbers might be useful.

ACTV – buses (☎ 041 272 27 23)

ACTV – vaporetti (☎ 041 272 21 79)

Municipio (town hall; ☎ 041 274 81 11)

Trenitalia (☎ 041 78 52 38)

MAPS

You should be able to get by with the maps in this book, but some of those on sale are also worthwhile investments. The free one handed out by the tourist office is next to useless.

Whichever map you buy, you will find inconsistencies. The *Venezianizzazione* (Venetianisation) of street names has created more problems than it could ever have solved. Most maps seem to take a haphazard approach to using Italian, Venetian or mongrel versions. Usually it's no great hassle to work out – but you need to use a little lateral thinking at times. We have tried to follow standard Italian rather than Venetian, but you may notice differences between spellings on the maps in this book and on the ground or on other maps. Where such discrepancies (most of them minor) occur, it is usually easy to work out what's what.

Try Lonely Planet's *Venice* map. If you can't find it, another good one is the wine-red-covered *Venezia* produced by the Touring Club Italiano (scale 1:5000).

If you plan to stay for the long haul, *Calli, Campielli e Canali* (Edizioni Helvetica) is for you. This is the definitive street guide and will allow you to locate to within 100m any Venetian address you need – saves a *lot* of shoe leather. Posties must do a course in it before being sent out to deliver the mail!

Online, try the maps on the Ombra.net site (www.ombra.net).

Street Numbering

Venice has its own style of street numbering: instead of a system based on individual streets, each *sestiere* (municipal division) has a long series of numbers. Thus a hotel might give its address as simply San Marco 4687. Because the *sestieri* are fairly small, wandering around and searching out the number is technically feasible and sometimes doesn't take that long. But there is precious little apparent logic to the run of numbers, so frustration is never far away. Most streets are named, so where possible we have provided street names as well as the *sestiere* number. Even where this is not the case, using the maps in this book in conjunction with the *sestiere* numbers should clear up any mysteries.

MEDICAL SERVICES
Medical Cover

All foreigners have the same right as Italians to free emergency medical treatment in a public hospital. EU citizens are entitled to the full range of health care services in public hospitals free of charge, but you will need to present your E111 form (enquire at your national health service before leaving home). Australia has a reciprocal arrangement with Italy that entitles Australian citizens to free public health care – carry your Medicare card.

Citizens of New Zealand, the US, Canada and other countries have to pay for anything other than emergency treatment. Most travel insurance policies include medical cover.

The Italian public health system is administered by local centres generally known as Unità Sanitaria Locale (USL) or Unità Socio Sanitaria Locale (USSL), usually listed under 'U' in the telephone book (sometimes under 'A'

for Azienda USL). Just for fun, the Venetian version is ULSS. Under these headings you'll find long lists of offices – look for Poliambulatorio (polyclinic) and the telephone number for *accettazione sanitaria* (medical appointments). You need to call this number to make an appointment – there is no point in just rolling up. Clinic opening hours vary widely, with the minimum generally being about 8am to 12.30pm Monday to Friday. Some open for a couple of hours in the afternoon and on Saturday morning.

If your country has a consulate in Venice, staff there should be able to refer you to doctors who speak your language. If you have a specific health complaint, obtain the necessary information and referrals for treatment before leaving home.

The following medical services may be of use to travellers.

Guardia Medica (☎ 041 529 40 60 Venice, 041 534 44 11 Mestre, 041 526 77 43 Lido) This service of night-time callout doctors (locums) operates from 8pm to 8am on weekdays and from 10am the day before a holiday (including Sunday) until 8am the day after.

Ospedale Civile (Map p259; ☎ 041 529 41 11; Campo SS Giovanni e Paolo) This is the main hospital. For emergency treatment, go straight to the casualty *(pronto soccorso)* section, where you can also get emergency dental treatment.

Ospedale Umberto I (Map p261; ☎ 041 260 71 11; Via Circonvallazione 50, Mestre) A modern mainland hospital.

METRIC SYSTEM

Italy uses the metric system. Like other continental Europeans, the Italians indicate decimals with commas and thousands with points. For a conversion chart, see the inside front cover of this book.

MONEY

As in 11 other EU nations (Austria, Belgium, Finland, France, Germany, Greece, Ireland, Luxembourg, the Netherlands, Portugal and Spain), the euro has been Italy's currency since 2002. During 2003 it rose to record levels against other major currencies like the US dollar and UK pound.

The seven euro notes come in denominations of €500, €200, €100, €50, €20, €10 and €5, in different colours and sizes. The eight euro coins are in denominations of €2 and €1, and 50, 20, 10, five, two and one cents.

Each participating state decorates the reverse side of the coins with its own designs, but all euro coins can be used anywhere that accepts euros.

See Economy & Costs, p16.

Changing Money

You can exchange money in banks, at post offices or in currency exchange booths (bureaux de change). Banks are generally the most reliable option and tend to offer the best rates. However, you should look around and ask about commissions: these can fluctuate considerably. You'll find most of the main banks in the area around the Ponte di Rialto and San Marco.

Keep a sharp eye open for commissions at bureaux de change. By way of example, Change (branches all over town) charges up to a staggering 11.9% on foreign-currency travellers cheques! Travelex (Thomas Cook) charges 4.5% for cash or travellers cheques (except Thomas Cook travellers cheques, which are commission-free).

There are a couple of bureaux de change in the arrivals hall of Marco Polo airport. A comparatively handy bank for both the train and bus stations is the Monte dei Paschi (Map pp250-2) on Fondamenta di San Simeon Piccolo.

American Express (Amex; Map pp254-5; ☎ 041 520 08 44; Salizzada San Moisè, San Marco 1471; 🕑 9am-5.30pm Mon-Fri, 9am-12.30pm Sat) Has an ATM for Amex cards.

Travelex (Thomas Cook; Map pp254-5; ☎ 041 528 73 58; Piazza San Marco 142 & Riva del Ferro 5126; 🕑 8.45am-8pm Mon-Sat, 9am-6pm Sun)

Credit/Debit Cards

Major cards such as Visa, MasterCard, Maestro and Cirrus are accepted throughout Italy. They can be used in many hotels, restaurants and shops. Credit cards can also be used in ATMs displaying the appropriate sign, or (if you have no PIN) you can obtain cash advances over the counter in many banks – MasterCard and Visa are among the most widely recognised for such transactions. Check charges with your bank.

It is not uncommon for ATMs in Italy to reject foreign cards. Don't despair or start wasting money on international calls to your bank. Try a few more ATMs displaying your credit card's logo before assuming the problem lies with your card rather than with the local system.

If your card is lost, stolen or swallowed by an ATM, you can telephone toll-free to have an immediate stop put on its use. For MasterCard the number in Italy is ☎ 800 870 866, for Visa it's ☎ 800 819 014 and for Diners Club it's ☎ 800 864 064.

Amex is also widely accepted (although not as commonly as Visa or MasterCard). The office in Venice (see Changing Money, earlier) has an express cash machine for cardholders. If you lose your Amex card, call ☎ 800 874 333.

Exchange Rates

See the Quick Reference (inside front cover) for exchange rates at the time of going to press. For the latest rates, check out www.oanda.com.

Travellers Cheques

These are a safe way of carrying your money because they can be replaced if lost or stolen. Most banks and exchange offices will cash them. Thomas Cook, Amex and Visa are widely accepted brands. If you lose your Amex cheques, call ☎ 800 872 000 (24-hour freephone). For Visa cheques call ☎ 800 874 155; for MasterCard or Thomas Cook cheques call ☎ 800 872 050.

Get most of your cheques in fairly large denominations to save on per-cheque commission charges. Amex exchange offices do not charge commission to exchange travellers cheques (even other brands) or cash equivalent to US$500 or above.

It's vital to keep your initial receipt, along with a record of your cheque numbers and the ones you have used, separate from the cheques themselves.

Take your passport when you go to cash travellers cheques.

NEWSPAPERS & MAGAZINES

A wide selection of national daily newspapers from around Europe (including the UK) is available at newsstands all over central Venice and at strategic locations like the train and bus stations. The *International Herald Tribune*, *Time*, the *Economist*, *Der Spiegel* and a host of other international magazines are also available.

Italian Press

There is no 'national' paper as such, but rather several important dailies published in major cities. These include Milan's *Corriere della Sera*,

Turin's *La Stampa* and Rome's *La Repubblica*. This trio forms what could be considered the nucleus of a national press, publishing local editions up and down the country.

Two papers dominate the local scene. *Il Gazzettino*, in business since 1887, brings out separate editions in each province across the Triveneto area (the Veneto, Friuli-Venezia Giulia and Trentino), each with a local supplement. If you are in Venice and want decent coverage of national and foreign news but with solid local content, this is probably the paper you want. Its competition is the tabloid-sized *La Nuova Venezia*, a more parochial paper.

Useful Publications

VeNews, a monthly magazine available at newsstands, has info on the latest events, cinema, music and the like, along with a hotchpotch of articles, some in English.

PHARMACIES

Most pharmacies in Venice open from 9am to 12.30pm and 3.30pm to 7.30pm and are closed on Saturday afternoon and Sunday. When closed, pharmacies are required to display a list of other pharmacies in the area that are open (on rotation) for extended hours. Information on all-night pharmacies is listed in *Un Ospite di Venezia*, available in tourist offices.

You can also check which pharmacies are open for 24 hours on any date at www .ombra.net.

POST

Le Poste (☎ 160; www.poste.it), Italy's postal service, is notoriously slow but has improved over the past few years.

Stamps *(francobolli)* are available from post offices and authorised tobacconists (look for the official *tabacchi* sign: a big 'T', often white on black).

The **main post office** (Map pp254-5; ◔ 8.30am-6.30pm Mon-Sat) is on Salizzada del Fondaco dei Tedeschi, just near the Ponte di Rialto. Stamps are available at windows No 1 to No 4 in the central courtyard. There is something quite special about doing your postal business in this former trading house. Stand by the well in the middle and try to imagine the bustle as German traders and brokers shuffled their goods around on the ground floor or struck

deals in their quarters on the upper levels back in the Republic's trading heyday.

Postal Rates

The cost of sending a letter airmail *(via aerea)* depends on its weight and where it is being sent. For regular post, letters up to 20g cost €0.41 within Europe and €0.52 to Africa, Asia, the Americas, Australia and New Zealand. Postcards cost the same.

Few people use the regular post, preferring the slightly more expensive priority mail service *(posta prioritaria)*, guaranteed to deliver letters sent to Europe within three days and to the rest of the world within four to eight days. Letters up to 20g sent *posta prioritaria* cost €0.62 within Europe and €0.77 to Africa, Asia, the Americas, Australia and New Zealand. Letters weighing 21g to 100g cost €0.77/1.24 (standard/priority) within Europe and €1.03/1.55 to Africa, Asia, the Americas, Australia and New Zealand.

Sending Mail

Officially, letters sent priority post within Italy should arrive the following working day; those posted to destinations in Europe and the Mediterranean basin within three days; and those to the rest of the world in four to eight days. The postal service claims an 85% success rate in meeting these targets.

Parcels *(pacchetti)* can be sent from any post office. You can purchase posting boxes or padded envelopes from most post offices. Padded envelopes are also available from stationery shops *(cartolerie)* and some tobacconists. Parcels usually take longer to be delivered than letters. A different set of postal rates applies.

Receiving Mail

Poste restante is known as *fermo posta* in Italy. Letters marked in this way will be held at the Fermo Posta counter in the main post office in the relevant town. At the main post office in Venice, you can pick up your letters at window No 40 – take your passport along as ID. Poste restante mail should be addressed as follows:

John SMITH
Fermo Posta
Posta Centrale
30100 Venice
Italy

Amex card or travellers cheque holders can use the free client mail-holding service at the main Venice office (see Money, p223).

RADIO

There are three state-owned stations: RAI-1 (1332kHz AM or 89.7MHz FM), RAI-2 (846kHz AM or 91.7MHz FM) and RAI-3 (93.7MHz FM). They offer a combination of classical and light music with news broadcasts and discussion programmes.

Local stations are not very inspiring. Radio Venezia (101.1MHz FM) is among the better ones, with news and, on balance, not a bad selection of music.

You can pick up the BBC World Service on medium wave at 648kHz, on short wave at 6.195MHz, 9.410MHz, 12.095MHz and 15.575MHz, and on long wave at 198kHz, depending on where you are and the time of day. Voice of America can usually be found on short wave at 15.205MHz.

RECEIPTS

Laws aimed at tightening controls on the payment of taxes in Italy mean that the onus is on the buyer to ask for and retain receipts for all goods and services. This applies to everything from a litre of milk to a haircut. Although it rarely happens, you could be asked by an officer of the fiscal police *(guardia di finanza)* to produce the receipt immediately after you leave a shop. If you don't have it, the officer may levy a fine of €50 to €1000.

TAXES

A value-added tax (known as Imposta di Valore Aggiunto or IVA) of around 19% is slapped onto just about everything in Italy.

Tourists who are resident outside the EU may claim a refund on this tax if they spend more than €155 in the same shop on the same day. The refund applies only to items purchased at retail outlets affiliated to the system – these shops display a 'tax-free for tourists' sign. If you don't see a sign, ask the shopkeeper. You must fill out a form at the point of purchase and have it stamped and checked by Italian customs when you leave the country (you will need to show the receipt and possibly your purchases). At major airports and some border crossings, you can then get an immediate cash refund at specially marked booths; alternatively, return the form by mail

to the vendor, who will make the refund, either by cheque or to your credit card.

For more information consult the rules brochure available in affiliated stores.

TELEPHONE

The orange public payphones liberally scattered about come in four types. The most common accept only phonecards *(carte/ schede telefoniche)*, although you will still find some that take both cards and coins. Some card phones also accept special credit cards produced by Telecom – the formerly state-owned telecommunications company – and even commercial credit cards. A few send faxes (see Fax, p226). If you call from a bar or shop, you may still encounter old-style metered phones, which count *scatti*, the units used to measure the length of a call.

There is a bank of telephones near the main post office on Calle Galeazza (Map pp254-5). Unstaffed Telecom offices can be found on the corner of Corte dei Pali and Strada Nuova in Cannaregio (Map p253); Ruga Vecchia San Giovanni, San Polo 480 (Map p253); Calle San Luca, San Marco 4585 (Map pp254-5); and at the train station (Map pp250-2).

You can buy phonecards (€2.50 or €5) at post offices, tobacconists and newsstands, and from vending machines in Telecom offices. To avoid the frustration of trying to find fast-disappearing coin telephones, always keep a phonecard on hand. Remember to snap off the perforated corner before using it.

Calling Venice from Abroad

Dial the international access code (00 in most countries), followed by the code for Italy (39) and the full number, including the initial 0. For example, to call the number ☎ 041 528 77 77 in Venice you need to dial the international access code followed by ☎ 39 041 528 77 77.

Costs

Call rates have been greatly simplified in Italy. A local call *(comunicazione urbana)* from a public phone costs €0.10 every minute and 21 seconds. For a long-distance call within Italy *(comunicazione interurbana)* you pay €0.10 when the call is answered and then €0.10 every 57 seconds.

The cost of calling abroad has fallen. A three-minute call from a payphone to most

European countries and North America will cost about €1.90. Australasia is a different proposition: three minutes chew up €4.10. Calling from a private phone is cheaper. Calling foreign mobile phones is more expensive to Europe and North America, but the same as a landline call to Australia and New Zealand.

Domestic Calls

Area codes are an integral part of Italian telephone numbers. The codes all begin with 0 and consist of up to four digits. You must dial this whole number, even if calling from next door. Thus, any number you call in the Venice area will begin with 041.

Mobile phone numbers begin with a three-digit prefix such as 330, 335, 347 or 368. Free-phone or toll-free numbers are known as green numbers (numeri verdi) and start with 800. National rate (one call rate that applies across the country) phone numbers start with 848 or 199. Some new six-digit national rate numbers are coming into use (such as that now used by Trenitalia for national rail information).

For national directory enquiries call ☎ 12.

Fax

You can send faxes from post offices and some tobacconists, copy centres and stationers. Faxes can also be sent from some Telecom public phones. To send a fax within Italy, expect to pay €1.30 per page. International faxes vary in cost. To the UK, for instance, you pay €2.46 for the first page and €2.15 per page thereafter.

The main post office operates a fax poste restante service – have faxes sent to you at Fax Fermo Posta, ☎ 041 522 68 20. To retrieve the fax you will need photo ID.

International Calls

Direct international calls can easily be made from public telephones by using a phonecard. Dial 00 to get out of Italy, then the relevant country and city codes, followed by the telephone number.

Useful country codes are: Australia 61, Canada and the USA 1, France 33, Germany 49, Ireland 353, New Zealand 64 and the UK 44. For international directory inquiries, call ☎ 176.

To make a reverse-charge (collect) international call from a public telephone, dial ☎ 170 (for European countries dial ☎ 15). It is easier and often cheaper to use the Country Direct service. You dial the number and request a reverse-charge call through the operator in your country. Numbers for this service include the following.

Australia (Telstra)	☎ 172 10 61
Australia (Optus)	☎ 172 11 61
Canada	☎ 172 10 01
France	☎ 172 00 33
New Zealand	☎ 172 10 64
UK (BT)	☎ 172 00 44
UK (BT Chargecard Operator)	☎ 172 01 44
USA (AT&T)	☎ 172 10 11
USA (IDB)	☎ 172 17 77
USA (MCI)	☎ 172 10 22
USA (Sprint)	☎ 172 18 77

International Phonecards & Call Centres

Several private companies distribute international phonecards offering cheaper rates on long-distance calls. Some are better than others but few are available in Venice. Keep an eye out at newsstands, tobacconists and the like.

Planet Internet (see Internet Cafés, p221) offers cheap-rate international calls.

Mobile Phones

You can buy SIM cards in Italy for your own national mobile phone (provided you have a GSM, dual- or tri-band cellular phone), as well as prepaid call time. This only works if your national phone hasn't been code blocked, something you might want to find out before leaving home. If you buy a SIM card and find your phone *is* blocked, you won't be able to take it back. You won't want to consider a full contract unless you plan to live in Italy for a good while, and even then the benefits are not always tangible. You need your passport to open any kind of mobile phone account, prepaid or otherwise.

Both Telecom Italia Mobile (TIM) and Vodaphone-Omnitel offer prepaid (prepagato) accounts for GSM phones (frequency 900 MHz). The card can cost €50 to €60, which includes some prepaid call time. You can then top up in their shops or with cards from outlets like tobacconists and newsstands.

TIM and Vodaphone-Omnitel retail outlets operate in virtually every Italian town. Call rates vary according to an infinite variety of call plans.

Wind and Blu are two smaller mobile phone operators with consequently fewer outlets around the country.

US mobile phones generally work on a frequency of 1900 MHz, so for use in Italy, your US handset will have to be tri-band.

TELEVISION

The three state-run stations, RAI-1, RAI-2 and RAI-3, are run by Radio e Televisione Italiane. Historically, each has been in the hands of one of the main political groupings in the country, although in the past few years these affiliations have become less clear cut. The appointment of station directors and senior staff remains highly politicised.

Of the three, RAI-3 tends to have some of the more interesting programmes. Generally, however, these stations and the private Canale 5, Italia 1, Rete 4 and La 7 tend to serve up a diet of indifferent news, tacky variety hours (with lots of near-naked tits and bums, appalling crooning and vaudeville humour) and game shows. Talk shows, some interesting but many nauseating, also abound.

There are also several regional channels, including Telenuovo, Italia 7, Antenna 3, TeleNordEst and Televenezia. Quality is generally indifferent at best, but all carry more news and cultural items on Venice and the Veneto than the main stations.

TIME

Italy (and hence Venice) is one hour ahead of GMT/UTC during winter and two hours ahead during the daylight-saving period from the last Sunday in March to the last Sunday in October. Most other Western European countries are on the same time as Italy year round, the major exceptions being the UK, Ireland and Portugal, which are one hour behind.

When it's noon in Venice, it's 3am in San Francisco, 6am in New York and Toronto, 11am in London, 9pm in Sydney and 11pm in Auckland. Note that in North America and Australasia, the changeover to/from daylight saving usually differs from the European date by a couple of weeks.

TIPPING

You are not expected to tip on top of restaurant service charges, but it is common to leave a small amount, say €1 per person. If there is no service charge, you might consider leaving a 10% tip, but this is by no means obligatory. In bars, Italians often leave any small change as a tip, often only €0.05 or €0.10. Tipping taxi drivers is not common practice, but you should tip the porter at higher-class hotels.

Bargaining is common in flea markets but not in shops, although you might find that the proprietor is disposed to give a discount if you are spending a reasonable amount of money. It is quite acceptable to ask if there is a special price for a room in a *pensione* or hotel if you plan to stay for more than a few days. Indeed, there is no harm in trying to bargain down room prices at any time.

TOILETS

Stopping at a bar or café for a quick coffee and then a trip to the toilet is the common solution to those sudden urges at awkward times. Make sure the bar actually has a toilet before committing yourself! Otherwise, public toilets (visitors €0.50, residents €0.25) are scattered about Venice – look for the 'WC Toilette' signs. They are generally open from 7am to 7pm.

TOURIST INFORMATION
Tourist Offices Abroad

Information on Venice is available from the following branches of the Italian State Tourism Board (Ente Nazionale Italiano per il Turismo; ENIT).

Australia (☎ 02-9262 1666; enitour@ihug.com.au; Level 26, 44 Market St, Sydney NSW 2000)

Canada (☎ 416-925 4882; enit.canada@on.aibn.com; Suite 907, South Tower, 175 Bloor St East, Toronto, ON M4W 3R8)

France (☎ 01 42 66 03 96; enit.parigi@wanadoo.fr; 23 rue de la Paix, 75002 Paris)

Germany (☎ 030-247 83 97; enit-berlin@t-online.de; Kontorhaus Mitte, Friedrichstrasse 187, D-10117 Berlin)

Germany (☎ 089-531 317; enit-muenchen@t-online.de; Goethestrasse 20, 80336 Munich)

Germany (☎ 069-259 126; enit.ffm@t-online.de; Kaiserstrasse 65, 60329 Frankfurt am Main)

Netherlands (☎ 020-616 82 44; enitams@wirehub.nl; Stadhouderskade 2, 1054 ES Amsterdam)

Switzerland (☎ 01 211 79 17; enit@bluewin.ch; Uraniastrasse 32, 8001 Zürich)

UK (☎ 020-7408 1254; italy@italiantouristboard.co.uk; 1 Princess St, London W1R 9AY)

USA (☎ 312-644 0996; enitch@italiantourism.com; 500 North Michigan Ave, Suite 2240, Chicago, IL 60611)

USA (☎ 310-820 1898; enitla@earthlink.net; 12400 Wilshire Blvd, Suite 550, Los Angeles, CA 90025)

USA (☎ 212-245 4822; enitny@italiantourism.com; 630 Fifth Ave, Suite 1565, New York, NY 10111)

Tourist Offices in Venice

Azienda di Promozione Turistica (APT; ☎ 041 529 87 11 central information line; www.turismovenezia.it) offices have information on the town and the province.

APT main office (Map pp254-5; Piazza San Marco 71/f; ⏰ 9am-3.30pm Mon-Sat) Staff will assist with information on hotels, transport and things to see and do in the city.

APT office (Map pp250-2; Santa Lucia station; ⏰ 8am-6.30pm) Open as late as 8pm in summer.

APT office (Map pp250-2; Next to Garage Comunale, Piazzale Roma; ⏰ 9.30am-6.30pm)

APT office (Arrivals hall at Marco Polo airport; ⏰ 9.30am-7.30pm)

APT office (Map pp262-3; Gran Viale Santa Maria Elisabetta 6/a, Lido; ⏰ 9am-12.30pm & 3.30-6pm Jun-Sep)

Chioggia APT office (☎ 041 40 10 68; www.chioggiatourism.it; Lungomare Adriatico 101, Sottomarina; ⏰ 8.30am-6.30pm, hours reduced in winter)

Infopoint (Map pp254-5; Venice Pavilion; ⏰ 10am-6pm) Next to Giardini ex Reali, a quick walk from Piazza San Marco.

The useful monthly booklet *Un Ospite di Venezia* (A Guest in Venice), published by a group of Venetian hoteliers, is sometimes available from tourist offices. If not, you can find it in most of the larger hotels. Similar, but a little less informative, is *Pocket Venice*, sometimes available from tourist offices.

Throughout the Veneto, you may come across increasingly common Informazioni e Assistenza ai Turisti (IAT) offices. These are the places to go for specific information about bus routes, museum opening times and so on.

Tourist Helpline & Complaints

The APT operates a free 24-hour tourist helpline in case you have a complaint to make about services poorly rendered (from hotels, restaurants, water taxis etc). Call ☎ 800 355 920 and follow the instructions. Alternatively, you can

contact the **Sportello di Conciliazione Turistica** (Map pp254-5; ☎ 041 529 87 23; complaint.apt@turismovenezia.it; Calle del Rimedio, Castello 4421; ⏰ 8.30am-1.30pm Mon-Fri).

Useful Websites

A plethora of websites is dedicated to all things Venetian. Some of the more useful sites:

APT (www.turismovenezia.it) The tourist office's website has a search function for tracking down addresses and phone numbers, information on sights and hotels, and a cultural events agenda.

Associazione Veneziana Albergatori (www.doge.it) This is a hoteliers' information directory (in English and Italian), with tips on hotels and eating options, upcoming events and links to other sites dealing with Venice.

Azienda Consorzio Trasporti Veneziana (ACTV; www.actv.it) This site contains all the local transport details you are ever likely to want and then some.

Comune di Venezia (www.comune.venezia.it) The city's town hall site has links to museum sites and other useful information.

Ente Nazionale Italiano per il Turismo (ENIT; www.enit.it) The Italian national tourist body's website has information on everything from local tourist office addresses, through town-by-town museum details and general introductions, to food, art and history. Look for upcoming cultural events too.

Ombra.Net (www.ombra.net) This site is bursting with information, but what makes it special is the interactive map, allowing you to zoom in on the precise location of the item you are searching – a handy tool in a place as complicated as this!

Rialto: The Venice Marketplace (www.rialto.com) Want to shop in Venice without going there? This could be a site for you. Many of the city's prestigious stores (and some perhaps not so prestigious) have contributed to this site. In many cases you can see catalogues and order online.

Sal.Ve (www.salve.it) This site, prepared by the Italian Ministry of Public Works, is dedicated to Venice's complex urban and environmental problems and the long history of discussion on what to do about them. It has links to related sites.

Trenitalia (www.trenitalia.it) Plan rail journeys, check timetables and prices and book tickets on Italy's national railways site.

Veneto (www.veneto.org) Information about the Veneto region, of which Venice is the capital, can be found here, including history, language and local news. You can read it in Venet (the language of the Veneto region) or English.

Venice in Peril (www.veniceinperil.org) For news on restoration going on in Venice and the latest on dangers facing the city, as well as general news.

VISAS

Italy is one of 15 member countries of the Schengen Convention, under which all EU member countries (except the UK and Ireland) plus Iceland and Norway have abolished checks at common borders. The other EU countries are Austria, Belgium, Denmark, Finland, France, Germany, Greece, Luxembourg, the Netherlands, Portugal, Spain and Sweden. Legal residents of one Schengen country do not require a visa for another Schengen country. Citizens of the UK and Ireland are also exempt and nationals of some other countries, including Canada, Japan, New Zealand and Switzerland, do not require visas for tourist visits of up to 90 days to any Schengen country.

Various other nationals not covered by the Schengen exemption can also spend up to 90 days in Italy without a visa. These include Australian, Israeli and US citizens.

All non-EU nationals entering Italy for any reason other than tourism (such as study or work) should contact an Italian consulate, as they may need a specific visa. They should also insist on having their passport stamped on entry as, without a 'stamp, they could encounter problems when trying to obtain a residence permit (permesso di soggiorno).

If you are a citizen of a country not mentioned in this section, check with an Italian consulate whether you need a visa. The standard tourist visa issued by Italian consulates is the Schengen visa, valid for up to 90 days. A Schengen visa issued by one Schengen country is generally valid for travel in all other Schengen countries. However, individual member countries may impose additional restrictions on certain nationalities. You should check visa regulations with the consulate of each Schengen country you plan to visit. These visas are not renewable inside Italy.

Permits

EU citizens do not need permits to live, work or start a business in Italy. They are, however, advised to register with a police station (questura) if they take up residence and apply for a residence permit (permesso di soggiorno). That is the first step to acquiring an ID card (carta d'identità). While you're at it, you'll need a tax-file number (codice fiscale) if you wish to be paid for most work in Italy. Go to the main police station (Map p259; ☎ 041 271 55 11; Fondamenta di San Lorenzo, Castello 5053) to obtain precise information on what is required. Study and work visas (required by all non-EU citizens) must be applied for in your country of residence.

WOMEN TRAVELLERS

Of the main destinations in Italy, Venice has to be the safest for women. The kind of bravado that has more southerly Italians strutting about in an effort to gain the attention of foreign women seems largely absent here. There are a couple of exceptions. The more popular Lido beaches have a bit of a reputation – local chaps of all ages try it on with local and foreign women. Some are said to 'work' Piazza San Marco. There is apparently even a club of men who compete with one another to pick up women! If you do get unwanted attention, whatever methods you use at home to deal with it should work. Following are a couple of organisations worth noting, especially if you are spending any length of time in the city.

Centro Donna (☎ 041 269 06 50; www.comune.venezia .it/c-donna, Italian only; Villa Franchin, Viale G Garibaldi 155/a, Mestre) A women's centre with a library and cultural events aimed at women, whether Italian or foreign.

Centro Anti-Violenza (☎ 041 269 06 10) Located in the same building as Centro Donna, this centre offers legal advice, counselling and support to women who have been attacked, regardless of nationality. The service is free.

WORK

It is illegal for non-EU citizens to work in Italy without a work permit (permesso di lavoro), but trying to obtain one through your Italian consulate can be a pain. EU citizens are allowed to work in Italy, but they still need to obtain a residence permit (permesso di soggiorno) from a police station. Immigration laws require foreign workers to be 'legalised' through their employers. This applies even to cleaners and babysitters. The employers then pay pension and health insurance contributions.

Employment Options

The best options are trying to find work in a bar, nightclub or restaurant during the tourist season. Another option is au pair work, organised before you come to Italy. A useful guide is The Au Pair and Nanny's Guide to Working Abroad, by Susan Griffith & Sharon Legg. Susan Griffith's Work Your Way Around the World is also worth looking at.

Art students and graduates might consider one other possibility. The Peggy Guggenheim Collection takes on foreign students to staff the museum, cloakroom and so on for periods of up to three months. This is most easily pursued through your art school.

The easiest source of employment for foreigners is teaching English (or another foreign language), but even with full qualifications, a non-EU citizen will find it difficult to secure a permanent teaching position. Most of the larger, more reputable schools will hire only those people who have work and/or residence permits, but their attitude can become more flexible if demand for teachers is high and they come across someone with good qualifications.

Translating and interpreting could be an option if you are fluent in Italian and a language in demand.

University students or recent graduates might be able to set up an internship with companies in Venice. The Association of International Students for Economics and Commerce (www.aiesec.org), with branches throughout the world, helps member students find internships in related fields. For information on membership, check out the website.

Language

Language

It's true – anyone can speak another language. Don't worry if you haven't studied languages before or that you studied a language at school for years and can't remember any of it. It doesn't even matter if you failed English grammar. After all, that's never affected your ability to speak English! And this is the key to picking up a language in another country. You just need to start speaking.

Learn a few key phrases before you go. Write them on pieces of paper and stick them on the fridge, by the bed or even on the computer – anywhere that you'll see them often.

You'll find that locals appreciate travellers trying their language, no matter how muddled you may think you sound. So don't just stand there, say something! If you want to learn more Italian than we've included here, pick up a copy of Lonely Planet's comprehensive but user-friendly *Italian phrasebook*.

SOCIAL
Meeting People
Hello.
Buon giorno.
Goodbye.
Arrivederci.
Please.
Per favore.
Thank you (very much).
(Mille) Grazie.
Yes/No.
Sì/No.
Do you speak English?
Parla inglese?
Do you understand (me)?
(Mi) capisce?
Yes, I understand.
Sì, capisco.
No, I don't understand.
No, non capisco.

Could you please ...?
Potrebbe ...?
repeat that	ripeterlo
speak more slowly	parlare più lentamente
write it down	scriverlo

Going Out
What's on ...?
Che c'è in programma ...?
locally	in zona
this weekend	questo fine settimana
today	oggi
tonight	stasera

Where are the ...?
Dove sono ...?
clubs	dei clubs
gay venues	dei locali gay
places to eat	posti dove mangiare
pubs	dei pub

Is there a local entertainment guide?
C'è una guida agli spettacoli in questa città?

PRACTICAL
Question Words
Who?	Chi?
What?	Che?
When?	Quando?
Where?	Dove?
How?	Come?

Numbers & Amounts
1	uno
2	due
3	tre
4	quattro
5	cinque
6	sei
7	sette
8	otto
9	nove
10	dieci
11	undici
12	dodici
13	tredici
14	quattordici
15	quindici
16	sedici

17	diciasette
18	diciotto
19	dicianove
20	venti
21	ventuno
22	ventidue
30	trenta
40	quaranta
50	cinquanta
60	sessanta
70	settanta
80	ottanta
90	novanta
100	cento
1000	mille
2000	duemila

Days

Monday	lunedì
Tuesday	martedì
Wednesday	mercoledì
Thursday	giovedì
Friday	venerdì
Saturday	sabato
Sunday	domenica

Banking

I'd like to ...
Vorrei ...

cash a cheque	riscuotere un assegno
change money	cambiare denaro
change some travellers cheques	cambiare degli assegni di viaggio

Where's the nearest ...?
Dov'è il ... più vicino?

| automatic teller machine | bancomat |
| foreign exchange office | cambio |

Post

Where is the post office?
Dov'è la posta?

I want to send a ...
Voglio spedire ...

fax	un fax
parcel	un pachetto
postcard	una cartolina

I want to buy ...
Voglio comprare ...

an aerogram	un aerogramma
an envelope	una busta
a stamp	un francobollo

Phone & Mobile Phones

I want to buy a phone card.
Voglio comprare una scheda telefonica.
I want to make ...
Voglio fare ...

| a call (to ...) | una chiamata (a ...) |
| reverse-charge/ collect call | una chiamata a carico del destinatario |

Where can I find a/an ...?
Dove si trova ...
I'd like a/an ...
Vorrei ...

adaptor plug	un addattatore
charger for my phone	un caricabatterie
mobile/cell phone for hire	un cellulare da noleggiare
prepaid mobile/ cell phone	un cellulare prepagato
SIM card for your network	un SIM card per vostra rete telefonica

Internet

Where's the local Internet café?
Dove si trova l'Internet point?

I'd like to ...
Vorrei ...

| check my email | controllare le mie email |
| get online | collegarmi a Internet |

Transport

What time does the ... leave?
A che ora parte ...?

bus	l'autobus
ferry (large)	la motonave
ferry (speedboat)	il motoscafo
plane	l'aereo
train	il treno
vaporetto	il batello/vaporetto

What time's the ... bus/vaporetto?
A che ora passa ... autobus/batello?

first	il primo
last	l'ultimo
next	il prossimo

Are you free? (taxi)
È libero questo taxi?
Please put the meter on.
Usa il tassametro, per favore.
How much is it to ...?
Quant'è per ...?
Please take me to (this address).
Mi porti a (questo indirizzo), per favore.

FOOD

breakfast	prima colazione
lunch	pranzo
dinner	cena
snack	spuntino/merenda
eat	mangiare
drink	bere

Can you recommend a ...
Potrebbe consigliare un ...?

bar/pub	bar/pub
café	bar
restaurant	ristorante

Is service/cover charge included in the bill?
Il servizio/coperto è compreso nel conto?

For more detailed information on food and dining out, see the Eating chapter, pp121–136.

EMERGENCIES

It's an emergency!
È un'emergenza!
Could you please help me/us?
Mi/Ci può aiutare, per favore?

Call the police/a doctor/an ambulance!
Chiami la polizia/un medico/un'ambulanza!
Where's the police station?
Dov'è la questura?

HEALTH

Where's the nearest ...?
Dov'è ...più vicino?

chemist (night)	la farmacia (di turno)
dentist	il dentista
doctor	il medico
hospital	l'ospedale

I need a doctor (who speaks English).
Ho bisogno di un medico (che parli inglese).

Symptoms

I have (a) ...
Ho ...

diarrhoea	la diarrea
fever	la febbre
headache	mal di testa
pain	un dolore

Glossary

Listed below are useful Italian terms. Some appear in the Venetian dialect (V). In a few instances, Italian words used only in Venice and perhaps elsewhere in the Veneto have been identified (Vz).

abbonamento – transport pass valid for one month
acqua alta, acque alte (pl) – high water (flooding that occurs in Venice during winter, when the sea level rises)
ACTV – Azienda Consorzio Trasporti Veneziano; bus and vaporetto company
affittacamere – rooms for rent (sometimes cheaper than a **pensione** and not part of the classification system)
AIG – Associazione Italiana Alberghi per la Gioventù; Italian Youth Hostel Association
alimentari – grocery shop
alloggio – general term for lodging of any kind; not part of the classification system
andata e ritorno – round trip
APT – Azienda di Promozione Turistica; provincial tourist office
arco – arch
ASL – Azienda Sanitaria Locale; provincial health agency
autostazione – bus station/terminal

bacaro – (V) traditional Venetian bar or eatery
batello – generic term for all types of vaporetto
battistero – baptistry

biglietteria – ticket office
biglietto, biglietti (pl) – ticket
binario – platform

calle, calli (pl) – (Vz) street
campanile – bell tower
campo – (Vz) square; equivalent to **piazza** elsewhere in Italy
cappella – chapel
carabinieri – police with military and civil duties
carnet – book of tickets
carta marmorizzata – marbled paper
cartapesta – papier-mâché, used to make Carnevale masks
cartoleria – shop selling paper goods
cartolina (postale) – postcard
casa – house
centro storico – (literally 'historical centre') old town
chiaroscuro – (literally 'light-dark') the use of strong light and dark contrasts in painting to put the main figures into stronger relief
chiesa – church
chiostro – cloister; covered walkway, usually enclosed by columns, around a quadrangle
cicheti – (Vz) traditional bar snacks eaten in bars and osterie
CIT – Compagnia Italiana di Turismo; Italian national travel agency
consolato – consulate

contorni – side orders
convalida – validation (of train ticket, for example)
coperto – cover charge (in restaurant)
corte – (Vz) blind alley
CTS – Centro Turistico Studentesco e Giovanile; student/youth travel agency
cupola – dome

deposito bagagli – left luggage
digestivo – after-dinner liqueur
doge, dogi (pl) – leader, duke

ENIT – Ente Nazionale Italiano per il Turismo; Italian State Tourist Office

ferrovia – train station
fiume – river
fondamenta – (Vz) street beside a canal
forcola – (V) wooden support for gondolier's oar
foresto – (V) stranger, foreigner (non-Venetian)
fornaio – bakery
FS – Ferrovie dello Stato; Italian State Railway

gabinetto – toilet, WC
gelateria, gelaterie (pl) – ice-cream shop

intarsia – inlaid wood, marble or metal

lago – lake
largo – (small) square; boulevard
lido – beach
locanda – inn, small hotel
lungomare – seafront road or promenade

malvasia – tavern (named after the wine imported from former Venice-controlled Greek islands)
merceria – haberdashery shop
motonave – big, interisland ferry on Venetian lagoon
motorino – moped
motoscafo – motorboat; in Venice, a faster, fully enclosed ferry

nave, navi (pl) – ship

oggetti smarriti – lost property
ombra – (Vz) small glass of wine
orario – timetable
ostello (per la gioventù) – (youth) hostel
osteria, osterie (pl) – traditional bar/restaurant

pala/pala d'altare – altarpiece; refers to a painting (often on wood) usually used as an ornament before the altar
palazzo, palazzi (pl) – palace, mansion; large building of any type, including an apartment block
panetteria – bakery
passeggiata – traditional evening or Sunday stroll

passerelle, passerelli (pl) – raised walkway
pasticceria – cake/pasty shop
pensione – guesthouse, small hotel
pescaria – (V) fish market; alternative spelling of the standard Italian *pescheria*
piazza – square
pietà – (literally 'pity' or 'compassion') sculpture, drawing or painting of the dead Christ supported by the Madonna
pinacoteca – art gallery
poltrona – airline-type chair on a ferry
ponte – bridge
portico – covered walkway, usually attached to the outside of buildings
porto – port
posta aerea – air mail
pronto soccorso – first aid, casualty ward
punto informativo – information booth

questura – police station

ramo – (Vz) tiny side lane
rio, rii (pl) – (Vz) the name for most canals in Venice
rio terrà – (Vz) street following the course of a filled-in canal
ruga – (Vz) small street flanked by houses and shops

sala – room, hall
salizzada – (Vz) street, the first type in Venice to be paved
salumeria – delicatessen
scalinata – staircase
servizio – service charge (in restaurant)
sestiere, sestieri (pl) – (Vz) term for the six 12th-century municipal divisions of Venice
spiaggia – beach
spiaggia libera – public beach
squero, squeri (pl) – gondola-building and repair yard
stazione (autobus) – (main bus) station
stazione marittima – ferry terminal
strada – street, road

tabaccheria, tabacchi (pl) – tobacconist's shop
traghetto – small ferry; in Venice, the commuter gondolas that crisscross the Grand Canal
trattoria, trattorie (pl) – cheap restaurant

ufficio postale – post office
ufficio stranieri – foreigners' bureau (in police station)

vaporetto, vaporetti (pl) – ferry
vetrai – glass-makers
via – street, road
vigili del fuoco – fire brigade
vigili urbani – traffic/local police

Language

Behind the Scenes

THE LONELY PLANET STORY

The story begins with a classic travel adventure: Tony and Maureen Wheeler's 1972 journey across Europe and Asia to Australia. There was no useful information about the overland trail then, so Tony and Maureen published the first Lonely Planet guidebook to meet a growing need.

From a kitchen table, Lonely Planet has grown to become the largest independent travel publisher in the world, with offices in Melbourne (Australia), Oakland (USA), London (UK) and Paris (France).

Today Lonely Planet guidebooks cover the globe. There is an ever-growing list of books and information in a variety of media. Some things haven't changed. The main aim is still to make it possible for adventurous travellers to get out there – to explore and better understand the world.

At Lonely Planet we believe travellers can make a positive contribution to the countries they visit – if they respect their host communities and spend their money wisely. Since 1986 a percentage of the income from each book has been donated to aid projects and human rights campaigns, and, more recently, to wildlife conservation.

THIS BOOK

This third edition of *Venice* was written by Damien Simonis, as were the previous two. The guide was commissioned in Lonely Planet's London office and produced by:

Commissioning Editor Fiona Christie

Coordinating Editor Stephanie Pearson

Coordinating Cartographer Valentina Kremenchutskaya

Layout Designer Margaret Jung

Editors Michelle Coxall, Barbara Delissen, Cherry Prior

Cover Designers Gerilyn Attebery, Andrew Weatherill

Series Designer Nic Lehman

Series Design Concept Andrew Weatherill & Nic Lehman

Managing Cartographer Mark Griffiths

Mapping Development Paul Piaia

Project Manager Ray Thomson

Language Editor Quentin Frayne

Regional Publishing Manager Katrina Browning

Series Publishing Manager Gabrielle Green

Thanks to Michala Green, Martin Heng, Jacqui Saunders, Pablo Gastar

Cover Carnevale mask, Jeff Cantarutti/Lonely Planet Images (top); moored gondolas, Glen Allison/Getty Images (bottom); Hotel Danieli, Damien Simonis/Lonely Planet Images (back)

Internal photographs by Juliet Coombe/Lonely Planet Images except for the following: p2 (#2), p8, p14, p18, p55, p57, p68 (#3), p69 (#3), p72 (#2), p73 (#4), p82, p85, p102, p108, p127, p150, p171 (#1, 2, 3), p174 (#4), p175 (#1, 2), p178 (#1, 2, 3), p186, p190, p201, p252, p258, p265 Damien Simonis/Lonely Planet Images; p2 (#5) Glenn Beanland/Lonely Planet Images; p2 (#4) Jenny Jones/Lonely Planet Images; p71 (#1) Olivier Cirendini/ Lonely Planet Images. All images are the copyright of the photographers unless otherwise indicated. Many of the images in this

guide are available for licensing from Lonely Planet Images: www.lonelyplanetimages.com.

THANKS
DAMIEN SIMONIS

I owe a major debt to Irina Freguia and Vladi Salvan, who not only rolled out the red carpet for me in their lagoon city home, but also helped out with all sorts of tips. Irina has unquenchable enthusiasm and a particular knack for connecting people, and so I ended up meeting Lucialda Lombardi of the Bucintoro rowing club, a city institution. Among other things, Lucialda has introduced me to the joys of rowing betwixt the isles of Venice. The Vogalonga was *longa* but memorable!

To other friends (in no particular order) eternal thanks for their help, tips and good company along the way: Antonella Dondi dall'Orologio, Caterina de Cesero and Francesco Lobina, Susanne Sagner, Federica Rocca, Alberto Toso Fei, Manuel Vecchina, Federica Centunali and Bernhard Klein, Roberta Guarnieri, Michela Scibilia (whose eating knowledge is always invaluable), Kristin Flood, Isabella Valenti and Rosa Caroli. In Padua *un abbraccio forte a* Dr Alberto Stassi, William Gasparini and Cristina Vallin. Thanks also to the staff of tourist offices in Venice and throughout the Veneto for their time-saving help.

Finally, the results of all the toil and sweat (summer struck early this year!) are for Janique, who, among other things, shared a blistering storm in an old-time tavern while joining me in a little Venetian exploration.

OUR READERS

Many thanks to the travellers who used the last edition and contacted us with helpful hints, useful advice and interesting anecdotes: Juliette Amielle, Angela and Brian Anderson, Jane Bentley, Bob and Cath Bolton, Sarah Chambers, Laine Cidlowski, Rich Clark, Rita Clayfield, Richard & Mary Coad, Michael Denslow, Aaron Fate, Chris & Marcelle Fileman, John Fink, Elaine and Rob Ford, Gerd Fricke, Grace Goodman, Meahan Grande, Debbie Hayball, Sandra Herrick, Adrian Hervey, Jessica Huter, Rudolf Komáromy, Caroline Lee, Bjorn Ljunghill, Marlene Lonergan, Peter and Delia Lucas, Andrew and Judy McManus, D Milton, Carolyn Mo, Peter & Judy Moore, Gail Packwood, Rachel Papworth, Jemma Pearce, Judith Pratt, Simon Rickman, Fiona Ross,

Amanda Scales, Sally-Ann Schiling, Cameron Scott, James Shields, Susan Shields, Jacalyn Soo, Saffron Swansborough, Ann Tuxford, Frank WJ Upton, Peter Walker, Demaris Wehr, Chris Wilkins, Monique Willis, Keefe Wong, Susan Wuchter-Stein.

SEND US YOUR FEEDBACK

We love to hear from travellers – your comments keep us on our toes and help make our books better. Our well-travelled team reads every word on what you loved or loathed about this book. Although we cannot reply individually to postal submissions, we always guarantee that your feedback goes straight to the appropriate authors, in time for the next edition. Each person who sends us information is thanked in the next edition – and the most useful submissions are rewarded with a free book.

To send us your updates – and find out about LP events, newsletters and travel news – visit our award-winning website: www.lonelyplanet.com.

Note: We may edit, reproduce and incorporate your comments in Lonely Planet products such as guidebooks, websites and digital products, so let us know if you don't want your comments reproduced or your name acknowledged. For a copy of our privacy policy, email privacy@lonelyplanet.com.au.

ACKNOWLEDGMENTS

Many thanks to the following for the use of their content: ACTV Network Map, © 2003

Behind the Scenes

Notes

Index

See also separate indexes for Eating (p245), Shopping (p245) and Sleeping (p246).

000 map pages
000 photographs

Index

Index

Index

Index

245

SLEEPING

000 map pages
000 photographs

LEGEND

ROUTES

	Tollway		One Way Street
	Freeway		Unsealed Road
	Primary Road		Mall/Steps
	Secondary Road		Tunnel
	Tertiary Road		Walking Tour
	Lane		Walking Tour Detour

TRANSPORT

	Ferry, Vaporetto		Rail
	Metro		Rail (Underground)
	Monorail		Tram

HYDROGRAPHY

	River, Creek		Canal
	Intermittent River		Water

BOUNDARIES

	Regional, Suburb		Ancient Wall

AREA FEATURES

	Airport		Cemetery, Christian
	Area of Interest		Land
	Beach, Desert		Mall
	Building, Featured		Market
	Building, Information		Park
	Building, Other		Sports
	Building, Transport		Urban

SYMBOLS

SIGHTS/ACTIVITIES
- Beach
- Buddhist
- Castle, Fortress
- Christian
- Hindu
- Islamic
- Jewish
- Monument
- Museum, Gallery
- Picnic Area
- Point of Interest
- Ruin
- Shinto
- Sikh
- Skiing
- Winery, Vineyard
- Zoo, Bird Sanctuary

EATING
- Eating

DRINKING
- Drinking
- Café

ENTERTAINMENT
- Entertainment

SHOPPING
- Shopping

SLEEPING
- Sleeping
- Camping

TRANSPORT
- Airport, Airfield
- Bus Station
- Cycling, Bicycle Path
- General Transport
- Taxi Rank

INFORMATION
- Bank, ATM
- Embassy/Consulate
- Hospital, Medical
- Information
- Internet Facilities
- Parking Area
- Petrol Station
- Police Station
- Post Office, GPO
- Telephone
- Toilets

GEOGRAPHIC
- Lighthouse
- Lookout
- Mountain
- National Park
- Well

NOTE: Not all symbols displayed above appear in this guide.

Map Section

VENICE

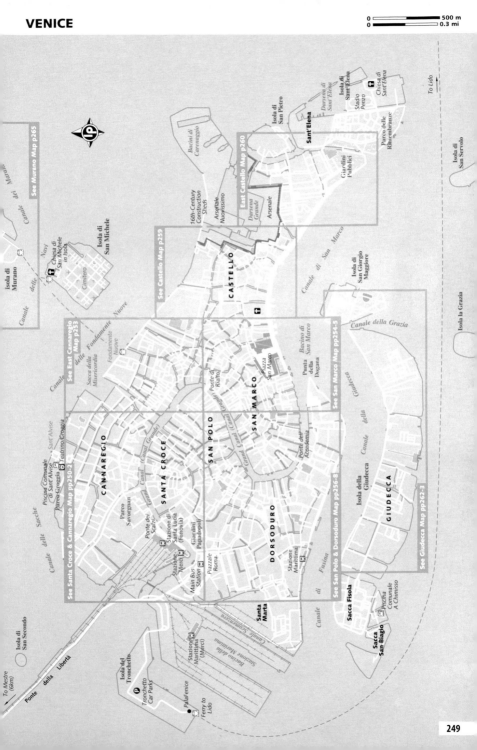

SANTA CROCE & CANNAREGIO

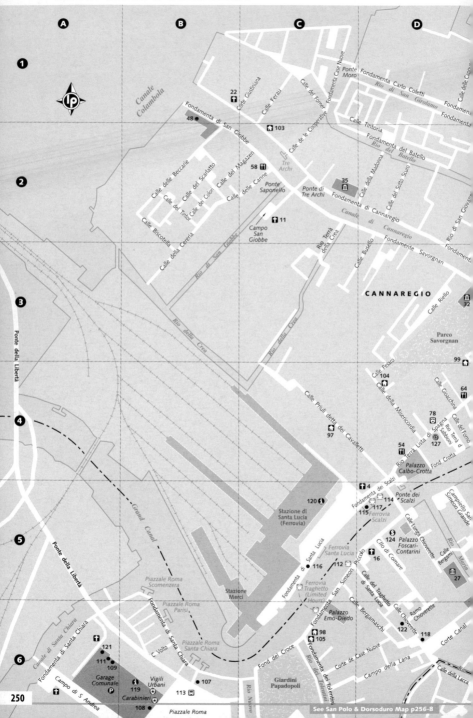

A   **B**   **C**   **D**

1

2

3

CANNAREGIO

Parco Savorgnan

4

Palazzo Calbo-Crotta

5

6

Canale Colombola

Fondamenta di San Giobbe

Fondamenta Case Nuove
Ponte Moro
Fondamenta Carlo Coletti
Calle della Cappuccine

22
48
103

Corte Giustiniana
Calle Ferau
Calle del Forner
Calle del Fumer
Calle delle Cooperative
Calle Tintoria
Rio di San Girolamo
Fondamenta
Fondamenta

Calle delle Beccarie
Calle delle Scarlatto
Calle del Colon
Calle del Tintor
Calle del Magazen
Calle delle Canne
58
Tre Archi
Ponte Saponello
35
Fondamenta del Batello
Rio del Batello
Calle della Madonna
Calle dei Sotti Scuri
Calle della Misericordia

Calle Biscotela
Calle della Cereria
Rio di San Giobbe
Campo San Giobbe
11
Ponte di Tre Archi
Fondamenta di Cannaregio
Canale di Cannaregio
Fondamente Savorgnan
Rio di San Giovanni

Rio Terrà della Crea
Calle Bucolo
Calle Riello
32

Ponte della Libertà

Rio della Crea

Calle Priuli detta dei Cavalletti
97

Calle Picaco
Calle della Misericordia
104
Calle Coascinia
64
78
Rio Terrà Lista di Spagna
127
54
Calle del Forno
Fond. Crotta

99

Grand Canal

Ponte della Libertà

Stazione di Santa Lucia (Ferrovia)
120

4
Fondamenta dei Scalzi
Ponte dei Scalzi
114
117
115
Ferrovia Scalzi

Campiello Santa Simeon Grande

Ferrovia Santa Lucia
116
Fondamenta di Santa Lucia
12
San Simeon Piccolo
Calle del Traghetto di Santa Lucia
Clio di Conure
16
124
Palazzo Foscari-Contarini
Calle Lunga Chioverete
Rio Marin
27

Piazzale Roma Scomenzera
Piazzale Roma Parisi
Stazione Merci
Ferrovia Traghetto (Limited Hours)
Fondamenta San Simeon Piccolo
Palazzo Emo-Diedo
98
105
Calle Bergamaschi
Calle Chioverete
Ramo Chioverette
122
118

Piazzale Roma Santa Chiara

121
111
109
Garage Comunale
P
Vigili Urbani
Carabinieri
108
107
113
119

C. Volto
C. di S Andrea
Canale di Santa Chiara
Fondamenta di Santa Chiara
Fondamenta di Santa Chiara

Fond. del Croce
Rio Nuovo
Corte de Case Nuove
Fondamenta dei Tolentini
Campo della Lana
Corte Corta
Calle della Lacca

Giardini Papadopoli

Piazzale Roma

250

See San Polo & Dorsoduro Map p256-8

EAST CANNAREGIO

0 _____ 200 m
0 _____ 0.1 mi

SIGHTS & ACTIVITIES	pp45-96
Ca' d'Oro	1 A5
Casino degli Spiriti	2 B2
Chiesa dei SS Apostoli	3 B5
Chiesa dei SS Giovanni e Paolo	4 D6
Chiesa di San Canciano	5 C5
Chiesa di San Felice	6 A4
Chiesa di San Giacomo di Rialto	7 B6
Chiesa di San Giovanni Elemosinario	8 A6
Chiesa di San Giovanni Grisostomo	9 B6
Chiesa di Santa Maria dei Miracoli	10 C6

Chiesa di Santa Maria della	
Misericordia	11 A3
Fabbriche Nuove	12 A6
Fabbriche Vecchie	13 A6
Galleria Franchetti	(see 1)
I Gesuiti	14 C3
Marco Polo's House	15 B6
Oratorio dei Crociferi	16 C4
Palazzo Bragadin-Carabba	17 C6
Palazzo Contarini del Zaffo	18 A2
Palazzo dei Camerlenghi	19 B6
Palazzo dei Dieci Savi	20 A6
Palazzo Dolfin Bollani	21 C6
Palazzo Loredan	22 C6
Palazzo Widman	23 C6
Pescaria	24 A5
Scuola Grande di San Marco	25 D6
Scuola Nuova della Misericordia	26 A3
Scuola Vecchia della Misericordia	27 A3
Squero	28 A3
Statue of Bartolomeo Colleoni	29 D6
Titian's House	30 C4

EATING	pp121-36
A La Vecia Cavana	31 B5
All'Arco	32 A6
Boccadoro	33 C5
Cantina do Mori	34 A6
Fiaschetteria Toscana	35 B6
In-Coop (Supermarket)	36 B5
McDonald's	37 A5
Ostaria al Ponte	38 D6

Osteria alla Frasca	39 C4
Osteria da Alberto	40 C6
Osteria dalla Vedova	41 A5
Pasticceria Puppa	42 C4
Vini da Gigio	43 A4

DRINKING	pp138-43
Algiubagiò	44 D4
The Fiddler's Elbow	45 A5
Zenevia	46 C5

ENTERTAINMENT	pp137-48
Centro Culturale Boldù	47 C6
Cinema Giorgione Movie d'Essai	48 B5
Teatro Malibran	49 C6

SHOPPING	pp149-60
Aliani	50 A6
Coin	51 B6
Drogheria Mascari	52 A6
Molin Giocattoli	53 B6
Nave de Oro	54 B5
Produce Market	55 A6
Produce Market	56 A6
Produce Market	57 A6

SLEEPING	pp161-82
Hotel Giorgione	58 B5
Locanda Leon Bianco	59 B5
Pensione Guerrato	60 A6

TRANSPORT	pp210-16
Fondamente Nuove ferry stop (To Murano, Burano & Treporti)	61 C3

INFORMATION	
Entrance to Ospedale Civile (Hospital)	(see 25)
Telecom Office	62 A6
Telecom Office	63 A4

OTHER	
Wooden Quay	64 B3

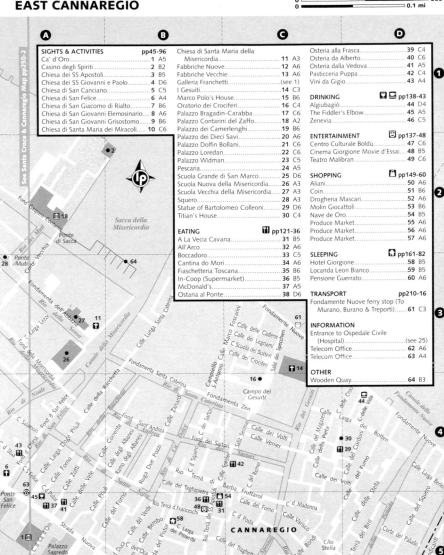

253

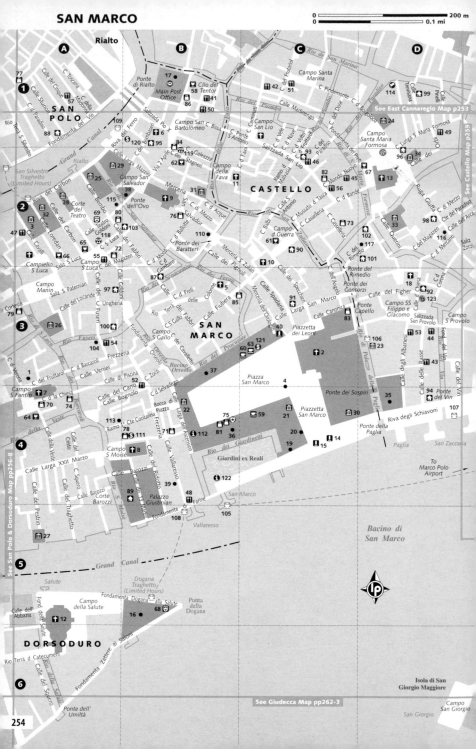

SAN POLO & DORSODURO

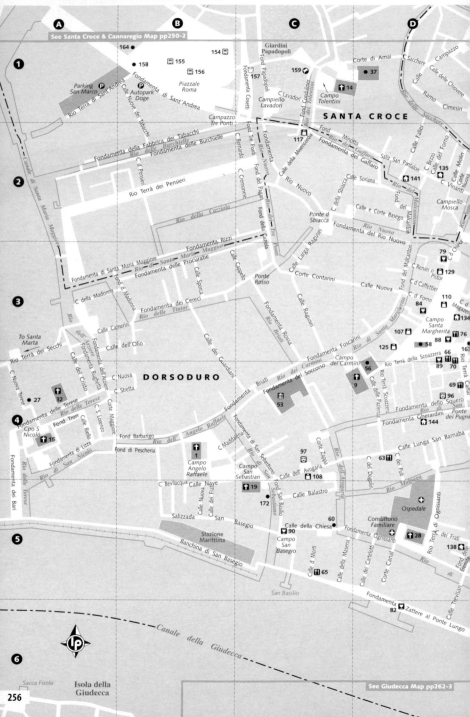

See Santa Croce & Cannaregio Map pp250-2

164

154

158

155

156

157

Giardini
Papadopoli

159

Corte di Amai

37

14

Sacchere

Campazzo

Calle delle Chiovere

Ramo

Calle

Cimesin

SANTA CROCE

Parking
San Marco

Autopark
Doge

Piazzale
Roma

Piazzale
di Sant'Andrea

Campazzo
Tre Ponti

Campiello
Lavadori

Campo
Tolentini

Calle Fallet

C Bezzo

Calle Molin

135

Vinanti

Fondamenta della Fabbrica dei Tabacchi

117

Saliz San Pantalon

141

Rio Terrà dei Pensieri

Rio Nuovo

Campiello
Mosca

Rio della Cazziola

Ponte d
Sbiacca

Calle e Corte Basego

79

Fondamenta del Rio Nuovo

129

Renier o
Pistor

Fondamenta Rizzi

Corte Contarini

C d'Affettier

110

Fondamenta delle Procuratie

Ponte
Rosso

Calle Nuova

C d
Forno

84

Magazen

DORSODURO

Fondamenta dei Cereci

Rio delle Tintor

Corte Contarini

Campo
Santa
Margherita

107

134

76

C della Madonna

58

125

88

Rio Terrà della Scoazzera

66

163

89

70

To Santa
Marta

Rio Terrà dei Secchi

27

32

Campo
dei Carmini

56

9

69

96

Fondamenta dello Squero

144

Ponte
dei Pugni

15

Fond Tron

Campo
Angelo
Raffaele

1

Campo
San
Sebastian

97

108

63

Calle Lunga San Barnaba

19

172

Calle Balastro

60

Consultorio
Familiare

28

Ospedale

138

90

Campo
San
Basegio

65

Stazione
Marittima

Banchina di San Basegio

San Basilio

82

Zattere al Ponte Lungo

Canale della Giudecca

Sacca Fisola

**Isola della
Giudecca**

See Giudecca Map pp262-3

256

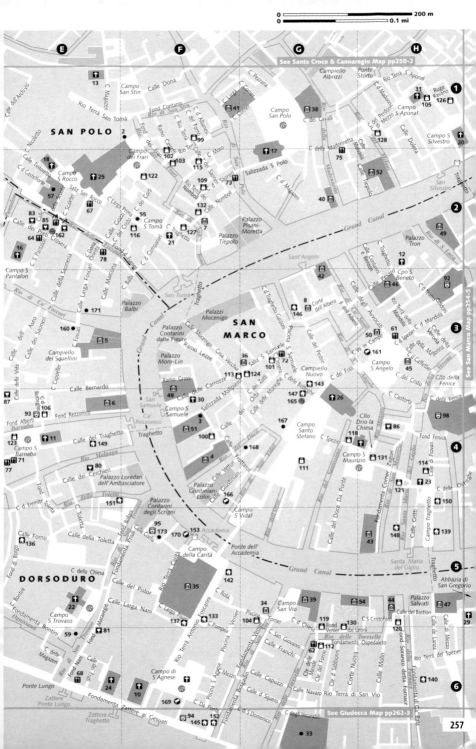

CASTELLO

0 ——————— 200 m
0 ——————— 0.1 mi

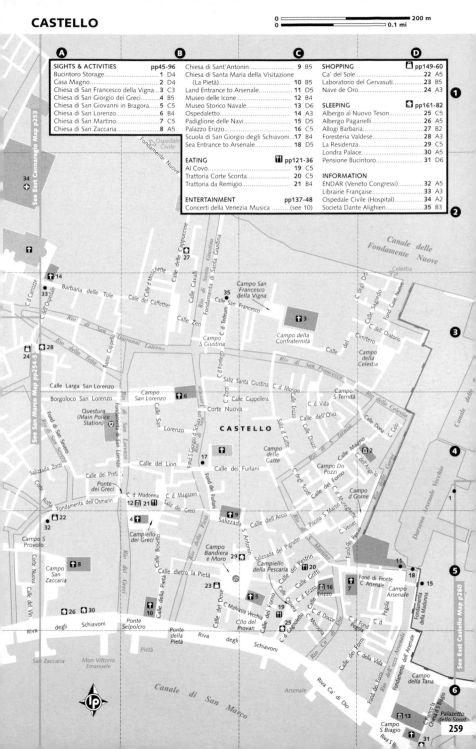

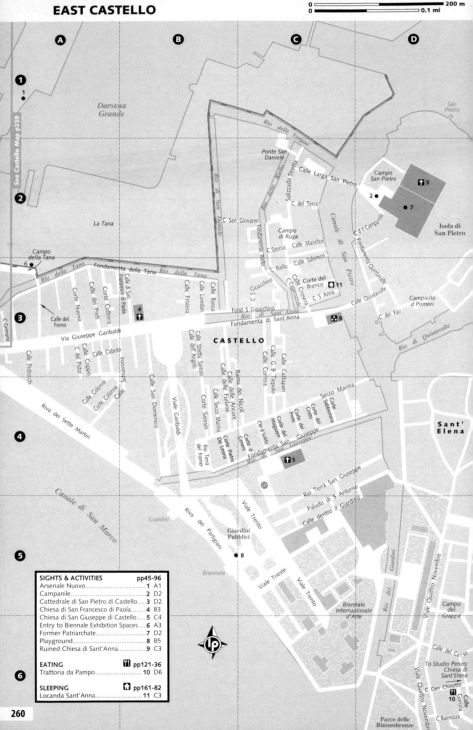

0   200 m
0   0.1 mi

A   **B**   **C**   **D**

See Castello Map p259

Darsena Grande

San Pietro

Rio delle Vergini

Ponte San Daniele

Calle Larga San Pietro

Campo San Pietro

Salizzada Stretta

C. del Terco

Isola di San Pietro

La Tana

C San Giovanni

Campo di Ruga

C d I Campanile

Fondamenta Quintavalle

C Sporca   Calle Marafani

Campo della Tana

Fondamenta della Tana   Rio della Tana

Calle di San Francesco di Paola

C Riello   Calle Salomon

Corte del Bianco

Campiello d Pomeri

C S Anna

C del Fari

Rio della Tana

Corte Coltrera

Calle dei Preti

Calle Bassa

Calle Loredan

Calle Frisiera

Gioacchino

Calle Crosera

C Capuzzorida

Calle Quintavalle

Rio di Quintavalle

C Grimana

Calle del Forno

Via Giuseppe Garibaldi

Fond S Gioacchino

Rio di Sant'Anna

Fondamenta di Sant'Anna

CASTELLO

Calle Nuova

Calle Coppo

C del Pistor

Calle Caboto

Sanuovo

Calle Colonne

Corte Colonne

Calle

Calle San Domenico

Viale Garibaldi

Calle Stretta Saresin

Calle dell'Angelo

Rama dei Nicoli

Calle delle Ancore

Calle delle Furlane

Calle G B Tiepolo

Calle Correra

Calle Cattapan

Secco Marina

Corte Salamona

Corte del Cristo

Corte del Magazen

Corte Prato

Fondamenta San Giuseppe

Rio di San Giuseppe

Calle Pedrocchi

Riva dei Sette Martiri

Corte Saresin

Calle Secco Marina

Corte Pietro Da Lesina

Rio Terà del Forner

Corte Cenese

Che d Solda

Sant' Elena

Canale di San Marco

Giardini

Riva dei Partigiani

Giardini Publici

Rio Terà San Giuseppe

Paludo di S Antonio

Calle dentro il Giardino

Viale Trento

Viale Trieste

Calle Quattro Novembre

Campo del Grappa

Biennale

Bennale Internazionale d'Arte

Rio dei

Giardini

Calle del Cai P

To Studio Penzo; Chiesa di Sant'Elena

C Gen Chinotto

Calle Gorizia

Calle Quattro Novembre

Parco delle Rimembranze

C Bainsizza

MESTRE

0 _____ 300 m
0 _____ 0.2 mi

GIUDECCA

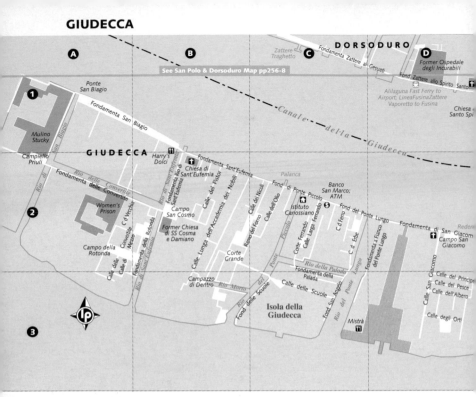

DORSODURO

A   B   C   D

Former Ospedale degli Incurabili

Zattere Traghetto

Fondamenta Zattere ai Gesuati

Fond. Zattere allo Spirito Santo

See San Polo & Dorsoduro Map pp256-8

Alilaguna Fast Ferry to Airport; LineaFusinaZattere Vaporetto to Fusina

Chiesa Santo Spi

Canale della Giudecca

Ponte San Biago

Fondamenta San Biago

Mulino Stucky

GIUDECCA

Harry's Dolci

Chiesa di Sant'Eufemia

Fondamenta Sant'Eufemia

Palanca

Banco San Marco; ATM

Campiello Priuli

Fondamenta delle Convertite

Women's Prison

Campo San Cosmo

Istituto Canossiano

Fond. di Ponte Piccolo

Fond. del Ponte Lungo

Fondamenta di San Giacom

Redem

Campo San Giacomo

Former Chiesa di SS Cosma e Damiano

Campo della Rotonda

Corte Grande

Fondamenta della Palada

Rio della Palada

Calle del Principe

Calle del Pesce

Calle dell'Albero

Campazzo di Dentro

Rio Marin

Calle delle Scuole

Isola della Giudecca

Calle San Giacomo

Calle degli Orti

Mistrà

LIDO DI VENEZIA

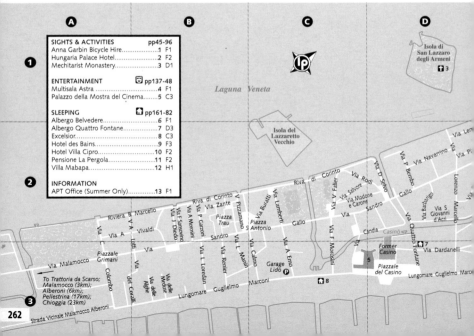

A   B   C   D

SIGHTS & ACTIVITIES   pp45-96
Anna Garbin Bicycle Hire..................1   F1
Hungaria Palace Hotel.....................2   F2
Mechitarist Monastery.....................3   D1

ENTERTAINMENT   pp137-48
Multisala Astra 4   F1
Palazzo della Mostra del Cinema.......5   C3

SLEEPING   pp161-82
Albergo Belvedere...........................6   F1
Albergo Quattro Fontane..................7   D3
Excelsior..8   C3
Hotel des Bains..............................9   F3
Hotel Villa Cipro............................10   F2
Pensione La Pergola........................11   F2
Villa Mabapa.................................12   H1

INFORMATION
APT Office (Summer Only)..............13   F1

Isola di San Lazzaro degli Armeni

Laguna Veneta

Isola del Lazzaretto Vecchio

Riva di Corinto

Via Lem

Via Navarrino

Via P Bembo

Via Pi

Via Rodi

Via D Selvo

Via V Faller

Via Salvore

Via Modone e Carone

Gallo

Lorenzo

Marcello

Via S Giovanni d'Acri

Via Barbaro

Riviera di Corinto

Riva Zante

V Pizzamano

V Zante

Via Buatri

Via Lamberti

Piazza Trau

Piazza S Antonio

Gallo

Via Candia

Casinò

Via F Morosini

Via Quattro Fontane

Via Dardanelli

Riviera B Marcello

Via A

Vivaldi

Via J Diedo

Via F Sanmicrini

Via A Morosini

Via P Garzoni

Via L Loredan

Via Renier

Via Buadri

Via Calmo

Via Masini

Sandro

Former Casino

Piazzale del Casino

Lungomare Guglielmo Marce

Via Malamocco

Piazzale Grimani

Via C

Via

Colombo

Via delle Alghe

Via delle Meduse

Lungomare Guglielmo

Marconi

Garage Lido

To Trattoria da Scarso; Malamocco (3km); Alberoni (6km); Pellestrina (17km); Chioggia (23km)

Strada Vicinale Malamocco Alberoni

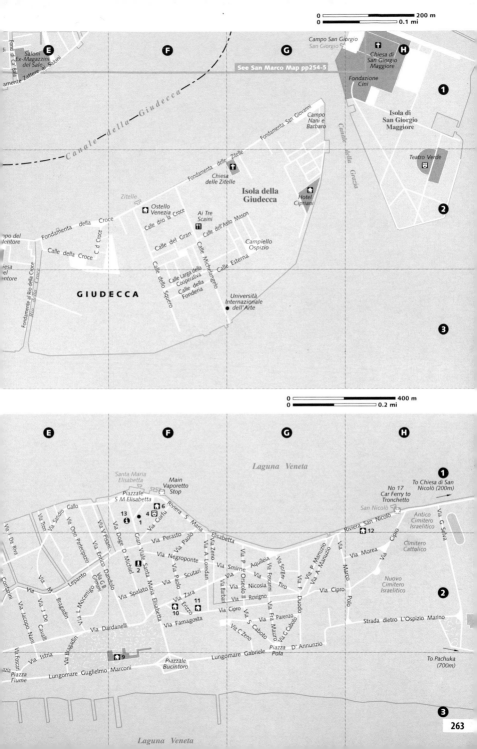

BURANO & TORCELLO

0 _____ 200 m
0 _____ 0.1 mi

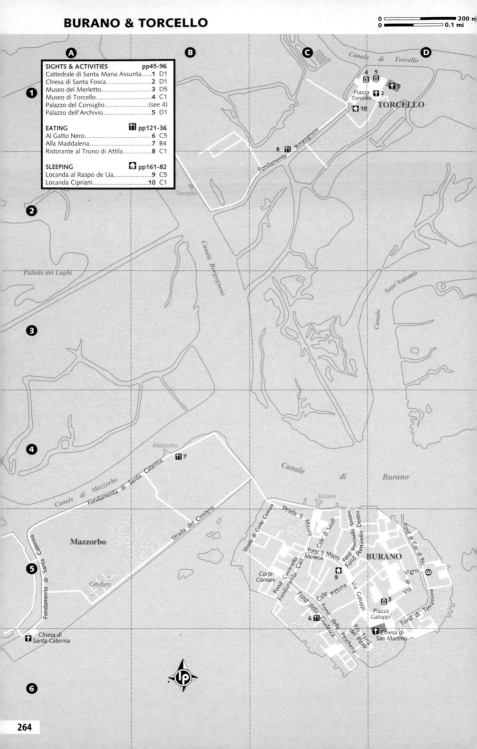

Canale di Torcello

Piazza Torcello

TORCELLO

Borgognoni

Fondamenta

Canale Borgognoni

Torcello

Palude dei Laghi

San'Antonio

Canale

Mazzorbo

Canale di Mazzorbo

Fondamenta di Santa Caterina

Strada del Cimitero

Canale di Burano

Burano

Mazzorbo

Strada di Corte Comare
Strada S. Mauro
Calle di Saludi

Fond S. Mauro
Fond Pontinello Destro
Fond Pontinello Sinistro
Fond di Cão del Rio

BURANO

Moleca
Corte Comare
Fond Cavanella
Fondamenta Cão
Calle Pittona
Via Galuppi
Vigna
Via

Cimitero

Fond. della Giudecca
Fond. della Pescheria
Rio Terà del Piazo
Rio Terà Nova
Fond di Terranova

Piazza Galuppi

Chiesa di Santa Caterina

Chiesa di San Martino

LP

MURANO

0 |======| 200 m
0 |■■■■■□| 0.1 mi

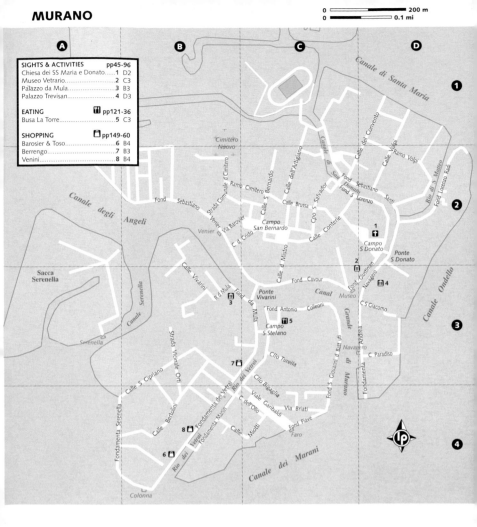

A **B** **C** **D**

SIGHTS & ACTIVITIES	pp45-96
Chiesa dei SS Maria e Donato......1 D2
Museo Vetrario.........................2 C3
Palazzo da Mula........................3 B3
Palazzo Trevisan.......................4 D3
EATING 🍴 **pp121-36**
Busa La Torre............................5 C3
SHOPPING 🛍 **pp149-60**
Barosier & Toso.........................6 B4
Berrengo..................................7 B3
Venini.....................................8 B4

Canale di Santa Maria

1

2

Cimitero
Nuovo

Canale degli Angeli

Fond Sebastiano

Strada Comunale d'Cimitero

Ramo Cimitero

Venier

Via Baroyer

C. d. Cristo

Calle S Bernardo

Campo
San Bernardo

Calle dell'Artigiano

Cpo S Salvador

Calle Brussa

Canale di San

Fond Sebastiano

Fond Donato
Fond S Lorenzo

Calle del Convento

Calle Volpi

Ramo Volpi

Rio di S Matteo

Fond Lorenzo Radi

Santi

1
🕈

Campo
S Donato

Ponte
S Donato

Sacca
Serenella

Calle Vivarini

R d Mula

Fond. da Mula

Ponte
Vivarini

3
🏛

Calle d Mistro

Fond Cavour

Canal

Grande

Museo
2🏛

🏛**4**

Canale Ondella

3

Canale
Serenella

SS
Serenella

Strada Vignale Orti

Fond Antonio

Colleoni

Campo
S Stefano

🍴**5**

Cllo Turella

C S Giacomo

di

Murano

Fond S Giovanni d Batt

un

Navagero
Andrea

C Paradiso

Fondamenta

Fondamenta Serenella

Calle S Cipriano

Calle Bertolini

7🛍

8🛍

6🛍

Fondamenta del Vetrai
Rio dei Vetrai
Fondamenta Marin

C dell'Olio

Calle Miotti

Cllo Bisaglia

Viale Garibaldi

Via Briati

Fond Piave

Faro

Colonna

Canale dei Marani

Ⓛⓟ

4

VENICE VAPORETTO ROUTES

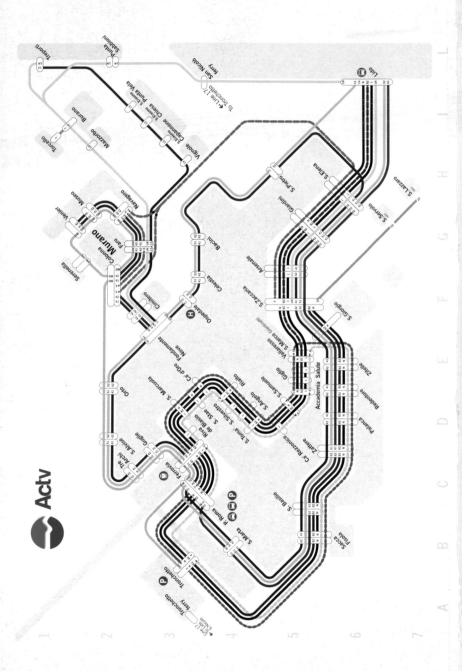